Teaching with the Internet:
Lessons from the Classroom

1999 Edition

We had just started a Masters class titled Current Issues: Technology in the Classroom. *We were Internet illiterate. Then our principal presented us with your book. It saved the day!*

Your easy to read lessons introduced us to the basic uses of the Internet. Your book provided us with a vast array of resources to explore.

Your book has motivated us to increase our knowledge and use of the Internet in our classrooms. Again, thank you for an excellent book!

-- Jill Newcomb and Cindy Ross
Ottawa Elementary School, Petosky, MI

Your book on using the Internet in the classroom is wonderful. I have learned so much from the book and look forward to using it.

--Dr Carol Moutray
Assistant Professor of Education and
Director of Graduate Reading Programs
King's College, Wilkes-Barre, PA

I had no idea that the Internet could be used so easily in the classroom or integrated into lessons.

--Chris Cameron
Intern at Oswego State, Oswego, NY

I really appreciate the E-mail for You sections and the classroom stories at the beginning of every chapter!

I have used the many web addresses to take my class to places they never dreamed possible.

--Kelly Oliphant Wise
Cherokee Elementary School, Memphis, TN

Teachers who are just beginning to explore the WWW will benefit greatly from the explanations included in these chapters.

--Mary Lou Balcom
Edward Smith School, Syracuse, NY

I think that Teaching with the Internet *meets the needs of teachers looking for a useful guide that will allow classroom use of the Internet to enhance student learning.*

--Anonymous

Teaching with the Internet *would serve as a much needed and valuable resource.*

One of the major challenges facing educators is developing students' skills and strategies such that they can make wise use of the Internet.

The reader-friendly, classroom-based orientation should prove not only non-threatening but also inviting to most readers.

--Phillip H. Loseby
Dzantik'i Heeni Middle School, Juneau, AK

This book would enable me to more effectively tap into a new and wonderful resource.
The book's philosophy fits nicely into current thinking about teaching and learning.

--Jonathan Dinkin
Edward Smith School, Syracuse, NY

The authors create a powerful argument for the use and methods to use the Internet with all their students and across subject areas.

--Anonymous

Teaching with the Internet:
Lessons from the Classroom

1999 Edition

Donald J. Leu, Jr. and Deborah Diadiun Leu
Syracuse University

with the assistance of

Katherine R. Leu

The George Washington University

Christopher-Gordon Publishers, Inc.
Norwood, Massachusetts

Credits

Every effort has been made to contact copyright holders for permission to reproduce borrowed material where necessary. We apologize for any oversights and would be happy to rectify them in future printings.

All e-mail correspondence, classroom web-sites and home-pages used with permission.

Chapter 1   Pi Mathematics Web-Site reproduced with the permission of Georgette Moore and Betty A. Ganas.

Chapter 2   Nueva Library Research Page used with the permission of Debbie Abilock and the Nueva Library Research Goal ©.

Netscape Images used with the permission of Netscape Communications Corporation ©.

Microsoft Explorer Images used with the permission of Microsoft ©.

Chapter 4   Internet Projects Registry used with the permission of Global Schoolnet ©.

Chapter 5   Jan Brett's Home Page reproduced with the permission of Jan Brett ©.

Bartlett's Familiar Quotations. Copyright © by Little, Brown and Company (Inc.). By permission of Little, Brown and Company.

Chapter 6   Kids' Web Japan used with permission of Japan Information Network, Illustration by Chitose Yamada ©.

Chapter 7   ENC Online reproduced with permission of the Eisenhower National Clearinghouse for Mathematics and Science Education.

Monarch Watch Home Page reproduced with permission of Monarch Watch ©.

Chapter 8   The Math Forum Home Page reproduced with permission of the Math Forum, a virtual center for Math Education, housed at Swarthmore College and funded by the National Science Foundation.

Chapter 9   Koala Trouble is an Alex Scribbles On-Line Production.

Chapter 11   Dave's ESL Cafe used with permission of Dave Sperling.

Chapter 12   Illustration on North Star Navigators used with permission. Copyright © 1997 Peter Reynolds.

Christopher-Gordon Publishers, Inc.
1502 Providence Highway, Suite #12
Norwood, MA 02062
(800) 934-8322

Printed in the United States of America

10 9 8 7 6 5 4 3 2 1   03 02 01 00 99

ISBN 0-926842-85-4
Library of Congress Number 98-073518

To our parents:
Rose, Anne, Don, and Dan.

Our first teachers, our best teachers.

Disclaimer

The authors and the publisher assume no responsibility for errors or omissions in the resources identified in this book. Moreover, the authors and publisher assume no liability for any damages resulting from the use of any information identified in this book or from links listed at sites that are described. As we indicate in this book, the best way to protect children from viewing inappropriate sites or receiving inappropriate messages is to implement a sound acceptable use policy and to carefully monitor student use of the Internet in your classroom, at school, and at home.

We have devoted much time and energy to providing accurate and current information in this book. Nevertheless, in an environment as constantly changing as the Internet, it is inevitable that some of the information provided here will also change. Information provided at one location may move to another, sometimes without any indication it has moved. Updated links are maintained at the web site for this book, Teaching with the Internet (http://web.syr.edu~djleu/teaching.html).

Contents

Preface

This book shows you how to effectively integrate the Internet into your classroom. The focus on teaching is what distinguishes this book from others. We have found that other books emphasize the technical side of the Internet, without considering how to actually use this technology for teaching. Our approach is very different. Instead of emphasizing the technology of the Internet, we focus on how to use the Internet for teaching and learning. The Internet is fundamentally changing the nature of classroom instruction, enhancing students' opportunities to learn about the world around them. This book shows you how teachers are developing classroom communities filled with the excitement of learning and discovery.

> *The focus on teaching is what distinguishes this book from others.*

We developed this book to save you time. Teaching is a profession that demands extraordinary amounts of time and we know you have little to spare as you explore this new context for learning. We seek to help you effectively integrate the Internet into your classroom in the shortest time possible.

The quickly changing nature of the Internet requires us to revise this book on an annual basis. Each year, we share new teaching ideas, new web sites, and new lessons from teachers. We also continually update the companion home page for this book, **Teaching with the Internet** (http://web.syr.edu/~djleu/teaching.html). This contains current links to every location we mention and will save you considerable time as you explore the many wonderful locations for teaching and learning on the Internet. We invite you to take advantage of this resource as you read.

> *We seek to help you effectively integrate the Internet into your classroom in the shortest time possible.*

Several assumptions have guided our work. First, we assume that the active role you play in orchestrating experiences with the Internet will determine the extent to which your students gain from this resource. Students left entirely on their own to "surf" the Internet will waste much time and learn little from their experiences. Students guided in their explorations of the Internet by a knowledgeable and thoughtful teacher will understand the world in new and powerful ways. We share useful ideas about how best to guide students in these explorations.

Second, we assume that understanding something as powerful, complex, and constantly changing as the Internet requires us to learn from one another; socially-mediated learning is central to success with the Internet. Our writing is guided by this assumption in several ways. We begin each chapter with a story of how a talented teacher uses the Internet in the classroom and then discuss the lessons each of us can learn from this experience. We also include over thirty e-mail messages to you from teachers around the world, describing the lessons they have learned from using the Internet. Finally, many chapters provide listservs and newsgroups to put you in touch with other teachers facing the same challenges as you are. We all learn from one another in this new electronic environment. We hope to support this learning so that you and your students may benefit.

The classroom episodes that begin each chapter were developed from multiple sources: e-mail conversations we have with teachers around the world, descriptions of Internet experiences posted on various listservs, ideas posted by teachers at Internet Project sites, classroom observations, and our own experiences as teachers. Each story represents a fusion of multiple sources; no story represents a single teacher's experiences. We feel, however, that each story faithfully represents the many outstanding classrooms we have encountered in our travels on the Internet.

Changes Appearing In This Edition

You will see many important changes in this second edition, many of which were suggested by teachers through their thoughtful e-mail messages to us.

- *Complete K–12 Coverage.*   We have expanded our coverage to include grades K–12. You will find resources and instructional strategies that immediately apply to your elementary, middle school, or high school classroom.

- *Macintosh and Windows-based Platforms.*   We have expanded our coverage to include Internet browsers on both Macintosh and Windows-based platforms. Chapters 2 and 3 contain directions for using both systems that are commonly found in schools.

- *Both Netscape and Internet Explorer Browsers.*   We now teach you how to use both major types of Internet browsers: Netscape Communicator (Navigator) and Internet Explorer.

- *Integrated Instructional Models for Teaching with the Internet.*   This edition also devotes special attention to an integrated set of instructional models we have developed for teaching with the Internet. They include Internet Workshop, Internet Activity, Internet Project, and Internet Inquiry. Chapters 4–11 will show you how to begin with easier instructional models and move to more complex and richer models as you feel increasingly comfortable with using the Internet in your classroom.

- *Great, New Central Sites.*   Teachers tell us one of their greatest challenges is locating information quickly on the Internet. We have included the best central sites from the first edition and added many new ones. Start your search at one of these locations. It is much faster than using a search engine.

- *A New Section on How to Save Time With Effective Search Engine Strategies.*   Search engines are often frustrating to new users looking for information. In Chapters 2 and 6 we show you a number of useful ideas to save you time.

We also update the companion home page for this book, Teaching with the Internet (http:// web.syr.edu/ ~djleu/ teaching.html).

- *A New Section on Citing Internet References.* Many teachers have told us that students need to know how to cite Internet resources in their reports and writing. We show you how to do this in chapter 4.

- *Expanded Coverage of Child Safety Strategies.* Throughout the book, we show you effective ways to protect children as they use the Internet. Chapters 4 and 9 have special sections about this important issue.

- *New Classroom Scenarios.* As we communicate with teachers around the world, we continually learn new lessons. We share these lessons through new stories about how teachers are using the Internet in their classrooms.

- *Strategies to Avoid the Growing Commercialization of Internet Sites.* Chapter 2 explores a new controversy being discussed in schools—the growing commercialization of the Internet and other information resources. We show you how to reconfigure your browser to minimize commercially motivated links. Moreover, our selection of sites minimizes much of the growing commercialism since we avoid those with extensive commercial messages.

- *Photographs of Teachers Who Share E-mail Messages.* You will also note the new photos of our e-mail contributors. We believe these communicate the human dimension of the Internet in a wonderful fashion. If you have a lesson to share with readers of our next edition, please send us an e-mail message. We would love to hear from you!

- *Many New Internet Resources for Teachers and Children.* And finally, of course, we have included many new sites that have appeared on the Internet to help you and your students. The Internet is changing quickly, providing many new opportunities for each of us to explore this exciting world for teaching and learning. Because this book is revised annually, we will continually bring you the most recent Internet resources we believe are useful.

We begin each chapter with a story of a teacher using the Internet in the classroom and then discuss the lessons each of us can learn from this experience.

The People Who Have Contributed to the Second Edition

We could not have completed a complex project like this without the assistance of many individuals. To each, we are profoundly indebted. We would like to thank as many of them as possible.

Many educators shared their experiences with the Internet, providing us with important insights that appear in this book. These include teachers from across the United States and Canada as well as educators from Argentina, Australia, Ecuador,

Finland, Japan, Germany, Great Britain, New Zealand, South Africa, and The Netherlands. Most are only known to us through their insightful e-mail messages and the descriptions they shared of their classes. We hope someday to have the opportunity to actually meet each person and personally express our gratitude for their important contributions.

We especially wish to thank the following educators who were kind enough to share their insights through the e-mail messages we include in this book: Nicole Boyce, Emily Buchanan, Celia Godsil, Barbara McInerney, Renata Svedlin, Lisa Brayton, Terrie Gray, Elizabeth Rohloff, Jeff Scanlan, Rina Hallock, Cindy Lockerman, Rachel Karchmer, Doug Crosby, Marjorie Duby, Brian Maguire, Jill Newcomb, Cindy Ross, Richard Love, Jeanette Kenyon, Maureen Salmon-Salvemini, Karen Auffhammer, Linda Shearin, Linda Swanson, Gary Cressman, Linda Hubbard, Jan Barth, Beverley Powell, Anton Ninno, Jodi Moore, Cathy Lewis, Angeles Maitland Heriot, Bill Farrell, Nicole Gamble, Anne Nguyen, and Mary Lou Balcom.

As we write this list, each name brings back an important memory of e-mail exchanges with a very knowledgeable educator. We thank each of you for sharing your wonderful lessons with us. Each of you is an outstanding educator, contributing in important ways to our increasingly global community. We have learned from your insights and we know our readers will too!

We also wish to thank our students and colleagues at Syracuse University who provided us with useful ideas as they responded to the first edition. Others at Syracuse also provided invaluable assistance. Joan Simonetta assisted with important aspects of communication and production. Karen Auffhammer and Allyson White provided valuable assistance in checking the accuracy of addresses for each web site. Allyson also assisted with web site development. Rachel Karchmer assisted with several projects involving e-mail, teaching us important lessons about this area.

Dr. Michael Hillinger of LexIcon provided important initial feedback about central ideas in this book. He has also been a valued colleague over the years as we have explored issues in electronic learning together.

Lynne Schueler of OutSide Services assisted in important ways to the final stages of this second edition. Her work in typesetting and layout can be seen on each page. We greatly appreciate her many contributions.

We especially wish to thank our good friends at Christopher-Gordon Publishers, Inc. without whom this second edition could not have been completed: Hiram Howard, Susanne Canavan, and Jacob Schulz. Hiram and Susanne shared our enthusiasm for this project at the beginning and have given us the freedom to complete this second edition in the way we envisioned it. They also picked up our spirits at several important points with their kind deeds and words. Besides his regular editorial duties, Jacob managed to obtain all of the many permissions required in a project as complex as this—a heroic task. The literary allusions in his e-mail messages always kept us smiling. Behind the scenes, others at Christopher-Gordon have also contributed to this project in important ways: Marcia Friedman, Laurie Maker, Paula Mazzone, and Linda Nevins. Authors could not ask for a more considerate and helpful publisher.

Finally, a special word of thanks is due our two daughters. Without the assistance of Caity and Sarah we could not have completed this book in a timely fashion. Caity contacted teachers around the world for us, identified a number of the sites we use in this book, and helped to develop the initial web site for the book. She also made several important suggestions at critical times. Sarah identified a number of important sites that we use in this book, especially those in Chapters 1 and 6. We greatly appreciate our daughters' many important contributions and their patience with parents who try very hard to be understanding . . . and sometimes succeed.

To everyone, our deepest thanks!

Don and Debbie Leu
Manlius, New York

1   Welcome to the Internet

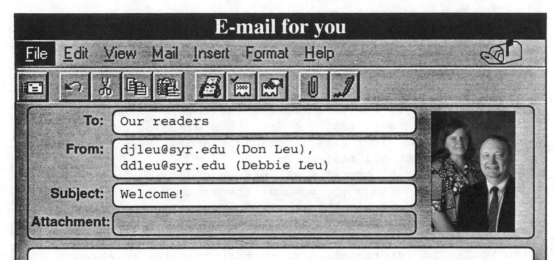

E-mail for you

File   Edit   View   Mail   Insert   Format   Help

To: Our readers

From: djleu@syr.edu (Don Leu),
ddleu@syr.edu (Debbie Leu)

Subject: Welcome!

Attachment:

Hi! Welcome to the second edition of Teaching with the Internet! This second edition contains a number of changes based on the many e-mail messages teachers have been kind enough to share with us. We have now expanded our coverage to include the entire K—12 curriculum and both PC and Mac platforms. We also have many new lessons from teachers and many new ideas to share with you. Most important, we have included the best new resources that have appeared on the WWW during the past year. We also have a new web site containing updated links to each of the locations mentioned in this book (http://web.syr.edu/~djleu/teaching.html). This will make it easier for you to locate the many locations we describe and easier for us to update these links. Come visit! We regularly add new items to this location, providing you with new ideas and new resources for your classroom.

Throughout this book, we will emphasize effective teaching practices while limiting the technical discussion of the Internet to basic essentials. Our focus is on using the Internet effectively in the classroom to support teaching and learning. Our approach is to show you how teachers and students use the Internet in their classrooms and then discuss the lessons we can learn from these experiences. Used thoughtfully, the Internet can make a powerful dif-

Document: Continued

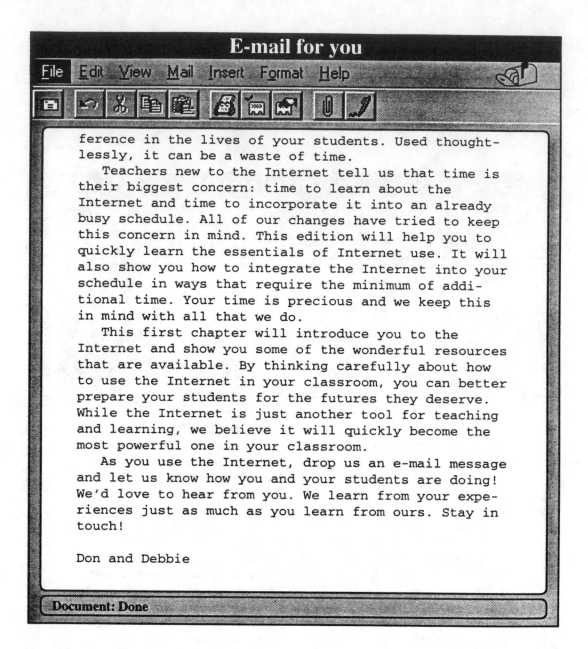

E-mail for you

File   Edit   View   Mail   Insert   Format   Help

ference in the lives of your students. Used thought-
lessly, it can be a waste of time.

Teachers new to the Internet tell us that time is
their biggest concern: time to learn about the
Internet and time to incorporate it into an already
busy schedule. All of our changes have tried to keep
this concern in mind. This edition will help you to
quickly learn the essentials of Internet use. It will
also show you how to integrate the Internet into your
schedule in ways that require the minimum of additional time. Your time is precious and we keep this
in mind with all that we do.

This first chapter will introduce you to the
Internet and show you some of the wonderful resources
that are available. By thinking carefully about how
to use the Internet in your classroom, you can better
prepare your students for the futures they deserve.
While the Internet is just another tool for teaching
and learning, we believe it will quickly become the
most powerful one in your classroom.

As you use the Internet, drop us an e-mail message
and let us know how you and your students are doing!
We'd love to hear from you. We learn from your experiences just as much as you learn from ours. Stay in
touch!

Don and Debbie

Document: Done

Teaching with the Internet: Tanisha Jackson's Class

It's Wednesday morning during the first week of school. Tanisha Jackson's tenth
grade class is just beginning their study of American history. Her class is working in
small groups today. Each group has a set of historical documents, books, and artifacts with information from one time period in American history. The activity calls
for them to use their materials to frame historical questions they will explore in
upcoming weeks. Tanisha uses this activity at the beginning of the year to whet her
students' interest in history and introduce them to the historical analysis of primary
source documents. She also uses the activity to develop important background knowledge, knowledge that will help her students throughout the year.

Each group has a single day to explore each of four sets of materials and develop their questions about the time period of their materials. The next day the groups rotate to the next set of historical materials. On Friday, they will share their questions and their discoveries in a whole-class discussion during Internet Workshop. Tanisha plans to organize their questions around the different time periods covered during the year, introducing themes and issues they will explore in upcoming units.

Three groups are working at their desks. A fourth group is working in pairs at the three Internet computers in her classroom, locating and analyzing original documents they find in cyberspace. Each day a different group completes an "Internet Activity" at the computer cluster, trying to develop important questions from the primary source documents they find on the Internet. Internet Activity is an instructional idea Tanisha learned last summer during a workshop session.

Tanisha looks up to observe the group at the Internet computers. This is the second year she has had an Internet connection in her classroom. One of the first lessons she learned was that students often spend their limited time at the computer just "surfing" for information on the World Wide Web (WWW) of the Internet, moving quickly from site to site trying to find something interesting. Often her students' time at the computer would run out before they had an opportunity to really read and learn anything. Or, they would sometimes end up at sites that were inappropriate for their work.

Therefore, Tanisha set the home page location on all three computers to open to **American Memory** (http://lcweb2.loc.gov/ammem/ammemhome.html) as soon as her students connected to the Internet. This outstanding resource from the Library of Congress contains a wonderful collection of original documents, photos, motion pictures, maps, and sound recordings for social studies education. Here, students can find all kinds of great resources including: original documents from the Continental Congress, a collection of 350 pamphlets providing insight into the African American experience from 1818–1907, movies, audio recordings of famous speeches, a collection of over 1,000 photographs from the Civil War, and much, much more. This was one of the central sites she discovered during her summer workshop. Setting the home page to a central site like this saved valuable time in a 40-minute period.

Tanisha also learned a second lesson very quickly—her students often taught one another about the Internet faster than she could teach them. After teaching the entire class some basic essentials about the computer and Internet use, Tanisha looked for ways to encourage students to exchange information and teach one another. Among other strategies, she set aside a portion of the bulletin board next to the computers for students to post information about the Internet. Students listed useful sites and shared other information about their current work. Some students even used the word processor on the computer to type these notes, so word processing skills were developed, too. And she had learned about using "Internet Workshop" at the end of each week to share discoveries and to ask questions. She quickly saw the potential of these activities for building a supportive classroom community.

Figure 1-1. American Memory, an outstanding location on the Internet for social studies developed by the Library of Congress. It contains an extensive collection of primary source documents including documents, photos, motion pictures, maps, and sound recordings.

American Memory (http://lcweb2.loc.gov/ammem/ammemhome.html)

"Cool," said Sarah. She and her partner Vanita had just found a site at American Memory that someone had described on the bulletin board. The site was called **"Votes for Women" Suffrage Pictures, 1850–1920** (http://lcweb2.loc.gov/ammem/vfwhtml/vfwhome.html), a collection of photographs and documents about the suffrage movement in the United States.

"Hey . . . sisters marching," Vanita said as the image in Figure 1-2 opened. They both laughed. Then they started reading **One Hundred Years toward Suffrage: An Overview** (http://lcweb2.loc.gov/ammem/vfwhtml/vfwtl.html), developing a greater appreciation for the struggles women have faced.

"Look, Seneca Falls. That's where they had the first women's rights convention. Cool! I went there last year."

At the computer next to Sarah and Vanita, Jonathon and his Internet partner, Josh, were working. "Hey, look! Jackie Robinson. We can study the history of baseball? That's phat!" Jonathon, had found a great source: **Jackie Robinson and other Baseball Highlights, 1980's–1960's** (http://lcweb2.loc.gov/ammem/jrhtml/

Figure 1-2. One of many images at American Memory is the exhibit **"Votes for Women" Suffrage Pictures, 1850–1920,** a collection of photographs and documents about the suffrage movement.

"Votes for Women" Suffrage Pictures, 1850–1920
(http://lcweb2.loc.gov/ammem/vfwhtml/vfwhome.html)

jrhome.html). They started reading about Jackie Robinson and viewing the extensive set of documents about this famous American.

"They got Larry Doby?" asked Jonathon. Clearly, Jonathon knew his baseball history.

At the third computer, Mircalla and Jessica had found the movie section. "Look at this movie. It's San Francisco and the real earthquake. Cool!" said Mircalla. "I was born there but I never saw something like this before."

"Don't forget to write down questions you want to explore in class this year," Tanisha reminded everyone. "We're going to have Internet Workshop on Friday."

The group at the Internet computers got together quickly to list their questions:

1. Why didn't people want women to vote?
2. Who were some of the important women? What did they do?
3. What were the Negro Leagues like and who were some of the best players?
4. How hard was it for Jackie Robinson when he played baseball?
5. What was San Francisco like before the earthquake?
6. How did they put the fire out in San Francisco?

Jonathon typed their questions at the computer as the others in his group dictated them. Then they printed their questions out for Ms. Jackson on the classroom printer.

Before they went back to their desks, Mircalla and Jessica typed and posted a short note on the bulletin board next to the computer. It said:

```
See the FANTASTIK movie about the San Francisco
earthquake on the internet. Check out where it says
motion pictures.

     Mircalla and Jessica
```

Lessons from the Classroom

This short episode illustrates a number of important lessons about using the Internet in your classroom; lessons that will guide us throughout this book. First, it illustrates how resources available to students on the Internet may be used in your classroom to support learning. Reading about the history of the Negro Leagues and then viewing a short movie about Jackie Robinson made this information come alive for Jonathon and Josh. They talked about it all day with other students and even shared this information at home. And, of course, they talked about this during Internet Workshop on Friday. The same was true for Sarah and Vanita and the documents about the suffrage movement as well as Mircalla and Jessica and the San Francisco Earthquake. The Internet provides a powerful new tool for you and your students to access information and then to communicate with others about what you have learned. Throughout this book you will find other sites on the Internet just as powerful for supporting your students' learning.

The Internet provides a powerful new tool for you and your students to access information and then to communicate with others about what you have learned.

The episode also illustrates how an insightful teacher can efficiently direct students to information and help them avoid endless "surfing" to find useful sites. By setting the computer to open to this location on the Internet, Tanisha made a number of resources immediately available to her students. Later, we will describe additional techniques to help students use their limited time wisely.

In addition, the episode shows how the Internet can be easily integrated into your current classroom activities. Using the Internet in your class does not need to take additional time. We will show you how Internet resources may be used with any of your current teaching practices: activity centers, writing process activities, author chair experiences, thematic units, cooperative learning groups, response journals, jigsaw grouping, and K-W-L, among others. We will also show you how to use several new instructional models in your class: Internet Workshop, Internet Activity, Internet Project, and Internet Inquiry.

An insightful teacher can efficiently direct students to information and help them avoid endless "surfing" to find useful sites.

Finally, the episode shows how Tanisha's planning encouraged her students to help one another as they searched for information. Social learning opportunities abound with Internet resources, and Tanisha developed several ways for students to support one another as they worked. The bulletin board told others where useful information was located on the WWW. Tanisha had encouraged all of the students to post information on the bulletin board when they came across something they thought others might be able to use. And, on Friday, she would be using Internet Workshop, where students could both share their discoveries and seek assistance. Needless to say, Tanisha's encouragement to assist one another on the Internet also helped to develop a very supportive classroom community. We will show you other ways in which you can assist your students to help one another with Internet resources, an excellent lesson for life.

Social learning opportunities abound with Internet resources.

The Times Are Changing

This story is not the first you have heard about the Internet. In just a few years, the Internet has become a central part of popular culture. Nearly every day we encounter stories in the press about the Internet and how it is changing our lives; ads in magazines and on television now carry World Wide Web addresses; we hear radio talk-show hosts mention the live "chat-rooms" where listeners can continue their conversations "on-line"; and we hear colleagues talking about all the e-mail they had to answer before going to bed last night.

In just a few years, the Internet has become a central part of popular culture.

You have also seen the changes taking place in your own school. Your classroom may already be connected and you are trying to find time to better understand these new resources for your students. Perhaps your district has recently completed a technology plan and new Internet connections are coming this year for your library/media center, the computer lab, and your classroom. Like many of us, you probably can recall the day when a student first showed you a print-out with Internet information for a class assignment and you began to wonder about the new world all of us are entering.

Undoubtedly, you have many feelings about these changes. You may be excited, skeptical, nervous, or, like us, you may experience all of these feelings, sometimes at the same time. We get excited when we discover a site like "American Memory" and think about how it can be used in the classroom. We become skeptical when we read about politicians who symbolically show their commitment by helping to wire schools, but disappear when it comes time to pay for computers or provide staff development time. We become nervous when we think about the speed of these changes and whether we can ever know everything there is to know about new technologies. After all, who had even heard of the Internet just a few years ago? And who can tell what new technologies will show up as soon as we begin to understand this one? Yes, the Internet prompts all of these thoughts.

What is the Internet?

It is sometimes hard to figure out what the Internet really is. Sometimes it sounds like a place to buy a car with a computer. Sometimes it appears to be a way of sending e-mail. Sometimes it sounds like a place to read the newspaper. Sometimes

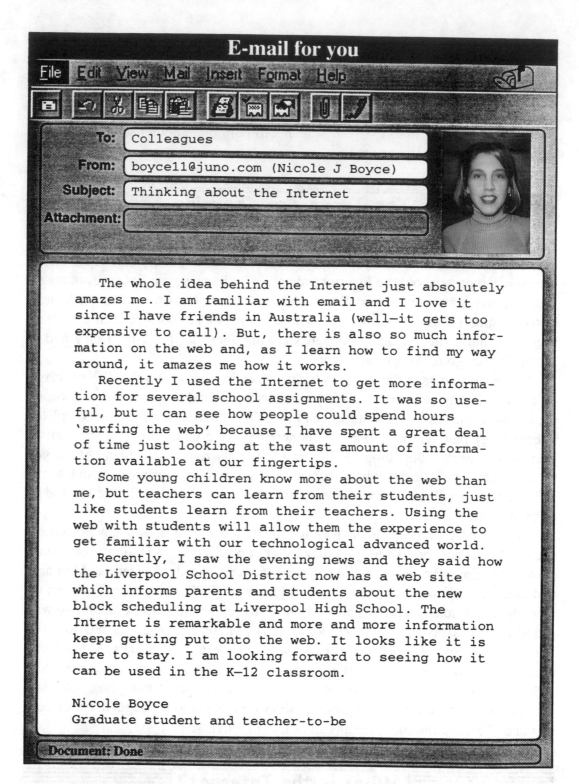

E-mail for you

File   Edit   View   Mail   Insert   Format   Help

To: Colleagues

From: boyce11@juno.com (Nicole J Boyce)

Subject: Thinking about the Internet

Attachment:

The whole idea behind the Internet just absolutely amazes me. I am familiar with email and I love it since I have friends in Australia (well—it gets too expensive to call). But, there is also so much information on the web and, as I learn how to find my way around, it amazes me how it works.

Recently I used the Internet to get more information for several school assignments. It was so useful, but I can see how people could spend hours 'surfing the web' because I have spent a great deal of time just looking at the vast amount of information available at our fingertips.

Some young children know more about the web than me, but teachers can learn from their students, just like students learn from their teachers. Using the web with students will allow them the experience to get familiar with our technological advanced world.

Recently, I saw the evening news and they said how the Liverpool School District now has a web site which informs parents and students about the new block scheduling at Liverpool High School. The Internet is remarkable and more and more information keeps getting put onto the web. It looks like it is here to stay. I am looking forward to seeing how it can be used in the K—12 classroom.

Nicole Boyce
Graduate student and teacher-to-be

Document: Done

it sounds like a way to talk with someone while you view them on your computer screen. It is all of these things, and more.

At heart, the Internet is simply a set of computers around the world connected to one another. You can go to one computer in Texas to check the price for a car, send e-mail to another computer in Tokyo, and read a newspaper that appears on yet another computer in London. Initially, only large computers at universities were connected to one another. Now, anyone with a desk-top computer and a telephone can get connected and become a part of the Internet. This is how the first connections were made in many districts. Increasingly, though, schools are moving away from separate phone connections and are beginning to directly wire classrooms to the Internet. This allows you and your students to link up with any other computer, anywhere in the world.

There are many different ways in which you may access information on computers linked to the Internet. You may use an e-mail program to send messages or documents back and forth. Most computers linked to the Internet have this ability because it is relatively simple. Other, richer sources of information are also available on the Internet including: music, video, audio, animation, color graphics, and even free software programs you can download to your computer. These are located on computers that are a part of the World Wide Web (WWW or, simply, the Web). You access the WWW through special software called a web browser. A web browser, like Netscape Navigator or Internet Explorer, allows you to read text, listen to music, watch a video clip, and view color graphics. The WWW of the Internet is an especially useful source of information for classroom learning.

Figure 1-3, for example, shows you the home page for **Journey Exchange** (http://www.win4edu.com/minds-eye/journey/), a location on the Web developed by a teacher in upstate New York for K–12 social studies. Small groups of students in one classroom develop a 5-day journey to different locations around the world, providing clues from their Internet research to another group of students. Students in the other classroom then research the clues, attempting to follow the trip that has been planned for them. When they think they have figured out the entire trip from the clues, they check with the classroom that posted it. The activity puts children in touch with one another around the world in wonderful ways as they study different geographical regions.

Being a part of this large network of computers allows you and your students access to information at any other computer located on the Internet. This is what makes the Internet such a powerful instructional tool for you and your students. There are many, many things you can do when you are connected to the Internet:

- **Send an E-Mail Message to anyone in the world.**   Students in a classroom in New Jersey were each doing an Internet Inquiry on a European country. They followed a K-W-L (Know, Want to Know, and Learn) model developed by Ogle, (1989). During their study, one student discovered **Web 66** (http://web66.coled.umn.edu/schools/Maps/Europe.html), a location where you could find web pages for schools from around the world, including most countries in Europe. The students quickly discovered how to send e-mail to schools in Europe from the web pages they located. Noticing what was taking place, the teacher decided to have each student write to students in their project country, asking them to describe what took place during a typical day in their part of the world. Students fol-

Being a part of this large network of computers allows you and your students access to information at any other computer located on the Internet. This is what makes the Internet such a powerful instructional tool for you and your students.

Figure 1-3. Journey Exchange is just one of many resources available on the Internet for you to use in your classroom.

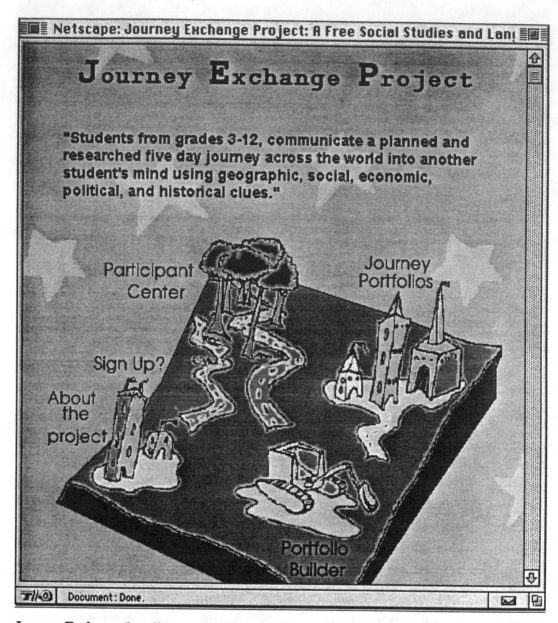

Netscape: Journey Exchange Project: A Free Social Studies and Lang

Journey Exchange Project

"Students from grades 3-12, communicate a planned and researched five day journey across the world into another student's mind using geographic, social, economic, political, and historical clues."

Participant Center

Journey Portfolios

Sign Up?

About the project

Portfolio Builder

Document: Done.

Journey Exchange (http://www.win4edu.com/minds-eye/journey/)

lowed traditional process writing procedures as they developed their letters: brainstorming, drafting, revising, editing, and publishing (sending). Within a few days everyone was receiving e-mail from Europe describing "typical days." This began a correspondence that lasted throughout the year for many of the students. The collection of "typical day" stories was printed out, included in each student's report, and displayed on a bulletin board for parents to see during the school's Open House. The experience provided a very special window to the cultures of Europe. It was also highly motivating. Students couldn't wait to check their mailboxes each morning to see if they had e-mail from their foreign friends. Many new understandings were developed about life in other cultures.

Internet FAQ

Who pays when I use my computer to communicate with another computer somewhere else in the world? We pay for telephone calls. Why don't we pay for the Internet?

With a few exceptions, no individual really pays for traffic on the Internet since everyone agrees to let everyone else travel through their network to get to other, connected networks of computers. The exceptions are Internet Service Providers like ATT, America On-line, or Local Service Providers in your community who charge people to connect to their computers in order to connect to the Internet. Your district will pay a fee to a Local Service Provider for Internet access. Recently, however, the FCC has determined that schools only have to pay a small percentage of the normal rate, depending upon the percentage of students receiving free or reduced lunches. The remainder will be provided by an annual pool in the United States of more than two billion dollars each year. This money is available to schools for telecommunications services, internal connections and Internet access. While the telecommunications industry is attempting to reduce the amount of the subsidy, this program will quickly increase the number of schools connected to the Internet. To find out more about federal support for schools interested in getting connected to the Internet, visit the WWW site the FCC has set up to keep schools informed about policy initiatives, **LearnNet** (http://www.fcc.gov/learnnet/). Information about the subsidy program for schools, known commonly as the e-rate program, is available at the **Schools and Libraries Corporation** (http://www.slcfund.org/), the not-for-profit corporation set up by the FCC to manage this program.

- **Discover Great Lesson Plans and Teaching Ideas.** There are many locations with outstanding lesson planning resources. Often these will let you search for lessons by topic and by grade level. If you are interested in integrating the Internet into literature experiences, pay a visit to **CyberGuides** (http://www.sdcoe.k12.ca.us/score/cyberguide.html). Here, you will find an extensive set of links to outstanding works of children's literature organized by grade level. Each link contains lesson plans, instructional ideas, links to other Web resources, and suggestions for how to use those resources. This location should be familiar to every teacher with an Internet connection in the classroom. Set a bookmark!

- **Acquire Information.** You may go to any other computer on the Internet and look for information put there for your use. You can read the complete works of Shakespeare, view a map of the world displaying earthquakes recorded during the past month, take a guided tour of the White House, view videos of different penguin species in the Antarctic, read the news and view news videos at sites operated by CNN, ESPN, or USA Today, and obtain photos of ancient Egyptian artifacts recently discovered in the Valley of the Dead. The list of information resources available to you and your students is nearly endless because people around the world are adding more each day. Most important, the information on the Internet is almost always more recent than that in any textbook in your classroom.

Information on the Internet is almost always more recent than that in any textbook in your classroom.

- **Communicate with Others Who Share a Similar Interest.** You can join a mailing list and receive messages from others who share a common interest. Are you interested in discussions with other teachers about science education, math education, music education, art education, literacy education, social studies education, ESL education, or special education? Mailing lists exist for each of these areas where teachers exchange teaching ideas and instructional resources. In addition to mailing lists, there are Newsgroups, and an increasing number of real-time, "chat" locations appearing on the Internet for teachers. At these locations, teachers can share ideas about instruction with other teachers around the world and immediately read what others think.

- **Acquire New Software.** A new teacher in Olympia, Washington was looking for a better way to keep track of grades in her social studies class. She heard about a free software program called **Eagle Gradebook** she could download onto her computer and then use to record and average her grades. She went to the sites at Virginia Tech (for Macintosh: http://tac.elps.vt.edu/htmldocs/mac.html; for Windows: http://tac.elps.vt.edu/htmldocs/ibm.html) that a friend had located, downloaded the software, and found that it met her needs perfectly. She also noticed programs at the same location for keeping track of attendance, making banners for the classroom, and making calendars. She downloaded these free programs and used them often during the year. Many locations on the Internet provide free and very useful software for classroom needs.

Many locations on the Internet provide free and very useful software for classroom needs.

- **Conduct a Video Conference.** Do you want to have a discussion between your class and a class in a foreign country about a book you have both read or an issue you have both studied? No problem. All you need is the right software and an inexpensive video camera for your computer. The interchange could provide your students with special insights into another culture. Or, conduct a video conference with an expert on the topic your students are studying. This might be a member of Congress, a scientist, a historian, or the author of a book they have recently read. Have your students do their research in advance and prepare their questions for this expert. If you would like to find out more about this technology, visit one of several sites explaining "CU-SeeMe" technology (http://CU-Seeme.cornell.edu/Welcome.html).

- **Publish a Page on the WWW for Your School and Your Class.** Many teachers are finding the WWW to be a useful location for publishing their students' writing and presenting other information about classroom activities. They find that publishing writing for the entire world to read motivates students to produce exceptional work. See, for example, the wonderful homepage developed by **Ms. Hos-McGrane's Grade Six Class** in The Netherlands (http://www.xs4all.nl/~swanson/origins/

intro.html). Teachers like Ms. Hos-McGrane quickly discover that other students, parents, and grandparents visit their classroom page to read their work and learn about classroom activities. Schools and classrooms with web pages also present an image of education that is different from the many critical images portrayed in the press. The importance of this positive image should not be overlooked by our profession.

These are just a few of the things you can do on the Internet in your classroom. While we will try to present a balanced view of the Internet and not get carried away with the hype of this new technology, it is easy to see why some people do get a bit excited. The information and communication resources available on the Internet are the beginning of a radical departure in the nature of information available to us and our students. Without trying to hype the technology, it is probably fair to say the Internet is fundamentally changing the nature of teaching and learning as it enters our classrooms (Kinzer & Leu, 1997; Leu, 1997; Leu, in press). Our response to these important changes will determine our students' ability to succeed in the world that awaits them. New challenges and new opportunities await us all.

Our response to these important changes will determine our students' ability to succeed in the world that awaits them.

Why is the Internet so Important to My Students?

The rapidly changing nature of technology affects each of us. More than anyone else, though, these powerful changes affect our students and the opportunities they will have in life. Let's think for a moment about the world our students will enter when they complete their formal education. This is where we should begin our plans for their education. As we think about this, let's make at least one assumption: Let's assume that many of our students will complete four years of education after completing high school, a consideration that is increasingly becoming a requirement for effective employment in a post-industrial society.

To begin our "thought experiment," let's add 17 years to the current year. This is the time when children who started kindergarten this year will enter the workplace to seek employment. For example, a student beginning kindergarten in 1998 will enter the workplace in 2015. What will it take to be successful in the world of 2015? While we cannot tell with absolute precision, there are several trends that give us a reasonable chance to anticipate the broad outlines for successful entry into society 17 years from now.

First, it is clear that economies around the world will be engaged in a competitive struggle for markets, jobs, and business. We see the beginnings of this now as areas of the world join regional economic groupings, as barriers to trade are lowered, and as companies compete for global markets. Successful societies will be those with individuals who can compete effectively in a global economy because their educational system prepared them for these economic realities.

Second, to succeed in an increasingly competitive global marketplace, organizations will have to change the way they work. In the past decade, many organizations

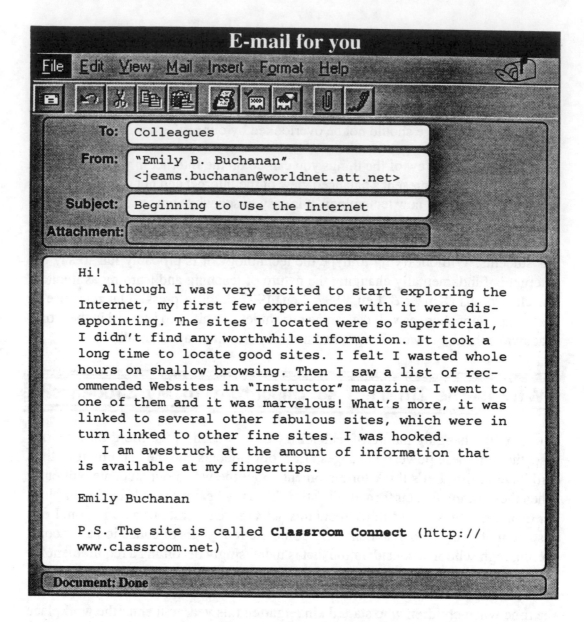

have worked to transform themselves into "high-performance" workplaces. In most cases, this means changing from a centrally planned organization to one that relies increasingly on collaborative teams at all levels to assume initiative for planning ways to work more efficiently.

There is also a third trend underway. Increasingly, problem-solving skills will be critical to successful performance. As collaborative teams seek more effective ways of working, they will be expected to identify problems important to their unit and seek appropriate solutions. Thus, when students leave school, they will need to be able to identify central problems, find the appropriate information quickly, and then use this information to solve the problems they identify as important.

Fourth, in "high performance" settings it appears that effective collaboration and communication skills will be central to success. The changes from a centralized to a decentralized workplace will require collaboration and communication skills so that the best decisions get made at every level in an organization and so that changes at one level are clearly communicated to other levels. Our students will need effective collaboration and communication skills when they leave us.

Finally, there is a fifth trend—effective information access and use will be increasingly important to success. Individuals who can access information the fastest and use it effectively to solve important problems will be the ones who succeed in the challenging times that await our students. This will make informational literacy a crucial determinant of success. We must prepare our students for the new information technologies that will become increasingly available as we change from an industrial to an information society.

What does all of this mean for our students? How can we support them to become effective individuals who make important contributions to society? We believe in the truth of the following maxim:

> In the information age in which we all live, the race will be won by individuals, groups, and societies who can access the best information in the shortest time to identify and solve the most important problems and communicate this information to others.

This is why the Internet and other electronic technologies are so important. We need to prepare our students to use these new information and communication technologies because they enable us to identify and solve important problems in the shortest time and communicate our ideas to others. Nothing is more important for the future of our students. This is the challenge we face as educators in the new world we are all entering. This is what we must prepare our students for as we think about their futures.

We need to prepare our students for the new information technologies that are available now and will become increasingly available as we change from an industrial to an information society.

Internet FAQ

I have heard a lot about children visiting sites on the WWW and seeing things they shouldn't be seeing. I have also heard stories about children being contacted by strangers for inappropriate purposes. Is this true? How can we protect our children from these things?

Schools have always taught children safety related to drugs, fire, earthquakes, school bus travel, strangers on the street, and other matters. As the Internet enters our worlds, schools are teaching safe Internet practices, developing "Acceptable Use" policies, and implementing other strategies to protect children. Our feeling is that Internet safety will be an important part of the curriculum as we seek to prepare children for their futures. We will describe more specific strategies to protect children in later chapters. If you wish to consider this issue now, you may want to read the Global School Network's tutorial, **Protecting Students: Guidelines and Policies** (http://www.gsn.org/web/issues/index.htm#begin). It shares many useful resources and strategies for developing an appropriate child safety policy for your school.

How Can I Use the Internet to Help My Students?

Throughout this book, we will help you to answer this important question. The Internet is an extensive resource of information and communication, but its effective use in the classroom will ultimately depend upon how *you* take advantage of this resource. Like every other area of education, it is not what the instructional materials are but what you do with them that determines the extent of your students' learning. No packaged set of materials can compete with a teacher who cares about students, understands their unique needs, and responds in effective ways to support their learning. As you begin to consider how to use the Internet with your students, it may be helpful to see specific examples of what is possible on the WWW of the Internet:

- **Dr. Seuss in Cyberspace.**   After reading *The Cat in the Hat* aloud to your class, have students visit **Seussville: Ask the Cat** to ask this mischievous character a question (http://www.randomhouse.com/seussville/askthecat/). The Cat in the Hat will send your students an e-mail message with the answer. Then, invite your students to play any of the great games located at **Seussville Games** (http://www.randomhouse.com/seussville/games/). Great fun! Set a bookmark!

- **Science Resources.**   The Science Learning Network is a group of museums and schools devoted to improving science teaching through the Internet. Use the **Science Learning Network** (http://www.sln.org/) to access descriptions of science units taking place in classrooms around the world based on the National Science Standards and inquiry learning. E-mail teachers who have classes doing the same units as yours to share ideas and resources. Have students use e-mail to discuss their results and compare them with the results from other students. Post science ideas and questions on a bulletin board and receive replies back from other teachers and students. Have your students complete interactive, multimedia units on topics such as: the physics of water, storm science, dissecting a frog or a cow's eye, using a scanning electron microscope (students can see the photos of objects they request), and much more.

- **Whales: A Thematic Web Unit.**   This incredibly rich resource (http://curry.edschool.virginia.edu/~kpj5e/Whales/) provides all the resources you will need for a cross-curricular thematic unit using cooperative grouping as your students study whales. Assign small groups to research a particular area and then report back to the whole class. After preliminary reports, decide upon additional questions to explore and develop new groups to explore these issues. Along the way, students can actually hear the voices of many different whale species, study the physics of echolocation, track several whales by satellite, and download a software program that provides basic information on all of the great whale species.

- **Pi Mathematics.** As students learn about Pi, use this site (http://www.ncsa.uiuc.edu:80/edu/RSE/RSEorange/buttons.html) to supplement your lessons. Have groups select an activity from this location and then share the results with the class. Some may choose to research and report on the history of Pi, others may wish to use Pi to determine the best deal at a pizza shop, others may wish to complete an activity measuring Pi using common objects, others may wish to calculate Pi out to one hundred decimal places and then show the class how this can be memorized by singing a popular tune, still others may choose to calculate the circumference of planets and then check their answers at other locations on the Internet. These and other activities are all clearly matched with standards from the National Council of Teachers of Mathematics. Set a bookmark!

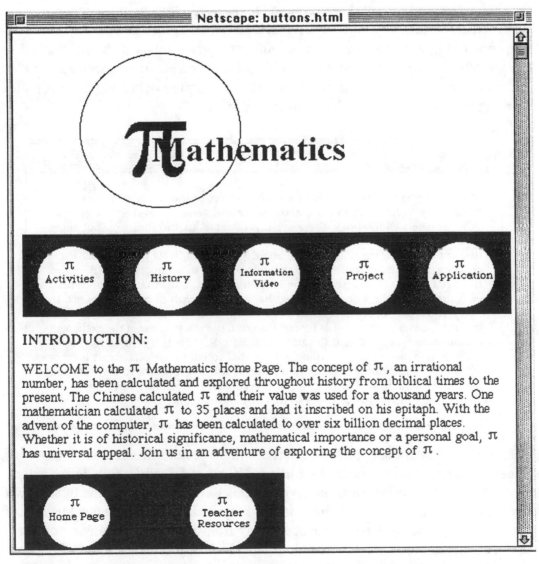

Figure 1-4. Pi Mathematics: A great location on the WWW for math classes

Pi Mathematics (http://www.ncsa.uiuc.edu:80/edu/RSE/RSEorange/buttons.html)

The many resources available on the Internet are the beginning of a radical departure in the nature of information available to us and our students. How we respond to these important changes will determine our students' ability to succeed in the world that awaits them.

- **Learn About Popular Authors.** Are your students looking for information about a favorite author? Have them visit **The Author Page** (http://ipl.sils.umich.edu/youth/AskAuthor/) at the Internet Public Library. This site provides biographies and interviews with many popular authors of children's and adolescent literature. It also provides links to many of the best author sites available on the Internet. Ask students to share the results of their discoveries with your class.

Teaching and learning are being redefined by the communication technologies that are quickly becoming a part of the information age in which we live (Negroponte, 1995; Reinking, 1995). We are experiencing a historic change in the nature of learning as digital, multimedia resources enter our world. The many resources available on the Internet are the beginning of a radical departure in the nature of information available to us and our students. How we respond to these important changes will determine our students' ability to succeed in the world that awaits them.

Internet resources will increase, not decrease, the central role you play in orchestrating learning experiences for your students. Each of us will be challenged to thoughtfully guide students' learning within information environments that are richer and more complex than traditional print media, presenting richer and more complex learning opportunities for both us and our students.

The Internet eliminates traditional walls that have prevented us from sharing the wonderful things happening in each of our classrooms.

TEACHING TIP

Many teachers find that the most powerful aspect of the Internet is the opportunity it provides them to learn about successful activities and resources from other teachers. Sometimes these are ideas related to Internet use, but more often they are ideas about traditional instructional issues: good works of literature for an upcoming unit, an idea about teaching radicals in mathematics, a great science demonstration on gravitational force, or an upcoming PBS video for social studies. The Internet eliminates traditional walls that have prevented us from sharing the wonderful things happening in each of our classrooms. In Chapter 3, you will see how to participate in these conversations by using mailing lists, newsgroups, and chat rooms. However, to see a preview of the exchanges taking place every day, visit the archives of **RTEACHER** (http://listserv.syr.edu/archives/rteacher.html), a mailing list devoted to conversations about literacy learning and technology. Notice how teachers use this resource to discover new ideas for instruction. The Internet is a very social environment, putting teachers in touch with other teachers so that all children benefit.

As but one example of how the Internet will make our role even more important, consider recent concerns raised by Birkerts (1995) and Stoll (1995). These authors worry that electronic information environments like the WWW of the Internet will encourage students to "surf" many unrelated topics on only a superficial level. Left on their own, students may be seduced away from reading and thinking critically about a single topic as they discover intriguing links to more and more locations and move farther and farther away from the initial topic. As a result, students will only skim the surface of many, unrelated, pieces of information, never integrating or thinking deeply about any of them.

We think this scenario is only possible, however, in classrooms where teachers do not actively guide the use of Internet resources and, instead, leave decisions about Internet use entirely to students. When students always determine their own paths through this rich and intriguing information resource, there is a powerful tendency to search for what students refer to as "cool," highly interactive and media-rich locations that quickly attract their attention but are unrelated to important learning tasks (Leu, 1996). These often include video, sound, animation, and other elements. As students search for "cool" sites, they are less likely to explore important topics in depth or think critically about the relation of this information to their own lives. Students end up viewing much but learning little.

On the other hand, when students are guided to resources and provided with important learning tasks to accomplish, they quickly focus on important information related to the issue at hand (Leu, 1996). This is not to say that students should be limited only to Internet resources that you select and complete tasks that only you devise. Clearly, if we wish students to become effective users of the Internet, we want them to develop independent strategies for searching and analyzing information. And, in order to do so we must provide them with learning experiences that they direct. Still, it points to the central role you will play with this new resource as you support their ability to independently acquire and evaluate information on the web.

Internet FAQ

How can I get my school connected to the Internet without spending a lot of money?

A national organization, Net Day, is a grassroots volunteer effort to wire schools so they can network their computers and connect them to the Internet. Labor and materials come from volunteers and support from companies, unions, parents, teachers, students, and school employees. This organization has been remarkably successful at coordinating efforts to get schools wired inexpensively with the support of the business community and others. Visit their WWW site and find out more about **Net Day** (http://www.netday.org/) resources and wiring kits.

A national organization, Net Day, is a grassroots volunteer effort to wire schools so they can network their computers and connect them to the Internet.

In this book, we will show you an integrated set of instructional models for teaching with the Internet. They include: Internet Workshop, Internet Activity, Internet Project, and Internet Inquiry. You will see how to begin with easier instructional models and move to move complex and richer models as you feel increasingly comfortable with using the Internet in your classroom.

Teachers who understand the Internet and thoughtfully integrate its many resources into their classroom curriculum will see students expand their understanding of important concepts and communicate these ideas more effectively to others in your class and around the world. Teachers who simply allow students to explore the

In this book, we will show you an integrated set of instructional models for teaching with the Internet. They include: Internet Workshop, Internet Activity, Internet Projects, and Internet Inquiry.

Internet on their own after their regular work is completed will see little change in student learning. In fact, this type of Internet experience may actually take students away from thinking critically about important ideas as they search for surface level "cool."

A central assumption of this book is that your role in orchestrating experiences with the Internet is central to your students' futures. Your instructional decisions will determine the extent to which your students gain from this resource. That is why we focus on effective teaching practices while limiting the technical discussion of the Internet to essential basics.

The Social Nature of Learning with the Internet

Much recent research suggests learning is best accomplished through social interaction in supportive social contexts. When students work together, they often are very effective at "scaffolding," or helping, one another on the way to important insights (Meyer, 1993). Theoretical perspectives established by Vygotsky (1978), Bahktin (1981), and others are often used to explain this process. Method frameworks such as cooperative learning (Johnson & Johnson, 1984), peer conferences (Graves, 1983), jigsaw activities (Aaronson, 1978), literature discussion groups (Leu & Kinzer, 1998), text set activities (Short, 1993), and others are thought to be particularly useful because they create situations where students help one another to learn important concepts.

A central assumption of this book is that your role in orchestrating experiences with the Internet is central to your students' futures.

This socially mediated learning may be especially important for learning within the Internet and other electronic information resources. Because these information resources are powerful, complex, and constantly changing, they often require us to communicate with others in order to make meaning from them. No one person knows everything there is to know about the Internet; each of us has useful information that can help others. I may know something about how to search for information but you may know a really good location for students who want to publish their work. By sharing our information, we can help one another learn about these rich information resources. Learning about the Internet is best accomplished through social interactions with others, perhaps even more naturally and frequently than in traditional print environments. This is one reason we have asked other teachers to share their insights with you through e-mail messages that appear throughout this book.

The instructional episode at the beginning of this chapter with Sarah, Vanita, Jonathon, Josh, Mircalla, and Jessica illustrates how an insightful teacher can take advantage of socially mediated learning with the Internet. Setting up a bulletin board next to the computer and encouraging students to help one another are simple ways you can support students in these efforts. So is instruction based on cooperation and collaboration.

We will also show you a powerful instructional model, Internet Workshop, to support students learning from one another. With a little encouragement from you, you will discover students helping one another and discovering new aspects of the

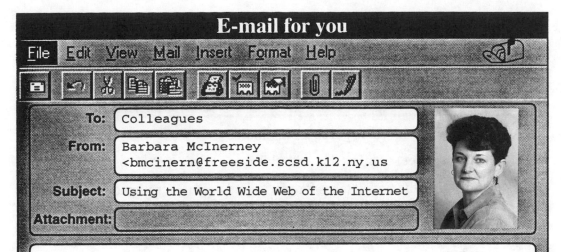

E-mail for you

File   Edit   View   Mail   Insert   Format   Help

To: Colleagues

From: Barbara McInerney
<bmcinern@freeside.scsd.k12.ny.us

Subject: Using the World Wide Web of the Internet

Attachment:

No one person knows everything there is to know about the Internet; each of us has useful information that can help others.

Hi!

I am really excited about the new doors opening to me as a teacher through use of the Internet. However, that excitement is tempered by some reservations and concerns. One of my biggest concerns is the application of the sources on the Internet. Will I be able to make the use of the Web integrated and meaningful to my students? Will I be able to instruct them correctly and completely in the use of the Web? Will their use of the Internet add to the completeness of the curriculum or just be a casual aside? I feel teachers need to be fully trained and capable in the workings of the Net before attempting to guide students in its use. We do so many "hit and miss" procedures in education—but this technology is here to stay and will be an integral part of their future so students need to learn its use completely and correctly to really enhance classroom experiences.

One of my students, when asked about the feelings they had about our school becoming hooked up to the Internet and what possibilities it presented for them, answered in this manner, "I think it's going to be really cool! I mean, if you are studying, say China, and you could communicate with students in China to really see what it is like there, that would be so cool! Or, if you needed to know some stuff about a topic and all your books were old, then you could go to the Internet and it could tell you new stuff."

Even students with no experience to date on the Internet have a general idea of what they would like to try to do with it—it shows they are thinking about the possibilities, as I am.

I am excited about using this in my class next year!!!!

Barbara McInerney

Document: Done

Internet to share with still other students. This can make Internet use an effective tool for community building as well as for learning.

The Purpose of this Book

We write this book with three purposes in mind:

- to help you feel comfortable with this new learning environment;

- to minimize the time it takes for you to find useful learning tools for your students; and

- to show you ways the Internet may be used in your classroom to support learning.

To those of us uncomfortable with technology, thinking about using the Internet in a classroom means sweaty palms, a dry throat, and a racing heart as our anxieties about technology start to overwhelm any thoughts of benefits for our students. How can we consider using the Internet when we are unable to set the time on our VCR? We will be sensitive to these concerns. We have had many long discussions about this issue as we planned this book. We will be supportive, inviting, and encouraging as we explain how to use the Internet to assist your students. What we will not do in this book is to describe esoteric aspects of the technology unrelated to instruction. We need to keep in mind that we use technology to support teaching, we do not use teaching to support technology. The focus on teaching is what distinguishes this book from others. If we get too far afield, emphasizing technology and not teaching, send us an e-mail message and let us know. Our learning is socially constructed, too!

The second purpose of this book is to minimize the time you must spend to find useful teaching/learning tools. Classrooms are busy places; teachers do not have much free time to look for locations on the Internet that fit their classroom needs. By identifying the most practical and useful locations on the Internet for teachers, we hope to save you time as you think about how to use this new tool to help your students.

We need to keep in mind that we use technology to support teaching, we do not use teaching to support technology.

Sharing the best locations on the Internet will assist us in accomplishing our third, and most important, purpose: To show you how the Internet may be used in your classroom to support learning. We will share several instructional models other teachers have used to successfully integrate the Internet into classroom learning, K–12. By showing you effective teaching practices, we hope to quickly get your students into using the powerful learning tool that is the Internet.

We have organized this book into several sections. The first section helps you to become acquainted with the Internet. In this first chapter we explore the potential of the Internet to support learning in your classroom. In the next chapter, we help you to understand the major tools for navigating the Internet. In the third chapter, we help you understand e-mail and other communication opportunities available through the Internet.

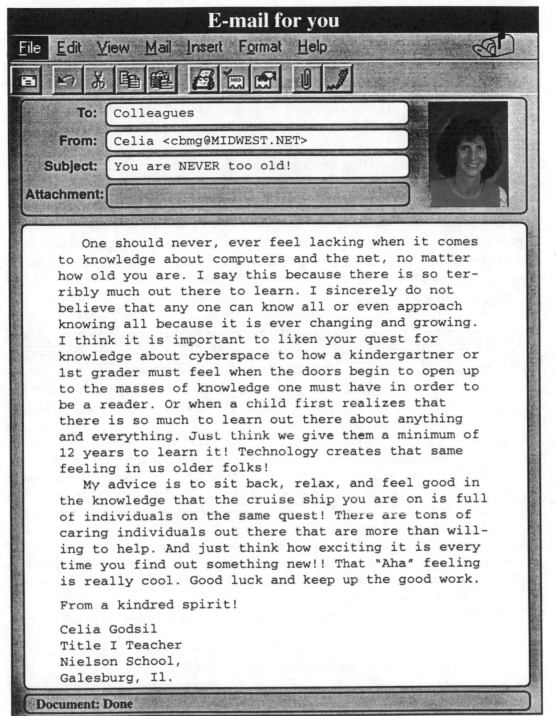

E-mail for you

File Edit View Mail Insert Format Help

To: `Colleagues`

From: `Celia <cbmg@MIDWEST.NET>`

Subject: `You are NEVER too old!`

Attachment:

> One should never, ever feel lacking when it comes to knowledge about computers and the net, no matter how old you are. I say this because there is so terribly much out there to learn. I sincerely do not believe that any one can know all or even approach knowing all because it is ever changing and growing. I think it is important to liken your quest for knowledge about cyberspace to how a kindergartner or 1st grader must feel when the doors begin to open up to the masses of knowledge one must have in order to be a reader. Or when a child first realizes that there is so much to learn out there about anything and everything. Just think we give them a minimum of 12 years to learn it! Technology creates that same feeling in us older folks!
>
> My advice is to sit back, relax, and feel good in the knowledge that the cruise ship you are on is full of individuals on the same quest! There are tons of caring individuals out there that are more than willing to help. And just think how exciting it is every time you find out something new!! That "Aha" feeling is really cool. Good luck and keep up the good work.
>
> From a kindred spirit!
>
> Celia Godsil
> Title I Teacher
> Nielson School,
> Galesburg, Il.

Document: Done

By identifying the most practical and useful locations on the Internet for teachers, we hope to save you time as you think about how to use this new tool to help your students.

The second section shows you how to integrate the Internet into your classroom for teaching and learning. It begins by describing instructional strategies we have found especially useful: Internet Workshop, Internet Activity, Internet Projects, and Internet Inquiry. Then, it explores specific teaching ideas within each of the major content areas: language arts and literature, social studies, science, and math. It also includes a separate chapter on instructional ideas for young children. Each of these chapters will describe a number of outstanding locations on the Internet and show you how to integrate them into your classroom.

The final section explores three areas important for putting all of this new information together in a busy and diverse classroom. One chapter will describe ways to increase multicultural understanding. A second will explore ways to include all students on the Internet. The final chapter will show you how to develop integrated, project-based units with the Internet by creating a home page on the WWW for your classroom.

Each chapter will contain a description of what we consider to be the most useful Internet sites for that topic. In addition, each chapter will contain several e-mail messages for you from other teachers. These teachers have been kind enough to take time from their busy schedules to welcome you into the Internet and share their experiences with you. You may wish to drop them an e-mail message to thank them and to share your own teaching ideas. Remember, we all learn from one another with these new technologies.

Welcome to the Internet!

> *Each chapter will contain several e-mail messages for you from other teachers.*

References

Aaronson, E. (1978). *The jigsaw classroom.* Beverly Hills, CA: Sage Publications.

Bahktin, M.M. (1981). *The dialogic imagination.* (C. Emerson & M. Holquist, Trans.) Austin: University of Texas Press.

Birkerts, S. (1995). *The gutenberg elegies.* New York: Ballentine Books.

Graves, D. (1983). *Writing: Teachers and children at work.* Portsmouth, NH: Heinemann.

Johnson, D.W., & Johnson, R. (1984). *Circles of learning: Cooperation in the classroom.* Alexandria, VA: Association of Supervision and Curriculum Development.

Kinzer, C.K., & Leu, D.J., Jr. (1997). The challenge of change: Exploring literacy and learning in electronic environments. *Language Arts, 74,* (2), 126–136.

Leu, Donald J., Jr. (in press). Literacy and technology: Deictic consequences for literacy education in an information age. In R. Barr, M. L. Kamil, P. Mosenthal, and P. D. Pearson (Eds.), *Handbook of reading research,* Volume III. White Plains, NY: Longman Publishing Group.

Leu, D.J., Jr. (1997). Caity's question: Literacy as deixis on the Internet. *The Reading Teacher, 51*(1), 62–67.

Leu, D. J., Jr. (1996). Sarah's secret: Social aspects of literacy and learning in a digital information age. *The Reading Teacher, 50* (2), 162–165.

Leu, D.J., Jr., & Kinzer, C. K. (1998). *Effective literacy instruction,* 4th edition. Upper Saddle River, NJ: Prentice Hall.

Meyer, D.K. (1993). What is scaffolded instruction? Definitions, distinguishing features, and misnomers. In D.J. Leu, Jr. and C. K. Kinzer (Eds.), *Examining central issues in literacy research, theory, and practice.* Forty-second Yearbook of the National Reading Conference. Chicago: National Reading Conference.

Negroponte, Nicholas (1995). *Being digital.* New York: Knopf.

Ogle, D. M. (1989). The know, want to know, learn strategy. In K.D. Muth (Ed.), *Children's comprehension of text* (pp. 205–223). Newark, DE: International Reading Association.

Reinking, D. (1995). Reading and writing with computers: Literacy research in a post-typographic world. In K.A. Hinchman, D.J. Leu, and C.K. Kinzer (Eds.), *Perspectives on literacy research and practice*. Chicago: National Reading Conference, Inc.

Short, K. (1993). Intertextuality: Searching for patterns that connect. In D.J. Leu, Jr. & C.K. Kinzer (Eds.), *Literacy research, theory and practice: Views from many perspectives*. Chicago: National Reading Conference.

Stoll, C. (1995). *Silicon snake oil: Second thoughts on the information highway*. New York: Doubleday.

Vygotsky, L.S. (1978). *Mind in society: The development of higher psychological processes*. (M. Cole, V. John-Steiner, S. Scribner, E. Souberman, Eds.). Cambridge, MA: Harvard University Press.

2 Developing Navigation Strategies With Your Students

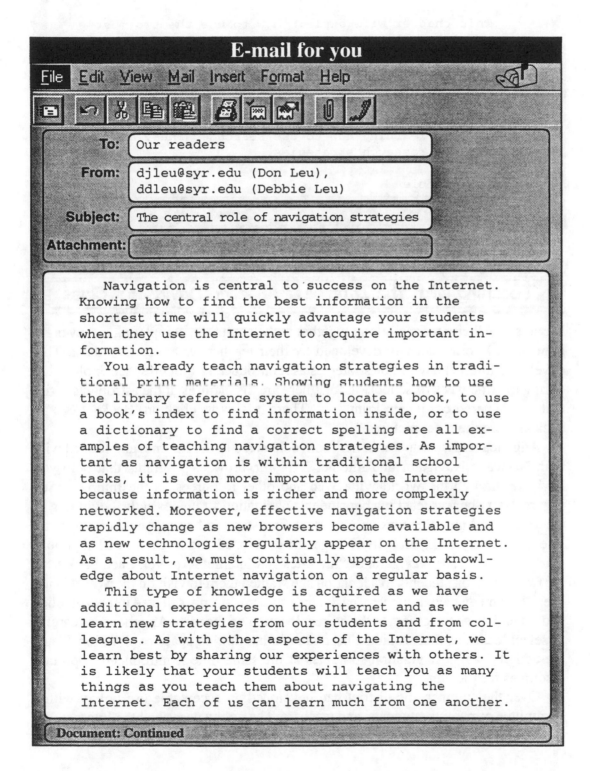

E-mail for you

File Edit View Mail Insert Format Help

To: Our readers

From: djleu@syr.edu (Don Leu),
ddleu@syr.edu (Debbie Leu)

Subject: The central role of navigation strategies

Attachment:

Navigation is central to success on the Internet. Knowing how to find the best information in the shortest time will quickly advantage your students when they use the Internet to acquire important information.

You already teach navigation strategies in traditional print materials. Showing students how to use the library reference system to locate a book, to use a book's index to find information inside, or to use a dictionary to find a correct spelling are all examples of teaching navigation strategies. As important as navigation is within traditional school tasks, it is even more important on the Internet because information is richer and more complexly networked. Moreover, effective navigation strategies rapidly change as new browsers become available and as new technologies regularly appear on the Internet. As a result, we must continually upgrade our knowledge about Internet navigation on a regular basis.

This type of knowledge is acquired as we have additional experiences on the Internet and as we learn new strategies from our students and from colleagues. As with other aspects of the Internet, we learn best by sharing our experiences with others. It is likely that your students will teach you as many things as you teach them about navigating the Internet. Each of us can learn much from one another.

Document: Continued

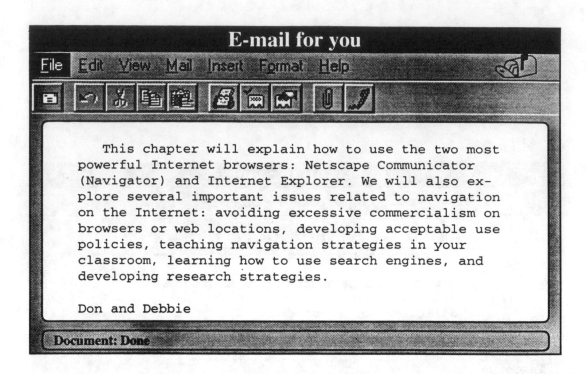

E-mail for you

File Edit View Mail Insert Format Help

```
      This chapter will explain how to use the two most
powerful Internet browsers: Netscape Communicator
(Navigator) and Internet Explorer. We will also ex-
plore several important issues related to navigation
on the Internet: avoiding excessive commercialism on
browsers or web locations, developing acceptable use
policies, teaching navigation strategies in your
classroom, learning how to use search engines, and
developing research strategies.

Don and Debbie
```

Document: Done

Teaching with the Internet: Angelica Davidson's Class

David and Alberto were working together at the computer, completing a scavenger hunt in an Internet activity developed by their teacher, Angelica Davidson. This developed Internet navigation strategies as it introduced a unit on space exploration during the first week of school. "Look, there are the pictures of the astronauts. Print that out. Where does it say 'Print?' . . . There it is! Now click on 'Back.' Let's go back and see the other pictures."

Angelica had a computer in her room connected to the Internet and loaded with both Netscape Navigator and Internet Explorer, browser programs that help you navigate through the World Wide Web and other resources on the Internet. (See Figure 2-1.) She was teaching her students navigation strategies at the beginning of the year. She knew this was an important first step. To begin, Angelica set up an Internet activity using an activity page she developed and a feature called "bookmarks" on Netscape Navigator or "favorites" on Internet Explorer. Each bookmark (or favorite) took students to a location she wanted them to visit on the World Wide Web. This made navigation very easy, since students simply selected items Angelica had set and these took them to the correct location on the web. Angelica was careful to select locations that would be used later in her unit on space exploration. Thus, the activity taught navigation strategies at the same time it introduced important resources for the unit.

Over the summer, the district had developed an acceptable use policy with a committee of parents, students, and teachers. The policy described the Internet, defined the "Do's" and "Don'ts" of Internet use, and defined sanctions for unacceptable

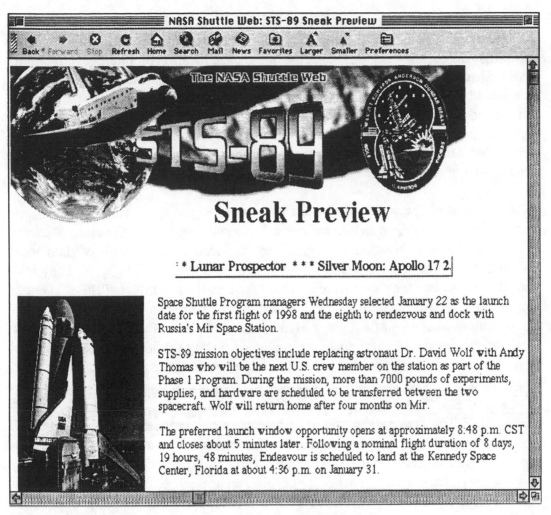

The NASA Shuttle Web page (http://shuttle.nasa.gov/index.html/)

Figure 2-1. The NASA Shuttle Web page students first saw on the Internet activity in Angelica Davidson's class

use. At the end of the form there was a location for everyone to sign, indicating they had read and understood the policy: student, parent/guardian, and teacher.

On the first day of class, Angelica introduced the computer and the Internet. She went over the acceptable use policy with her students, explaining each item. Then she had them sign the form and take it home to obtain the signature of their parent or guardian.

As students returned the forms, she introduced small groups to the fundamentals of navigation using Internet Explorer, a program used to navigate on the Internet. First, she showed her students how to connect to the Internet using this program. Then she showed them how to go to a site on the Internet by using preset "favorites" on Internet Explorer. Next, she showed her students how to move to locations with related information by clicking on a hypertext link. These colored, or underlined words, take you to additional locations on the Internet. She also showed students how to use the **Back** button (see Figure 2-1) to move back to the previous location they had just visited and the **Forward** button to move ahead. Finally, she introduced

Developing an acceptable use policy will head off a number of problems.

the Internet activity and scavenger hunt in Figure 2-2, designed to be completed in pairs. She wanted students to support one another as they developed initial navigation skills. Before they began, she set the home page location on Internet Explorer to **NASA Shuttle Web: STS-89 Sneak Preview** (http://shuttle.nasa.gov/index.html/). This would always be the first page to appear when students connected to the Internet and started their Internet activity. Setting the home page location like this was an important new strategy Angelica recently learned about from another teacher at school. This saved time and helped to ensure that students visited only appropriate locations. It also avoided some of the commercialism at the Start Up Page on Internet Explorer.

At the end of the week, after students completed the space navigation assignment, Angelica organized an Internet workshop session with the entire class. Students shared additional navigation strategies they had learned as a result of their tour, teaching each other new ways of navigating on the World Wide Web. They also shared information they discovered about space as they completed the scavenger hunt. Everyone was excited as they talked about the people at NASA they had met, the upcoming Space Shuttle flight, and the incredible photos from the Hubble Space Telescope they printed out to share during the workshop session. It was a wonderful start to the new school year and to using the Internet in the classroom.

Lessons from the Classroom

There are a number of important lessons in this episode as you think about developing navigation strategies with your students. First, this district had worked carefully with parents, students, and teachers to develop an acceptable use policy for Internet use. Developing an acceptable use policy will head off a number of problems including the viewing of inappropriate sites, using inappropriate language on the Internet, and receiving inappropriate e-mail from strangers. Moreover, because both students and parents/guardians signed the policy statement, everyone received important information about the Internet and how it was going to be used at school. We will discuss acceptable use policies later in this chapter.

Time was precious in Angelica's class with only one computer connected to the Internet. As a result, she wanted students to know how to use their time efficiently.

This episode also illustrates a second lesson—how important it is to systematically teach navigation strategies at the beginning of the year. Angelica realized that navigational strategies were important; students gather more information in a shorter time when they know how to navigate through the Internet. Time was precious in Angelica's class with only one computer connected to the Internet. As a result, she wanted students to know how to use their time efficiently. She developed a thoughtful plan to accomplish this and started with teaching essential navigation strategies through Internet Activity and Internet Workshop.

Another important lesson is how Angelica strategically combined two elements: an introduction to the first thematic unit of the year and a scavenger hunt to learn and practice navigation strategies. Again, this saved time in a busy classroom; students were learning background information important for the upcoming unit at the same time they were developing important navigation strategies.

Figure 2-2. An Internet activity used to develop navigation knowledge at the beginning of the year.

Navigating through Space: Using the World Wide Web of the Internet

Space Traveler: _____ **Date:** _____

Preparing for Your Mission: Learning from the Apollo Missions to the Moon

1. Start your journey by double clicking on Internet Explorer to connect to the World Wide Web. You should soon see the home page for the **NASA Shuttle Web: STS-89 Sneak Preview** (http://shuttle.nasa.gov/index.html/).

2. Locate the reference information near the bottom of the page. Read the FAQs. Take notes and bring one new piece of information you discovered to Internet Workshop.

3. Click on the "Back" button to return to STS-89 Sneak Preview page. (Use the favorites menu if you get lost.) Take a look at the pre-flight photos and videos from Kennedy Space Center. Print out one and staple it to this page. Bring this page and your photo to Internet Workshop.

4. Explore other areas of this site. This will get you ready for your flight on the Space Shuttle as you learn about earlier space programs.

Space Team Online

Visit **Space Team Online** (http://quest.arc.nasa.gov/shuttle/) by using "Favorites." Explore as many resources here as you have time. Pay special attention to the opportunities to chat with space engineers and scientists about this flight. Also note the many projects we could do. Write down your best ideas about which of these activities you would like to do during the next two weeks. Bring your ideas to Internet Workshop and be prepared to share them with the class.

_____

_____

Look through the Hubble Space Telescope (HST) into Deep Space

1. Ready to take a look at deep space? You may need to make observations of space during your flight. Open the favorites folder at the top of the page and choose **HST's Latest Pictures** (http://oposite.stsci.edu/pubinfo/Latest.html).

2. View some of these pictures from the Hubble telescope. Print out your favorite. Write a description of what you can see on the back and attach it to this page.

View the Earth from a Satellite

1. What will it look like outside your shuttle window? You can get an idea by seeing recent photographs from one of more than a hundred satellites circling our planet. Open the bookmark to **View from a Satellite** (http://www.fourmilab.ch/earthview/satellite.html).

2. Be certain the satellite ACTS is highlighted, or select another satellite if you wish.

3. Click on "View Earth from Satellite." Print out this photo of our Earth. Mark the location of our school on this picture. Bring it to Internet Workshop to share with others.

Good Work! You are now ready to begin our unit on space exploration. Staple all your space artifacts together and bring them to Internet Workshop. You should be certain you have the following:

- notes from the STS FAQs;
- your ideas for shuttle activities during the next two weeks;
- your favorite Hubble photograph and
- a description;
- your photograph of Earth with our school located on the photograph;
- this page.

Angelica strategically combined two elements: an introduction to the first thematic unit of the year and a scavenger hunt to learn and practice navigation strategies.

Designating the NASA site as the home page location took students immediately to the location she wanted them to visit. Time was not wasted looking for the right page.

Having Internet Workshop at the end of the experience tied everything together for her class, allowing each student to share new navigation strategies they had learned with other members of the class.

This episode also illustrates how Angelica saved time by designating a home page location on her Internet browser. Designating the NASA site as the home page location took students immediately to the location she wanted them to visit. Time was not wasted looking for the right page. This strategy also helped to prevent inappropriate surfing to other sites on the Internet.

There is also a final lesson: how Angelica used three methods (group introduction, paired learning, whole class workshop) to teach navigation skills. These worked in a complementary fashion to take advantage of social learning opportunities inherent with Internet use. Her initial group presentation explained essential elements for students to practice as they completed the tour in pairs. Working in pairs after the group presentation led to many new learning experiences as students helped one another when they were stuck, discovering new ways of navigating the Internet. Sometimes other students would even stop by the computer to assist a pair having difficulty; this saved Angelica time as she worked with students in other areas of the classroom. Finally, having Internet Workshop at the end of the week tied everything together for her class, allowing each student to share new navigation strategies they had learned with other members of the class.

Internet Workshop led to many new ideas for navigating the Internet. Someone, for example, had discovered the "Home" button and explained how this worked to take you back to the home page location, the NASA Space Shuttle site. Someone else had discovered how the browser saved a list of the locations visited during each session. This student took the class to the computer and showed them how they could return to any site that had already been visited, even one without a favorite (or bookmark), by looking under the menu item labeled "Go." Someone else had noticed that only single clicks were necessary with the mouse to activate any link; double clicking was unnecessary. In fact, double clicking often caused the program to be confused about what you wanted. All of these new strategies were shared and discussed. It was a very productive session.

It is clear we can learn many things from Angelica's classroom. Her classroom contains many lessons for us to consider: helping students develop navigation skills on the Internet, establishing an acceptable use policy for schools, teaching navigation strategies early in the year, using a scavenger hunt to simultaneously teach navigation strategies and introduce the first unit, designating a home page location to save time, using a combination of methods to teach navigation strategies, and supporting students as they shared navigation strategies with one another.

Important Tools for Navigating the Internet

How, exactly, do we navigate through the Internet? Many books have already been written on this topic and many online tutorials can provide assistance. Our discussion will focus on the most important navigation elements for teachers and students in busy classrooms. As you become more adept at using the Internet in your classroom, you may wish to explore this issue in greater detail. We list a number of sites on the WWW at the end of this chapter to provide you with additional information.

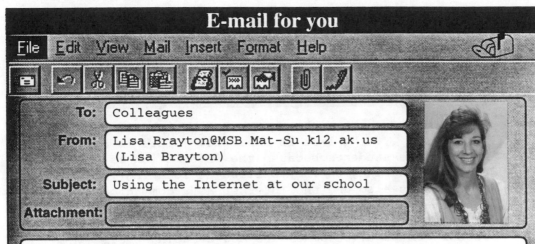

E-mail for you

File   Edit   View   Mail   Insert   Format   Help

To: Colleagues

From: Lisa.Brayton@MSB.Mat-Su.k12.ak.us
(Lisa Brayton)

Subject: Using the Internet at our school

Attachment:

Greetings Educators!

My name is Lisa Brayton. I am a fifth grade teacher at Cottonwood Creek Elementary School in Wasilla, Alaska. Our school has been using technology for a long time. We are making a natural progression to using the Internet in our classrooms.

Since the last printing, Cottonwood has gone from having one terminal with Internet access (in our lab) to having a shared line for 4th and 5th grade classrooms, to now having our own free line in each classroom! We also have four lines in the computer lab and one in the library. At this point, our Internet access is unlimited! This has made a positive impact in many ways.

The Internet has become more than a "cool, awe inspiring unknown entity" in the computer lab. Our principal, Marie Burton, is the visionary! The Internet is as familiar (and easier to access) as any reference book. Students log on and find information otherwise unavailable.

I started this year by entering my class in an Internet contest . . . **Cybersurfari** (http://spa.org/ cybersurfari). This was an excellent way to teach students how to surf for information. It was, in a sense, a scavenger hunt. Students went from site to site through links, looking for clues. This contest is held annually in October, although you can practice at other times. My students learned navigational skills, neat facts and felt excited and successful.

We have found other contests to enter, such as the **Acts of Kindness** (http://www.webstock96.com/ districtb/forum/k&j/index.html) where the students log the number of kind acts they perform. Contests really excite and motivate the students.

Students use the Internet as a resource. During our Colonial study we've gathered historical informa-

Document: Continued

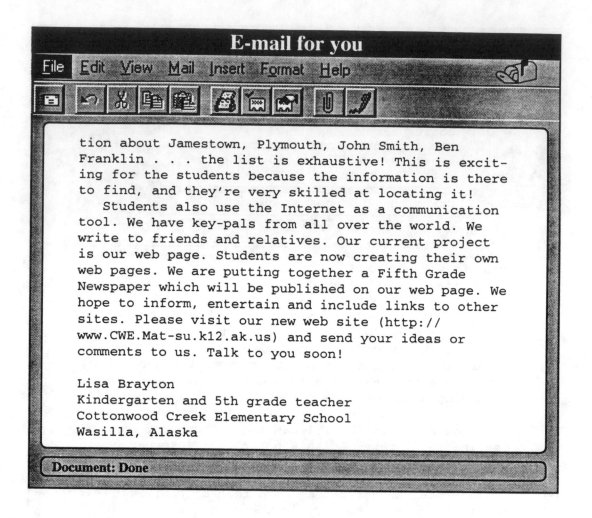

```
                    E-mail for you
File  Edit  View  Mail  Insert  Format  Help

tion about Jamestown, Plymouth, John Smith, Ben
Franklin . . . the list is exhaustive! This is excit-
ing for the students because the information is there
to find, and they're very skilled at locating it!
    Students also use the Internet as a communication
tool. We have key-pals from all over the world. We
write to friends and relatives. Our current project
is our web page. Students are now creating their own
web pages. We are putting together a Fifth Grade
Newspaper which will be published on our web page. We
hope to inform, entertain and include links to other
sites. Please visit our new web site (http://
www.CWE.Mat-su.k12.ak.us) and send your ideas or
comments to us. Talk to you soon!

Lisa Brayton
Kindergarten and 5th grade teacher
Cottonwood Creek Elementary School
Wasilla, Alaska

Document: Done
```

The most important tool for navigating through the Internet is a browser. A browser is a software program on your computer allowing you to connect to locations on the Internet.

The most important tool for navigating the Internet is a browser. A browser is a software program on your computer allowing you to connect to locations on the Internet. The two most popular browsers are Netscape Navigator and Internet Explorer. Each comes in at least two flavors: Windows and Macintosh. This section will explain the essential elements of Netscape Navigator 4 (Communicator) for both Macintosh and Windows-based computers. The following section will explain the essential elements of Internet Explorer 4, again for both types of computer systems. You only need to read the section that applies to the type of browser on your computer.

Netscape Navigator and Internet Explorer are the most powerful browsers available because each allows you to access multimedia information (graphics, audio, video, animations) on the WWW. In addition, each comes packaged with a number of very powerful features such as e-mail. The other nice thing is that both are free to educators. You simply download them from the Internet to load them onto your computer. The latest version of Netscape Navigator (Communicator) for either Windows or Macintosh may be downloaded at Netscape's home page (http://www.netscape.com). The latest version of Internet Explorer may be downloaded at Microsoft's home page for Internet Explorer (http://www.microsoft.com/ie/).

A Few Thoughts at the Beginning

Before you read the section appropriate for your needs, we wish to share three important thoughts with you. The first is that the images you see here may be slightly different from the images you see on your computer screen. New releases for each browser appear frequently, resulting in minor changes in the appearance of windows the browser displays. New releases also appear frequently for your operating system (Macintosh or Windows), causing even more changes. Between changes in browsers and changes in operating systems, it is impossible to visually keep up with each permutation. Fortunately, even if the images change slightly, the main functions of each browser are remarkably stable, at least for periods of up to a year or so. Thus, you will be able to follow along just fine, even if the images are slightly different from what you see on your computer.

Both Netscape Communicator and Internet Explorer are free to educators.

Second, in the upcoming description of browsers we will only present basic fundamentals to get you started using the WWW quickly and effectively in your class. With these basics firmly in hand, you will discover many more useful features and functions as you explore on your own and as you learn from colleagues and students. Learning new ways of exploring the Internet is one of the exciting aspects of the journey ahead of you. Take full advantage of these moments. Exploring new features of a browser, e-mail, or a web site is how all of us learn to navigate on the Internet. Be certain, too, to share your discoveries with others. They will appreciate it and share their own discoveries with you.

The final thought is an important one. It concerns a developing controversy within the educational community. You will need to decide, perhaps with guidelines from your district, about the amount of advertising you wish to expose your students to. This happens through the choice and configuration of your browser and the locations you ask students to visit for classroom assignments. Increasingly, browsers build in links to commercial sites favoring their products and companies with which they have formed strategic alliances. Increasingly, sites on the WWW include banner advertising along with the information they provide.

You will need to decide, perhaps with guidelines from your district, about the amount of advertising you wish your students to view.

Some see this as inevitable and worthwhile. Exposing students to commercial messages helps initiate conversations about how best to critically view information on the Internet. Commercial images are seen as tools for teaching students about the increasingly commercial nature of the information they will encounter in their lives. Others see the intrusion of commercial images as inconsistent with the traditional, commercial-free nature of most educational materials.

We tend to favor exposing students to fewer, not more, commercial images. We believe it is important to engage students in discussions about these matters, but not when we have other educational goals in mind. As a result, we have tried to avoid commercial sites in the recommendations and examples of WWW locations we provide. In some cases, this is not always possible. Nevertheless, as we made decisions about which WWW locations to include in this book, we have favored those developed by professional organizations, governmental organizations, non-profit organizations, federally funded sites, and others who limit or exclude advertising at

We tend to favor exposing students to fewer, not more, commercial images.

their locations. In some cases, you will find that the WWW locations we mention contain advertising or commercially motivated links. In these cases, we decided the information resources were much more important than the advertising. You will need to make similar decisions, as it is difficult to be entirely commercial-free in the locations you select for classroom use.

This issue also affects your choice of browser in important ways. Both Netscape Navigator 4 and Internet Explorer 4 have commercially motivated links. Often these appear in subtle ways, ones you would not immediately consider. We have found Internet Explorer to be especially problematic in this area. This is a shame, since Internet Explorer has several nice features. Our presentation will show you how to remove most of the commercially motivated links built into this browser. If you choose to use Internet Explorer, this should enable your students to focus more on the information at a web location and less on commercially motivated links that appear as part of the browser.

Netscape Navigator: A Powerful Internet Browser

Figures 2-3 and 2-4 show the home page for Netscape Navigator 4 in a Macintosh and a Windows format. Something like this will appear when you first start this program. Netscape Navigator 4 is one of several components of Netscape Communicator.

In this section, we will assume you have Netscape Navigator on your computer and your computer is connected to the Internet. If you have not loaded Navigator onto your computer or you do not know how to obtain Internet access, seek the assistance of a person at your school who can provide technical support. In many schools, this may be a colleague in the room next door who is already connected and beginning to explore the Internet. Sometimes you will be fortunate and have a technology specialist for teachers at your school to assist you.

Launch Netscape Navigator by double clicking the icon for this program on your computer or follow along by using the illustrations in this chapter. Now, let's take a look at the Internet!

A Quick Orientation

At the top of Figure 2-3 (or Figure 2-4), you see a title bar with the words: "Netscape: Welcome to Netscape". The label on this bar will change as you navigate through the Internet. It will always tell you the title of the page on the WWW you are looking at. Right now, it indicates that you are looking at the "Netscape: Welcome to Netscape" page.

Beneath the title bar you will see a toolbar, a row of objects with labels underneath each object. Items in the toolbar let you do things with your browser. The toolbar includes items such as **Back, Forward, Reload, Home, Search, Guide, Images, Print, Security,** and **Stop**. We will explain each below.

Beneath the toolbar is the location window. In this white window, you will see the address for your current location on the Internet. The location showing in Figures

The home page of Netscape Navigator on the Macintosh (http://home.netscape.com/)

Figure 2-3. The home page of Netscape Navigator, a WWW browser if you use a Macintosh system.

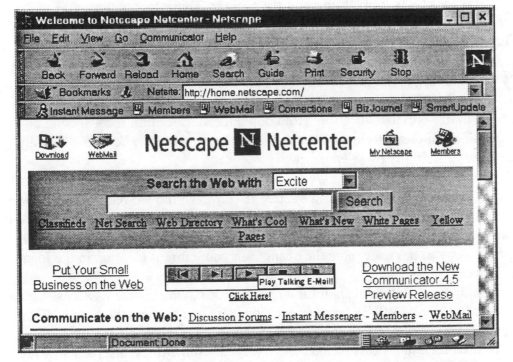

The home page of Netscape Navigator for Windows (http://home.netscape.com/)

Figure 2-4. The home page of Netscape Navigator, a WWW browser if you use a Windows system.

2-3 and 2-4 (http://home.netscape.com/) is the address for Netscape's "Welcome to Netscape" page. There is no need to know the technical aspects of the language used to mark locations now. Just note that the address of your current location will appear here.

Now look at the viewing window containing the Netscape welcome page. Note how some words are underlined and written in a distinctive color (usually blue). Words that are underlined and/or marked in a distinctive color signal a key navigational feature on the WWW, a hypertext link. If you single click on an underlined or specially colored word with your mouse, a hypertext link will take you to the site on the Internet linked to that item(s). The same is true for many of the pictures and graphic elements you find on the Internet. If you are at your computer, try clicking (only once) on a hypertext link and notice how a new screen appears with information related to the word(s) or picture you selected. Also note the new address in the location window. You are now at this new location on the Internet and this location probably contains several more hypertext links. You could keep clicking on hypertext links and travel to different locations throughout the Internet, seemingly forever.

Figure 2-5.
The Toolbar
for Navigator.

The Toolbar

*The first button, **Back**, allows you to move back from where you are currently.*

Now let's take a closer look at items in the toolbar. These tools allow you to do things as you navigate through the WWW. The first button, **Back**, allows you to move back one location from where you are currently. This is only active after you move to a location beyond the first page, the Netscape Welcome Page. If you haven't already tried moving to another location by clicking on a colored hypertext link, do so now. Then, try clicking on the Back button on the toolbar and notice how you return back to the previous location. Hold down the Back button for a second and you will notice that previous locations are listed in a new window. You can go to any of these locations simply by selecting it.

The next button, **Forward**, moves you forward one location in your travels through the Internet. Note this is only active if you have moved back at least one location and can really move forward to places you have visited. Try using the Back and Forward buttons. You may also wish to try using the hypertext links at some of these pages. As you navigate, note the changes in your current location in the location window.

The next button, **Reload**, is helpful when you are having problems accessing a popular location on the WWW because everyone else wants to get there, too. When this happens, you will receive a message that says Netscape was unable to connect to your desired location. Press Reload and try again. Sometimes, a screen will not transmit completely to your computer for one reason or another. Press Reload when this happens and you should receive a complete screen. Reload also works well for locations that are regularly updated, such as newspapers. To receive a completely fresh version of news screens that are regularly updated, just hold the "shift" key down while you press reload.

Home is the next button on the toolbar. This button always takes you back to the location you have designated as the first one to show in your viewing window. Right now, this has been designated as the Welcome to Netscape page. Your home location is an important feature. You may designate another location, such as a content site central to an instructional unit, as your home location. This is what Angelica did to save time in a busy classroom and to avoid the commercially motivated links at the Netscape home page. More on this later.

Often we need to search the Internet for very specific information. The button **Search** will take you to a location with "search engines," computers on the Internet that search for sites containing words or phrases you specify. Are you looking for information about origami for next week's unit on Japan? Click on the Search button and the search engine window will appear. Click in the white keyword window and then type in the word "origami." Press return (or click the Search, Find, or "Go get it!" button next to "origami") and a list of sites on the WWW will appear, each with information about origami. Often, they will also contain short descriptions of the contents at each location. You may find a great location, **Joseph Wu's Origami Page** (http://www.origami.vancouver.bc.ca/), with directions for creating many wonderful paper objects as well as information about this Japanese art form. To go to this site, or any other location the search engine found, just click on the appropriate hypertext link. If you do not find this location from your search, you may need to do a more precise search. Type "Joseph Wu's Origami Page" in the search engine's keyword box and do another search. When you find this location, pay a visit. It is an amazing location if you are interested in this art from Japan.

After clicking the **Net Search** button you will notice there are many different search engines available at this location: Yahoo, InfoSeek, HotBot, Lycos, and others. Each searches in a slightly different fashion. If you develop a preference for one, just click on the hypertext link to the search engine you prefer.

Notice that some search engines also have a set of categories listed, in case you wish to search by category rather than by a word or phrase. When you click on a category like "Education," a more specific subdirectory will appear containing additional categories within education. Click on a category such as "K-12," for example, and you will find more specific subcategories like "Science," "Math," "Art," or "Social Studies." Continue until you find the types of items you seek.

We will explore search engines a bit later. For now, just play around a bit with one of the search engines and notice the types of features you will find.

Guide will guide you to different parts of the Internet. Click on this button and hold it down. You will see a window open with several options: The Internet, People, Yellow Pages, What's New, and What's Cool. Selecting one of these options will take you to a guide book for that area. Each will help you to find useful and interesting items on the Internet simply by clicking and exploring various hyperlinks. Some

Words that are underlined and/or marked in a distinctive color signal a key navigational feature on the WWW, a hypertext link.

The button Search will take you to a location with "search engines," computers on the Internet that search for sites containing words or phrases you specify.

will have search engines of their own. Each will have a number of hyperlinks. Go ahead and explore a bit.

Images is a button to open up images that have been turned off. Why would you turn images off? Sometimes teachers will turn off images in order to speed up the transmission of text information. To see the pictures on any page when they have been turned off, simply press the Images button and the graphic images will appear after a short time.

Internet FAQ

How do I turn off images to speed up the transmission of information?

You may turn images off by selecting the Edit menu (with both Windows and Macintosh systems) and selecting "Preferences." Click on the item "Advanced" and then uncheck the box, "Automatically load images and other data types." This will turn off images. Recheck the box in your preferences or options window if you wish to turn images back on.

Print does pretty much what it says. You may print out pages on the Internet that appear in your viewing window with this button. This is often helpful in scavenger hunts when students need evidence that they have found a location you specified. It also comes in handy in other situations as well. Need a lesson plan for tomorrow? Find a nice collection at **AskERIC Lesson Plans** (http://ericir.syr.edu/Virtual/Lessons/) and print out ones that meet your needs.

You will also see a button on your toolbar called **Security**. Go ahead and click on this button, opening the security window. You will see a number of options here. Basically, this area allows you to set up Navigator to send and receive confidential information so others may not see it. While this is becoming increasingly important for businesses, the security area is probably one you will not immediately use in your classroom.

Stop will abort any transmission to your computer that is in progress. This is helpful when it is taking too long to get into a web site; sometimes too many people want to go to the same place at once. If you don't wish to keep waiting to connect to a web location, press Stop. Then move on to another location. Come back in a few minutes and the line may be open.

Figure 2-6.
The location
window.

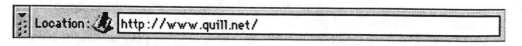

Location: http://www.quill.net/

Location Window

Your current location on the Internet is indicated in the location window. This contains the "Uniform Resource Locator" (URL), or address, of the site that appears in the viewing window. Note, for example, the URL for **The Quill Society** (http://

www.quill.net/) in Figure 2-6, one of the finest locations for middle and high school students who are serious about their writing.

You may also use the location window to travel to any location on the Internet, as long as you know its address. Perhaps, for example, an article you recently read listed the URL for **Harriet Tubman: An Unforgettable Black Leader** (http://www.acusd.edu/~jdesmet/tubman.html) and you wish to find out more about this famous African American. How do you visit this site to see if it will be helpful during an upcoming unit? Simply highlight the current address in the location window with your mouse, type in the address, and press return. This will open any location on the WWW when you know the address in advance. Be careful though! The address must be typed exactly as you find it. A missing period or even the wrong case for a letter (e.g., upper case instead of lower case) may give you an error message.

Highlight the current address in the location window with your mouse, type in the address, and press return. This will open any location on the WWW when you know the address in advance.

Internet FAQ

Why does my computer sometimes "freeze" when students are using Netscape Navigator? The computer won't respond to commands or the cursor is stuck in one position.

There are several possibilities when something like this happens. There may be a conflict between different software programs on your computer, for example. This type of problem will usually require technical assistance to resolve. Often, however, we have found a simple cause to the problem: students freeze the cursor because they click the mouse too often and too quickly, trying to get something to happen on the screen, without allowing Netscape Navigator or Internet Explorer a chance to keep up with their commands. Students are used to the double-click techniques and rapid response typical of most computers. Navigator and Internet Explorer only require a single click to activate a hypertext link. When students use double-click strategies and click quickly on multiple items it sometimes causes the computer to "freeze" because the computer they are trying to reach on the Internet, say in Australia, can't keep up. We have found that it is important to explain this to students, reminding them to only click once on a hypertext link and encouraging them to wait until it says "Done" at the bottom of the browser window before clicking on a new item.

Using Bookmarks: An Important Navigation Aid for Your Class

Navigator has a special feature to assist you and your students as you navigate the Internet: the bookmark menu feature. The bookmark menu allows you to set a bookmark when you are at a useful location on the WWW. You may then come back to this location quickly at a later time by simply selecting the bookmark you set. If you are at your computer and Netscape Navigator is running, look at the top of your screen with a Macintosh or just under the toolbar in Windows. Here you will find a special item that looks like a blue-green bookmark. (It may only contain the word "Bookmark" in some Windows systems.) If you open this menu item with your mouse, you will see an item that says "Add Bookmark." Selecting "Add Bookmark" will set a bookmark for your current location. The bookmark will be listed inside the

The bookmark menu allows you to set a bookmark when you are at a useful location on the WWW. You may then come back to this location quickly at a later time by simply selecting the bookmark you set.

Bookmarks window. At a later time, if you wish to return to this location on the Internet all you need to do is to click on the image of the bookmark in your menu and select the location where you wish to return.

Bookmarks are useful in a classroom. During a unit, you may set bookmarks for sites you wish students to visit and use in their studies. This saves time finding resources and also limits the possibility of extensive "surfing" to sites you do not wish students to visit. Simply make a rule that students may only visit sites where you have set a bookmark or sites that are no more than a few links away.

You may manage the organization of your bookmarks in a number of ways. This is accomplished with a Macintosh computer by selecting the menu item at the top of your window with the Communicator icon and then choosing "Bookmarks." A window will open up on your screen as in Figure 2-7, listing each of your bookmarks. You may do a number of things once this window is open. You may delete a bookmark by selecting it and pressing the delete key or selecting "Clear" or "Delete" in the Edit menu. You may also move bookmarks around in the list in your bookmark window by dragging them with your mouse and dropping them to another location in your list. Other features and functions may be explored on your own by looking at each of the menu items at the top of your screen when you have the "Bookmarks" window open. When you finish, close the "Bookmarks" window. With a Windows computer, you can edit your bookmarks by going to the menu item "Communicator," selecting "Bookmarks," and then selecting "Edit Bookmarks."

Figure 2-7. The bookmark window in Netscape Navigator.

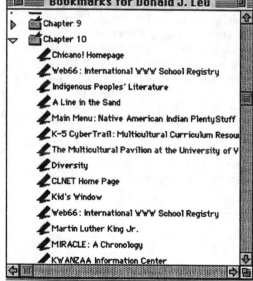

Bookmarks for Donald J. Leu
- ▷ 📁 Chapter 9
- ▽ 📁 Chapter 10
  - Chicano! Homepage
  - Web66: International WWW School Registry
  - Indigenous Peoples' Literature
  - A Line in the Sand
  - Main Menu: Native American Indian PlentyStuff
  - K-5 CyberTrail: Multicultural Curriculum Resour
  - The Multicultural Pavilion at the University of V
  - Diversity
  - CLNET Home Page
  - Kid's Window
  - Web66: International WWW School Registry
  - Martin Luther King Jr.
  - MIRACLE: A Chronology
  - KWANZAA Information Center

TEACHING TIP

It is often very useful at the beginning of the year to have a workshop session devoted to the use of bookmarks (favorites with Internet Explorer). At one session, share information about how bookmarks/favorites work. Then, encourage students to try out some of the additional features described there. At the next workshop session have students share what they have discovered.

Designating a Home Page Location

It is important to designate a home page location on your classroom computer related to content your class is studying. A home page location is the page that shows up first on your screen each time students connect to the Internet with Netscape Navigator. As Angelica Davidson discovered, this saves time in a busy classroom; students begin immediately with the site you want them to visit first, perhaps one with important content for your unit. To change the home page location from Netscape's Welcome Page, go to the menu item "Edit" and select "Preferences." A window similar to that in Figure 2-8 will appear.

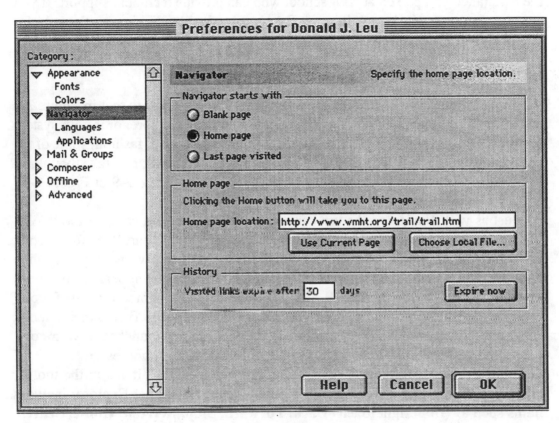

Figure 2-8. Opening the preferences window and setting the home page location in Netscape Navigator. This saves your students time and helps them to begin their work at a useful location.

In the middle of this window, type in the Internet address you wish to designate as your home page location or click the "current page" button. In this example, the teacher is designating a site called **K-5 Cyber Trail** (http://www.wmht.org/trail/trail.htm), a nice introduction to navigating the Internet.

Also note several other options in the General Preferences window in Figure 2-8. Selecting any of the items at the left will take you to windows where you may set preferences for other items: Appearance, Fonts, Colors, Navigator, Languages, Applications, Mail & Groups, Composer, Offline, and Advanced. One useful preference is located in the "Appearance" window. If you wish to save a bit of space on your screen, select the button "Show Toolbar as Text Only." This will eliminate the pictures in the tool bar, take up less room on your screen, and display more information

During a unit, you may set bookmarks for sites you wish students to visit and use in their studies. This saves time finding resources and also limits the possibility of extensive "surfing" to sites you do not wish students to visit.

in the viewing window. Often this is helpful with the smaller monitors purchased for classrooms; every bit of extra space in the main window helps you to see more information without having to scroll down the window.

Internet Explorer: Another Powerful Browser

Another popular browser for the Internet is Internet Explorer. If you are reading this section, we will assume you are using this browser. If you have not loaded Internet Explorer onto your computer or you do not know how to obtain Internet access, seek the assistance of a person at your school who can provide technical support. If you are at your computer, launch Internet Explorer by double clicking on the icon for this program. If not, simply follow along by using the illustrations in this section.

A Few Words at the Beginning

When you connect to the Internet, you will see a screen similar to that in Figure 2-9 or Figure 2-10. If you have a different version of Internet Explorer or if your system administrator has configured your system at school in a special fashion, some of the buttons at the top may be slightly different. It will be similar enough, though, to follow our discussion. Take a close look at the screen in Figure 2-9 or Figure 2-10 and let's go over several navigational elements that appear here.

Another popular browser for the Internet is Internet Explorer.

Just as with Navigator, the top bar contains the title of the page on the WWW you are currently viewing. Right now, you are looking at the Start Page for Internet Explorer 4. Beneath the title bar you will see the address bar with a narrow white window. The address for your current location on the Internet appears in this window. The address in Figure 2-9 and Figure 2-10 (http://home.microsoft.com/runonce.asp) is the initial screen most people will see when they first launch Internet Explorer. (If Internet Explorer has already been loaded and launched at your computer, you will see a different screen with a different URL, or address.)

Items in the toolbar allow you do things with your browser.

Below (or above) the address bar you will find a toolbar. Items in the toolbar allow you do things with your browser. The toolbar for Internet Explorer includes items such as (from right to left) **Back, Forward, Stop, Refresh, Home, Search, Mail, New, Favorites, Larger, Smaller,** and **Preferences.** This toolbar may be slightly different on some systems. Don't worry. We will explain each in just a bit.

Below the address bar is a favorites bar. These contain buttons that can take you to favorite locations on the Internet. As you can see in Figure 2-9, this contains commercially motivated links. It is possible to change the buttons on this bar to locations you plan to use in class assignments instead.

Now look at the window containing the Start Page for Internet Explorer 4. This is the viewing window. Before we go any further, if you see the item marked "New to the Internet," go ahead and select the box to add an Internet guide to your start page. Then enter your zip code or geographical designation in the other boxes.

When you click on words or images in the viewing window that are underlined or distinctively marked, you will notice that Internet Explorer takes you to another

The Start Page for Internet Explorer 4, a WWW browser (http://home.microsoft.com/ runonce.asp)

Figure 2-9.
The Start Page for Internet Explorer 4, a WWW browser on a Macintosh System

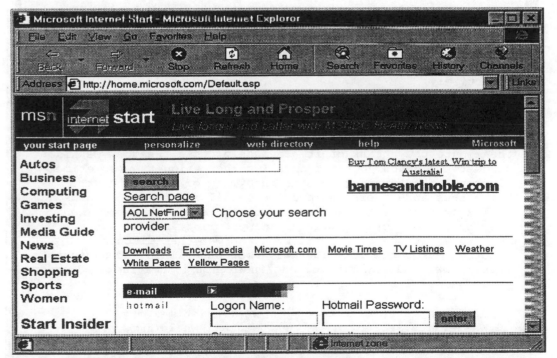

The Start Page for Internet Explorer 4, a WWW browser (http://www.microsoft.com/microsoft.htm)

Figure 2-10.
The Start Page for Internet Explorer 4, a WWW browser on a Windows System

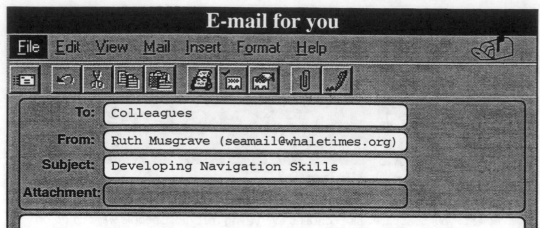

E-mail for you

File   Edit   View   Mail   Insert   Format   Help

To: Colleagues

From: Ruth Musgrave (seamail@whaletimes.org)

Subject: Developing Navigation Skills

Attachment:

Hi! My first bit of advice is, "Play, play, play and play some more, on the Internet first before you do anything." If you're "playing" you'll relax, take all sorts of twists and turns and find many exciting sites (and some you won't visit again!).

Try the various search engines like Yahoo, Lycos . . . etc. You'll find that the search engines vary in style and content. Our favorite is "AltaVista"; we've found it to be by far the most comprehensive search engine available. Using key words or phrases you can find just about anything.

Now you're ready to allow your students access. Be certain to allow your students time to play, too. If you feel you need to structure the "play" (due to time limitations or other concerns), create a scavenger hunt that encourages students to use the various search engines. Take them all over the world (with a tie-in to geographic studies by pairing with a world map). Have them find locations like **The White House for Kids** (http://www.whitehouse.gov/WH/kids/html/kidshome.html), **USA TODAY** (http://www.usatoday.com), or visit a computer in France and take a tour of the Louvre at the **Virtual Tour of the Louvre** (http://www.smartweb.fr/louvre/globale.htm). Once they're comfortable traveling via the computer they can begin to use it effectively.

The biggest challenge is to allow students room to explore without allowing too much freedom. The Internet is this amazing open world. Scientists, authors, and artists . . . from all over the world allow students to send them questions directly—the minute they think of it. Because of this freedom, we also suggest you teach your students Internet etiquette (sometimes students take advantage of the anonymity of the computer). Scientists and others who provide e-mail addresses or forms will answer student's letters, but become disenchanted when they begin to receive silly or inappropriate notes. You may want to visit one of the sites on the web that discusses Internet etiquette like **The Net: User Guidelines and Netiquette** (http://www.fau.edu/rinaldi/net/index.htm). Good luck and enjoy this wonderful tool for classrooms!

Ruth Musgrave, Director   www.whaletimes.org
WhaleTimes SeaBed   seamail@whaletimes.org

Document: Done

location related to the item you clicked. These are a key navigational feature on the WWW, a hypertext link. If you single click on an underlined or distinctively marked element with your mouse, a hypertext link will take you to the site on the Internet linked to that item(s). If you are at your computer, try clicking (only once) on the "Done" box in Figure 2-9. If you do not see this item, simply click on any other hypertext link you can see. Notice how a new screen appears with information related to the word(s) or picture you selected. You may wish to also note the new address in the location window. You are now at this new location on the Internet and this location probably contains several more hypertext links. You could keep clicking on hypertext links and travel to different locations throughout the Internet, seemingly forever.

Also note the Explorer bar on the left side of the viewing window with a Macintosh platform. This contains tabbed items such as "Channels," "Favorites," "History," and "Search." Sliding your cursor to any of these locations without clicking will open up a folder for each item. You may wish to explore these. Many of these items have commercially motivated items. Your students will be able to navigate just fine without them. A little later we will show you how to drop this feature.

Figure 2-11. The Toolbar for Internet Explorer.

The Toolbar

Take a look at the items in the toolbar. These tools allow you to do things as you navigate through the WWW. Many are similar to the tools in the toolbar for Netscape Navigator. The first button, **Back**, allows you to move back one location from where you are currently. Note that this is active only after you move to a location beyond the first page. If you haven't already tried moving to another location by clicking on a hypertext link, do so now. Explore the page you see on your computer and try to locate hypertext links by clicking on them. Then, try clicking on the Back button on the toolbar and note that you return back to the previous location.

The next button, **Forward**, moves you forward one location in your travels through the Internet. Note that this is only active if you have moved back at least one location and can really move forward to places you have visited. Try moving back and forward. You may also wish to try using the hypertext links at some of these pages. As you navigate, note the changes in your current location in the location window.

Stop will abort any transmission to your computer that is in progress. This is helpful when it is taking too long to get into a web site; sometimes too many people want to go to the same place at once. If you don't wish to keep waiting to connect, press Stop. Then move on to another location. Come back in a few minutes and the line may be open.

Often we need to search the Internet for very specific information. The button "Search" will take you to a location with "search engines", computers on the Internet that search for sites containing words or phrases you specify.

The next button, **Refresh**, is helpful when you are having problems accessing a popular location on the WWW because everyone else wants to get there, too. When this happens, you will receive a message indicating that you were unable to connect to your desired location. Press Refresh and try again. Sometimes, a screen will not transmit completely to your computer for one reason or another. Press Refresh when this happens and you should receive a complete screen. Refresh also works well for locations that are regularly updated, such as newspapers.

Home is the next button on the toolbar. This button always takes you back to the location you have designated as the first one to show in your viewing window. This saves time in a busy classroom. Right now, Home will take you to a Microsoft location, perhaps your start page. We will show you how to change the home location to one more appropriate for your students. More on this later.

Often we need to search the Internet for very specific information. The button **Search** will take you to a location with "search engines," computers on the Internet that search for sites containing words or phrases you specify. Are you looking for information about origami for next week's unit on Japan? Click on the Search button and the search engine window will appear. You will find that one of several search engines has been selected for you. There will also be a white rectangular box in which you can type in a keyword for a search. Click in this box to activate your cursor within the box. Then type in the word "origami." Press return (or click the Search, Find, or "Go get it!" button next to the keyword window. A list of sites on the WWW will appear, each with information about origami. Often, the locations found by the search engine will also contain short descriptions of the contents for each location. You may find a great location, **Joseph Wu's Origami Page** (http://www.origami.vancouver.bc.ca/), with directions for creating many wonderful paper objects as well as information about this Japanese art form. To go to this location, all you need to do is click on the hypertext link that takes you there. If you do not find this location from your search, you may need to do a more precise search. Type all of the words "Joseph Wu's Origami Page" in the search engine's keyword box and do another search. When you find this location, pay a visit. It is an amazing location if you are interested in this art from Japan.

You will find that your list of "favorites" will be a very useful feature for your classroom. This makes it easier for students to find important locations during your instructional units. It may also be used to limit the sites children may visit.

After clicking the **net Search** button you will notice there are many different search engines available at this location: Yahoo, InfoSeek, Magellan, Lycos, or others. Each searches in a slightly different fashion. If you develop a preference for one, all you need to do is click on the circle next to the name of the search engine you prefer. We will explore search engines a bit later. For now, just play around a bit at the search engine site and notice the types of features you will find.

Mail is a button that will take you to the e-mail program used with Internet Explorer. We will show you how to use this in the next chapter.

Favorites is the next button. This will open a window containing links to favorite sites so that you can quickly return to them later. You will find that your list of "favorites" will be a very useful feature for your classroom. This makes it easier for students to find important locations during your instructional units. It may also be used to limit the sites children may visit. Some teachers only allow students to visit sites on the "favorites" list. The next section will explore the "favorites" feature in greater detail.

You may also find buttons called **Larger** and **Smaller** if you use a Macintosh platform. These allow you to display information in your viewing window in a larger or smaller sized font. Each time you click one of these buttons, the print will quickly be set to a different font size. Setting the print to a larger size is especially helpful for children experiencing vision difficulties. It makes information in the viewing window easier to read.

You may also find a button on your toolbar called **Preferences**. Go ahead and click on this button, opening the preferences window. (With some Windows systems, changing preferences may be accomplished by choosing "Internet Options" from the View menu.) You will see a number of options here. These allow you to configure the browser to satisfy your individual needs. Go ahead and explore this area to see some of the features you may set. Don't change any settings yet, though. We will come back to this in a moment.

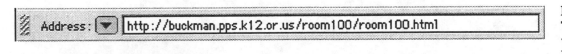

Figure 2-12. The location window for Internet Explorer.

The Location Window

Your current location on the Internet is indicated in the location window. This contains the "Uniform Resource Locator" (URL), or address, of the site that appears in the viewing window. Note, for example, the URL for **Room 100 at Buckman School** (http://buckman.pps.k12.or.us/room100/room100.html) in Figure 2-12, one of the finest home pages for a primary grade classroom we have ever seen.

You may use the location window to travel to any location on the Internet, as long as you know its address. Perhaps, for example, you came across the web site called **Harriet Tubman: An Unforgettable Black Leader** in an article. The article listed the URL, or address: (http://www.acusd.edu/~jdesmet/tubman.html). You want to review this resource for your upcoming unit on heroes. How do you visit the site? Simply highlight the current address in the location window with your mouse, type in the correct address, and press return. This will open any location on the WWW as long as you know the address in advance. Be careful though! The address must be typed exactly as you find it. A missing period or even the wrong case for a letter (e.g., upper case instead of lower case) will give you an error message. If this happens, go back to double check the URL, making certain you have typed it in correctly.

Using the Favorites Feature with Internet Explorer: An Important Navigational Aid for Your Class

Internet Explorer has a useful feature to assist you and your students as you navigate the Internet: the favorites menu feature. If you are at your computer and Internet Explorer is running, look at the menu at the top of your screen (not on your toolbar). In your menu, you should find an item called "Favorites." If you open this menu item with your mouse, you will find an item that says "Add to Favorites." Selecting this will place your current location on the WWW into your folder of favorite sites. If you wish to return at a later time, click on Favorites in your menu and select this location.

A second way to return to a location is to click on the "Favorites" item in your toolbar and a window with the complete list of your favorites will appear, similar to the image in Figure 2-13. Just click on one of your favorite locations and Internet Explorer will take you to that location on the WWW.

Figure 2-13. The "favorites" window with Internet Explorer. This helps you to organize your list of favorite sites on the WWW and to find favorite sites.

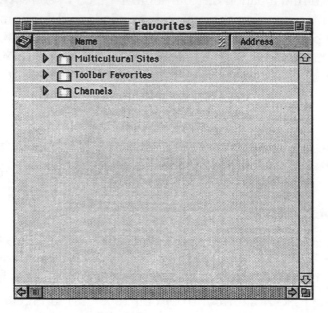

You may add new folders to your favorites window and rearrange favorite sites. Simply use the options in the "Favorites" menu item at the top of the screen to add new folders. Once you have established a new folder, use the "favorites" button on your toolbar to open up a window listing all of your favorites. This is where you can rearrange the organization of your "favorites" folders. You may move items into new folders by simply clicking and dragging them to the desired location. You may also delete items by clicking once on the item and then selecting "Clear" from the "Edit" menu item. On a Windows computer, you may make these changes by selecting "Organize Favorites" from the "Favorites" menu item.

Favorites are very useful in a classroom. During a unit, you may set favorites for sites you wish students to visit and use in their studies. This saves time finding resources and also limits the possibility of extensive "surfing" to sites you do not wish students to visit. Simply make a rule that students may only visit sites where you have set a favorite, or sites that are no more than one, two, three, or four links away.

Designating a Home Page Location

It is helpful to designate a home page location for the content your class is studying. A home page location is the page that shows up first on your screen each time students connect to the Internet with Internet Explorer. As Angelica Davidson discovered, this saves time in a busy classroom; students begin immediately with the site you want them to visit first, perhaps one with important content for your unit. To change the home page location from the one that first appears on Internet Explorer, click on the "Preferences" button in the toolbar and then select "Home/Search." (With Windows systems, changing preferences may be accomplished by choosing "Internet Options" from the View menu.) This will take you to a window that looks like Figure 2-14. Simply type in the URL of the location you wish to designate as your home page location. Note that you may also use this window to designate the URL for a search engine, if you have a preference. The search engine you designate will appear whenever you click the Search button in the toolbar. Later, after you have had a chance to try out various search engines, note the URL of your favorite and enter it here.

To change the home page location from the one that first appears on Internet Explorer, click on the "Preferences" button in the toolbar and then select "Home/Search."

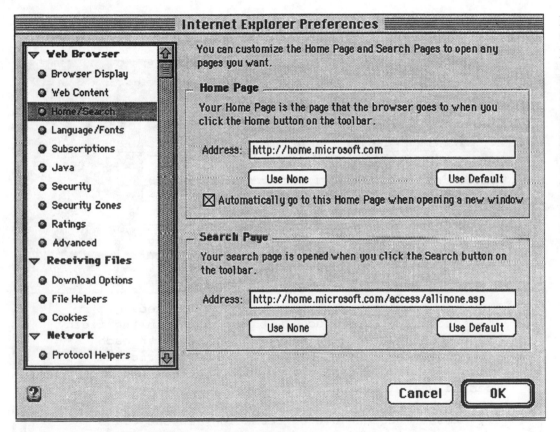

Figure 2-14. Opening the preferences window and setting the home page location in Internet Explorer. This saves your students time and helps them to begin their work at a useful location.

Content Advisor: Censoring Web Sites Based on Content

Internet Explorer 4 contains a feature enabling you to block student access to web sites with inappropriate content: Content Advisor. If you wish to explore this feature, you may find it by selecting Preferences from your toolbar and then choosing "Ratings." (In Windows, you may need to choose Internet Options from the View Menu, select the Content tab.) In both systems, a window appears containing settings for the RSAC Ratings Service. You may set each content filter to different

We believe the best solution to viewing inappropriate content is a solid acceptable use policy at your school that is consistently applied and a teacher who carefully monitors student use of the Internet.

levels. Then, if your students visit a site that includes a rating from the RSAC service, it will determine whether or not to allow access, depending upon the levels of access you have set. If the site has not been rated, this feature will block access. Thus, your students will be unable to access many inoffensive, and potentially useful, sites. You may provide access to unrated sites by selecting "Options" and turning this feature off. However, this tends to defeat the purpose of the screening function. You should explore the Content Advisor on Internet Explorer and decide if you wish to use it. Your district may also have established a policy about this feature.

We feel Internet Explorer's Content Advisor is more problematic than helpful. We believe the best solution to viewing inappropriate content is a solid acceptable use policy at your school that is consistently applied and a teacher who carefully monitors student use of the Internet. In an upcoming section we will explore these alternatives.

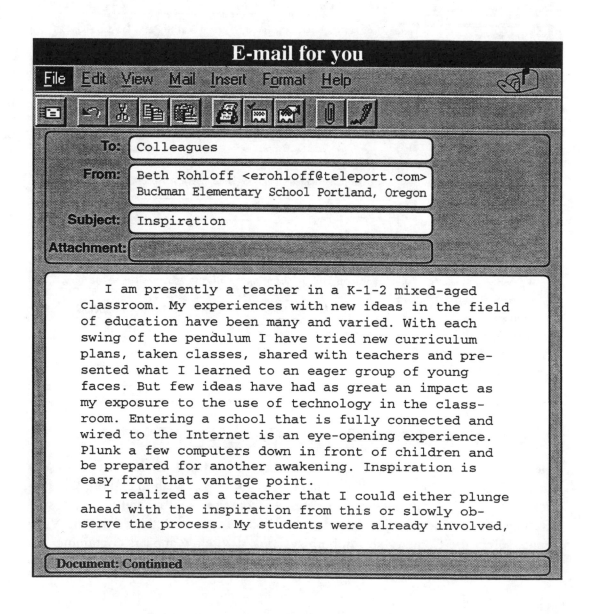

E-mail for you

File   Edit   View   Mail   Insert   Format   Help

To: Colleagues

From: Beth Rohloff <erohloff@teleport.com>
Buckman Elementary School Portland, Oregon

Subject: Inspiration

Attachment:

>   I am presently a teacher in a K-1-2 mixed-aged classroom. My experiences with new ideas in the field of education have been many and varied. With each swing of the pendulum I have tried new curriculum plans, taken classes, shared with teachers and presented what I learned to an eager group of young faces. But few ideas have had as great an impact as my exposure to the use of technology in the classroom. Entering a school that is fully connected and wired to the Internet is an eye-opening experience. Plunk a few computers down in front of children and be prepared for another awakening. Inspiration is easy from that vantage point.
>   I realized as a teacher that I could either plunge ahead with the inspiration from this or slowly observe the process. My students were already involved,

Document: Continued

I might as well join in. Rarely fearing new ideas, I embraced technology the first time I saw another teacher communicating to our classroom over a CU-See Me Camera. This was connecting, this was networking, and this was sharing!

My enthusiasm spread the first time I completed a web page of our students' poetry. We were studying a science unit on weather. Using the Internet, my teaching partner and I were able to share weather data with the students. Included in the unit were some rare (for our region) snow and ice storms and a series of wind storms. My literary focus for the 7 and 8 year-old was the use of rhyming words. With my focus intact, they produced a collection of poems and drawings.

My task was to put it all together for use on our Home Page. It was so inspiring to take a project from the very beginning of process, the study of a science/literature unit, to an end product, an art product that linked and integrated many subjects. I was hooked on technology and its use with the kids. I'm not sure who was more excited, the students or I.

I have this new found source to use with my students when I teach. I do my homework and research the information I plan to use; previewing sites and coordinating written material with the skills I want to teach. Technology (the Internet) does not replace my other outstanding resources, but its connections to the "big world" are empowering for all of us. We can communicate with our neighbors in the city and talk to someone in another part of the world. We can see the world as a smaller place and feel connections with others doing the same or different things. As for myself, it is an opportunity to be a learner along with my students pioneering this vast new arena.

Good luck on your journey!

Experience is not what happens to you;
experience is what you do with what happens to you.
Aldous Huxley

+++

ElizaBeth Rohloff
http://buckman.pps.k12.or.us/room100/room100.html

Document: Done

Removing Commercially Motivated Aspects of Internet Explorer 4

If you use a Macintosh computer, it is possible to remove several aspects of Internet Explorer 4 containing commercially motivated links without limiting students' ability to navigate the Internet and access resources important to classroom learning projects. If you are concerned about commercial aspects of this browser, we suggest that you do the following:

- disable the Explorer bar;
- set your home page for an appropriate content page, not the Microsoft Start page; and
- remove all items from the favorites toolbar, replacing these with your own favorites for classroom learning.

We will explain how to take each of these actions and make your classroom browser a little less commercial.

How do you disable the Explorer bar? The Explorer bar consists of the tabbed items on the left side of your viewing window: Channels, Favorites, History, and Search. To disable the Explorer bar, simply uncheck this item in the View menu. It's that simple. If you wish to enable the Explorer bar, simply select it again in the View window. Disabling the Explorer bar also frees up a bit of space on your viewing window, allowing you to view more information at one time.

The Microsoft Start Page is a nice feature for home use. It allows you to configure your start up page to include any resources you wish. We especially like the weather feature, the quote of the day, and the "Your Links" section. Nevertheless, it is not impossible to remove the links to several commercially motivated items from Microsoft. As a result, we prefer to designate a location on the WWW related to current work in your classroom, a classroom home page, or your school's home page. You will recall the strategy for designating your home page location: click on the "Preferences" button in your toolbar, and then select "Home/Search." (With Windows systems, changing preferences may be accomplished by choosing "Internet Options" from the View menu.) Type in the address for the page on the Internet you wish to appear when you first launch Internet Explorer and you should be all set. For suggestions, see some of the central sites listed in Figure 2-15.

Multimedia Tools for Your Computer: Using All of the Resources on the Internet

OK. You are all set. Your computer is connected to the Internet with Netscape Navigator or Internet Explorer, you have figured out the essentials for navigating around the world and visited the **Galileo Project** at Rice University (http://es.rice.edu/ES/humsoc/Galileo/) to discover a vast amount of historical material about this famous scientist, **Poetry HiFi** (http://www.poetryhifi.com/index2.html) to hear modern poets read their work and discover the nature of a poetry "slam", and **Multicultural Book Reviews** (http://www.isomedia.com/homes/jmele/homepage.html) where students can read and post reviews of wonderful multicultural literature. At some locations, the pages even contain audio and video, in addition to graphics. Sometimes, these came through and sometimes they didn't. Why?

First, a little background. Each location on the Internet may require slightly different tools to read its graphics, audio, and video information. Netscape Navigator and Internet Explorer have plug-ins and helper tools that let you read many items. Often, though, you reach a site where the person wasn't very thoughtful and used a multimedia tool you do not have. As a result, you discover you cannot hear the audio or view the video or graphic without adding the appropriate tool to Netscape Navigator or Internet Explorer.

When this happens, a message will usually appear directing you to extend your capabilities by adding a new plug-in tool to your plug-in file. You may be directed to a central location for plug-in programs and be encouraged to download the appropriate program. Go ahead and follow these directions, restart your computer, and visit the multimedia site you had located earlier. You should then be able to view, read, or listen to the appropriate multimedia element.

Internet FAQ

I have heard that some Internet sites collect information about me. Can I prevent this?

Some sites on the WWW do collect information about you with what are called "cookies." Cookies are requests for information from web site administrators who may record and request information about you whenever you visit their site. Sometimes this is information they collect to direct you to locations you visit most often. Sometimes web sites gather information about you for statistical purposes in order to determine how many people visit their site.

Internet Explorer and Netscape Navigator may be set to warn you when a cookie is being requested. Here are the directions for Windows systems:

> In Netscape Navigator, go to the Edit menu and click on "Preferences." Click on the "Advanced" tab and check the box that says "Warn me before accepting a cookie." In IE, go to the View menu item, choose "Internet Options," and then select the Advanced tab. Go down to the Cookies section, which is nested in the Security section. Select, "Prompt before accepting cookies." Click OK.

Here are the directions for Macintosh systems:

> In Netscape Navigator 4, go to the Edit menu and select Preferences. Click on Advanced and check the box that says, "Warn me before accepting a cookie." In Internet Explorer 4, select Preferences from your toolbar, click on Cookies in the section called Receiving Files, then find the pull down menu and select "Ask for each cookie."

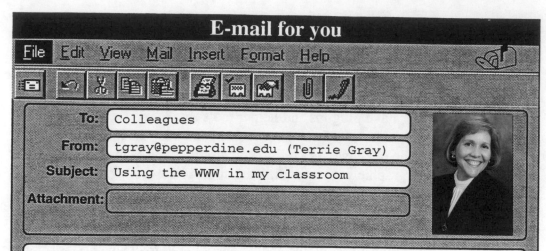

E-mail for you

File   Edit   View   Mail   Insert   Format   Help

To: Colleagues

From: tgray@pepperdine.edu (Terrie Gray)

Subject: Using the WWW in my classroom

Attachment:

Hi! My 7th and 8th-grade students and I were fortunate to work in a classroom with 15 Macintosh computers and a teaching workstation all connected to the Internet via an ISDN line, which means we have fast access. We used Netscape Navigator for our browser.

Using the web for research requires navigation skills. When we first started, 4 school terms ago, the search engines weren't as easy to use as they are now, nor were the resources available to the degree they are currently. Nevertheless, even at this date, I still find that students of this age tend to become easily frustrated. Many have not developed skills for selecting likely sites from a long list. They are not patient readers. Or, they get distracted by something that looks intriguing, but is off topic.

Because of this response to my early web projects, I tried to steer students first to a page I've created which contains links to sites that will most likely be useful. In the spring I involved the students in a research project on an animal of their choice. They were required to search multiple resources, including the Internet, for information. The page I created for this assignment (the first one I ever made!) is located at http://www.chicojr.chico.k12.ca.us/staff/gray/animals.html.

Since its original creation students and contacts from all over the world have contributed links to this collection. 8th grade students studying the weather were involved in multiple web-based activities this last year. Our most successful was one involving lessons and resources located at: http://athena.wednet.edu/curric/weather/index.html.

This site contains directions for activities as well as the links to up-to-date weather maps for collecting data about current conditions. The project we focused on required the students to choose 3 cities, read and chart the weather for those cities over a period of a week or two. Then they researched the topology of the surrounding areas,

Document: Continued

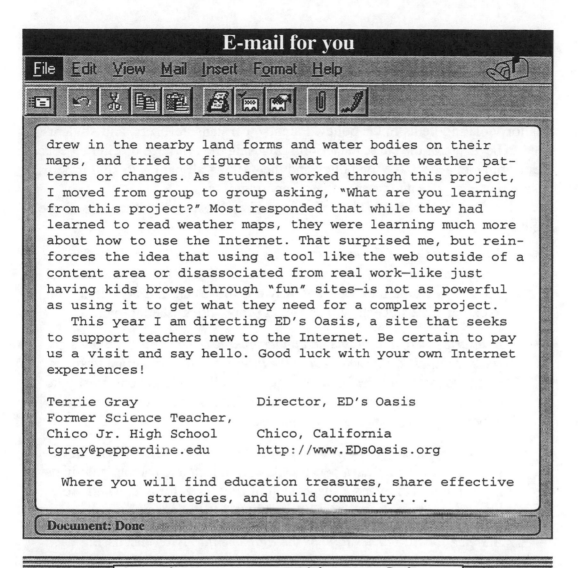

To respond to the viewing of inappropriate sites, some schools use software filters that deny students access to certain Internet sites.

Developing Acceptable Use Policies

Because the Internet is so powerful, it has the potential for great good. At the same time, however, this power may also be abused. Students may travel to sites that are inappropriate for them to view, they may send out an offensive e-mail message, or they may interfere with the running of a computer system.

To respond to the viewing of inappropriate sites, some schools use software filters that deny students access to certain Internet sites, especially in the younger grades. These filters deny access to locations where certain words appear. Teachers and parents may edit the list of words used in the blocking software. You may find out more about these software programs and download evaluation copies for free at the following commercial locations:

Cyber Patrol—(http://www.cyberpatrol.com/);
Net Nanny—(http://www.netnanny.com/);
SurfWatch—(http://www1.surfwatch.com/).

Whether your system uses a software filter or not, it is important for your district to develop an acceptable use policy as part of a comprehensive program of Internet navigation. An acceptable use policy is a written agreement signed by parents/guardians, students, and teachers which specifies the conditions under which students may use the Internet, defines appropriate and unacceptable use, and defines penalties for violating items in the policy. Parents/guardians, teachers, and students all need to be aware of the consequences for misusing the privilege of Internet access. Developing an acceptable use policy and then asking all parties to sign it helps to ensure that everyone understands these important issues.

What does an acceptable use policy look like? Most contain the following elements:

- *An explanation of the Internet and its role in providing information resources to students.* It is important to explain to parents/guardians and students what the Internet is and why it is important. It is also important to explain that students will be taught proper use of the Internet.

- *A description of acceptable and unacceptable behavior that emphasizes student responsibility when using the Internet.* It is important to supervise student use of the Internet, but ultimately each student must take responsibility for his or her own actions. This section describes what is appropriate and inappropriate behavior.

- *A list of penalties for each violation of the policy.* Often this will describe increasing levels of penalties: a warning letter to parents/guardians for a first violation and a suspension of privileges for a repeated violation. A panel may sometimes be established to review cases.

- *A space for all parties to sign the agreement.* After discussing each element carefully with students, the form is usually sent home for parents and students to sign. Teachers will also sign this form before it is carefully filed in an appropriate location.

You may find out more information, print out sample acceptable use policies, and read about other teachers' experiences by visiting the following Internet sites:

Houston Independent School District's Acceptable Use Page—
(http://chico.rice.edu/armadillo/acceptable.html)

Acceptable Use Policies—
(http://www.erehwon.com/k12aup/)

Child Safety on the Information Highway—
(http://www.larrysworld.com/child_safety.html)

Global School Network's Guidelines and Policies for Protecting Students—
(http://www.gsn.org/web/issues/index.htm#begin)

Internet FAQ

It takes a long time to go back more than one or two locations. Is there a faster way to go back to a site I visited a while ago?

Sure! Take a look at your menu in either Netscape Navigator or Internet Explorer. Find the "Go" menu item and then click and hold this down. You will see a list of sites you have already visited since you launched your browser. Just come down to a location you wish to return to and you will go there immediately. With a Windows computer, simply select the item in your toolbar called "History." Internet Explorer will even show you a list of places you have visited many days ago, a nice feature.

Instructional Strategies for Developing Navigation Skills

Renata Svedlin's message from Finland shares a wonderful story about the importance her nation places on developing familiarity with Internet and other information technologies. Finland is leading the world in developing a national plan for teacher education in this area. Like Finland, we need to carefully consider how best to help our students navigate this rich information resource.

If your students are new to the Internet, the weekly structure developed by Angelica Davidson may be a useful model. Each week consisted of small group meetings at the beginning to introduce a new navigation strategy, followed by paired work on the Internet to use the strategy as they completed a weekly classroom assignment. The week concluded with Internet Workshop to share experiences.

If you are just starting to use the Internet in your classroom and only have a single computer linked to the Internet, begin each week with brief small group instruction at the computer on an important navigational strategy such as one of the following:

- the use of search engines;
- how to use directories;
- printing strategies;
- how to use graphic elements from the WWW in your writing projects;
- using the location window to type in a new address;
- using the "Go" menu item;
- helping others effectively;
- understanding the meaning of addresses on the Internet; and
- strategies for staying on task.

During this time, show 5 or 6 students a new aspect to navigating the Internet. Introduce the strategy, show students why it is useful and when it might be used, and then give one or two students an opportunity to practice it while others watch. As you move through the year, you may wish to turn this responsibility over to the groups

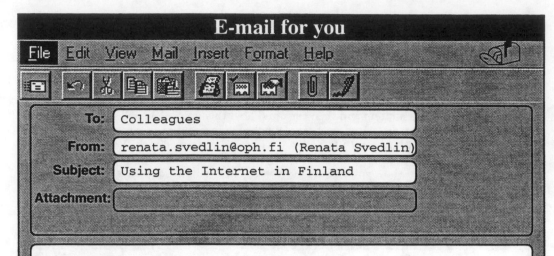

E-mail for you

File   Edit   View   Mail   Insert   Format   Help

To: Colleagues

From: renata.svedlin@oph.fi (Renata Svedlin)

Subject: Using the Internet in Finland

Attachment:

By the end of 1997 approximately 3500 schools in Finland have Internet connections and the number is increasing quickly. That means around 60% of all primary, secondary and high schools in Finland have Internet connections.

In 1996 the Ministry of Education launched a new three-year program supporting the use of information technology. The program is carried through by the National Board of Education. We have started a large program supporting the development of new teaching methods in the schools, methods where we use the advantages of information technology. The aim is to have all schools Internet connected before the year 2000, and for all pupils to have the basic skills in using information technology.

To reach this goal the state is financially supporting the schools (municipalities) in buying micro-computers, establishing connections, and offering a 5 week in-service training course in how to integrate the use of information technology in teaching. The courses have been a success and the knowledge and skills among teachers is increasing—will probably be as good as among the pupils!! Our goal is for every tenth teacher to receive this training. Last autumn there was a call for schools to increase their number of home pages with information in English and other foreign languages. A few hundred of our schools answered the request. If there is more information that would be of interest to you, you are welcome to visit our homepage: http://www.edu.fi/english/.

Sincerely,

Renata Svedlin, senior adviser at the National Board of Education
Finland

Document: Done

themselves. Each week, make a different group responsible for teaching the other groups a new skill they have discovered recently.

During the week, students can integrate the new strategy as they complete content work in one of the subject areas or on a thematic unit. While some schools may have sufficient computer resources to allow students to work alone on the Internet during the week, it is often preferable to have students work together in pairs since this provides more teaching/learning opportunities. Seldom do two students know the same navigation strategies for using the Internet. When students work together, they exchange information and teach each other navigation skills. Rotating partners each week or so ensures that all students have a chance to learn from every other student in the class. This increases opportunities for sharing information about navigation strategies.

At the end of each week, an Internet Workshop will help to consolidate the navigation strategies you introduced at the beginning of the week. It will also raise new navigation issues that you may then explore in subsequent weeks, again in small groups at the beginning of the week, in pairs during the week, and with the whole class at the end of the week.

It is important to note that time used to develop Internet strategies need not be great. Small group sessions at the beginning of the week should take no more than 5–10 minutes. The learning that takes place as students work in pairs occurs during regular content learning experiences; this takes little time. Finally, Internet Workshops need not take more than 20–30 minutes as you share navigational experiences and raise questions that came up during the week. You will find that time devoted to developing navigation skills at the beginning of the year pays rich dividends as your students develop confidence and expertise at navigating the Internet on their own.

As your students become more experienced on the Internet, you should think about modifying this initial structure for developing navigation knowledge. Spend a little time observing students working together on the Internet, looking for those students who have not acquired all of the basic navigational strategies. Then, gather these students together in small group sessions at the beginning of each week according to the strategies they need to refine. One group may need additional assistance on using search engines, while a second group may need additional assistance on using the location window to go to a known address. This additional small group work ensures that all of your students will have the opportunity to develop the essential skills of navigation. It probably won't take more than a week or two to accomplish this. During this time, students may continue to work in pairs on classroom assignments, helping one another. Within a short period of time, your students will have all of the basic navigation strategies in place. When this happens, new strategies may be successfully handled during Internet Workshop, with the entire class sharing ideas they have discovered.

As students develop the ability to navigate on their own, you will find yourself devoting less time to this area and more time to content projects. Questions during Internet Workshop, for example, will gradually and naturally move from navigation issues to useful content locations that students have discovered on the Internet for

It is often preferable to have students work together in pairs since this provides more teaching/learning opportunities.

classroom work. As you move through the year, you will find less and less time devoted to navigation and more and more time devoted to useful information students have discovered on the Internet.

Internet FAQ

When I try to go to a location on the WWW, it sometimes gives me a message that the server is not responding. What should I do?

The server (computer) where this web page is located may be down for servicing, someone may have turned it off, or too may people may be trying to get in at once. Our strategy in these cases is to try a location three times; often you can sneak in, even if it is very busy. If this fails, try again at a later time, especially if it sounds like a good site.

Research and Search Engine Strategies: Saving Time in Busy Classrooms by Navigating Efficiently

As we indicated in Chapter 1, time is a critical component on the Internet. We often hear this concern expressed in several ways:

- How do I find the time to learn about the Internet?
- How do I find the time to teach the Internet in addition to everything else?
- How do I quickly locate good sites on the Internet?

The answer to the first question is one each of us must determine in our own way. Clearly, you are taking time out of your busy schedule to learn about the Internet as you read this book. It is important to recognize, though, that we cannot possibly keep up with all the changes taking place alone. We need to organize our classrooms to take advantage of opportunities for each of us to learn from one another. By making Internet Workshop a part of your instructional program, you can help everyone in your class learn from one another. Often, our students will teach us as much about navigation as we will teach them. This is the one of the new realities of life with the Internet. In Chapter 4, we will show you how to use Internet Workshop along with several other strategies to help you learn together with your students.

Except for initial instruction at the beginning, the Internet should not require extra instructional time during the day.

The second question is also important: How do I find the time to teach the Internet in addition to everything else? The answer to this is to be certain you make the Internet a resource, not a subject. The Internet is just a tool that provides you and your students with information resources. It is no more and no less than a book, a library, an encyclopedia, a video. The Internet should not become a permanent, separate subject for your students. Except for initial instruction at the beginning, the Internet should not require extra instructional time during the day. Even Internet Workshop should be seen as a time to learn about subject areas, not a time to focus exclusively on the Internet, especially after students develop beginning navigation skills.

The third question is important, too: How do I quickly locate good sites on the Internet? We need to learn to become efficient in finding useful resources on the Internet. There are two types of strategies that should assist you in this area: central site strategies and search engine strategies.

Locating Information with a Central Site Strategy

As you begin your journey with the Internet, consider using a central site strategy. A central site is a location on the Internet with extensive and well-organized links about a content area or important subject. Most are located at stable sites that will not quickly change. Most are not commercial sites. As you explore the Internet, you will discover these well-organized treasure troves of information. They will become homes to which you will often return. We take this approach in this book. Each of the content area chapters will share the best central sites we have found. Set a bookmark or a "favorites" marker and begin your explorations at these central locations. This will save you much time and frustration during the period when you are developing effective strategies for using search engines. In fact, you could use only central sites and find everything you require for your class.

As you begin your journey with the Internet, consider using a central site strategy.

We have found the locations in Figure 2-15 to be the most useful central site locations for different subject areas. You may wish to visit some of these now and set a bookmark (favorites) for those you find useful. We will discuss each in upcoming chapters.

TEACHING TIP

Set bookmarks for each of the central sites listed in Figure 2-15. This will save you important time when you, or your students, are looking for good resources in a content area. You might also wish to designate one of these sites as your home page location. You will recall that your home page location is the first screen to appear each time you launch your Internet browser. With most browsers, this can be set from your preferences window. See the earlier discussions for Navigator or Internet Explorer to see how this may be done with either a Windows or a Macintosh system.

Locating Information with a Search Engine Strategy

There are many, many search engines on the Internet to help you find information you require. A search engine locates sites on the Internet containing the key word(s) you enter. Each search engine seems to have its own style, its own strengths, its own weaknesses. You should become familiar with how each engine searches for information and displays the information it finds. As you use search engines, you will develop a favorite for your work. When this happens, be certain to set a bookmark/favorites so that you can return to this search engine whenever you require it.

You should become familiar with how each engine searches for information and displays the information it finds.

Figure 2-15.
Central sites
on the Internet
for teaching
and learning.

Area	Central Internet Sites
Literature (all ages)	**Children's Literature Web Guide** (http://www.ucalgary.ca/~dkbrown/index.html)
Science (general)	**Eisenhower National Clearinghouse: Action** (http://www.enc.org:80/classroom/index.htm) **Science Learning Network** (http://www.sln.org/index.html)
Math (general)	**Eisenhower National Clearinghouse: Action** (http://www.enc.org:80/classroom/index.htm) **The Math Forum** (http://forum.swarthmore.edu/)
Social Studies (general)	**History/Social Studies Web Site for K-12 Teachers** (http://www.execpc.com/~dboals/boals.html) **Nebraska Department of Education Social Science Resources HomePage** (http://www.nde.state.ne.us/SS/ss.html)
Multicultural Curriculum Resources	**Cultures of the World** (http://www.ala.org/parentspage/greatsites/people.html#b **Multicultural Pavilion** (http://curry.edschool.Virginia.EDU:80/go/multicultural/) **K-5 Cybertrail: Multicultural Curriculum Resources** (http://www.wmht.org/trail/explor02.htm)
African American Culture	**Multi-Cultural Paths: African American Resources** (http://curry.edschool.Virginia.EDU:80/go/multicultural/sites/afr-am.html)
Chicana/o Latina/o Culture	**Latin American Network Information Center** (http://www.lanic.utexas.edu/la/region/k-12/)
Native American Culture	**Native American Indian Resources** (http://indy4.fdl.cc.mn.us/~isk/mainmenu.html)
Special Education	**Special Education Resources on the Internet (SERI)** (http://www.hood.edu/seri/serihome.htm) **Family Village** (http://www.familyvillage.wisc.edu/)

For now, it is useful to be able to match one of several search engines with the needs you might have in a search. If, for example, you wish to search a broad topic and gradually narrow down the resources you find, you should begin with the search engine **Yahoo** (http://www.yahoo.com/). Yahoo organizes information hierarchically, providing you a general category as well as a specific site for each match of the key word(s) you entered. This is useful as you explore different broad categories, looking for specific treasures.

Sometimes, though, you know the exact phrase or a very narrow key term you wish to find and you do not wish to explore higher-level categories. Perhaps, for example, you wish to find the home page for the Smithsonian Institution and you know it is called The Smithsonian Institution Home Page. For narrow searches, the best search engines are **AltaVista** (http://www.altavista.digital.com/) or **HotBot** (http://www.hotbot.com/), especially if you take advantage of some of their advanced search features to refine your search. Each will quickly find your key word if it exists on the Internet.

If you are interested in the quality of sites found by a search engine, you should use either **Magellan** (http://www.mckinley.com/), **Lycos** (http://www.pointcom.com/), or **WebCrawler** (http://webcrawler.com/). Each of these search engines reviews sites and ranks them in terms of quality. This is often helpful for busy teachers who are looking for central sites in a particular area.

If you are most interested in reading summaries of sites located in your search, you should probably use **Excite** (http://www.excite.com/). This search engine is known for providing a more limited number of items containing very descriptive summaries of the information at each location. When you find a site that interests you, you can then link to additional locations like the one you found.

A Central Site for Internet Research and Search Engine Use

These suggestions, though, just provide you with the beginning steps in your journey as you discover effective research and search engine strategies. If you wish to explore this topic more thoroughly, pay a visit to a computer at Nueva School in the San Francisco Bay area. At the **Research** (http://www.nueva.pvt.k12.ca.us/~debbie/library/research/research.html) page of the Nueva School Library, Debbie Abilock and Marilyn Kimura have developed an outstanding resource for helping you and your students understand more about effective research and search engine strategies. Stop by and explore the wonderful work they have accomplished for all of us. Drop a note, too, and let these good folks know about the wonderful work they are doing.

If you are interested in the quality of sites found by a search engine, you should use either Magellan.

To discover effective research and search engine strategies, pay a visit to a computer at Nueva School in the San Francisco Bay area: Research.

Navigation Resources on the Internet

Adam Rosen's Quick Guide to Viewing the World Wide Web—
(http://www.cgicafe.com/~ajrosen/guide.html)
Have you been working hard trying to figure out how to navigate in the WWW and need of a little humor? Visit this (very) quick guide to viewing the WWW and enjoy the joke. Cute.

AskERIC Virtual Library: Educational Questions—
(http://ericir.syr.edu/Qa/userform.html)
At this location you may ask any question regarding educational research or practice and receive a personalized response back via e-mail within 48 hours. The "Educational Questions" site is a part of the Educational Resources Information Center (ERIC), a federally-funded national information system. Many other useful resources are also located here. Take advantage of this important resource.

Beginners Central—(http://www.northernwebs.com/bc/)
This is an outstanding guide to the Internet, especially if you are just starting out. It takes you through everything you need to know to successfully navigate the Internet. This guide is updated regularly, a real bonus. This might also be a useful location to direct your class to at the beginning of the year. Set a bookmark/favorite!

Exploring the Internet—(http://www.screen.com/start/guide/)
If you are just beginning your travels on the Internet, this is a good location to assist you with information about navigation issues. In addition to an easy-to-read style, it includes many useful links to locations that will be helpful to you as a new user.

Glossary of Internet Terms—(http://www.matisse.net/files/glossary.html)
This is an extensive set of Internet terms, precisely defined for your use. A nice resource.

Internet 101—(http://www2.famvid.com/i101/internet101.html)
Here is one of the best on-line guides to the Internet we have discovered. It covers everything you, or your student, need to know. Be certain to visit this location. Set a bookmark/favorite!

K-5 Cyber Trail—(http://www.wmht.org/trail/trail.htm)
This is a great location to develop navigation skills as you see how other teachers are using the Internet in their classrooms. Developed in the Albany, NY area, it is a wonderful resource for every teacher. Set a bookmark/favorite!

Net Lingo—(http://www.netlingo.com/)
Here is a great location if you want to find out about all the new vocabulary the Internet is generating. Need to know the meaning of a word you came across? Here is the location for you!

RealNetworks—(http://www.realaudio.com/)
This is a commercial site but we find it very useful. You can download most versions of their wonderful plug-ins for free. These will allow you to listen to radio stations around the world (see Chapter 12), or receive audio and video from an increasing number of locations on the Internet. This is wonderful technology that everyone should download to their browser. Currently, you only have to pay for the

latest version of their software. We hope this continues! The older versions work just fine. Best of all, they are free!

Teacher Talk—(http://www.mightymedia.com/talk/working.htm)
A useful discussion area for teachers to talk about issues of instruction and technology. If you have a question, post it here and you will receive answers from other teachers. You will be asked for your name and a password to enter. Do not use your e-mail password or another password you use on a computer. Use a different one to prevent anyone from accessing your accounts.

The Internet Index—(http://www.openmarket.com/intindex/)
Here you will find a collection of interesting Internet statistics. Interesting reading.

The Net: User Guidelines and Netiquette—
(http://www.fau.edu/rinaldi/net/index.html)
This Internet book provides a useful discussion about socially responsible ways of using the Internet. It provides useful background before developing an acceptable use policy. It is also useful as required reading for older students at the beginning of the year. Included is a list of Ten Commandments for Computer Ethics from the Computer Ethics Institute. This might be printed out and posted next to each computer in your classroom.

WWW Viewer Test Page—http://www-dsed.llnl.gov/documents/WWWtest.html
At this location you may test many common helper applications to see if you have them on your browser. If they are not, this location will connect you to a location on the WWW where you may download them onto your computer. A nice resource.

3 Communicating on the Internet: E-mail, Mailing Lists, and Other Forms of Electronic Communication

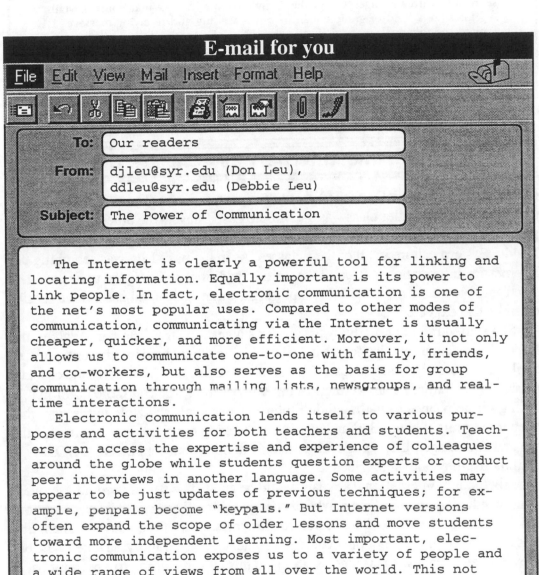

E-mail for you

File   Edit   View   Mail   Insert   Format   Help

To: Our readers

From: djleu@syr.edu (Don Leu),
ddleu@syr.edu (Debbie Leu)

Subject: The Power of Communication

The Internet is clearly a powerful tool for linking and locating information. Equally important is its power to link people. In fact, electronic communication is one of the net's most popular uses. Compared to other modes of communication, communicating via the Internet is usually cheaper, quicker, and more efficient. Moreover, it not only allows us to communicate one-to-one with family, friends, and co-workers, but also serves as the basis for group communication through mailing lists, newsgroups, and real-time interactions.

Electronic communication lends itself to various purposes and activities for both teachers and students. Teachers can access the expertise and experience of colleagues around the globe while students question experts or conduct peer interviews in another language. Some activities may appear to be just updates of previous techniques; for example, penpals become "keypals." But Internet versions often expand the scope of older lessons and move students toward more independent learning. Most important, electronic communication exposes us to a variety of people and a wide range of views from all over the world. This not only broadens perspectives, but also develops analytical and critical thinking as students integrate new and diverse ideas with their own experiences.

Using e-mail is not just another way to get information; it is an opportunity to increase our understanding and share our ideas.

Don and Debbie

Document: Done

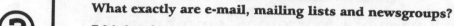

Internet FAQ

What exactly are e-mail, mailing lists and newsgroups?

E-Mail is electronic mail, messages sent electronically from one computer to another. Special software programs allow any person who has an e-mail address to send and receive messages to any other individual who has an e-mail address. Mailing Lists are a kind of group e-mail in which sending and receiving messages is limited to individuals who are listed as members of a particular group formed to discuss a specific area of interest. Newsgroups are also a kind of group e-mail focused on a specific topic. However, there are no membership lists; anyone can read and reply to messages.

Teaching with the Internet: Lily Chang's Classroom

Lily Chang was especially excited about the upcoming school year. The first major unit for her social studies class was the Middle East. She and the other seventh grade teachers were working together so that the students could study various aspects of Middle Eastern culture in all of their classes. As in the past, Lily was searching the Internet for information related to the unit; in addition, she decided to expand her electronic communication skills by exploring a variety of e-mail uses. It was easier than she had expected.

She started rather casually by asking for suggestions from Barbara Walker, the leader of a recent in-service for the district. Although they lived in different cities, e-mail made it easy to communicate. Lily didn't have to call at a certain time or leave messages on Barbara's answering machine. In addition, she felt more comfortable asking for help since e-mailing didn't interrupt Barbara's schedule in the way that telephoning might have. Barbara suggested checking out some keypal sites on the net and encouraged Lily to ask for advice from other teachers on **SCHOOL-L**, a mailing list they both subscribed to.

Lily thought international keypals would be great. The students could ask questions, conduct interviews, and maybe exchange photos. They could learn a lot about other cultures. When she did a search for "keypals," Lily found several sites. She was pleased to find that not only could her students look for individual keypals, but she could also request a partner class. She did this by subscribing to a mailing list at one of the sites, **Intercultural E-mail Classroom Connections** (http://www.stolaf.edu/network/iecc/index.html), and then posted an e-mail message introducing herself and her class and asking if there were any teachers from Middle Eastern countries who might want to partner their class with hers in the fall. It might be very convenient to have keypals all from one class and a co-teacher to share ideas with.

Next, Lily sent a message to the SCHOOL-L mailing list asking for suggestions about sites and resources on the Middle East. Although she had subscribed to SCHOOL-L for some time, she had never posted a message. She had read many helpful replies to others, however, so she wasn't surprised when she received many e-mail responses over the next few days. Several teachers sent information about Middle East sites and Internet activities their students had done the previous year. One teacher recommended working on a project with a partner class, and mentioned several project sites. He also gave her the address for a projects discussion group. Another message suggested checking out newsgroups on related topics. Two teachers mentioned how they had used Internet resources to help their middle school students develop research skills. Another teacher gave information about how he had arranged for his students to e-mail questions to a professor of Japanese history, and suggested that Lily might be able to do the same with a Middle East expert.

As Lily noted ideas from her e-mail messages, she began thinking about the most effective way for her class to present their ideas to a partner class. One of the e-mail messages, from a teacher who had just returned from Kuwait, had focused on cultural differences, and ended with a suggestion that she discuss diversity and cross-cultural interaction. That seemed like a good idea. Lily also wanted to be make full use of e-mail's capabilities. Just exchanging facts that could easily be found in an encyclopedia wouldn't be very effective. Perhaps she could get two partner classes from different countries. Then, the students could get information on specific topics and compare the different viewpoints. Maybe they could even do some sort of analysis in math class. She kept notes on index cards about several ideas so that she could share them with the other seventh-grade teachers and with the students in order to get their input before final decisions were made. It was a good beginning.

In addition to thinking about content, Lily had been working with the other teachers to develop a plan to help the students expand their computer skills and manage their time on the computer. Each classroom had only one computer, but this year students would have their own e-mail accounts; this would be a big change from last year when they had sent their messages from their teacher's account. Last year's teacher had kept an electronic folder for each student in his account, so he could easily monitor what was sent and received. Lily would have to use a different system. She didn't really want to print out all the students' messages, but she wouldn't have time to read each one as it was sent either. Perhaps they could have a discussion about manners on the net, relating to themselves as well as to their keypals. She could even do a workshop and maybe some role plays about how they would feel if they received a mean message. Lily was looking forward to the new year, but there was still a lot to do.

Lessons from the Classroom

This scenario illustrates several lessons for using electronic communication effectively. First, as a teacher, Lily Chang used e-mail, mailing lists and newsgroups to get suggestions for herself on sites, resources, and activities from other teachers. This is one of the most powerful ways for teachers to expand their knowledge and learn from others' experiences. Many lists have hundreds of members, and newsgroups may have thousands of readers; together, their composite expertise covers almost every topic and point of view. Having e-mail is almost like having access to an individualized in-service program anytime you need it.

Second, Lily had clear goals and purposes. She didn't see the Internet as an end in itself but as a tool whose use could be incorporated into the curriculum to help students develop certain skills and meet desired objectives. In this case, electronic communication would help increase understanding of other cultures, provide practice in collaborative teamwork, develop critical thinking, and encourage tolerance and respect for others.

Third, her students' ages and previous computer experience played a large role in Lily's planning. She planned age-appropriate activities that included student participation in choosing activities. This would expand their e-mail skills and foster better decision-making, both of which would help prepare them to use electronic communication more independently in the future.

Fourth, by planning activities and projects that involved not only obtaining information, but also analyzing and synthesizing it, Lily was helping her students develop their critical thinking skills. Her district was emphasizing critical thinking skills and e-mail experiences seemed to fit nicely into the program they were developing in this area.

Finally, Lily planned lessons on netiquette. As an e-mail user herself, she knew the importance of good Internet manners. With a younger group of students, she would have posted a list of rules. However, because she recognized the seventh graders' developing ability to understand the need for order and safety, she would have them participate in discussions to formulate their own netiquette guidelines.

Getting Started with E-Mail

In order to use electronic communication effectively, you need to integrate Internet knowledge and skills with your own beliefs and teaching practices. You will want to reflect on which types of communication—individual e-mail, mailing lists, newsgroups, and real-time interactions—fit in with your approach to education, as well as consider which uses seem more suitable for students and which are better for teachers. If you haven't used e-mail before, allow yourself extra time to practice various functions before trying them out with your students in the classroom. The more proficient you are, the easier it will be to anticipate your students' needs and develop effective teaching and learning strategies.

In these next sections, we provide an overview of electronic communication from a classroom perspective. We will focus on the basics and use as little technical jargon as possible. Our goal is to help you get started and provide you with a jumping off point for your own future exploration. We encourage you to work cooperatively with other teachers, and when necessary, to seek help from technical resource people for more detailed information.

We will begin with e-mail, the basis of electronic communication on the Internet. You need only two things to get started: an e-mail account and an e-mail software program. Then, identify yourself to the program, and you are ready to receive and send electronic messages.

Your E-Mail Account

The first step is to request an e-mail account from your Internet service provider (ISP), who will then give you an e-mail address and an e-mail password. E-mail addresses follow a standard, three-part format:

UserID@host.domain

1. UserID (pronounced *user I.D.*) is the name or identifying number of the account user.

2. @ is the "at" sign.

3. host.domain is the name and location of the computer that handles the user's account and the type of group which hosts the account.

Here is an example: ddleu@mailbox.syr.edu

The last part of the address (.edu) means that the host is an educational institution. Other common categories are: .com for commercial; .gov for government; .org for organization; and .net for network. Some addresses, especially those outside the United States are followed by a country code such as .ca for Canada or .au for Australia.

Your e-mail password will be a number, word, or some combination of these. It is known only to you, somewhat like a PIN number for your bank account. Most programs allow you to change your password, but do not choose an easily guessed word or number, because your password provides security for your account. For this reason, you should memorize it and keep it secret. Never let anyone else use your password.

TEACHING TIP

E-Mail Security In The Classroom

Unless you have your own computer in a secure place, it's a good idea to shut it down, or at least sign off your e-mail account, when you leave the terminal. That way, no unauthorized person can read your e-mail files or use your e-mail account. If your students will send and receive e-mail through your account rather than have their own individual accounts, it is also a good idea to discuss security and privacy issues with them.

We will explain e-mail using examples from Netscape Communicator 4 and Internet Explorer 4, two popular browsers available in both Mac and Windows.

E-Mail Software

Your second step is getting an e-mail software program. There are several different programs, so check with your technical resource person for information about which ones are supported by your service provider. We will explain e-mail using examples from Netscape Communicator 4 and Internet Explorer 4, two popular browsers available in both Mac and Windows platforms, which include e-mail software. Don't be concerned if you notice some differences between your screen and our examples or have another version of these browsers. Companies are continually improving their software, which results in small changes between upgrades (version 4.01 vs. 4.02, for example). Even if you have a different version or use a different software program altogether, you should be able to follow or adapt the procedures described below because most programs perform the same basic functions and use similar terminology.

Internet FAQ

There are so many different e-mail programs and hosts. Do I need different kinds of software to communicate with everyone?

No, any e-mail software will allow you to communicate with anyone else who has an e-mail address, regardless of their location or software program. There may be some minor differences, such as how attachments are handled. Generally speaking, though, all e-mail systems are compatible.

Identifying Yourself by Setting Preferences

Before you actually communicate via e-mail, you must let your software program know who you are and where to get and send your mail. This is done by "setting preferences." Most programs offer many options for organizing your mail, but there are only a few that must be set in order to begin sending and receiving messages. Later, when you are more familiar with e-mail, you can customize your system. For now, you will need the information listed in the box below. You may wish to write it down here for easy reference. Contact your technical resource person or service provider for any information you are not sure of.

Your name: _____

Your reply-to address: _____

Your organization: _____

Your outgoing (SMPT) mail server: _____

Your incoming mail server: _____
(usually the same as the outgoing server)

Your POP ID: _____
(usually the same as your UserID—a few providers request IMAP instead of POP)

Now, depending on which Internet software you use, read one of the following two sections about using e-mail with either Netscape Communicator or Internet Explorer. Then continue with the section headed Moving On, which appears later in this chapter on page 95.

Read one of the following two sections about using e-mail with either Netscape Communica- tor or Internet Explorer. Then continue with the section: Moving On.

Using Netscape Communicator for E-Mail

Netscape Communicator 4 is an integrated program that handles mail and news functions through its Messenger and Collabra components. Because Communicator gives users the opportunity to set all preferences when first opening it and creating user profiles, you may already have set your e-mail preferences, or they may have been set by your technical resource person. If so, move on to the next section: Receiving and Reading Messages. If you haven't set your mail preferences, or aren't sure whether they are set, continue reading here.

The first time you want to use e-mail, open Netscape Communicator and set your e-mail preferences by choosing Edit from the main menu and selecting Preferences. [To choose and select, move the cursor to Edit, depress the mouse button, move the mouse down to Preferences, and release the button.] This opens the Preferences window and shows a Category frame on the left. Look for the item "Mail and Groups" in the Category list. Within this category will be a subcategory called "Identity." Select this subcategory. This will open the Identity preference box. Enter your name, e-mail address, and reply-to address in the appropriate boxes. You may wish to enter your organization name; if you don't, Netscape will enter the name of your Internet service provider. Leave the other boxes empty for now. Then click OK. An example is provided in Figure 3-1.

Internet FAQ

What should I do if I don't see "Identity" in the Category list?

This means that the sub-categories are collapsed. To reveal them, click the icon next to "Mail and Groups." You may reverse this process by clicking the icon again, which closes the sub-category list. In Mac systems, the icon is a triangle that points down to show categories and to the right to hide them; in Windows, the icon is a minus sign (-) to show categories and a plus sign (+) to hide them.

Next, return to the Category list and click "Mail Server" within "Mail and Groups." This opens the Mail Server box. Enter your mail server user name (which is usually your UserID); also enter your outgoing (SMPT) mail server and your incoming mail server addresses (these are usually the same). Select the type of server (which is usually POP3) by clicking the appropriate button. Click OK to close the Preferences window. Your required mail preferences are now set, but you may change or further customize them by returning to the Preferences window at another time.

Figure 3-1.
Setting Preferences in the Mail and Groups Identity window for Netscape Communicator.

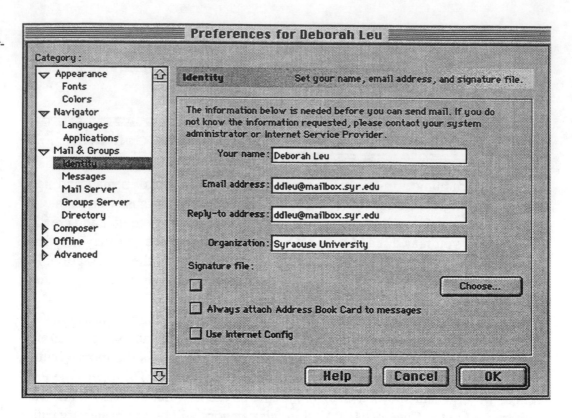

Receiving and Reading Messages

Now you are ready to communicate using your e-mail account. This may be done by choosing and selecting items from the Netscape Communicator menu at the top of your screen. However, many people find it easier to click on icons or buttons, which is the process we describe in the following sections. To receive new messages, you must be connected to the Internet. Since Netscape Communicator does allow you to use some features off-line, make sure you are connected. Then, begin by clicking the Messenger Inbox icon in the Component Bar as illustrated in Figure 3-2 which shows the icons for Navigator, the Inbox, the Message Center, and Composer. The Messenger Inbox icon contains a small image of a letter and a mailbox. The Component Bar is usually located in the lower right corner of the Netscape Communicator window. If the Component Bar is hidden, choose the Netscape Communicator icon in the main menu and select Messenger Inbox to reveal it.

Figure 3-2.
The Component bar in
Netscape Communicator.

Netscape Communicator/Messenger will attempt to check with the mail server to see if you have any new mail. In order to retrieve your mail, it will ask for your password by opening a dialog box. Just type your password and click OK.

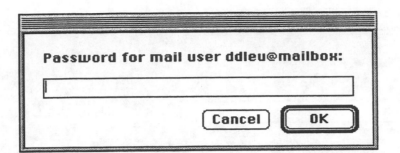

Figure 3-3.
This is the
Password
Request win-
dow.

This opens the Messenger window with your Inbox selected as shown in Figures 3-4 and 3-5, for Macintosh and Windows systems, respectively. In addition, these figures illustrate the Messenger toolbar as it appears in Macintosh (Figure 3-4) and Windows systems (Figure 3-5).

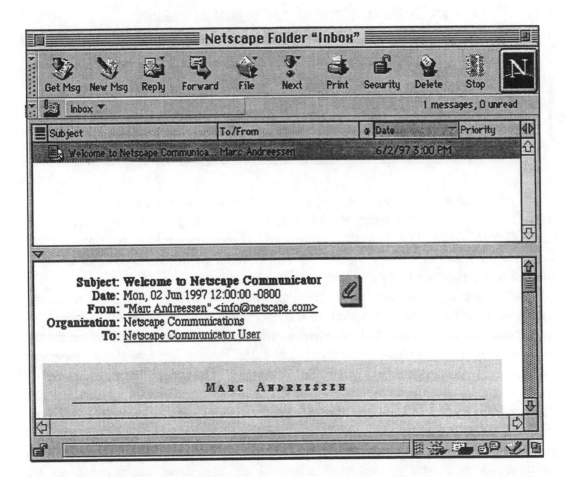

Figure 3-4.
The Messenger Inbox
window in
Netscape
Communicator, as it
appears in a
Macintosh
system.

Notice that the mail screen is divided into several sections. The top section contains the main menu. In both Macintosh and Windows systems it will include the Messenger toolbar, and other headings. The middle section, the listing pane, lists your messages. The bottom section, the message pane, displays the messages you highlight in the listing pane.

Figure 3-5.
The Messenger Inbox window in Netscape Communicator, as it appears in a Windows system.

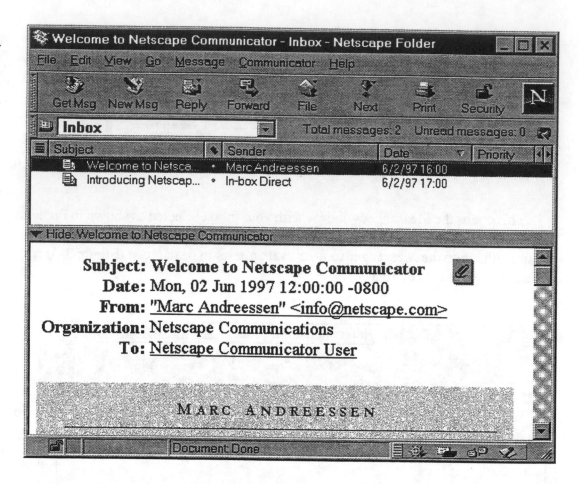

Look directly below the toolbar. On the left, you will see the folder selection box with Inbox selected and a small black triangle just to the right of the box. (Later, you may click this triangle to select different folders from your folder list, but for now, keep Inbox selected.) The total number and number of unread messages are displayed to the right on this same line.

Next, look at the listing pane. The first time Messenger is opened, a welcome message from Netscape will appear in the pane. In addition, if any other messages have been sent to you, they will be retrieved from the server and appear in the listing pane with their subject headers, senders, and dates. New messages always appear in bold type. Additional message information can be found in various columns to the right. A green diamond next to a message indicates the message is unread. The diamond disappears when a message is read, but you may return it by clicking in the diamond column next to the message you want to mark. Do this if you intend to re-read a message. You may also flag important messages by clicking in the red flag column next to a message you want to mark. Flags also disappear as messages are read, but may be returned by clicking. Other columns include Priority, which may be marked if the sender has indicated a priority level (urgent, normal, or slow) for the message. If you can't see some of the columns mentioned above or want to see additional message information, click the small triangles in the top right corner of the listing pane to move the pane left or right, which reveals and hides the columns.

The display pane may be closed until you click the small triangle in the left corner at the bottom of the listing pane. Clicking this triangle opens the pane and displays any message which you have highlighted above in the listing pane so that you may read it.

From now on, Messenger will automatically check for new messages the first time in each session that you open the Messenger Inbox window. Follow the procedures mentioned above, and enter your password if you want to read your messages or click Cancel if you don't. Remember, you may also get your mail at any time during a session by clicking Get Msg in the Inbox toolbar. If you have more than one message, click on a succeeding or preceding message in order to display and read it in the bottom pane. You may also select messages by clicking the Next button in the Messenger toolbar.

Replying to a Message

In many cases after reading a message, you will want to respond. First, make sure that the message you want to reply to appears in the message display pane. Then, click and hold down the Reply button in the toolbar and select from the sub-menu that appears. If the message you want to reply to was sent by one person and has only one address, select To Sender Only. If the message contains multiple addresses, and if you want to reply to all of the addressees, select To Sender and All Recipients. Either selection opens the Message Composition window as shown in Figure 3-6.

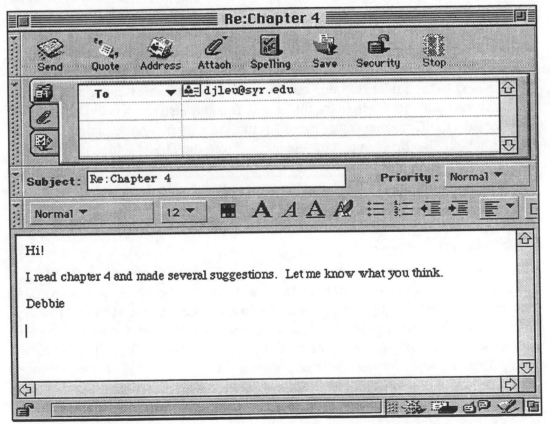

Figure 3-6. The Message Composition window with the "To" and "Subject" items already entered for a reply message.

Notice that the subject and address(es) are already entered. However, you may edit any entry by moving the cursor to the appropriate box and deleting or adding information. Next, move the cursor to the bottom pane of the Message Composition window and type your message.

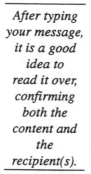

Internet FAQ

What are the icons in the toolbar directly below the subject line of the Message Composition window?

These icons allow you to design your message using color, various fonts, underlining, images, and other features using a special HTML (HyperText Mark-up Language) tool. While these features can add a special look to your message's appearance, it is probably best to send simple, text-only messages unless you know that your recipient(s) can receive messages containing these special features available in Netscape Communicator /Messenger. If your recipient's e-mail program doesn't support graphical messages, your message will be unreadable.

After typing your message, it is a good idea to read it over, confirming both the content and the recipient(s).

After typing your message, it is a good idea to read it over, confirming both the content and the recipient(s). If you are sure your message is the way you want it, click the Send button. Once you click this button, if you are working on-line, it is impossible to stop or retrieve your message; it is immediately sent to the server. If you click Send while you are working off-line, your message will be put in the Unsent Messages folder for later delivery. The next time you come online, Messenger will ask if you want your unsent messages sent.

If you aren't ready to send your message, you can save it by clicking the Save button. This will hold it in your Drafts folder until you are ready to finish it. When you want to work on your message again, you can retrieve it by clicking the black triangle next to the folder selection box (directly below the Messenger toolbar) and selecting the Drafts folder from the folder list. You may also reach your Drafts folder by choosing the Communicator icon from the main menu and selecting Message Center, which also brings up your folder list. From the Drafts folder, double click the message you want to work on. This brings the saved message up in the Message Composition window where you can continue working on it. When you are finished you can send it or save it again for further editing.

The Quote Button

The Quote button in the toolbar of the Message Composition window (see Figure 3-7) can also be useful when replying to a message. Whether to use it, however, is a matter of personal choice. Some people like to always include the original message within their reply message to provide context and to enable others to refer to it easily if necessary. [You may set up your mail to automatically quote the original message every time you reply by selecting that option from Preferences.] Other e-mail users feel using quotes is inconsiderate because it takes up time and Inbox space for recipients, and adds extra charges for those who pay for e-mail by the line. Some people quote only a few important lines. In any case, using the Quote button is easy. Clicking it adds the original message which is shown in the display screen to your reply message. Depending on the default settings of your program, the quote will be shown with the original author's name and either a greater-than sign (>) at the beginning of each line (for text-only messages), or a vertical blue line along the left side of the quoted message (for html/graphical messages). You may edit the quote by moving the cursor and adding and deleting information as in any message.

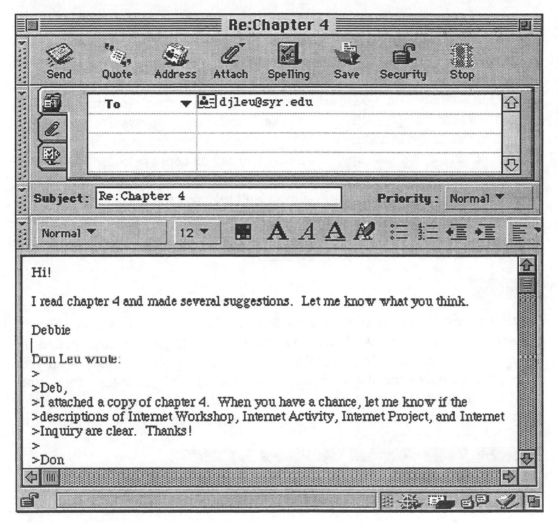

Figure 3-7. The Message Composition window, showing the use of the Quote button when replying to a message.

Forwarding Mail

Sometimes you receive messages you know would be useful for colleagues. It's easy to share these messages by using the Forward button in the Messenger Inbox toolbar. Before forwarding a message, however, consider whether the original sender would want the message relayed to other people. You may want to ask for permission. If you decide to share a message, click the Forward button while the message you want to forward is in the message display pane. This will bring up the Message Composition window with the subject box filled in, and the forwarded message (shown as a quoted message) in the lower pane of the window. All you need to do is enter the recipient's e-mail address on the To: line. If you wish, you may also type a message of your own above or below the forwarded message. Then click Send. The message will be forwarded to the person you have designated.

Composing and Sending a New Message

It's a good idea to type in a subject for your messages. A subject isn't required, but it's helpful for recipients who like to skim their messages for content prior to opening and reading them.

Composing and sending a new message is basically the same as replying, but you begin in a different way. Start by clicking the New Msg button in the Messenger Inbox toolbar. This will open the Message Composition window (like Figure 3-6). You must enter the name and e-mail address of the person you wish to contact on the To: line. You may send your message to more than one person by typing additional names and addresses on the same line, separating each person's information with a comma. You can also press Return on the keyboard to bring up new To: lines and fill them in individually. In addition, clicking on To: will show a sub-menu from which you can select Cc (carbon copy) and Bcc (blind carbon copy) options.

It's a good idea to type in a subject for your messages [except when subscribing or unsubcribing to a mailing list]. A subject isn't required, but it's helpful for recipients who like to skim their messages for content prior to opening and reading them. After entering the name(s), address(es), and subject, proceed with your new message in the same way as for a reply message.

Printing

Printing a message is one of the easiest features. Just click the Print button in the Messenger Inbox toolbar while the message you want to print is displayed in the display screen. Although it isn't really necessary to have paper copies of all your messages, you may want to use this feature to print out e-mail messages for posting on a bulletin board so that the whole class can read them. It's also nice to print some e-mail messages for students to share with their parents at home or at an open house.

Managing Your Mail and Working with Folders

The Message Center helps you to organize your e-mail messages. It keeps a list of your folders for e-mail messages and helps you delete, save, and move messages from one folder to another. It also allows you to create new folders. The Message Center initially contains five default folders: Inbox, Unsent Messages, Drafts, Sent, and Trash. Clicking on any of these folders will display its contents.

- The *Inbox folder* is where Messenger stores new, incoming messages as well as any old messages that you have not deleted or filed elsewhere.

- The *Unsent Messages folder* holds finished messages for sending at a later time. For example, you may want to compose or reply to messages when you are not connected to the Internet. After you write them, instead of sending them immediately, you can save them in the Unsent Messages

Figure 3-8.
The Message Center window for Netscape Communicator, showing the five initial folders: Inbox, Unsent Messages, Drafts, Sent, and Trash.

folder and then send them the next time you connect to the Internet by choosing File from the main menu and selecting Send Unsent Messages.

- The *Drafts folder* saves unfinished messages that you intend to work on later.
- The *Sent folder* holds copies of messages that you have sent or forwarded.
- The *Trash folder* temporarily holds deleted items until you are ready to remove them permanently.

After you read a message, it remains in your Inbox folder unless you remove it. As a result, the Inbox becomes crowded and disorganized, and when it gets too full, you can't receive any new messages. Moreover, if you want to refer back to a message, it can be difficult to find it in a long list. Therefore, it is a good idea to get in the habit of moving messages out of your Inbox as you read them. One way to do this is by deletion.

Deleting Messages

Deleting messages is very easy. If you don't need to keep a message after reading it, simply click the Delete button in the toolbar. This removes the current message from the listing and display panes and transfers it to the Trash folder. If you want to delete a message at a later time, highlight it by clicking its subject header in the listing pane; then click the Delete button. If you have several messages, you can "block delete" them as a group by clicking on each one while holding down the

If you don't need to keep a message after reading it, simply click Delete in the toolbar.

keyboard shift key. This highlights a group of messages. Click the Delete button and the whole group will be removed from the listing pane and transferred to the Trash folder.

The Trash Folder

Be careful; once you click Empty Trash Folder, the messages and folders in the trash at that time are permanently deleted.

At this point, although you have deleted your messages, they are not really gone from your mail service. They are in the Trash folder. This can be a convenient feature if you have accidentally deleted a message that you need. To retrieve a message, click the Trash Folder, then click the message you want. Next choose the File button on the toolbar and select the folder to which you want to save the retrieved message. This will move your message to the appropriate folder. It's a good idea to open the new folder and make sure that your message does actually appear there.

In order to actually get rid of your deletions, you must empty the Trash folder. Do this by going to the main menu, choosing File, and selecting Empty Trash Folder. Be careful; once you click Empty Trash Folder, the messages and folders in the trash at that time are permanently deleted.

Saving Sent Messages

Netscape Messenger automatically saves copies of messages that you send, including forwarded messages, to the Sent folder in the Message Center. This provides a convenient record of your sent messages and allows you to easily re-send a message to others if necessary. However, this folder can become very large if you are an active e-mailer. Therefore, you may wish to create additional folders (by month, for example) and transfer your sent messages accordingly. Or if you do not want to save them, simply delete as explained above.

Saving Received Messages

To save a message after you have read it, click the File button. This brings up the list of your folders. Click the folder in which you want to save the message. This removes the current message from the listing and display panes and transfers it to the selected folder.

If you want to save a message at a later time, highlight it by clicking its subject header in the listing pane; then proceed as above. You can "block save" messages just as you block delete them by clicking each one while holding down the keyboard shift key. Then choose File from the toolbar and select the folder in which you want to save the messages. The whole group will be removed from the listing pane and transferred to the selected folder.

At this point, any messages you have kept have been saved to one of the five default folders mentioned above. Since these folders do not offer much flexibility, it is likely that your mail is not organized as effectively as possible. You can improve the situation by creating new folders that suit your individual needs.

Creating New Folders

To create a new folder, choose the Communicator icon on the main menu and select Message Center. From the Message Center window, click on the toolbar item New Folder. This brings up a dialog box that asks for the name of the new folder as shown in Figure 3-9. Windows users can also open the Message Center directly by clicking the Message Center icon which is located directly below the Netscape logo in the upper right of the Messenger window.

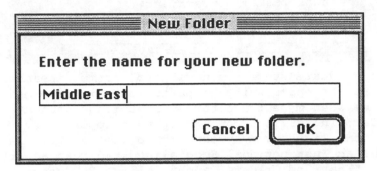

New Folder

Enter the name for your new folder.

Middle East

Cancel   OK

Figure 3-9. This is the New Folder dialog box. Type the name of your new folder and click OK.

Just type the name of your new folder and click OK. The new folder will then appear in your list of folders. As you accumulate more messages, you can create additional folders to further organize your mail.

If you have younger students, or only one computer in your classroom, student mail will probably be sent through your e-mail account. To help manage these mail messages, you may want to create folders labeled with each student's name. You can keep track of their messages and monitor their correspondence if you wish, or teach them how to save and delete messages for themselves depending on the ages of your students. In addition, you will most likely want to discuss privacy issues and remind students to use only their own folders.

Read the e-mail message on the following page to see how one pre-service teacher made use of electronic communication.

If you have younger students, or only one computer in your classroom, you may want to create folders labeled with each student's name to help manage their messages.

Using Internet Explorer for E-Mail

Microsoft's Internet Explorer 4 contains an integrated program that handles mail and news functions through its Outlook Express component. When Explorer is first opened, it gives users the opportunity to set all preferences; thus, you may already have set your e-mail preferences, or they may have been set by your technical resource person. If so, move on to the next section: Receiving and Reading Messages. If you haven't set your e-mail preferences, or aren't sure whether they are set, continue reading here.

In Macintosh systems, first access the e-mail program, Outlook Express, by clicking the Mail icon in the toolbar of the Internet Explorer window or by clicking the Outlook Express icon in the Microsoft Internet Applications folder. Then, set your

Microsoft's Internet Explorer 4 handles mail and news functions through its Outlook Express component.

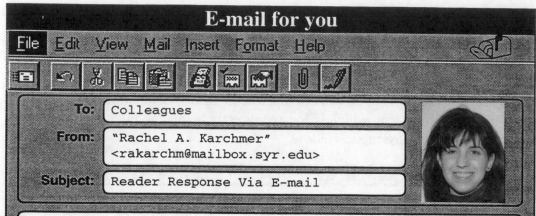

E-mail for you

File Edit View Mail Insert Format Help

To: Colleagues

From: "Rachel A. Karchmer"
<rakarchm@mailbox.syr.edu>

Subject: Reader Response Via E-mail

As a graduate student studying to become a teacher, I jumped at the opportunity to participate in an e-mail exchange between myself and three first grade students in North Carolina. I found out about this opportunity via an educational listserv my professor told me about. Linda Shearin, an Instructional Specialist, had read an article called, "What 2nd Graders Taught College Students and Vice Versa," by Curtiss and Curtiss. The article described a project which linked teacher education students with second graders via e-mail. At the time, Ms. Shearin was working with first graders who were reading at an advanced level. In order to enrich their reading program, she put a request on the RTeacher listserv looking for graduate students to correspond with her students about the books they were reading in class.

This was an enlightening experience for me. I had the chance to submerge myself in children's literature such as Ramona the Pest and Child of the Silent Night. I would send a separate letter to each of my key pals at least twice a week. In the beginning I would tell my new friends about myself and ask them general questions such as, "What is your favorite color?" Once we were familiar with each other, I concentrated more on the book by modeling open-ended questions and responses to the stories. My key pals were very excited about telling me their ideas about the books and they were very good about asking related questions. We ended the project by collaborating on a chapter book which Ms. Shearin typed up and the children illustrated. They even videotaped themselves reading the story and shared a copy with me!

Computer technology is just beginning to shape the lessons in our classrooms. This reader response project is just one way e-mail can be integrated into the school day. As a preservice teacher, it gave me a hands-on opportunity to learn how to integrate such technology into the curriculum.

Rachel Karchmer
Syracuse University

Document: Done

e-mail preferences by clicking the Preferences folder in the toolbar for Outlook Express. This opens the Preferences window showing a category frame on the left and the preferences identify box on the right. If another category is highlighted, click E-mail in the left frame to show the identity box.

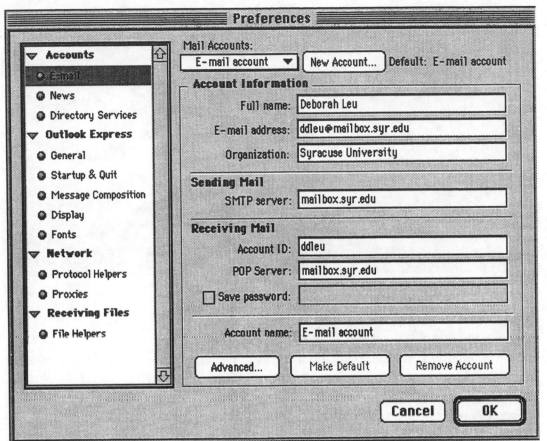

Figure 3-10. In Internet Explorer, with Mactintosh systems, you set your e-mail preferences by clicking on the Preferences folder in the toolbar for Outlook Express and then completing the information in the Preferences window.

Enter your name, e-mail address, the address of your SMTP server, your account ID and the POP server address. Then Click OK to close the Preferences window.

In Windows systems, first access Internet Explorer. Choose View and Internet Options from the Main Menu at the top of the screen. Then, select the connection tab. Select the appropriate connection method. This brings up a series of Internet Connection Wizard boxes that help you set your preferences step by step. The first box is shown in Figure 3-11.

Simply fill in the required information for each box; then click Next to go to the next screen. You will need to enter your name, your e-mail address (your UserID), your incoming and outgoing servers, and your password. (If you are the first person on your system to use Outlook Express, you may need to specify additional information. If this is the case, please check with your technical resource person.) Click Finish in the final dialog box. Your required mail preferences are now set, but you may change or further customize them by returning to the Internet Connection Wizard at another time.

Figure 3-11:
In Internet
Explorer with
Windows
systems, set
your e-mail
preferences
using Internet
Connection
Wizard boxes
such as this.

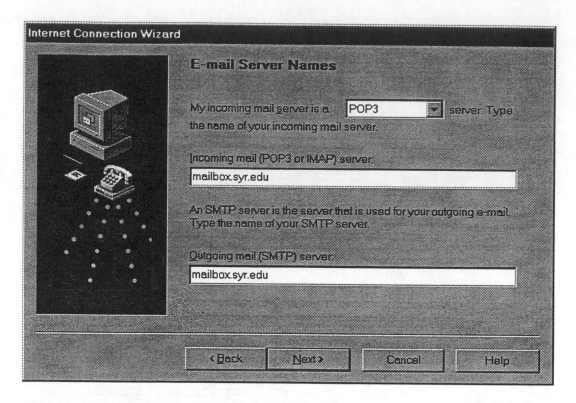

Receiving and Reading Messages

Now you are ready to communicate using your e-mail account. Remember, in order to receive new messages you must be connected to the Internet; since Internet Explorer allows you to use some features offline, make sure you are connected to the Internet. Then click the Mail icon (an image of a mailbox) in the Main Menu at the top of your screen (Macintosh systems) or the Mail icon (an image of a letter in front of an "e") in the Quick Launch toolbar at the bottom of the screen (Windows systems). This opens Outlook Express, which will look similar to Figure 3-12 if you use a Macintosh system, and similar to Figure 3-13 if you use a Windows system.

In addition, depending on your default settings, Outlook Express may attempt to check with the mail server to see if you have any new mail. It may also ask for your password by opening a dialog box. The dialog box also offers you a Remember Password option. If you want Outlook Express to enter your password automatically each time, click the Remember Password box. You should only do this, however, if you have your own computer or are not concerned about privacy, because the automatic entry of your password will cause your mail to be retrieved and displayed for anyone who clicks Send & Receive from the Outlook Express toolbar.

Notice that the Outlook Express Mail window is divided into several sections. The top section contains the Outlook Express toolbar. The left section shows a list of your Outlook Express folders. The upper right section, the listing pane, lists messages you have received; and the lower right section, the display pane, displays the text of a highlighted message.

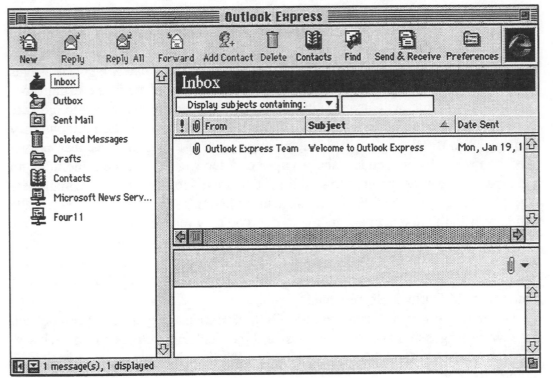

Figure 3-12.
The Outlook Express window in Internet Explorer, as it appears in a Macintosh system.

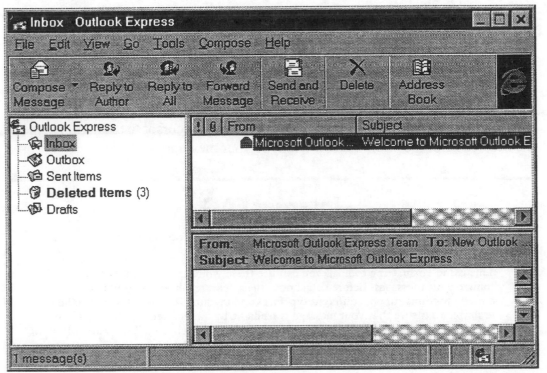

Figure 3-13.
The Outlook Express window in Internet Explorer, as it appears in a Windows system.

We will return to the folder list later. For now, look at the listing pane on the upper right. The first time Outlook Express is opened, a welcome message from Internet Explorer will be listed here. Any other retrieved messages will also appear in the listing pane with their subject headers, senders, and dates. New messages always appear in bold type, while previously read messages are in the usual typeface. Windows users will also see either an open or closed envelope icon to indicate the read/unread status of a message. In both platforms, two additional icons may also appear in the listing pane: an exclamation point if a message has been prioritized as urgent by its sender, and a paper clip icon if the message includes an attachment. [An attachment is an additional document included with an e-mail message.] If you click on the title of a message in the listing pane, the text of the message will appear in the display pane below so that you may read it.

If you have more than one message, double click on a succeeding or preceding message in order to display and read it in the bottom pane. In Macintosh systems, you may also read messages by choosing View and then selecting Next or Previous from the main Outlook Express menu.

Depending on your default settings, Outlook Express may automatically check for new messages and ask for your password the first time you open it in each session. Remember, you may also get your mail at any time during a session by clicking Send & Receive.

Replying to a Message

After reading a message, you may wish to reply. First, make sure the message you want to reply to appears in the message display pane. Then, click the Reply button in the Outlook Express toolbar (Macintosh systems) or the Reply to Author button (in Windows) if the message you want to reply to was sent by one person and has only one address. If the message contains multiple addresses, and you want to reply to all of the addressees, click the Reply to All button. Clicking either button opens the Message Composition window as shown in Figure 3-14.

Notice that the subject and address(es) are already entered. However, you may edit any entry by moving the cursor to the appropriate box and deleting or adding information. To reply to any message, simply move the cursor to the bottom pane of the Message Composition window and type your message.

Internet FAQ

What are the boxes and icons in the toolbar directly below the subject line of the Message Composition window?

This is the Formatting toolbar. You can use these word-processing features to customize your messages. Before you choose these features, keep in mind that not all e-mail programs support different typefaces and layouts. It's probably best to keep it simple to insure that your message is readable by all recipients unless you know that someone can take advantage of these features in their e-mail software; otherwise, your message may be unreadable.

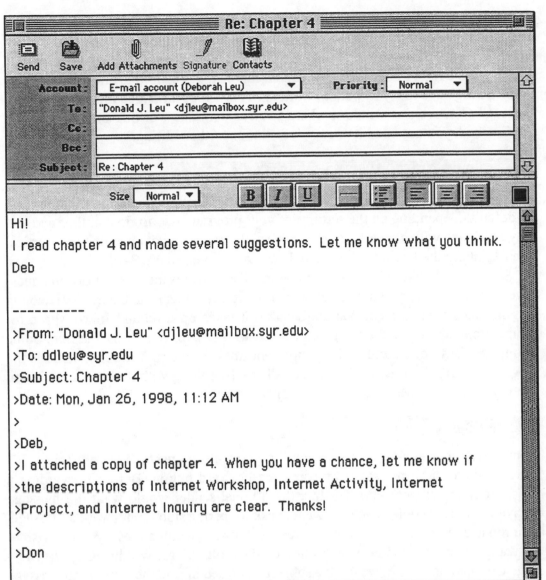

Figure 3-14.
The Message
Composition
Window in
Internet
Explorer's
Outlook Ex-
press showing
a reply to a
message,
ready to be
sent.

After typing your message, it is a good idea to read it over, confirming both the contents and the recipient(s). When you are sure your message is the way you want it, click the Send and Receive button (Macintosh) or Send (Windows). This immediately sends your message to the server if you are working online. If you are working offline, your message will be temporarily sent to the Outbox for later delivery. The next time you are online and click the Send and Receive button (in both Macintosh and Windows platforms), your Outbox messages will be sent out immediately without any additional action by you. This is because the sending and receiving functions share one icon; you may click the icon to retrieve messages for reading, but remember that this also immediately sends Outbox messages. Therefore, it's a good idea to be very sure that any messages left in the Outbox at the end of a session are ready to be sent.

It's a good idea to be sure that any messages left in the Outbox at the end of a session are ready to be sent.

If you aren't ready to send a message at the end of a session, you can save it by clicking the Save button, which holds it in your Drafts folder until you are ready to finish it. When you want to work on your message again, you can retrieve it by clicking the Drafts folder in the left pane folder list. Then, double click the message in the listing pane that you want to work on. This brings the saved message up in the Message Composition window, where you can continue working on it. When you are finished, you can send it or save it again for further editing.

Including Original Messages with Your Reply

In Outlook Express, original messages are automatically included with your reply by default. Depending on the settings of your program, the original author and text may be shown with a greater-than sign (>) at the beginning of each line or a vertical line (|) along the left side. An example can be seen in Figure 3-14.

Some people like this automatic feature. They always include the original message in their reply to provide context for the recipient. Other e-mail users feel quoting original messages is inconsiderate because it takes up time and Inbox space for recipients, and adds extra charges for those who pay for e-mail by the line. Some people prefer to quote only a few important lines. If you prefer not to include the original message, you can delete part or all of it by editing with the cursor while you are working in the Message Composition window.

Forwarding Mail

Sometimes you receive messages you know would be useful for colleagues. It's easy to share these messages by using the Forward button. Before forwarding a message, however, consider whether the original sender would want the message relayed to other people. You may want to ask for permission. To forward a message, you must first be in the Outlook Express window. Select the message you wish to forward. Then click the Forward button on the toolbar. This will bring up the Message Composition window with the subject box filled in, and the forwarded message in the lower pane of the window shown as a quote. All you need to do is enter the recipient's e-mail address on the To: line. If you wish, you may also type a message of your own above or below the quoted message. Then click Send and Receive (Macintosh) or Send (Windows).

Composing and Sending a New Message

Composing and sending a new message is basically the same as replying. To begin, you must first be in the Outlook Express window. Go to the toolbar and click the New button (in Macintosh systems) or the Compose Message button (in Windows). This will open the Message Composition window, but unlike a reply message, the subject and address boxes will be empty. You must enter the name and e-mail address of the person to whom you are sending the message. You may send your message to more than one person by typing additional names and addresses on the same line, separating each person's e-mail address with a comma. You may also enter the addresses for others to receive a Cc (carbon copy) or Bcc (blind carbon copy). You may see these options in the message composition window in Figure 3-14.

It's also a good idea to type in a subject [unless you are subscribing or unsubscribing to a listserv.] A subject isn't required, but it's helpful for recipients who want to skim their messages by subject or know a bit about the contents of each message in order to prioritize their reading. After entering the name(es), address(es), and subject, proceed in the same way as for a reply message.

Printing

Printing a message is very easy. Make sure the message you want to print is displayed in the bottom pane of the Outlook Express window. Then choose File from the main menu and select Print. Although it isn't really necessary to have paper copies of all your messages, you may want to use this feature to print out e-mail messages for posting on a bulletin board for the whole class to read. It's also nice to print out some of a student's messages to share with parents at home or at an open house.

Managing Your Mail and Working with Folders

Now that you understand the basic e-mail functions of receiving and sending, and are familiar with most of the buttons in the toolbars, let's look at using folders to manage your e-mail. Outlook Express includes five default folders: Inbox, Outbox, Sent Mail (Macintosh)/Sent Items (Windows), Deleted Messages/Deleted Items, and Drafts. These may be seen in Figure 3-11 (Macintosh) and 3-12 (Windows).

- The *Inbox folder* stores new, incoming messages as well as any old messages that you have not deleted or filed elsewhere.
- The *Outbox folder* holds finished messages for sending at a later time.
- The *Sent Mail/Sent Items* folder holds copies of messages that you have sent or forwarded.
- The *Deleted Messages/Deleted Items* folder temporarily holds deleted items until you are ready to remove them permanently.
- The *Drafts folder* saves unfinished messages that you intend to work on later.

After you read a message, it remains in your Inbox folder unless you remove it. As a result, the Inbox becomes crowded and disorganized, and if it gets too full, you can't receive any new messages. Therefore, it is a good idea to get in the habit of moving messages out of your Inbox as you read them. One way to do this is by deletion.

Deleting Messages

Deleting messages is very easy. If you don't need to keep a message after reading it, simply click the Delete button in the toolbar. This deletes the message appearing in the display pane and transfers it to the Deleted Messages/Items folder. If you want to delete any other message, highlight it by clicking its subject header in the listing pane; then click the Delete button.

The Deleted Messages/Items Folder

At this point, although you have deleted your messages, they are not really gone from your mail service. They are in the Deleted Messages/Items folder. This can be a convenient feature if you have accidentally deleted a message that you need. To retrieve a message, click the Deleted Messages/Items Folder, then highlight the message you want to retrieve in the right listing pane, and drag it to the folder in which you want to save it. It's a good idea to open the new folder and make sure that your message does actually appear there.

In order to actually get rid of your deletions, you must empty the Deleted Messages/Items folder. Do this by clicking once on the Deleted Messages/Items folder, choosing Edit from the main menu, and selecting Empty Deleted Messages/Items. Be careful; once you do this, all messages and folders in the Deleted Messages/Items folder are permanently removed.

Saving Sent Messages

Outlook Express automatically saves copies of messages that you send, including forwarded messages, to the Sent Messages folder. This provides a convenient record of your messages and allows you to easily re-send a message to others if necessary. However, this folder can become very large if you are an active e-mailer. Therefore, you may wish to create additional folders (by month, for example) and then transfer your sent messages accordingly. Or if you do not want to save them, simply delete as explained above.

Saving Received Messages

The easiest way to save a message after you have read it is to drag its subject header from the right listing pane to the folder in which you want to save it. You can "block save" messages just as you block delete them by clicking each message while holding down the keyboard shift key. Then drag this group of messages to the folder where you want to save them. The whole group will be removed from the listing pane and transferred to the selected folder. In Windows you can also save messages by choosing File from the main menu and selecting Save As. Then work your way through the lists of folders and files and save the message in the desired location.

Up to this point, any messages you have saved have been kept in one of the five default folders mentioned above. Since these folders do not offer much flexibility, it is likely that your mail is not organized as effectively as possible. You can improve the situation by creating new folders that suit your individual needs.

Creating New Folders

The procedure for creating new folders is somewhat different, depending upon the type of system you use: Macintosh or Windows. For Macintosh users, choose File from the Main Menu, select New, and release on Folder. This creates a new folder in the left pane folder list. Type the new folder's name in the highlighted box next to the folder.

For Windows users, right click any folder in the folder list and then click New Folder. This displays the New Folder box. Type the name of the new folder in the name box and then click the Outlook Express icon to add the new folder to the Outlook Express folder list in the left pane.

If you have younger students, or only one computer in your classroom, student mail will probably be sent through your e-mail account. To help manage mail messages, create a folder labeled for each student. You can keep track of their messages and monitor their correspondence if you wish, or teach them how to save and delete messages for themselves. You may also want to discuss privacy issues and remind students to use only their own folders.

Moving On

Reading about e-mail can get tedious, and like swimming, you don't really know how to do it until you try it. So take some time for hands-on practice. Try one or two things at first and work at your own pace. You may wish to work with a partner. If your school doesn't have a media specialist or technology coordinator, try to find someone a bit more experienced who can help out. Remember, everyone was a beginner once and no one knows it all, not even the experts.

As you become more familiar and confident with the basic features of e-mail, you can customize your mail service further. Explore other toolbar selections. Go back to Preferences or the Internet Connection Wizard and set additional options. Create an automatic signature or a personal address book. Learn how to send attachments or reconfigure windows. Get really organized by using the Thread Messages feature in Netscape. If you are a Windows user, find out about short-cuts using the right-side mouse button.

Reading about e-mail can get tedious, and like swimming, you don't really know how to do it until you try it. So take some time for hands-on practice.

Using E-mail in the Classroom

Learning how to use e-mail does take some time, but it is well worth the effort when you consider the many ways e-mail can help you in the classroom. Perhaps the most common way is to communicate with people you already know—just like a letter. However, communicating electronically adds special excitement as it brings the world into your classroom and lets you and your students interact with new people and new cultures.

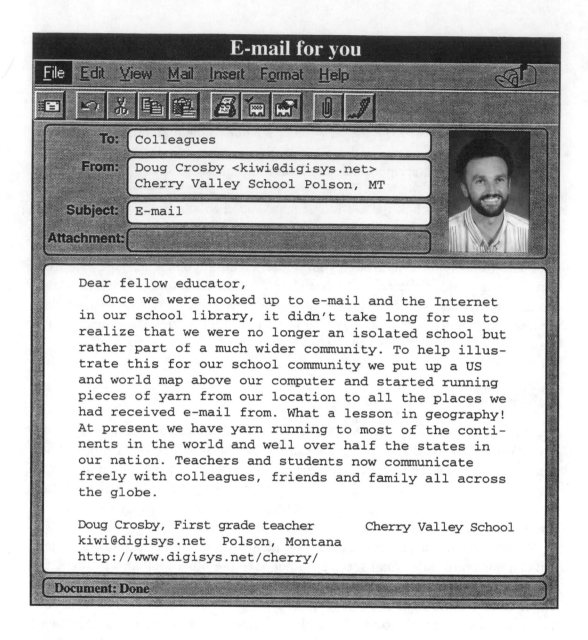

One of the most common ways for students to interact with new people has been to write to penpals. The Internet equivalent, e-mailing keypals, is equally exciting and beneficial: it can provide motivation, improve writing skills, increase knowledge, and broaden perspectives. E-mail's greatest feature, however, is that it reduces the time between messages to just a few seconds or minutes. Because of this speed, students can do much more than simply correspond once or twice a month. Very quickly, they can get almost any kind of information by asking questions and conducting interviews with other students in their own country or abroad; they can practice a second language; they can share cool web sites; they can work on joint projects; they can even help each other with homework.

Keypals

Central Sites for Keypals

There are numerous sites for locating keypals and partner classes. Some of them are commercial sites that charge fees, but many of the best sites are free. The sites included below are ones that we have found to be especially useful; nevertheless, it is best to think of them, and of all our recommendations, as starting points for your own exploration. The Internet changes quickly and often; some of these sites may disappear; certainly new ones will come online. Most important, you will know best which sites meet your needs. Therefore, we encourage you to move on from our sites and make your own list of favorites.

- **Intercultural E-Mail Classroom Connections**
  (http://www.stolaf.edu/network/iecc/index.html)
  This site, located at St. Olaf's College, is one of the best sources especially for linking with keypals and partners from different countries. IECC is their mailing list for K-12 teachers who are looking for partner classrooms. They also have a mailing list for discussing the applications of intercultural e-mail communications, IECC-DISCUSSION. You can subscribe directly from their web page.

- **Pitsco's Launch to Keypals**
  (http://www.pitsco.com/keypals).
  Another excellent keypal site, containing a master list of mailing lists from different organizations. There are lists that link teacher to teachers, students to students, and classes to classes. On most lists you can post your own as well as read others' requests. You can subscribe directly from their web locations.

- **Rigby/Heinemann Global Keypals**
  (http://www.reedbooks.com.au/heinemann/global/global1.html)
  This site is located in Australia and updates its offerings every week. Both teachers and students can make contacts and enter their own messages for students in the following age groups: 5–10, 11–13, and 14–18. This site also includes its own Netiquette Guide for Keypals.

- **eMail Classroom Exchange**
  (http://www.epals.com/)
  This is a site for partner classes where you can search by category: school name, location, language, or grade level.

Keypals are only one of the ways you can use e-mail. We hope you are getting excited about its potential for your classroom. You may be wondering, though, how to get started, especially if you and your students have never used electronic communication before. Perhaps the e-mail message from Jeanette Kenyon will help.

Very quickly, students can get almost any kind of information; they can practice a second language; they can share cool web sites; they can work on joint projects; they can even help each other with homework.

There are numerous sites for locating keypals and partner classes.

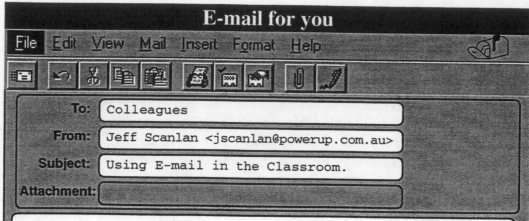

E-mail for you

File Edit View Mail Insert Format Help

To: Colleagues

From: Jeff Scanlan <jscanlan@powerup.com.au>

Subject: Using E-mail in the Classroom.

Attachment:

Hi!

This year our school in Australia is being connected to the Internet. It is good to see all the discussions and talk that I have been involved with in our school are bearing fruit. Furthermore I expect, going by past experiences, that I will then be the resource person for all who will want to use it, to which requests I will happily accede!

My experience with the Internet is limited mainly to e-mailing other schools around the world. Here are several ideas I would like to share with you. First, if you want to correspond with a school in another country, make contact with several schools. Teachers everywhere are busy people with lots of responsibilities and although they might not intend it, they may not get the time to organize the replies. (It can be quite a task in making sure that all kids get their replies away and you really don't want to disappoint anyone at the other end).

Also, think about how to integrate your total English program into an e-mail project before you begin to e-mail other schools. I am a great believer in getting children to write reflectively and express feelings. It is important that children in writing to other children know to write more than just basic information about their life circumstances. You really need to explain and show children how this can be done.

Finally, when you are corresponding with another classroom, don't be afraid to share snail mail addresses and telephone numbers. Kids get quite a buzz from an intercontinental phone call! A lesson or two on time zones and time differences does not go astray here! In any case it is something of which in future we will all need to be more aware. Best wishes with all your e-mail projects!

Yours sincerely,
Jeff Scanlan
Year 3 teacher (7-8 year olds),
Alexandra Hills State School   Queensland Australia

Document: Done

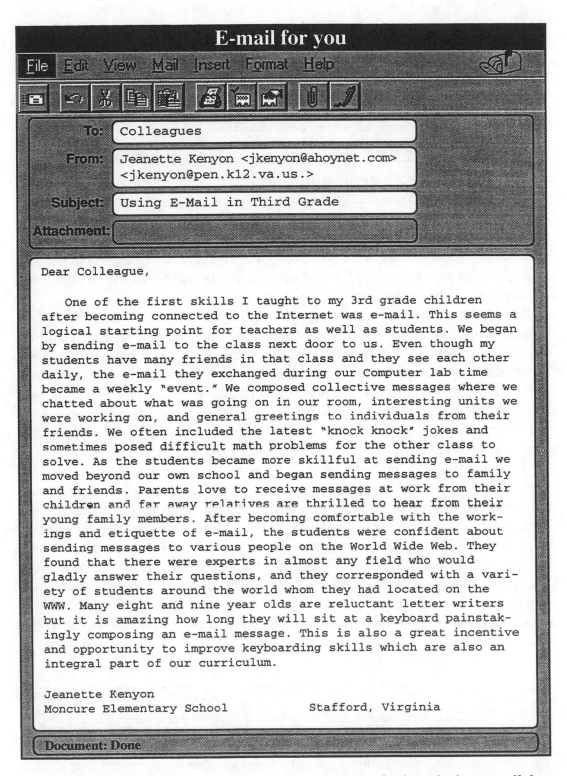

E-mail for you

File Edit View Mail Insert Format Help

To: Colleagues

From: Jeanette Kenyon <jkenyon@ahoynet.com>
<jkenyon@pen.k12.va.us.>

Subject: Using E-Mail in Third Grade

Attachment:

Dear Colleague,

One of the first skills I taught to my 3rd grade children
after becoming connected to the Internet was e-mail. This seems a
logical starting point for teachers as well as students. We began
by sending e-mail to the class next door to us. Even though my
students have many friends in that class and they see each other
daily, the e-mail they exchanged during our Computer lab time
became a weekly "event." We composed collective messages where we
chatted about what was going on in our room, interesting units we
were working on, and general greetings to individuals from their
friends. We often included the latest "knock knock" jokes and
sometimes posed difficult math problems for the other class to
solve. As the students became more skillful at sending e-mail we
moved beyond our own school and began sending messages to family
and friends. Parents love to receive messages at work from their
children and far away relatives are thrilled to hear from their
young family members. After becoming comfortable with the workings and etiquette of e-mail, the students were confident about
sending messages to various people on the World Wide Web. They
found that there were experts in almost any field who would
gladly answer their questions, and they corresponded with a variety of students around the world whom they had located on the
WWW. Many eight and nine year olds are reluctant letter writers
but it is amazing how long they will sit at a keyboard painstak-
ingly composing an e-mail message. This is also a great incentive
and opportunity to improve keyboarding skills which are also an
integral part of our curriculum.

Jeanette Kenyon
Moncure Elementary School   Stafford, Virginia

Document: Done

Jeanette Kenyon's message might serve as a primer for introducing e-mail, beginning simply within the classroom and gradually expanding its scope to include
the world. Depending on the age and experience of your students, you might want to
start out with a message composed jointly by the students, but entered by you. The
message and any responses could be printed out and kept in a binder or put up on a

Depending on the age and experience of your students, you might want to start out with a message composed jointly by the students, but entered by you.

bulletin board near the computer. Later, students could work in pairs or small groups to send their own messages to other students in their school. Then they could move into their community by e-mailing questions to local businesses and organizations. Finally, they might each have their own international keypal.

Netiquette

Jeanette's message also brings up an issue that becomes important as students begin to use e-mail more independently and extensively: Internet etiquette, or "netiquette" as it is called. With e-mail communication, we are unable to share facial expressions, voice tone, and body language as we can with face-to-face oral communication. As a result, e-mail messages are prone to miscommunication. Thus, it is important to help students develop good Internet manners and become sensitive to how their messages might be misinterpreted.

We are not talking here about actions that are dangerous or illegal but about politeness and courtesy. Because the Internet is not run by any single group or government, there are no official rules to teach, nor is there a single source of information about what constitutes acceptable behavior. Nevertheless, we need to help our students realize that the Internet, as a place of social interaction, has its own traditions and customs. We can discuss Internet use as a privilege not a right, and together with our students develop guidelines that encourage tolerance and acceptance of the diversity of people, languages, and viewpoints that exists on the net.

People often talk about netiquette in terms of "common sense," but common sense varies depending on factors such as age, culture, and experience. Therefore, before you discuss this issue with your students, you may want get some background information from this excellent location: **Netiquette Homepage** by Arlene H. Rinaldi (http://www.fau.edu/rinaldi/netiquette.html). This is the most comprehensive site we've found on Netiquette. It's fairly detailed, giving netiquette advice on e-mail, lists, newsgroups and other areas of the net. It includes a question and answer section as well as a bibliography. Depending on the level of your students, you might choose appropriate sections for them to read and discuss. For example, "The Ten Commandments for Computer Ethics" is a straightforward list of "thou-shalt-nots" which would probably be effective with all but the youngest students.

We need to help our students realize that the Internet, as a place of social interaction, has its own traditions and customs.

Mailing Lists

In addition to using e-mail for one-to-one style communication between individuals, an e-mail address also allows you to participate in one-to-many communication by joining mailing lists. You can think of mailing lists, also called listservs, as group e-mail, where a message sent to one address is automatically forwarded to a whole group of individuals without the need to make older style carbon copies or photocopies. This is accomplished by a special computer program that maintains a list of people, the subscribers, who have joined a particular list in order to discuss a specific interest area. Subscribers participate by sending and receiving e-mail messages that come directly to their electronic mailboxes. Some lists are moderated by the owner or another person who screens and selects the messages that are sent out.

There are several thousand mailing lists covering almost every interest area. Most are intended for a specific audience, but are open for anyone to subscribe. There are some closed lists, however. List activity varies; some lists have thousands of members and are very active. Others are quite small and generate only a few messages a month. Many mailing lists are useful in education. As was the case for Lily Chang, mailing lists are great places to ask questions, get information, locate resources, and share information.

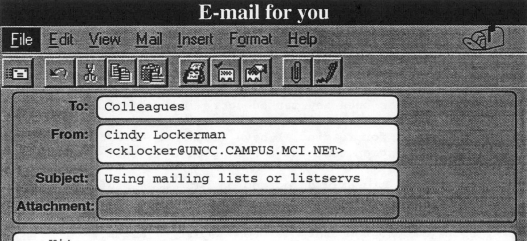

There are several thousand mailing lists covering almost every interest area.

Mailing lists are great places to ask questions, get information, locate resources, and share information.

E-mail for you

File Edit View Mail Insert Format Help

To: Colleagues

From: Cindy Lockerman
<cklocker@UNCC.CAMPUS.MCI.NET>

Subject: Using mailing lists or listservs

Attachment:

```
Hi!
    I want to share with everyone my recent experi-
ences with using e mail on the RTEACHER listserv that
illustrate an important point: The opportunity to
make important connections is useful, informative,
and tremendously satisfying as I see concerns and
opinions that I hold echoed by voices worldwide. It
truly affirms the concept of a shrinking planet! I
will try to relate concisely a couple of electronic
experiences.
    First, I needed some help with a biography on
Marie Clay, the New Zealand educator. Clay's work is
a mainstay at the school where I teach and so I am
quite familiar with her work, but I needed some bio-
graphical information for a course I was taking. I
posted my needs on the RTEACHER listserv and another
member quickly sent me the e-mail address of Profes-
sor Yetta Goodman (another prominent literacy educa-
tor), suggesting that I ask her for the information.
I sent a query and within an hour, she wrote back
with biographical information from her personal expe-
rience with Dr. Clay. Not only was I able to get
information "that inquiring minds want to know," but
```

Document: Continued

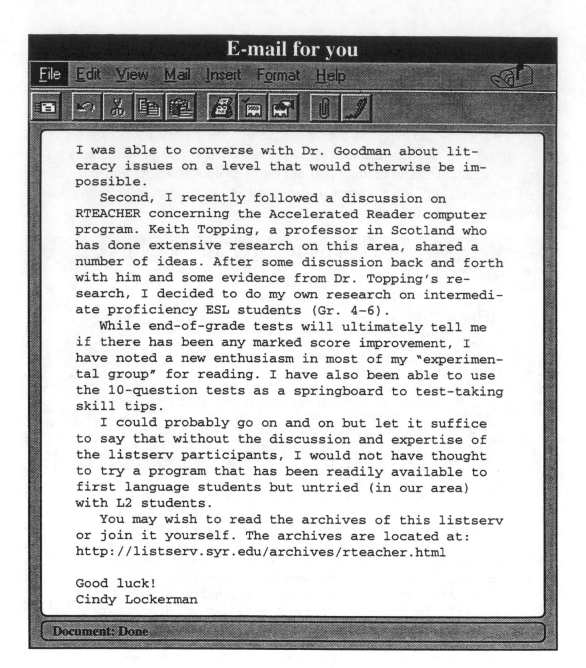

Although mailing lists can be useful for students as well as teachers, some care should be taken when deciding how to use lists in the classroom because there is no way to know in advance what will appear in individual messages. If a list is moderated, obvious problems such as bad language will probably be avoided, but there may still be topics or viewpoints which not everyone feels comfortable with. There are lists especially for kids and other education-oriented lists where kids can participate with interested adults. Still, almost anyone can subscribe to an unmoderated list, and even moderated lists may not be able to screen with 100 percent effectiveness. Thus, it is possible that even an appropriate list might occasionally have postings containing inappropriate material for some students. There is also the chance of encountering unsuitable topics as well. Nevertheless, lists are great resources and many teachers do use them effectively with their students. As always, it is best for you to check out the situation for yourself. Subscribe to a mailing list for awhile before deciding how it might be used in your situation with your students.

Here is a message from a teacher who has used several different mailing lists.

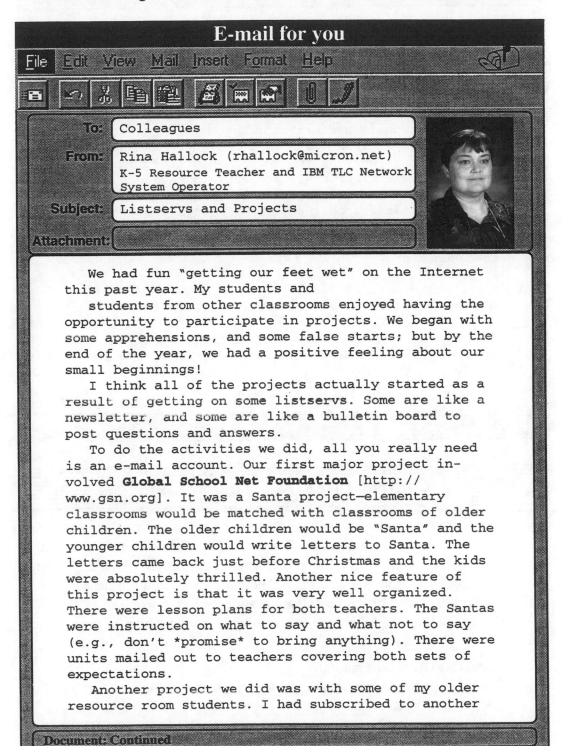

E-mail for you

File Edit View Mail Insert Format Help

To: Colleagues

From: Rina Hallock (rhallock@micron.net)
K-5 Resource Teacher and IBM TLC Network
System Operator

Subject: Listservs and Projects

Attachment:

> We had fun "getting our feet wet" on the Internet
> this past year. My students and
>
> students from other classrooms enjoyed having the
> opportunity to participate in projects. We began with
> some apprehensions, and some false starts; but by the
> end of the year, we had a positive feeling about our
> small beginnings!
>
> I think all of the projects actually started as a
> result of getting on some listservs. Some are like a
> newsletter, and some are like a bulletin board to
> post questions and answers.
>
> To do the activities we did, all you really need
> is an e-mail account. Our first major project in-
> volved **Global School Net Foundation** [http://
> www.gsn.org]. It was a Santa project—elementary
> classrooms would be matched with classrooms of older
> children. The older children would be "Santa" and the
> younger children would write letters to Santa. The
> letters came back just before Christmas and the kids
> were absolutely thrilled. Another nice feature of
> this project is that it was very well organized.
> There were lesson plans for both teachers. The Santas
> were instructed on what to say and what not to say
> (e.g., don't *promise* to bring anything). There were
> units mailed out to teachers covering both sets of
> expectations.
>
> Another project we did was with some of my older
> resource room students. I had subscribed to another

Document: Continued

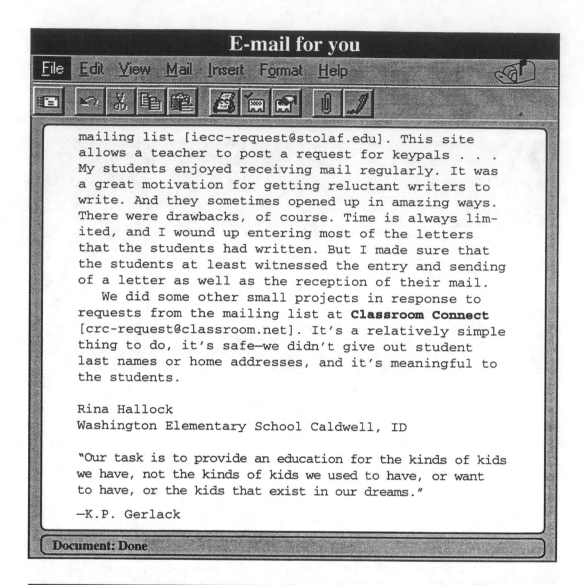

E-mail for you

File Edit View Mail Insert Format Help

mailing list [iecc-request@stolaf.edu]. This site
allows a teacher to post a request for keypals . . .
My students enjoyed receiving mail regularly. It was
a great motivation for getting reluctant writers to
write. And they sometimes opened up in amazing ways.
There were drawbacks, of course. Time is always limited, and I wound up entering most of the letters
that the students had written. But I made sure that
the students at least witnessed the entry and sending
of a letter as well as the reception of their mail.

   We did some other small projects in response to
requests from the mailing list at **Classroom Connect**
[crc-request@classroom.net]. It's a relatively simple
thing to do, it's safe—we didn't give out student
last names or home addresses, and it's meaningful to
the students.

Rina Hallock
Washington Elementary School Caldwell, ID

"Our task is to provide an education for the kinds of kids
we have, not the kinds of kids we used to have, or want
to have, or the kids that exist in our dreams."

—K.P. Gerlack

Document: Done

Central Sites for Mailing Lists

If you wish to try out the use of mailing lists, the first step is to find the name and e-mail address of a list you want to join. There are thousands of lists, so you might begin by checking with colleagues and professional organizations or looking through journals. Thankfully, there are also many Internet sites containing master lists of mailing lists. Go to one of the central sites below, select a list, and follow their directions, or read on and follow the general steps for subscribing in the next section.

- **Liszt** (http://www.liszt.com/)
  This is the most comprehensive site we've found. It contains over 50,000 lists, including some managed by listserv, listproc, and majordomo, as well as almost 2,000 independently managed lists (other master lists usually contain only listserv-managed lists). You can either do a search for

lists in your interest area, or click the Liszt select box, for a much smaller, annotated list of sites picked by Liszt.

- **TileNet** (http://tile.net/lists/)
  This is another comprehensive list, but it contains only listserv lists. You can search for lists alphabetically by name, host country, sponsoring organization, most popular, or subject categories.

- **Publicly Accessible Mailing Lists**
  (http://www.neosoft.com/internet/paml/)
  This site organizes lists by subject or name.

- **Reference.com** (http://www.reference.com/)
  A very detailed site.

- **Pitsco's Launch to Lists** (http://www.pitsco.com/p/listinfo.html)
  This site doesn't have search capabilities, but it is focused on education.

- **L-Soft International** (http://www.lsoft.com/lists/listref.html)
  This site contains only listserv lists. You can search by host site, country, or list size as well as alphabetically.

- **EdWeb** (http://sunsite.unc.edu/edweb/lists.html)
  This is a somewhat smaller but useful list that focuses on K-12 issues, educational technology, and education reform. It also has a little background on mailing lists and an example for subscribing.

Subscribing to a Mailing List

In order to subscribe to a mailing list, you need to send an e-mail message to the server that manages the list. It's very important to send your request to the correct address. Mailing lists have two addresses, one for administration, which begins with the name of the server that manages the list; and another for "posting" (sending contributions to the list members), which usually begins with the name of the list. Make sure you subscribe to the administration address. Most of these begin with "listserv@ . . .", the most common server. However, some addresses being with "listproc@ . . ." or "majordomo@ . . .", or less frequently with some other server.

Send an e-mail message to the administrative server of the list. Type the administrative address in the address box of the message composition window. Leave the subject line blank. Then type a subscribe message in the first line of the message pane. Usually upper and lower case is not significant, but people often type the name of the list in capitals. Your message should look like this, but with your name, and without the brackets:

```
subscribe [list name] [your first name] [your last name]
```

For example, if I wanted to subscribe to the SCHOOL-L list, it would look like this:

```
subscribe SCHOOL-L Deborah Leu
```

Mailing lists have two addresses, one for administration, which begins with the name of the server that manages the list; and another for "posting," which usually begins with the name of the list.

Don't put any other information, such as an automatic signature for example, in the message pane. Any extra information is rejected by the server and usually invalidates the request. Rarely a list has a different procedure, but this is usually indicated on the master list or on the list's web page.

The Welcome Message

Shortly you should receive a return message that welcomes you to the group and details its procedures. Save this message! It contains important information about expectations for members, how to get help and, most important, how to get off the list.

Usually you can leave a list by sending a message similar to your subscription request. Some lists do have special procedures, though. To leave a list, type "unsubscribe" or "signoff" instead of "subscribe." For example:

```
unsubscribe SCHOOL-L
```

Remember to send this message to the administrative address, not the posting address.

Internet FAQ

I have tried to unsubscribe from a list several times, but I keep getting mail. I am using the administrative address. What's going on?

First, if you have more than one e-mail account, be sure to unsubscribe using the same account that you used to subscribe. The server is a computer, not a person, and it won't recognize you if you try to unsubscribe from a different address, use a nickname, or spell your name differently. Occasionally, there may be a problem even if you have only one account. If you access your account from different computers, at home and at work for example, it sometimes prevents successful unsubscription. Somehow, the server seems to differentiate messages from the two computers, even if the address is the same. Therefore, it's probably safest to try to always subscribe and unsubscribe from the same account and the same machine.

Mailing List Netiquette

Netiquette is especially important for mailing list subscribers because their messages may be read by hundreds or thousands of people from all over the world. In addition, a list is a bit like a club where you may run into other members at any time—you don't want to offend someone that you know you will be "meeting" (electronically) several times a week.

In order to get a feel for the culture and "personality" of the list, it is strongly recommended that you "lurk" for a week or two, that is, just read the list for awhile before posting any messages. This will give you a chance to see how the group operates and find out answers to some of your initial questions. Most group members are tolerant and helpful to beginners. However, the introduction of an inappropriate topic or the tenth repetition of a basic question sometimes receives a nasty response, called "flaming."

Posting a Message

When you feel ready to make a contribution to the discussion, you should send your message to the posting address, which usually (but not always) begins with the name of the mailing list—for example, rteacher@listserv.syr.edu. The address for posting a message to a list is usually included in the welcome message—another reason to save it. If your message is a response to an individual's question, it is often better to send your reply directly to him/her rather than to the whole list. However, there are some lists that request that you always respond to the whole list in order to improve the discussion. Again, check your welcome message for information on what is expected.

It is easy to reply to either an individual or the group because most e-mail programs give you the option of addressing your reply to either an individual or to the group. (Netscape offers the options of "To Sender Only" to reply to an individual, and "To Sender and All Recipients" to reply to the group. Internet Explorer has "Reply to Author" and "Reply to All" options.)

In order to get a feel for the culture and "personality" of the list, it is strongly recommended that you "lurk" for a week or two, that is, just read the list for awhile before posting any messages.

TEACHING TIP

Double Check The "Reply-To" Address

It's a good idea to double-check the "reply-to" address of any reply message before you actually send it. Make sure the address box contains the address you want, either an individual's name and address or the listserv name and address. We have run across a few mailing lists that are configured so that a reply message is sent to the whole list when the individual reply button is clicked.

Privacy

The issue of privacy is often overlooked by newcomers to the Internet. Perhaps because we often use e-mail in private, we believe it is private. Actually it may be even less private than regular mail. Just as in the regular mail system, electronic communications occasionally get missent or lost. In addition, virtually all e-mail is archived somewhere, "indefinitely" as we have been told. It is most likely kept in an out-of-the-way file, known only to a system administrator, so it is unlikely that anyone would search through thousands of messages to see what you have written, but it is possible.

Postings from mailing lists are more accessible and thus even less private. Many lists are archived in easily accessed places. Some lists keep their own archives, which are available only to members, but that could be a number in the thousands. Some education lists are archived at ERIC and easily accessible through a net search. Other lists are posted to Usenet newsgroups, which may be read by thousands of people around the world. Finally, there are search engines that can bring up an individual's postings when that individual's name is entered for a search.

This information is not meant to alarm you, but only to caution you to think about what you write. Think of an e-mail message as a postcard, not a sealed letter. We have heard that you should never write anything that would embarrass you if it happened to be announced at your next town meeting. We think this is sound advice.

Internet FAQ

What about viruses? I've heard that I can get them through e-mail.

Computer viruses are programs that can infect your computer with small annoying problems, destroy files, or even cause a major crash. You can "catch" them by transferring files from one infected computer to another. For example, using a program at school, saving files to a disk, and then using that disk at home can let a virus into your system. In most situations, it is not possible to transmit a virus by e-mail. However, if an e-mail message has an attached document which includes an infected file you can release it, but only if you if you download the document to your hard drive. You could avoid the problem by never reading attachments or by investing in one of several anti-virus software programs. As this book goes to press, a second problem has appeared with e-mail attachments. It is called the Long Filename vulnerability. This security lapse exists on the e-mail programs used within Netscape 4.0 and Internet Explorer 4.0 (Outlook Express). It is important to recognize and fix. This security problem permits the transfer of a virus in a lengthy filename of an attachment. It is especially important to fix if you use a Windows machine or Internet Explorer. You may download patches for this problem at the following sites: Internet Explorer (http://www.microsoft.com/ie/security/oelong.htm) or Netscape (http://www.netscape.com/products/security/resources/bugs/longfile.html?hom07prt1). These locations will also tell you when later versions of these programs have been updated with the remedy. In addition to true viruses, there are also many virus hoaxes which appear on the Internet regularly. You can find out more about viruses at CIAC, the U.S. Department of Energy's Computer Incident Advisory Capability (http://ciac.llnl.gov/ciac/CIACHome.html). We will also update information about this problem in less technical language at the web site for this book: Teaching with the Internet (http://web.syr.edu/~djleu/teaching.html).

Useful Mailing Lists

It's difficult to recommend mailing lists because everyone's needs and expectations are different, but we have found the following general lists to be especially useful while writing this book. In addition, there are mailing lists at the end of each of the chapters that follow this one.

- **KIDSPHERE**—(listserv@vms.cis.pitt.edu).
  This active list provides an opportunity for kids, parents, teachers, and administrators and other interested people to discuss anything related to education. People post news items, share good books, ask for help and give suggestions, and discuss the advantages and disadvantages of various educational practices.

- **SCHOOL-L**—(listserv@listserv.hea.ie)
  Another active site that is really useful for primary and secondary school discussion. Most subscribers seem to be teachers and technology coordinators. Teachers request and share all kinds of information. There are often postings about other good sites and useful resources.

- **MIDDLE-L**—(listserv@postoffice.cso.uiuc.edu)
  Sponsored by ERIC, this list is for classroom teachers, administrators, parents, and anyone else interested in middle schools and middle school students. People share ideas, resources, advice, and problems.

- **WWWEDU**—(listproc@ready.cpb.org)
  This is a moderated list whose stated purpose is ". . . to offer educators, webmasters and policy makers a continuous discussion on the potential of World-Wide Web use in education. WWWEDU is targeted for use by educators, as well as webmasters and web providers, but anyone with a keen interest in the use of Web methodology in education is welcome to join." This list seems a bit more focused and has fewer postings of individual requests for resources than the ones above.

- **EDTECH**—(listserv@h-net.msu.edu)
  This is a very active list about the use of technology in education. It's not for everyone as it is quite technical, but there seemed to be quick and friendly responses for set-up and equipment problems.

Usenet Newsgroups

Another popular use of e-mail is reading the postings in Usenet newsgroups. Usenet is a world-wide network of distributed discussions. It consists of thousands of newsgroups that are organized hierarchically by category and topic. Like mailing lists, newsgroups are a one-to-many type of e-mail-based communication. However, they differ from mailing lists in several important ways.

First, access is different. While mailing lists are limited to individual subscribers, newsgroups are available to almost everyone. Earlier we compared mailing lists to group e-mail, saying it was like copies of a letter being sent to each person on a list. Usenet is more similar to a bulletin board where anyone who is in the vicinity can read whatever is posted over a period of days or weeks. The length of posting time varies by newsgroup, and many groups also archive their messages. This allows you to browse a large number of messages quickly and read at your convenience rather than having to check your mail every day.

A second difference is that messages are not sent to individual mailboxes. They are sent and stored on computers at Usenet sites around the world, where they can be accessed by other computers. In a way, you can think of your service provider as a kind of subscriber in that providers select the newsgroups that they will access and make available on their servers. This means you have access to hundreds of messages without worrying about your mailbox becoming too full.

Finally, there is a difference in the users. Many more people from all around the world participate in newsgroups than in mailing lists. In addition, unlike mailing list subscribers, newsgroup readers are not necessarily posting to their major interest groups; they may just be skimming when they find a group they want to contribute to. This, together with the fact that very few newsgroups are moderated, results in an incredible variety of topics and viewpoints.

Using Usenet Newsgroups in the Classroom

The wide open readership and diversity of views found in newsgroups makes them an excellent source of information and a great way to broaden horizons. These same characteristics, however, can cause serious concern in the classroom since there are sure to be some topics, language use, and discussions that are unsuitable for students. Moreover, several of the newsgroup "alternate" categories contain explicit discussions of sex-related topics. Many of these areas may not present problems for you, however, depending on your service provider. If your provider is your school district or a state network, for example, chances are they will not carry controversial newsgroups. On the other hand, even the unavailability of certain groups cannot totally guarantee appropriateness because it is still possible for almost anyone to post to any group, so even "appropriate" groups may carry inappropriate messages from time to time.

Even though the number of obviously unsuitable newsgroups is relatively small compared to the total, our experience and the e-mail messages we have received indicate that many teachers have reservations about using newsgroups with their students. There are a few teachers, however, who point out that having older students compare the diverse viewpoints presented in newsgroups can be very helpful in improving critical thinking skills, as long as there is guidance and supervision.

In short, opinions on newsgroups vary. Therefore, as with all Internet activities, we encourage you to make your own decision. You are the best judge of what suits your situation and meets your and your students' needs.

Reading Newsgroups with Netscape Communicator and Internet Explorer

One of the benefits of using Netscape Communicator or Internet Explorer is that they have closely integrated their mail and news functions. This means it is relatively easy to explore newsgroups using either Netscape Collabra or Internet Explorer Outlook Express News if you already use one of their respective e-mail programs. We will give a brief overview here.

First, just as with e-mail, before you begin to read News, or Groups as they are referred to in Netscape, you must set preferences. This may already have been done by your technical resource person, or you may have set your news preference when you set your mail preferences. If you need to set your news preferences, the only additional information required is the name of your news server. If you don't know it, check with your service provider or technical support person. You can also try adding "news." before your provider's address; for example: news.syr.edu. You may wish to write your news server here for easy reference: _____

Setting Preferences

In Netscape Communicator, choose Edit from the main menu and select Preferences. This brings up the Preferences list. Click on Groups Server and fill in the dialog box that appears. Click OK to save your preferences.

In Internet Explorer for Macintosh users, click the Preferences button in the Outlook Express toolbar. Then click News, which opens the News preferences box. Fill in the information and click OK to save your preferences. For Windows users, the first time you click Read News in Internet Explorer, the Internet Connection Wizard will display a dialog box. Fill in the information and click Next. In the last box, click Finish to save your preferences.

Newsgroup Names and Hierarchies

Before you explore newsgroups, take a moment to look at the format of their names. They may appear confusing at first, but they are actually hierarchical categories and topics. They are always written in lower-case letters with dots between the words. It is usually easy to figure out the topic of any group by reading its name from left to right as in the following examples:

`news.announce.newusers`

This group is in the "news" hierarchy and its topic is "announcements" for "news users."

`k12.ed.comp.literacy`

This group is in the "education" hierarchy and its topic is "computer literacy." Other common Usenet hierarchies include:

- alt   alternative (just about any topic)
- bit   bitnet (a network)
- biz   business
- comp   computers
- k12   primary and secondary education
- misc   miscellaneous
- news   Internet news
- sci   science research
- soc   social issues and world cultures
- talk   discussion of controversial issues

Newcomer's Groups

There are three groups especially for newcomers:
- news.announce.newusers
- news.newusers.questions
- news.answers

As you have time, you should look over the postings in these three groups because they contain helpful information about participating in newsgroups and also answer FAQs (Frequently Asked Questions). Many of the messages in these groups are reposted on a regular basis, often monthly, so that they are always available to newcomers and others for reference.

Reading News/Groups

Begin by selecting All Newsgroups from the menu or toolbar. This will download all of the newsgroups offered by your provider. This process usually takes several minutes. When the list is complete, scroll down and skim through the names of groups; double click on one or more that seem promising and read a few messages.

Triangle and Plus/Minus Icons

You may notice that some of the newsgroups in the list have triangle icons (Netscape in both platforms) or plus/minus sign icons (Explorer for Windows) next to their names. Just as with e-mail, these icons indicate nested or collapsed sub-groups. Clicking the icons will alternately hide and reveal the sub-groups. It should be mentioned that as of this writing, the way newsgroups are listed in Internet Explorer for Macintosh systems is far less detailed and organized than either Internet Explorer for Windows or Netscape Communicator for both platforms. For example, Explorer for Macintosh shows only a simple alphabetical list of newsgroup names compared to the multi-layered, integrated lists of the other news programs.

Subscription to Newsgroups

If you think you may be interested in following up on a particular group's messages, you should "subscribe." (It is actually the service provider who subscribes by agreeing to carry various groups and providing access to them.) For individuals, subscription actually means identifying certain newsgroups as ones they are interested in and would like to read again. If you subscribe, the next time you check News, you can click Subscribed Groups and only the groups you are interested in will be downloaded, which saves considerable time. Of course, you can still select All Newsgroups if you want to view the whole list again.

To subscribe to groups in Netscape you can click the gray dot in the subscribe column next to the newsgroup you want, which changes the gray dot to a check. To unsubscribe, click the check, which then becomes a gray dot again. In Explorer for Windows, highlight the group you want, then click the subscribe button on the right side of the dialog box that appears. In Explorer for Macintosh, choose Tools from the main menu and select Subscribe or Unsubscribe.

Replying and Composing

Replying to messages in either Netscape or Explorer is very easy, since both use the same Message Composition windows for replying to mail and news. You can refer back to the Reply and Composing New Messages sections earlier in this chapter if necessary. If you are composing a new message, be sure to add an explanatory subject title. Remember, readers will be looking for messages in their interest area. There are so many messages on news servers that many readers ignore non-descriptive titles such as "question," so be as informative as possible in a few words.

Newsgroup Netiquette

In general, newsgroup netiquette is similar to that for e-mail and mailing lists. You can get more specific information, however, by reading the postings in the news hierarchies for news users. Another good place to look is at **Usenet FAQs** (http://www.cis.ohio-state.edu/hypertext/faq/usenet/). This site lists all of the FAQs that are in news.answers. They are alphabetized by topic. Finally, it is always helpful to lurk (just read) for awhile until you have a sense of the culture of the new group.

Central Sites for Newsgroups

As we have said, the newsgroups that are available to you depend on your service provider. You can download that list as well as the list of newsgroups accessible from your browser e-mail program. Consequently, it is not really necessary to search the web for newsgroups. However, if you would like to see a more complete list, check the following sources. If you find an interesting site that is not accessible through your service provider, you can ask your provider to consider adding it.

- **Liszt Select**—(http://www.liszt.com/news/)
  This site allows you to search its huge database by topic.

- **TileNet**—(http://www.tile.net/news)
  This site has an alphabetical index and also lets you search by description or by hierarchy.

- **Reference.com**—(http://www.reference.com/)
  Search and read several thousand newsgroups.

Real-Time Communication

E-mail, mailing lists, and newsgroups are non-synchronous forms of electronic communication. There are, in addition, several types of real-time, live communication available on the Internet, including RealAudio, for listening to radio programs; MOOs, text-based "virtual rooms" where you can "move around" and "converse" with other participants; IRC/Internet Relay Chat and Web Chat, which allow you to discuss various topics with people around the world by reading and writing simultaneous messages; and audio and video conferencing (maven and cu-SeeME). These areas of the Internet are changing especially rapidly, and may require special software or access; they can be confusing to use at first, especially for newcomers. As a result, you may want to seek help from a more experienced user or from your technical resource person when exploring these forms of electronic communication.

On a positive note, real-time interaction is getting easier as various sites offer step-by-step instructions or click-on capabilities for participants. You may wish to visit the following sites for more information.

- **The University of Oregon's Babel—**
  (http://babel.uoregon.edu/yamada/interact.html),
  for definitions.

- **Liszt—**(http://www.listzt.com/chat)
  a chat directory

- **The Teacher's Network—**(http://www.teachnet.org/),
  for discussion with other teachers.

- **Teachers Helping Teachers Chat Area—**
  (http://www.pacificnet.net/~mandel/ircinfo.html)
  for discussion with other teachers, good how-to information.

- **How to connect to a MUSH/MOO/MUD—**
  (http://fly.ccs.yorku.ca/mush/con-into.htm/)

- **IRCLE—**(http://www.ircle.houseit.com/),
  for information about Mac chat software.

- **mIRC—**(http://www.mirc.co.uk/),
  for information about Windows chat software.

Real-time interaction is getting easier as various sites offer step-by-step instructions or click-on capabilities for participants.

4 Effective Instructional Strategies: Internet Workshop, Internet Activity, Internet Project, and Internet Inquiry

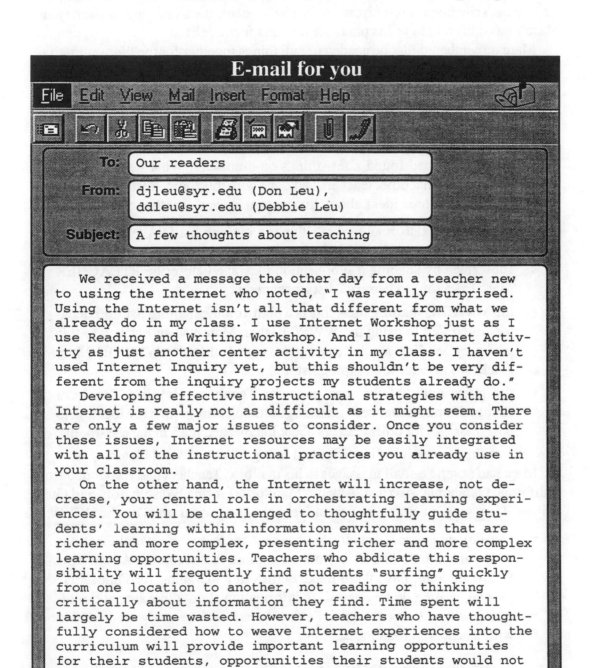

E-mail for you

File Edit View Mail Insert Format Help

To: Our readers

From: djleu@syr.edu (Don Leu),
ddleu@syr.edu (Debbie Leu)

Subject: A few thoughts about teaching

We received a message the other day from a teacher new to using the Internet who noted, "I was really surprised. Using the Internet isn't all that different from what we already do in my class. I use Internet Workshop just as I use Reading and Writing Workshop. And I use Internet Activity as just another center activity in my class. I haven't used Internet Inquiry yet, but this shouldn't be very different from the inquiry projects my students already do."

Developing effective instructional strategies with the Internet is really not as difficult as it might seem. There are only a few major issues to consider. Once you consider these issues, Internet resources may be easily integrated with all of the instructional practices you already use in your classroom.

On the other hand, the Internet will increase, not decrease, your central role in orchestrating learning experiences. You will be challenged to thoughtfully guide students' learning within information environments that are richer and more complex, presenting richer and more complex learning opportunities. Teachers who abdicate this responsibility will frequently find students "surfing" quickly from one location to another, not reading or thinking critically about information they find. Time spent will largely be time wasted. However, teachers who have thoughtfully considered how to weave Internet experiences into the curriculum will provide important learning opportunities for their students, opportunities their students would not be able to have otherwise. Moreover, they will have provided students with a better understanding of our increasingly interdependent and global community.

Don and Debbie

Document: Done

Teaching with the Internet: Marc Erickson's Class

Marc Erickson said good-by to the last few students as they left for their buses. He went around the room straightening things up a bit, checking the hamsters, and writing the schedule for tomorrow on the chalk board. It was the end of the day and Marc's thoughts turned to his plans for the next few weeks.

Marc remembered that he needed to pull things together for the dinosaur unit he was planning for his third grade class. It would start soon. He was gathering resources and ideas from a number of sources: his folder from last year's unit, the school library, and the Internet. He went to his classroom computer to see what he could find.

First, he checked his e-mail. He had been using several search engines to locate information and he had found a few things on dinosaurs. What he really wanted, though, was to see what other teachers had done with this topic. Yesterday he posted requests for instructional ideas about dinosaurs at several locations:

- the **RTEACHER** mailing list—this is a mailing list for literacy educators run in conjunction with the journal *Reading Teacher.* Marc had just subscribed by sending a subscription message (subscribe RTEACHER Marc Erickson) to listserv@listserv.syr.edu

- the **WWEDU** mailing list—this is a high volume mailing list for educators interested in using the WWW. Earlier, Marc had subscribed to this group by sending a subscription message (subscribe WWEDU Marc Erickson) to listproc@listproc.listproc.net

- the guest book of the web page for **Teachers Helping Teachers** (http:www.pacificnet.net/~mandel/guestbook.html)—this is a location to post messages for other teachers about Internet activities in the classroom.

Now it was time to see if his inquiries had brought in any useful ideas.

Marc had several e-mail messages in his mailbox. Teachers had responded from California, Oklahoma, Arizona, Alberta, Manitoba, Florida, Washington, and Great Britain. They shared a number of great ideas about dinosaur units on the WWW:

- *Develop an Internet Activity.* Set a bookmark to one of several locations with guided tours and have students explore that resource. As students follow the tour, have them make entries in a "Digging for Dinosaurs" journal, writing down interesting information about dinosaurs and indicating where it was obtained. Several locations for tours were included with teachers' e-mail messages:

  - the University of California's Museum of Paleontology's **Tours Through Time** (http://www.ucmp.berkeley.edu/education/life/tournew.html);
  - the Field Museum of Natural History's **Dinosaurs!** tour (http://www.fmnh.org/exhibits/dino/Triassic.htm);

- and a wonderful central site for dinosaurs from the Illinois Department of Natural Resources, **Dino Russ's Lair** (http://www.isgs.uiuc.edu/isgsroot/dinos/dinos_home.html).

- *Conduct an Internet Workshop session.* After students have completed their Internet Activity, conduct an Internet Workshop session by having students read and share the information they gathered in their journals using the classroom's "author's chair." Use this to initiate discussion about what each student learned.

- Print out a list of books on dinosaurs, a dinosaur crossword puzzle, a word search puzzle, a dinosaur flip book, and blackline masters for drawing full-scale outlines of several dinosaurs provided by the Field Museum of Natural History in Chicago. All of these great resources are available at **Life Over Time Teacher's Guide** (http://www.fmnh.org/education/LOTguide1.htm).

- Have students view animations of dinosaurs and play several interactive games at the **Media** page (http://www.fmnh.org/exhibits/lot_media/Media1.htm) of the Life Over Time exhibit, again at the Field Museum of Natural History.

- Provide time for students' independent exploration of the WWW for dinosaur resources. Direct this exploration by setting a bookmark to **Yahooligans** (http://www.yahooligans.com/) and limiting their search to resources at this location. Yahooligans is a central site for children where the information has been screened for child safety. Have students share their search strategies and the information they find about dinosaurs during Internet Workshop sessions.

- Have students create an image of their own dinosaur at the web page for **Create-a-saurus** (http://www.adventure.com/kids/dinosaurs/createasaurus/). Then have students paste the picture into their word processor and either write a story about it or use the picture in a report about that species.

- Request the excellent classroom packs for dinosaur study provided by the Field Museum of Natural History at the **Teacher's Guide** location (http://www.fmnh.org/education/LOTguide1.htm) for the Life Over Time exhibit. These are available for short-term loans to teachers in the Chicago area.

- Help students become what a teacher from Texas called "healthy skeptics." Require them to cross reference claims from several sources before accepting them as accurate. She noted that anyone can publish information on the Internet and one is never certain about the accuracy of information found there. Show students how to reference information found on the WWW by visiting **Citing Internet Resources** (http://www.classroom.com/resource/citingnetresources.asp).

As he read these ideas, Marc went to his web browser, found each location, and quickly reviewed the contents, determining whether they would fit his goals for the unit. He made a bookmark for **Dino Russ's Lair** (http://www.isgs.uiuc.edu/isgsroot/dinos/dinos_home.html) and decided to use the journal activity, "Digging for Dinosaurs." He also made a bookmark for **Create-a-saurus** (http://www.adventure.com/kids/dinosaurs/createasaurus/); he would have students use this site, too. He also set a bookmark for **Yahooligans** (http://www.yahooligans.com/) to provide independent exploration time in an area of the web that would be safe for his students. He copied and pasted the list of children's books on dinosaurs into an e-mail message and sent the list to the school librarian. He asked that any of these books in the school library be sent down to his class. Then, he printed out the activity pages he found at the Field Museum. He especially liked the flip book and the idea of drawing full-size patterns of several dinosaurs on the walls of the classroom using an overhead projector. Since he lived in Chicago, he also called to order the classroom packs from the Field Museum. These would come in handy during his unit. Things were coming together nicely.

Earlier in the year, Marc had developed a schedule for students to use with the single computer he had linked to the Internet. Having only a single Internet computer limited access for students but this schedule provided equal access for each student. Each week, every student received half an hour alone on the computer and half an hour on the computer with a partner. If students needed more than an hour of Internet access, they would sometimes go down to the media center and use the connection there. While he always wanted more time on the Internet for his students, Marc noted that students quickly learned to use their Internet time efficiently. This appeared to help them develop useful strategies for navigation. You can see his schedule in Figure 4-1.

Marc's computer schedule had worked well in other units, so he planned to continue its use. However, he was going to reassign partner pairs. He wanted each student to have an opportunity to work with different classmates.

During the first two weeks of the unit, Marc decided to have students take tours and keep journal entries for each session. This Internet Activity sounded like a good one. Later, students would do Internet Inquiry about a dinosaur species or another issue of paleontology they had selected using the resources at Yahooligans.

He also liked the idea of having an Internet Workshop session where students could share the results of their dinosaur research. He would schedule a workshop session for 30 minutes each week. Students could share information they had acquired and the new locations they had found during Internet Inquiry. He would do this on Mondays.

Yes, the unit was coming together. Now, if he could find another class on the Internet that would like to do a collaborative Internet Project on dinosaurs. Maybe they could each share the results of classroom Inquiry projects. This would help his students develop written communication skills.

Marc decided to see if any other teachers were on the **Live Chat Area at Teachers Helping Teachers** (http://www.pacificnet.net/~mandel/ircinfo.html). Yes, the

	Monday	Tuesday	Wednesday	Thursday	Friday
8:30–9:00	Michelle	Michelle/ Becky	Chris/ Emily	Shannon/ Cara	Cynthia/ Jennifer
9:00–9:30	Chris	John/Peter	Jeremy/Dave	Kati	Patti
9:30–10:00	Ben	Aaron	Lisa	Julia	
10:00–10:30	**Internet Workshop** Shannon	**PE**	Paul	**PE**	Andy
10:30–11:00	**Library**	Mike	Scott	Faith	Melissa
11:00–11:30	Cynthia	Eric	James	Linda	Sara
11:30–12:30	**Lunch**	**Lunch**	**Lunch**	**Lunch**	**Lunch**
12:30–1:00	Jennifer	Dave	Peter	Cara	Emily
1:00–1:30	Becky	Jeremy	Ben/Sara	Mike/Linda	John
1:30–2:00	Eric/James	Aaron/ Melissa	**Music**	Paul/Scott	**Class Meeting**
2:00–2:30	Kati/Lisa		Faith/Andy	Patti/Julia	

Figure 4-1. Marc Erickson's computer schedule posted next to his Internet computer.

chat sessions were going strong. They were often active after school. He located a third grade teacher in Detroit who was interested in doing something together. They were going to think about joint projects tonight and share ideas later via e-mail. It was time to get off the computer and prepare a few things for tomorrow.

Lessons from the Classroom

The episode with Marc Erickson provides us with a number of important lessons as we consider effective instructional strategies with the Internet. First, it is clear that developing a weekly schedule for Internet use in single computer classrooms helps to ensure that all students receive access to this important resource. Sometimes, certain students will tend to dominate access to the Internet and other students will have their time curtailed. It is important to guarantee time for all students to use the resources on the Internet.

Second, Marc discovered how easy it was to use Internet Activity. Using Internet Activity was a simple way to integrate the Internet into the regular classroom day. Setting a bookmark and then developing a short assignment was easy to do. Moreover, it focused student use of the Internet on important information. Marc found

Developing a weekly schedule for Internet use in single computer classrooms helps to ensure that all students receive access to this important resource.

Using Internet Activity is a simple way to integrate the Internet into the regular classroom day.

this simple technique engaged students actively in their learning. He often noticed several students at the computer talking about the information for that week's Internet Activity. It was a great suggestion.

Third, the weekly use of Internet Workshop provides students with an opportunity to share important information they discover. We have already mentioned the use of this procedure for developing navigation skills; it is also highly effective for sharing and discussing content information.

The weekly use of Internet Workshop provides students with an opportunity to share important information they discover.

Marc's story also reminds us how important it is to help students evaluate the accuracy of information they find on the Internet. Since anyone can publish nearly any information they wish on the Internet, it is hard to be certain the information you find is accurate. We need to help students become "healthy skeptics" if we wish them to become effective consumers of information on the Internet. We also need to show them how to reference the information they use in their writing.

It is also important to note the special opportunities on the Internet for Internet Project. Developing a collaborative project with classrooms in other parts of the country leads to important learning outcomes as information is shared and new questions are developed. Internet Project requires advance planning between teachers, but the rewards are often well worth the additional time.

Note, too, how Marc provided opportunities for his students to search for information on their own. After students have developed initial navigation strategies, it is important to provide opportunities for independent navigation through the Internet. This encourages students to discover, and then share, even more useful strategies. Providing opportunities for independent research on the Internet, as Marc did with Internet Inquiry, accomplished this.

It is also important to realize that Internet use may be easily integrated with other instructional practices with which you are already familiar. Marc's use of a journal while students took a dinosaur tour is but one example of this. He also wove in a practice found in many classrooms, the use of an "author's chair." Nearly every instructional activity you currently use in your classroom may also be used with the Internet.

We need to help students become "healthy skeptics" if we wish them to become effective consumers of information on the Internet. We also need to show them how to reference the information they use in their writing.

Finally, while the Internet is a tool to support students' learning, it is also a powerful resource for planning instructional activities. In a short session after school, Marc quickly gathered resources and ideas for an extensive, thematic unit. As you become more familiar with the Internet, you will also develop efficient strategies for using the Internet to plan activities. After a short time, you will wonder how you ever taught without this resource.

Teaching with Internet Workshop, Internet Activity, Internet Project, and Internet Inquiry

It is essential to thoughtfully plan how to integrate Internet experiences into your classroom curriculum. Sometimes we abdicate this responsibility when we make Internet experiences available only after students' regular classroom work is completed, providing little direction for what should be done. Using the Internet like this makes it one of several "free choice" activities in the classroom. There are several problems with this approach.

Equity is one of the problems. Making the Internet available only when regular work has been completed, ultimately results in more advanced students having greater Internet access. This ends up helping the rich get richer, as advanced students, who finish their regular work first, become more advanced in their ability to access and analyze information on the Internet. Meanwhile, weaker students, often last in completing work, are denied these opportunities to improve their abilities.

Another problem is that students often simply "surf the net" when they do not have a purpose for Internet use. When the Internet is used without direction and guidance, it often takes students away from thoughtful integration and analysis of information and involves them instead in random, unconnected surfing experiences. You will see this pattern, too, in your classroom unless students have a clear purpose each time they sit down to use the Internet. Internet experiences should always have a purpose; they should always be an integral part of your instructional program. This requires you to thoughtfully plan this integration.

How can you integrate the Internet into your classroom to avoid these problems? Developing effective instructional strategies with the Internet is not difficult. We will share an instruction model we have found useful in many classrooms. It contains four instructional frameworks:

- Internet Workshop
- Internet Activity
- Internet Project
- Internet Inquiry

What is especially useful about this model is that it is developmentally sensitive, so you can begin with Internet Workshop, a framework that is easiest to use, and gradually build to more complex and powerful instructional strategies as you feel comfortable. You will probably find many similarities between elements in this model of Internet use and the instructional strategies you already use in your classroom. This should also make it easier to integrate Internet use into your classroom. Let's take a look at each of the elements in this instructional model.

Using Internet Workshop in Your Classroom

Internet Workshop is a regularly scheduled time used to support students' ability to acquire information from the Internet and to think critically about the information they obtain. During Internet Workshop, students share what they have learned, ask questions about issues they do not understand, and seek information to help them in upcoming work. As such, Internet Workshop provides a perfect opportunity to make explicit the many "hidden" strategies we use to comprehend and analyze written information, strategies that often apply in books, articles, and other traditional texts as well as on the Internet. Engaging children in discussions about these matters during Internet Workshop can be a central part of your instructional program.

The nature of Internet Workshop activities differs depending on the teacher and the students who use it. Often, however, it shares several common characteristics.

During Internet Workshop, students share what they have learned, ask questions about issues they do not understand, and seek information to help them in upcoming work.

First, it takes place during a regular time period, usually at the beginning or the end of the week. A regularly scheduled time period allows all members to anticipate the session and prepare for it. Second, Internet Workshop provides opportunities for both you and your students to share navigation strategies as well as content information. Internet Workshop provides an important opportunity for everyone to learn from one another about the Internet and the information they find.

Teachers usually direct the first few sessions of Internet Workshop to model what they wish to take place. After students understand the process, teachers turn over responsibility for the session to students.

Teachers usually direct the first few sessions of Internet Workshop to model what they wish to take place. After students understand the process, teachers turn over responsibility for the session to students. When you are modeling the first few sessions, Internet Workshop might consist of these two steps:

1. Share something new you recently learned using the Internet and invite others to respond.

2. Share something you are still trying to figure out and invite others to respond.

During the first step, share with your students something you discovered while working on the Internet. This might be a navigational strategy such as how to contact an expert in colonial history to answer a question about the Boston Massacre. It might also be a content issue such as what you discovered about the Boston Massacre. After you share what you have recently learned, invite students to ask questions or share their experiences related to your item. They might, for example, be interested in locations where they can contact an expert in the area they are studying. Or, they might share their experiences with contacting experts and perhaps several new web locations where these experts are located.

During the second step, share something about the Internet (either navigation or content) that you want to learn but haven't quite figured out. After you share what it is you wish to learn, invite others to respond and see if anyone knows how to do this. If a student does, encourage him/her to share the information. This will allow others to try it out after the workshop session to see if it works.

Sometimes, the solution will not work as the student described it. When this happens, encourage students to bring their experiences to the next workshop to see if the problem can be solved by others or if the solution was misinterpreted. In either case, the discussion that occurs during the second step is often the most productive learning time about the Internet that will take place in your classroom.

After one or two sessions modeling Internet Workshop, encourage students to follow the same procedures as you: sharing something they learned about the Internet and inviting others to respond; sharing something they want to learn about the Internet and inviting others to respond. Gradually, encourage students to assume ownership of Internet Workshop so the class is always focused on items that students find most helpful in their work. You should, though, always come to Internet Workshop prepared to share your items if students do not have something they wish to share. After you begin the use of Internet Workshop, this will seldom happen.

Often teachers will add a rule for everyone to follow during Internet Workshop: each student may only respond twice until everyone else has had a chance to contribute a response. This rule prevents individuals from dominating the conversation and will encourage quieter students to contribute.

It is important to recognize that both navigation issues (e.g., "How do I set a bookmark so I can come back to a location?") as well as content issues (e.g., "Has anyone found information about volcanoes?") are appropriate topics for Internet Workshop. Initially, you will find students more interested in navigation issues. As the year progresses, however, and they become more skilled in navigating the Internet, content issues will dominate.

There are many variations to this structure. You already saw how Marc Erickson used Internet Workshop as an opportunity for students to share the results in their dinosaur journals. Other strategies are also possible. Internet Workshop works especially well when you combine it with Internet Activities, Internet Project, and Internet Inquiry. Internet Workshop may be combined with each of these method frameworks, providing students with opportunities to share discoveries and sharpen critical thinking skills.

Internet Workshop works especially well when you combine it with Internet Activities, Internet Project, and Internet Inquiry.

TEACHING TIP

Often it is useful to vary the structure of Internet Workshop. There are probably as many ways to organize Internet Workshop as there are teachers with creative ideas. One way to increase social learning opportunities in your class is to have several small groups engage in Internet Workshop at the same time. This gives everyone a greater chance to speak and share ideas. As you circle around, listen to the discussions. You will hear many new ideas being learned as students share their Internet experiences with one another.

Using Internet Activity with Internet Workshop

You have just received several Internet connections in your classroom along with several new computers. How do you begin to integrate the Internet into your instructional program? Many teachers start by using Internet Activity. This is the easiest way to begin using the Internet for instruction. Internet Activity is especially useful to introduce students to sites that will be used in your class for an upcoming unit.

Many teachers start by using Internet Activity. This is the easiest way to begin using the Internet for instruction.

Internet Activity turns your Internet computer into a traditional learning center activity. All you need to do is to locate a site on the Internet with content related to the learning you have planned for that week in your classroom. Then you develop an activity related to that site and assign this activity to your students and have them complete it during their weekly session(s) on the computer. Often, teachers will develop several different activities related to the site they have selected and ask students to pick one, or several, from the list to complete during the week.

Internet Activity has many variations. Generally, though, it contains these steps:

1. Locate a site, or several sites, on the Internet with content related to a classroom unit of instruction and set a bookmark for the location(s).

2. Develop an activity requiring students to use the site(s).

3. Assign this activity to be completed during the week.

4. Have students share their work, questions, and new insights at the end of the week during Internet Workshop.

The first step is to locate a site on the Internet with content related to the learning you have planned for that week in your classroom. As you consider which site on the Internet to use, it is helpful to begin your search at a central Internet site, a location on the Internet with extensive and well-organized links about a specific topic. Visiting a central site such as those listed in Chapter 2 will often give you many useful resources for your instructional unit, some of which may be used for Internet Activity. When you find a location you wish to use in your activity, set a bookmark.

Internet FAQ

Is there some way I can automatically update my bookmark list? Web sites are constantly changing or disappearing. Is there some way that the updating of a bookmark file can be automated and that I can be told that a bookmarked site has changed, moved or disappeared?

There are several new types of "Push Technologies" that will update your bookmarks automatically for you. You may wish to visit **NetMind Services Inc.** (http://www.netmind.com/) and download their free program called URL Minder. This program will automatically notify you when the URL for a bookmark changes.

The second step is to develop an activity related to the learning goals of your unit, using the site you have bookmarked. Sometimes this activity will introduce students to a site you will be using in your instructional unit. Sometimes the activity will develop important background knowledge for your unit. And, sometimes the activity will develop navigation strategies for Internet use. Often, teachers prepare an activity page for students to complete and then bring to Internet Workshop.

The third step is to assign the activity to be completed during the week. If you have only a single Internet connection in your classroom, you may wish to have students work in pairs to complete the assignment.

The fourth step is to have students share their work, questions, and new insights at the end of the week during Internet Workshop. This is a time for the class to get together and share the learning they completed during Internet Activity and to ask questions about issues that came up during their work on the Internet.

Often, Internet Activity is used by teachers to develop important background knowledge for a unit of a topic they will be exploring in class. These teachers will locate a central site about the topic and then develop an activity designed to explore the site, a location that will also be used throughout the unit. In these cases, the activity page invites students to explore the web site and bring their discoveries to Internet Workshop, where they are shared and used to initiate important discussions about the topic. At other times, Internet Activity is used during a unit to explore an idea or an issue that is central to your curricular goals.

The activity page in Figure 4-3 was developed by two teachers to develop background knowledge about Japan. They developed the activity to begin a unit for an interdisciplinary global studies course in the 9th grade, team taught by a social studies teacher and an English teacher. These teachers located **Kids Web Japan** (http://www.jinjapan.org/kidsweb/) and set a bookmark to this central site on the classroom computers. Notice how the tasks on the activity page are open-ended, inviting students to make their own discoveries at this location and bring these to Internet Workshop to share at the beginning of the unit. This is a critical aspect of any activity sheet prepared for Internet Activity. Open-ended questions invite students to bring many different types of information to Internet Workshop for discussion.

Often, Internet Activity is used by teachers to develop important background knowledge for a unit of a topic they will be exploring in class.

Kids Web Japan (http://www.jinjapan.org/kidsweb/)

Figure 4-2. A portion of the screen at **Kids Web Japan**, a central site used to introduce a classroom unit on Japan with Internet Activity.

Figure 4-3. A page developed for Internet Activity to introduce a unit on Japan.

EXPLORING JAPAN

Internet Researcher: _____ Date: _____

News About Japan

Go to the bookmark I have set for *Kid's Web Japan* (http://www.jinjapan.org/kidsweb/) and scroll down to the bottom of this page. Now click on the button "Monthly News" (http://www.jinjapan.org/kidsweb/news.html) and read several recent news stories from Japan. Write notes about some of the news you discovered and be ready to share this with us during Internet Workshop.

_____
_____
_____
_____

Nature and Climate

Click on the button "Nature and Climate" and read a description of what it is like to live in Japan. Be certain to read answers to some of the questions at the bottom of this article. Write down notes about what you learned about the nature and climate of Japan. We will share these during Internet Workshop.

_____
_____
_____
_____

What's Cool in Japan?

Now let's find out what are some of the biggest fads among children in Japan your own age. Visit "What's Cool in Japan" (http://www.jinjapan.org/kidsweb/cool.html) and find out what kids are doing. Write down notes about what you discovered is most popular among kids and be ready to share this information during Internet Workshop.

_____
_____
_____
_____

Virtual Japanese Culture: Origami

Now let's discover a small piece of Japanese culture. Visit "Virtual Japanese Culture" (http://www.jinjapan.org/kidsweb/virtual.html) and follow the directions to make an origami (folded paper) object. Use the special origami paper I placed next to the computer. Read the directions and make an airplane, a crane, or a soldier's helmet. Bring this to Internet Workshop so we can see how well you followed directions.

_____
_____
_____
_____

Your Choice

Visit at least one of the many other locations at Kids Web Japan. You decide where to go! Write down notes of what you discovered and share your special discoveries with all of us during Internet Workshop.

_____
_____
_____

E-mail for you

File   Edit   View   Mail   Insert   Format   Help

To: Colleagues

From: Jill Newcomb
   newcomb@voyager.net
Cindy Ross
   jross@sunny.ncmc.cc.mi.us

Subject: My Hero Project

   For our first experience using the Internet in the classroom, we decided to choose a small group to work on an activity called "Heroes." We used two web sites, **"My Hero"** (http://myhero.com/) and **"The Giraffe Project"** (www.giraffe.org/giraffe/).

   The students first read about well known heroes described on these web sites. Then the students read about local heroes which were submitted by other students to these web sites. The group discussed qualities and characteristics of the heroes using the analytical skills of comparing and contrasting.

   Students then choose their own personal hero and wrote an essay about this person. These essays were submitted to the "My Hero" web site to be published on the Internet for other students to read.

   To further practice writing and communication skills, the students chose a hero from their school or community. Collaboratively they wrote interview questions. After practice and role playing, the students interviewed their hero. The interview was videotaped.

   For a culminating activity we held a "Hero Celebration." Students invited their parents and the community hero. At the celebration, the students read their essays, introduced their hero, and all participants viewed the videotaped interview.

   Using the Internet was highly motivating for these students. They eagerly shared their findings of heroes with their teachers and classmates. We noticed their enthusiasm carried over to other areas. For instance, when checking out library books, these students now choose biographies over easy to read fiction. We are looking forward to other activities using the Internet in the classroom.

Jill Newcomb newcomb@voyager.net
Cindy Ross jross@sunny.ncmc.cc.mi.us
Ottawa Elementary School Petoskey, Michigan

Document: Done

Communicating with others around the world on a common classroom project provides special opportunities for your students, opportunities they will not experience without the Internet.

Using Internet Project with Internet Workshop

As you use the Internet in your class, there will come a time when you feel confident enough to explore collaborative learning possibilities with others at locations around the world. Collaborative projects may take place as you work with another class on a common project, with students and teachers communicating extensively about the topic both classes are exploring. Collaborative projects also take place when classes contribute data to a common site and then, after the data are analyzed, see how their data compare with others. Often there will also be discussion between participating classes about the meaning of the results and even opportunities to use the data for further analyses. Each leads to rich learning opportunities.

Communicating with others around the world on a common classroom project provides special opportunities for your students, opportunities they will not experience without the Internet. You should seek out these opportunities for your students and integrate them into your curriculum for several reasons. First, communicating with students from a culture other than their own helps your students to develop a greater appreciation for the diversity that characterizes our world. Understanding diversity leads children to respect differences, a value increasingly important in a global community. Moreover, writing takes on a different meaning as students learn that messages must be perfectly clear for others to understand what they mean. Communication in writing requires meaning to be very explicit; children come to learn this through misunderstandings from poorly written e-mail messages. It serves to help them learn important lessons about correct spelling, sentence structure, and organization, since each may get in the way of effective communication. In addition, reading information from other places on our planet becomes an exciting way to learn. In fact, all of your curriculum will suddenly come to life when you are able to share work with students in another location who have similar interests. These special opportunities for communicating and learning from others comprise an important advantage of Internet use. You should seek them out as often as you can.

There are two approaches to the use of Internet Project in a classroom: web-site Internet projects and spontaneous projects developed by teachers who find one another on the Internet. Web-site projects are more permanent projects, coordinated by an individual at a web site. They are a good starting point for teachers new to the Internet because they are often precisely defined, with clear directions for participation and a complete package of instructional resources. There is not yet a central Internet site for web-site Internet projects. You will discover them in your explorations on the Internet. Figure 4-4 lists several examples of web-site Internet projects. To participate, you simply need to visit the site and follow the directions.

A second type of Internet Project consists of spontaneous projects developed by teachers who find one another on the Internet. Spontaneous projects are more common on the Internet. These projects are created by an individual teacher who then advertises for collaborating classrooms at one of several locations. After one or several teachers communicate their interest by e-mail, students in each classroom

Good News Bears (http://www.ncsa.uiuc.edu: 80/edu/RSE/RSEyellow/gnb.html)	A stock market activity for high school or middle school students. Students manage a portfolio and compete with others to see who manages their portfolio best to maximize earnings.	**Figure 4-4.** Examples of web-site Internet projects and their locations
Monarch Watch (http://www.MonarchWatch.org/)	Raise Monarch butterflies, tag them, release them, record observations about Monarchs in your area, then watch as your data and those compiled by others are used to track the annual migration of this wonderful creature!	
Mind's Eye Monster Project (http://www.win4edu.com/ minds-eye/monster)	Useful for primary grade classrooms. Classrooms and students are matched. Then one student draws a monster and writes a detailed description. The description is sent to the student's partner, who must draw the monster from the description. Then, both pictures are posted in the monster gallery. Both reading and writing skills are supported. Much fun!	
Journey Exchange Project (http://www.win4edu.com / minds-eye/journey/)	Students research and develop a five-city journey around the world. Then they exchange clues to the locations with their Internet partner. Each attempts to discover the cities and the travel itinerary.	
Earth Day Groceries (http://www.halcyon.com/arborhts/ earthday.html)	Students decorate grocery bags with environment-friendly messages and distribute at local grocery stories just before Earth Day. Classrooms report on their experiences.	

complete the project together and share their work. Spontaneous projects recently developed by teachers on the Internet include:

- **Neighbors to the North and South.**   Posted by a middle school teacher in Illinois, this project sought collaborating classrooms in Canada and Mexico to learn more about each other's country and cultures. Each week, classes would exchange information on one topic: What is your school like? Which holidays do you celebrate and what is the significance of each? What is unique about the economy in your state or province? What are current political issues that people in your state/province do not agree on? How do you spend a typical weekend?

- **Passage to Hiroshima.**   Developed by a teacher in Nagoya, Japan, this class sought other secondary classrooms interested in studying about the importance of peace and international cooperation. They proposed to begin by exchanging useful sites on the world wide web related to peace. This class also indicated they would be visiting Hiroshima in November and sought interview and research questions from a collaborative classroom. They volunteered to interview citizens of Hiroshima and then share the results, including photos, upon their return.

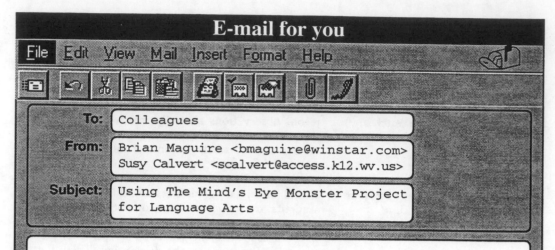

E-mail for you

File Edit View Mail Insert Format Help

To: Colleagues

From: Brian Maguire <bmaguire@winstar.com>
             Susy Calvert <scalvert@access.k12.wv.us>

Subject: Using The Mind's Eye Monster Project
             for Language Arts

The Internet has become an invaluable vehicle for teaching. We have not been able to find a better tool for removing the walls of the classroom and opening it to an incredible learning environment. It makes a vast amount of information available to the class, provides real-life experiences, and allows kids to publish their work to a worldwide audience.

I (Brian) began incorporating the Internet into my classroom about two years ago when I created a writing project that I believed would meet many curriculum goals and, at the same time, excite the students. By means of a bulletin board message in CompuServe's education forum, I looked for a classroom that would participate in a Monster Exchange Program. This called for students in two classes to form small groups and design a monster, vividly describe their monster, and then e-mail their descriptions to the other class. Then the student groups in the partner class would attempt to recreate the monster solely from the descriptions. The two classes would finally exchange their pictures to compare the originals with the new ones. John Thompson, the dedicated parent of a Brunner Elementary student in New Jersey loved the idea. He suggested that we publish the monster pictures and descriptions on the WWW and committed to help his home school become involved in the project.

The project was met with enthusiasm by both classes and proved to be a multifaceted learning activity. Students were introduced to and were given the opportunity to practice various computer skills such as word processing, e-mailing, and digital scanning. They were also challenged to refine and integrate their descriptive writing, creative design and drawing skills, and to work together as a team.

What began as a project for two classes increased to a party of over 100 classes from the entire world (Siberia, Japan, Australia, etc.). So, not only did we become par-

Document: Continued

ticipants, but we also took on the task of organizing. I suggest teachers first find an already existing Internet project that meets their current classroom goals, is well organized, and offers curriculum integration. It should also require computer skills that you already have. Good features that one should look for are tools such as listings of frequently asked questions, electronic bulletin boards, chat capabilities, and a support team to answer questions.

When participating with a cooperating class or school, always remember to maintain a common timeline, especially with foreign countries. Many countries have opposite seasons, different school schedules, vacation dates, and time zones.

If they are well planned it can actually be to everyone's advantage. Try a collaborative project. We are certain it will excite your students and lead to important learning experiences! A group of excellent projects that are free, offer curriculum integration, communication tools such as chat and WebBoards, are extremely well planned and documented include the MindsEye Projects. The Insect Ecology Exchange, Journey Exchange, Fish N Chips, the Monster Exchange, and Tidal Passages are all free projects that focus on many curriculum areas and really hit home with the kids. They can be visited at http://www.win4edu.com/minds-eye/ for the MindsEye Projects and http://www.tidalpassages.com for Tidal Passages.

```
Brian Maguire
bmaguire@winstar.com
****************************************************************
Project Manager—WinStar for Education
Former Grade 3 Teacher at Gilbertsville—Mount Upton CSD
http://www.win4edu.com/
WinStar MindsEye Projects
Project Director
http://www.win4edu.com/minds-eye/
****************************************************************
Susy Calvert, Coordinator/Teacher of Gifted Programming
****************************************************************
Raleigh County Schools, Beckley, West Virginia
scalvert@access.k12.wv.us
****************************************************************
```

- **Culture and Clues.**   In this project for 7–9 year olds, a teacher proposed exchanging boxes of cultural artifacts from the culture where each participating school is located. Students would use these artifacts to make inferences about what life was like at each location and then write descriptions of this culture. These would be exchanged by e-mail and then students would compare how close their guesses were.

Spontaneous Internet projects have many variations. Generally, they follow these procedures:

1. Plan a collaborative project for an upcoming unit in your classroom and write a project description. The description should contain a summary of the project, a clear list of learning goals, expectations you have for collaborating classrooms, and a projected timeline for beginning and ending the project.

2. Post the project description and timeline several months in advance at one or several locations, seeking collaborative classroom partners.

3. Arrange collaboration details with teachers in other classrooms who agree to participate.

4. Complete the project, using Internet Workshop as a forum in your own class for working on the project and exchanging information with your collaborating classrooms.

The first step requires you to do some advance planning, at least several months before you wish to begin the project. A clear description with explicit goals and timelines will make it easier for everyone to understand what will be expected of them.

The second step is to post the project description and timeline at one of several locations of the Internet where teachers advertise their projects, seeking collaborating classrooms. This should be done several months in advance so that other teachers have time to find your project. Project descriptions may be posted at several locations, including:

- **Global SchoolNet's Internet Project Registry—** (http://www.gsn.org/pr/index.html)

- **Classroom Connects's Teacher Contact Database—** (http://www.classroom.com/teachercontact/)

- **The Global School House—**(http://www.gsh.org/class/default.htm)

- **Intercultural E-mail Classroom Connections—** (http://www.stolaf.edu/network/iecc/)

Figure 4-5 provides an example of a project description posted recently at Global SchoolNet's Internet Project Registry.

Project Name: Latitude and Shadow Length

Contact Person: Helen Schrand

E-mail Contact: schrandh@ride.ri.net

Description: Students will measure the length of the shadow of a 2 meter pole at three times during a school day on three dates over the course of the school year. We would like to receive similar data from schools in other locations so students can compare their findings with those from a variety of places.

How Long: 7 months

Objectives: Students will

1. learn to use meter sticks to measure accurately

2. locate places on a world map or globe using latitude and longitude

3. graph and analyze data

4. determine the effect of latitude and time of day on shadow length

Share: We will compile a table of results we receive and e-mail it to participating classes.

Figure 4-5. An example of a project description posted at Global SchoolNet's Internet Project Registry.

The third step in an Internet Project is to arrange collaboration details with teachers in other classrooms who agree to participate in the project with you. Internet projects require close coordination. It is important to confirm procedures and timelines with everyone involved.

Finally, you complete the activities in the project, exchanging information with all of the collaborative classrooms. This step provides you and your students with opportunities to read, write, and critically evaluate information related to the project. Internet Workshop often provides a supportive forum for organizing and developing much of your classroom's efforts on the project.

Internet projects require close coordination. It is important to confirm procedures and timelines with everyone involved

TEACHING TIP

Are you interested in discovering more information about a project approach to Internet use? Pay a visit to **NickNacks Telecollaborate!** (http://www1.minn.net:80/~schubert/NickNacks.html). This site contains a wealth of suggestions and a number of great examples. Before developing your own project description and posting it to seek partners, you may wish to review the project descriptions at **Global SchoolNet's Internet Project Registry** (http://www.gsn.org/pr/index.html). You may also wish to participate in one or two Internet projects as a collaborating classroom before developing your own. This will help you develop insights about this approach as you seek to exploit its special opportunities for classroom learning.

Figure 4-6.
The home page for Global SchoolNet's Internet Projects Registry, a useful place to find examples of Internet projects developed by teachers around the world.

Global SchoolNet's Internet Projects Registry (http://www.gsn.org/pr/index.html)

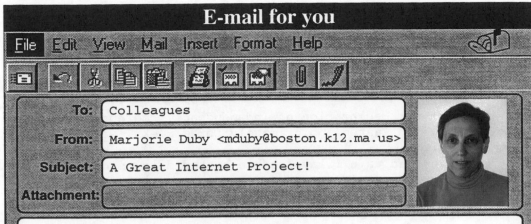

E-mail for you

File Edit View Mail Insert Format Help

To: Colleagues

From: Marjorie Duby <mduby@boston.k12.ma.us>

Subject: A Great Internet Project!

Attachment:

Dear Risk-takers and Experimenters,

   For the past 7 years, I have been enriching my classroom content as I participated in online projects. I have met global friends online, one of whom even visited Boston . . . from Australia! I have involved my students and myself, as part of our team, in collaborative problem-solving projects, information/database collections, and e-mail exchanges.

   The most rewarding project was a colonial simulation taking place in the 18th century. It was totally student-centered as my class members kept a portfolio of their colonial character identities, families, and friends.

   That project began with a posting to a mailing list. Carolyn Burt, an educator in Washington, was looking for a fifth grade class studying colonial America to collaborate in a simulation. She had in mind for each class to select a colonial area—the northeast, middle Atlantic, or south. Students in each class would then describe the charter for that colony and populate the colony with characters appropriate for the time and place. Our students would "be" those characters as they faced challenges or problems created by the other colonies, as events led to the Revolutionary War and the creation of our original Declaration of Independence.

   Each educator would independently use materials and strategies in her classroom as her students learned about the period leading to independence. I used many children's literature resources and primary source documents as I explored "the invisibles" of the time which included women, servants, Africans, apprentices, and Native Americans around the theme of condoned mob actions.

   Carolyn recruited another individual on the Internet to "be" the authority in England, adding intrigue and suspense as he sent electronic mail obstacles which needed to be addressed.

   Other than the first introduction of characters with photographs and text done through snail mail and the final

Document: Continued

signing of our Declaration of Independence, the entire project, which lasted approximately three weeks, was done by e-mail.

My class had us all involved in heated discussions as our characters, in incoming e-mail messages, received "challenges" from our collaborating classrooms. Characters were named as slave traders, made ill with a mysterious sickness, and jailed for non-payment of taxes. Using their knowledge of the times, they "saved" themselves.

An asset for us in the project was living in Boston, with the Freedom Trail and the colonial resources at our feet. I told Carolyn that if selected for the project, my class would represent the Massachusetts Bay area. We would populate the area, not just Boston, with characters appropriate to the time and place and with appropriate jobs and interests.

We were accepted into the project. Carolyn chose to be a middle colony, Newportia, in the area of Philadelphia.

My students and I took off on a memorable adventure where one's imagination can soar within the bounds of facts!

Living in Boston, we have access to many primary source documents and resources associated with the National Park Service and the sites on the Freedom Trail. My class, during the school year, visited the Old State House, the Paul Revere House, Faneuil Hall, the Old South Meeting House, Granary Burying Ground, Bunker Hill Monument, and the John Adams Homestead. With educators at these sites, we simulated the Boston Massacre Trial, met the poetess Phillis Wheatley, discussed mob actions, and visited the sites of the Boston Tea Party and the Liberty Tree. We had a wealth of real information. In discussions, our "characters" referred back to the geography of Boston, the artifacts we handled, the sense of history we experienced on our trips as we had our probing questions answered by site educators familiar with the time and events.

Independently, Carolyn and I set about creating a series of "challenges" related to the 18th century without alerting each other to what was about to come. As one challenge was sent and another received, we set to solving the situation to give a response. The challenges our characters had to face ranged from the danger of fire in the meeting house when a beam hit and killed the minister, a smallpox epidemic, our reaction to the triangular trade, and an in-

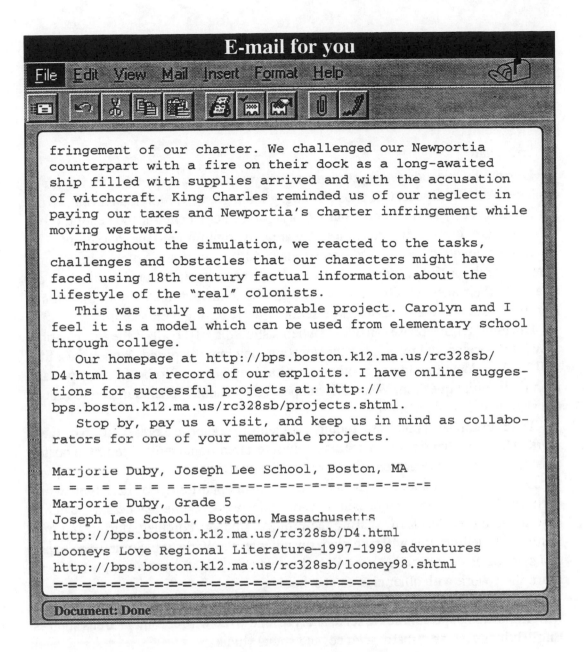

E-mail for you

File   Edit   View   Mail   Insert   Format   Help

fringement of our charter. We challenged our Newportia
counterpart with a fire on their dock as a long-awaited
ship filled with supplies arrived and with the accusation
of witchcraft. King Charles reminded us of our neglect in
paying our taxes and Newportia's charter infringement while
moving westward.

Throughout the simulation, we reacted to the tasks,
challenges and obstacles that our characters might have
faced using 18th century factual information about the
lifestyle of the "real" colonists.

This was truly a most memorable project. Carolyn and I
feel it is a model which can be used from elementary school
through college.

Our homepage at http://bps.boston.k12.ma.us/rc328sb/
D4.html has a record of our exploits. I have online suggestions for successful projects at: http://
bps.boston.k12.ma.us/rc328sb/projects.shtml.

Stop by, pay us a visit, and keep us in mind as collabo-
rators for one of your memorable projects.

Marjorie Duby, Joseph Lee School, Boston, MA
= = = = = = = = =-=-=-=-=-=-=-=-=-=-=-=-=-=
Marjorie Duby, Grade 5
Joseph Lee School, Boston, Massachusetts
http://bps.boston.k12.ma.us/rc328sb/D4.html
Looneys Love Regional Literature—1997-1998 adventures
http://bps.boston.k12.ma.us/rc328sb/looney98.shtml
=-=

Document: Done

Using Internet Inquiry with Internet Workshop

Once your students have become familiar with locating Internet resources, Internet Inquiry may be a useful means to develop independent research skills and allow students to pursue a question that holds a special interest for them. Internet Inquiry may be developed by small groups or by individuals. They usually begin with students identifying a topic and a question they wish to explore related to the current unit. The question may be as specific as "What happened to Benedict Arnold after he betrayed his country in the Revolutionary War?" or as general as "What is it like to live in Japan?" The most important aspect of Internet Inquiry is that the students should do research on a question that they find to be important.

The most important aspect of Internet Inquiry is that the students should do research on a question that they find to be important.

Internet Inquiry consists of five phases:
1. question
2. search
3. analyze
4. compose
5. share

During the question phase, students identify an important question they wish to explore. You can support this phase by engaging in group or individual brainstorming sessions or by setting a bookmark to a central Internet site for the general topic area and allowing students to explore the area, looking for an issue to explore.

Once students have decided upon a question they wish to explore, the second phase, search, begins. Students may search on the Internet for useful information related to their question. Students should also be reminded to use more traditional resources found in their classroom or school library during their search.

During the third phase, analyze, students should analyze all of the information they have located and respond to the question they initially posed. Sometimes, this will lead students to address another question they discover to be more important than their initial question. When this happens, they should be encouraged to repeat the search and analyze phases.

The fourth phase, compose, requires students to compose a presentation of their work. There are many ways to do this, including a traditional written report, a poster session, a multimedia presentation, or an oral report.

During the final phase, share, students have an opportunity to share their work with others and respond to questions about their work. Some teachers set aside a regular time each week for sharing the projects students complete during Internet Inquiry. Sometimes this will take place during Internet Workshop. Sometimes a special science or social studies fair will be held where students have an opportunity to share their work with other classes at school.

Internet Inquiry can be an exciting part of your curriculum, providing students with important opportunities to read, analyze, and write within content areas such as English/language arts, math, science, and social studies.

Special Instructional Considerations:

Scheduling Internet Use in a Single Computer Classroom, Information Accuracy, Citation Styles, and Child Safety

Most of your current practices work well with the Internet. There are only a few issues you need to consider as you plan for Internet integration in your class:

• scheduling computer time appropriately;

- helping students become healthy skeptics about information accuracy;
- becoming familiar with new citation strategies for Internet references; and
- developing independent search strategies while being sensitive to child safety concerns.

Once you consider these issues, Internet resources may be easily integrated with nearly all of the instructional practices you already use in your classroom.

Scheduling Computer Time Appropriately in Single Computer Classrooms

There are many different ways in which Internet access is provided to schools. In some cases, Internet computers will be available for the entire school to use in the library or media center. In other cases, a lab or cluster will contain many Internet computers in a single room; your class will have a scheduled time for using these computers. In still other cases, each classroom will have at least one computer connected to the Internet. In very unusual cases, five or more computers will be linked to the Internet in each classroom.

Having a single Internet computer in your classroom presents a special challenge as you consider how to effectively schedule time for its use. One of the best solutions to this situation is the one developed by Marc Erickson. You will recall that Marc devised a schedule so that each of his 28 students had one-half hour on the Internet with a partner and one half-hour on the Internet by themselves. Each student had a minimum of one hour per week to use the Internet for class projects. While not ideal, this is the best solution we have seen for providing equity in classrooms with only a single Internet connection. It will, however, usually require you to adjust your organizational patterns slightly to optimize Internet use. You will need to be sufficiently flexible so that, at any time during the day, one student or student pair will miss regular, on-going instruction. That is, students will need to leave the regularly scheduled class or group activity to work on the Internet during their assigned time. In most cases, this is a minor matter; both teachers and students adjust to the situation remarkably well.

There are, however, a few issues you should consider. First, be certain that you periodically rotate the assigned times on the computer schedule so that the same students do not miss their time because of regular conflicts with the school's special functions (e.g., regularly scheduled school assemblies, student council meetings, or special activity meetings). It would be unfair, for example, to have a student miss her Internet time on Monday of each week because she had to attend music class.

Second, rotate partners regularly at the computer so that all of your students have an opportunity to work with many different individuals in your class. This increases opportunities for improving social skills at the same time it increases opportunities to learn new things from other students about Internet use.

Developing a regular schedule for Internet use will help you to manage equity issues in your classroom. In the future, this problem will be resolved as additional connections are made to school classrooms. For now, we need to develop strategies such as this to accommodate our students' learning needs.

Having a single Internet computer in your classroom presents a special challenge as you consider how to effectively schedule time for its use.

Be certain that you periodically rotate the assigned times on the computer schedule so that the same students do not miss their time because of regular conflicts.

TEACHING TIP

If you develop a schedule like that described in this chapter for a single computer classroom, consider scheduling students who are strong at math during math time, students who are strong in language arts during language arts time, and so forth. This prevents students who really need assistance in a subject from missing important instructional time in that area. You may wish to read how Mark Ahlness uses this strategy in his classroom at Arbor Heights Elementary School in Seattle, Washington. Visit his spotlight page at **Ed's Oasis** (http:/ /www.EDsOasis.org/Spotlight/Ahlness/Ahlness.html) to see how Mark uses the Internet in his class.

Helping Students Become Healthy Skeptics about Information Accuracy

Traditional forces, guaranteeing some degree of control over the accuracy of information in published books, do not exist on the Internet where anyone may publish anything.

While the Internet makes more information available to more classrooms, it also presents new challenges to both students and teachers. One of the important challenges we face is that we are never certain about the accuracy of the information we find on the web. Traditional forces, guaranteeing some degree of control over the accuracy of information in published books, do not exist on the Internet where anyone may publish anything. As a result, searches for information may sometimes turn up web pages created by people who have political, religious, or philosophical stances that influence the nature of the information they present to others. Or, sometimes a person simply gets the facts wrong on a web page.

As a result, we need to help our students become healthy skeptics so that they can evaluate the nature of any information they find on the web and be confident about its reliability. Such skill has not always been necessary in classrooms where the textbook is always assumed to be correct.

There are a number of strategies used to help students become healthy skeptics, including:

- Ask students to provide at least two references for major claims they make in their written or oral reports, especially when these come from the Internet.

- Keep a bulletin board entitled "Discrepant facts: Who is right?" Encourage students to post copies of material they find containing contradictory information. These may come from the Internet or from printed material. You will be surprised how quickly students will find different spellings, different dates for events, different birth dates for famous individuals, and other information that differs between two sources.

- Discuss this issue in your Internet Workshop sessions and see if students can come up with additional strategies for evaluating the accuracy of information. Strategies might include looking to see if document references are provided, considering the reputation of the source (an individual you do not know versus a source with a commercial reputation to protect), or detecting any biases the author may display.

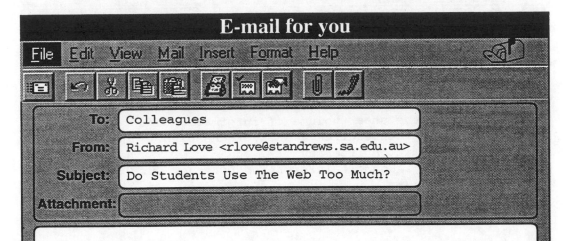

E-mail for you

File Edit View Mail Insert Format Help

To: Colleagues

From: Richard Love <rlove@standrews.sa.edu.au>

Subject: Do Students Use The Web Too Much?

Attachment:

My conversations with colleagues always help me to see things from a fresh perspective. Barbara Michaels, a Year 7 teacher at our school, and I recently had a very productive discussion about an important issue: the authentication of Web sites. Even if we KNOW that a Web site is 'reliable,' what are the issues surrounding students using this site for all of their research instead of traditional sources like our library?

One issue we discussed was WHO does the verification? If teachers do the verification and leave a list of bookmarked sites that have been verified, is that OK? Or does that mean that s/he has intentionally or non-intentionally performed some 'editing' according to his/her 'beliefs' (social, racial, political, or whatever).

Another important issue is how to evaluate the accuracy of information at a site. Students in Ms Michaels class were doing research on the solar system. One site that was bookmarked in Navigator was **The Nine Planets Tour** (http://seds.lpl.arizona.edu/billa/tnp/). Students found a wealth of information about many aspects of our solar system that resulted in debate, discussion, and a great deal of learning! This is a terrific site—well planned and clearly well resourced! But the site cannot be verified by the reputation or qualifications of the author, institutional affiliation, etc. So should it be a site that students could use? Yes—it is terrific! But how do students know that?

The issue of where to source information had been raised in a number of Curriculum Meetings at school during the development of our Information Literacy Curriculum Statement. Our current policy statement on Information Literacy, however, only provides general guidance about this issue:

Document: Continued

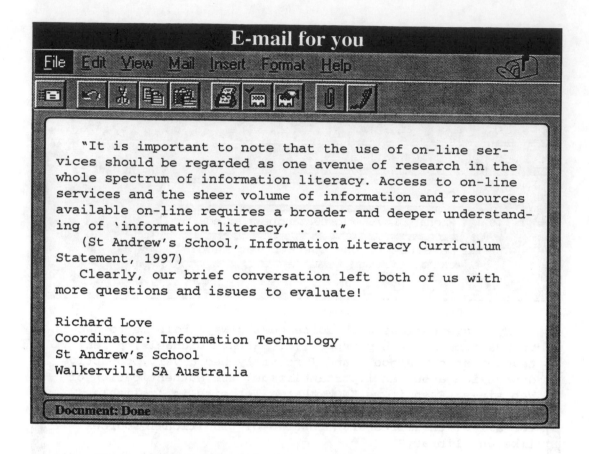

A common question many of us have these days is how to cite information resources on the Internet. The question is so new that definitive guidelines for citation style do not exist. The problem is compounded because so many different types of media sources are available on the Internet: film, video, audio clips, photographs, data bases, and many others.

The best location on the Internet for information about how to cite Internet resources may be found at the **Learning Page of the Library of Congress: Citing Electronic Sources** (http://lcweb2.loc.gov/ammem/ndlpedu/cite.html). This resource provides examples of how to cite the wide variety of media now available to our students. It also contains links to other citation style resources on the Internet. Another location containing links to many different citation guides is located at the Internet Public Library's, **Citing Electronic Resources** (http://www.ipl.org/ref/QUE/FARQ/netciteFARQ.html). A third useful location may be found at Classroom Connect's **Citing Internet Resources** (http://www.classroom.com/resource/citingnetresources.asp).

Generally, style manuals favor including the following information in a reference to Internet resources:

*The best location on the Internet for information about how to cite Internet resources may be found at the **Learning Page of the Library of Congress: Citing Electronic Sources**.*

```
Author's Last Name, Author's First Name. "Title of
Document." Title of Complete Work (if applicable).
Version or File Number, if applicable. Document date
or date of last revision (if different from access
date). Protocol and address, access path or directo-
ries (date of access).
```

For example:

```
The U.S. Library of Congress. "Learning Page of the
Library of Congress: Citing Electronic Sources." May
8, 1997. http://www.ipl.org/ref/QUE/FARQ/
netciteFARQ.html (May 1, 1998).
```

Often the order of this information will change, depending upon which manual you use. And, keep in mind these conventions are changing quickly as the Internet, it-self, changes. Regularly checking the citation manuals listed above will keep you current as these styles evolve.

Internet FAQ

How can I find out the date when a page on the Internet was last revised? Often, I like to know how recently something was created. It helps me to evaluate the accuracy of the information. Then, too, this information is usually required for a reference citation.

If you use Netscape Navigator, it is easy to find the date when a document was created or the date of its latest revision. Select "View" from the top menu bar and then select "Page info." This will open a window telling you when a page was created and when it was last revised.

Developing Independent Search Strategies While Being Sensitive to Child Safety Concerns

There is an inherent tension between child safety on the Internet and helping children to develop the independent search strategies necessary for effective Internet use. If we protect children by restricting their access to the Internet, they fail to develop comprehensive search strategies and do not learn how to use the full power of Internet resources. Many districts are beginning to resolve this tension by developing a graduated access policy; older students are provided with greater access while younger students are restricted in what they may access on the Internet. Some districts purchase commercial solutions with built-in graduated access to the Internet that may be set by teachers or administrators. Most districts are also developing acceptable use policies and requiring teacher supervision of Internet use.

It is impossible to completely protect children from viewing sites they should not see. The best policy, in the long run, is to educate children, parents, and guardians about how to use the Internet safely, develop an acceptable use policy, and

It is impossible to completely protect children from viewing sites they should not see. The best policy, in the long run, is to educate children, parents, and guardians about how to use the Internet safely, develop an acceptable use policy, and always supervise student use of the Internet.

always supervise student use of the Internet. This is your best insurance for all child safety issues.

One way that teachers often guide very young children's Internet experiences is to bookmark safe items and limit children's Internet use to these items. This makes it less likely for young students to view sites that are inappropriate for their age.

In addition, some teachers, especially in the primary grades, limit their children to certain areas in the WWW selected with attention to child safety issues. There are a few sites on the WWW that attempt to do this. None, however, are able to guarantee that children will not be able to view inappropriate sites, since links within sites change on a daily basis. Moreover, the nature of the WWW is that sites are linked to sites, which are linked to still other sites, and on and on. No area or commercial solution will guarantee the appropriateness of third level links or greater. Still, if you wish to limit the resources your students view but still allow them to develop independent search strategies, you may wish to designate certain areas as appropriate for your younger children to explore. The best site we have found that does not charge a fee is **Yahooligans** (http://www.yahooligans.com/). This is a special area with a vast set of information resources for students and a search engine that allows them to search sites approved for children's use. You may wish to make a bookmark for this location or designate it as your home page location (see Chapter 2). Another wonderful site is one developed by the American Library Association, **700+ Great Sites: Amazing, Spectacular, Mysterious, Colorful Web Sites for Kids and the Adults who Care About Them** (http://www.ala.org/parentspage/greatsites/amazing.html).

As children become older and more aware of child safety issues, you will want to allow them to view more of the Internet and to begin to use search engines for finding information they are researching for projects. After all, as students grow older, we want them to develop effective strategies for finding information efficiently. You will need to make this decision or, perhaps, it may be specified in your school's acceptable use policy.

Adapting Your Current Instructional Strategies to the Internet

*If you would like to see examples of how other teachers are using the Internet in their K-12 classrooms, be certain to visit **Spotlight on Successful Teachers**.*

Once you consider these issues, most of your current instructional practices may be easily integrated with Internet resources as you modify Internet Workshop, Internet Activity, Internet Project, or Internet Inquiry to meet your own needs. In many ways, the Internet is simply another information resource for your classroom, much like a very powerful encyclopedia. Certainly it also has special potentials, especially in the area of communicating with distant locations or with experts in the area you are studying. But, by and large, the Internet is just another information resource for your students to exploit as they engage in classroom learning activities.

If you would like to see examples of how other teachers are using the Internet in their K-12 classrooms, be certain to visit **Spotlight on Successful Teachers** (http://www.EDsOasis.org/Spotlight/Spotlight.html). This wonderful site contains great stories of how teachers have integrated the Internet into their classroom programs.

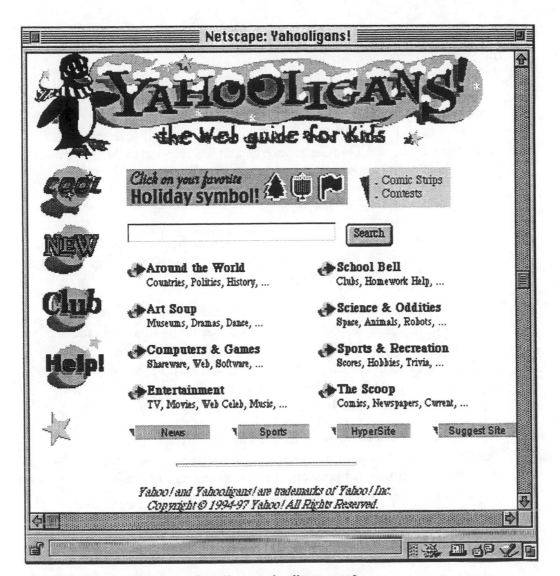

Figure 4-7. The Yahooligans Home Page on the WWW, a central site with links screened for children.

The Yahooligans Home Page (http://www.yahooligans.com/)

There are stories from teachers at all levels: elementary, middle school, and high school.

Using the Internet to Plan Instruction: Sources of Support for Teachers

As you have seen from the example with Marc Erickson, the Internet can be an important tool for planning instructional activities and units for your class. You may contact other teachers, read about projects other schools have used, find useful sites for instructional activities, collaborate with another teacher at a distant location, and read professional articles. All of these will provide important assistance as you plan for instruction. You may wish to visit some of these general resource sites as you explore ways in which the Internet may assist you with planning:

- **The Staff Room of Canada's SchoolNet—**
  (http://www.schoolnet.ca/adm/staff/)
  This is one section of a rich teaching resource, Canada's SchoolNet. The Staff Room contains links to lesson plans and teaching resources as well as other areas. This is especially nice for teachers in Canada or for teachers who wish to link up with Canadian schools, though all teachers will find these resources useful. One Canadian educator has referred to this as Canada's "crown jewel." We agree.

- **Ed's Oasis: Classroom Support for Classroom Internet Use—**
  (http://www.EDsOasis.org/)
  Here is a great new resource for teachers who wish to use the Internet in their classroom. It contains many planning and instructional resources as well as a listserv to discuss issues with other teachers.

- **Teachers Helping Teachers—**(http://www.pacificnet.net/~mandel/)
  The goals of this site include: to provide basic teaching tips to inexperienced teachers, ideas that can be immediately implemented into the classroom; to provide new ideas in teaching methodologies for all teachers; and to provide a forum for experienced teachers to share their expertise and tips with colleagues around the world. It does each very well.

- **Global SchoolNet Foundation Home Page—**(http://www.gsn.org/)
  This non-profit organization has connected teachers and students around the world in many important projects. This is an especially useful location for developing cooperative projects with other teachers.

Sometimes it is also helpful to see the lesson plans developed by other teachers for classroom projects. These sites will give you many useful ideas:

- **SCORE Cyberguides—**
  (http://www.sdcoe.k12.ca.us/score/cyberguide.html)

- **Teacher Talk Forum: Lesson Plans—**
  (http://education.indiana.edu/cas/ttforum/lesson.html)

- **Teachnet.com—**(http://www.teachnet.com/lesson.html)

Other teachers, of course, are often the best source of information, especially about Internet use in the classroom.

Finally, there are times when it is helpful to be able to talk to another teacher. Other teachers, of course, are often the best source of information, especially about Internet use in the classroom. You may wish to subscribe to any of the mailing lists at the end of each chapter in this book. Or, you may wish to visit these locations where you can read and post comments on bulletin boards or engage in chat sessions:

- **The Teacher's Network—**(http://www.teachnet.org/)
  The "Let's Talk" area at this site contains bulletin boards for teachers.

- **Teachers Helping Teachers Guestbook—**
  (http:www.pacificnet.net/~mandel/guestbook.html)
  A bulletin board with ideas posted by teachers.

- **Teachers Helping Teachers Chat Area—**
  (http://www.pacificnet.net/~mandel/ircinfo.html)
  At this location you may download Internet Relay Chat software by following directions and then participate in chat sessions with other teachers around the world.

A Final Word

Earlier we made an important point: It is not the resources available on the Internet, though these are considerable, that will make a difference for your students. Instead, your students' success at life's opportunities will be determined by what you decide to do with these resources. As you begin to incorporate the Internet into your classroom, making it an integral part of teaching and learning, you will develop new ideas and new ways of teaching. We want to encourage you to share these ideas with other teachers who are also learning about this new resource for education. Though we have no evidence, we suspect the Internet will have its greatest impact on teaching and learning through the new ideas that teachers share with one another and the new connections that are formed between teachers and students around the world. For too long, teachers have spent much of their time in school, isolated from other teachers by the walls of their classrooms. The Internet allows us to transcend these walls and learn from one another about best instructional practices. We want to encourage you to take the time to support others and to learn from others as you begin your journey to fulfill the potential the Internet provides for new ways of learning and new ways of teaching.

> *It is not the resources available on the Internet, though these are considerable, that will make a difference for your students. Instead, your students' success at life's opportunities will be determined by what you decide to do with these resources.*

Instructional Resources on the Internet

AskLN—(http://ericir.syr.edu/AskLN/)
This location, sponsored by ATT, provides an online answering service for teachers, administrators, media specialists, and anyone who is interested in using the Internet and other technologies as effective classroom tools. AskLN promises to answer any question related to Internet use in the classroom within 48 hours. Got a question? AskLN has answers!

ATT Learning Network—(http://www.att.com/learningnetwork/)
This is a nice central site for teachers with links to all kinds of valuable resources including Internet projects, acceptable use policies, classroom management, grants and funding opportunities, WWW links for teaching and learning, and much more! Set a bookmark!

Busy Teachers' Web Site—(http://www.ceismc.gatech.edu/BusyT/)
Just what it says! If you are busy, stop by. Great locations to wonderful sites organized by subject area.

Children's Literature Web Guide—(http://www.ucalgary.ca/~dkbrown/)
This is the most comprehensive location on the web for links to children and young adults' literature. A great resource for teachers and students.

Civil War Photograph Collection—(http://rs6.loc.gov/cwphome.html)
This site at the Library of Congress contains over 1,000 photographs from the Civil War, many by Mathew Brady. Viewing these images makes you feel the national conflict and struggle during this period.

Classroom Connect—(http://www.classroom.net/)
A commercial site but one of the better on-line resources for teachers. Includes the "Classroom Web" (a database of school Web sites), "Teacher Contacts" (a database of teachers online), and a great set of K-12 web sites.

Digital Dozen—(http://www.enc.org/classroom/index.htm)
Each month the 13 best sites for math and science are carefully selected by the team at the Eisenhower National Clearinghouse for Math and Science and posted here. One of the finest sites for great ideas on the web! Set a bookmark!

KidsConnect—(http://ericir.syr.edu/kidsconnect/)
If your students really like to ask challenging questions about the Internet, here is the resource for you and for them. KidsConnect is a question-answering, help and referral service for K-12 students using the Internet. The goal of the service is to help students access and use the information available on the Internet effectively and efficiently. KidsConnect is a component of ICONnect, a technology initiative from the American Association of School Librarians (AASL), a division of the American Library Association (ALA). Many students are using this service to assist with homework assignments!

Reading Online—The Electronic Classroom—
(http://www.readingonline.org/electronic/index.html)
Devoted solely to teachers, this is a section of the International Reading Association's electronic journal, *Reading Online*. In addition to great articles and a discussion forum, this site contains a wealth of resources for teachers including lists of Internet projects, useful WWW sites, and tips for technology use.

The Exploratorium—(http://www.exploratorium.edu/)
A palace of hands-on science learning in San Francisco, this site makes outstanding interactive adventures in science available to the world. A great location for science, fun, and learning.

The Nine Planets Tour—(http://seds.lpl.arizona.edu/billa/tnp/)
This is the best tour through the solar system that exists. At each stop, beautiful photographs of each planetary object are displayed along with information about the object. Short sound clips and videos are also available. Many links take you to related sites. A wonderful journey!

The United Nations Electronic Field Trip—(http://www.pbs.org/tal/un/)
It used to be that only students in New York City could take a field trip to the United Nations. No longer. Many classroom activities.

VolcanoWorld—(http://volcano.und.nodak.edu)
Study volcanoes around the world, talk to a vulcanologist, obtain real-time data on active volcanoes, and many more fun activities for kids and adults.

Listservs/Mailing Lists for Teaching with the Internet

EDsOasis—(EDsOasis@listserv.syr.edu)
A mailing list for teachers assisting teachers in using the Internet. Run in conjunction with the ED's Oasis web site. Directions for subscribing are located at http://www.EDsOasis.org/Listserv.html.

K12ADMIN—(listserv@listserv.syr.edu)
A mailing list for K-12 administrators, but the conversations focus largely on instructional issues. Over 1,000 members. The archives may be viewed at http://listserv.syr.edu/archives/k12admin.html.

RTEACHER—(listserv@listserv.syr.edu)
A mailing list devoted to conversations related to literacy education as well as the use of Internet and other technologies for literacy and learning. The educators on this list are very supportive of teachers new to the Internet. The archives may be viewed at http://listserv.syr.edu/archives/rteacher.html.

Web66—(listserv@tc.umn.edu)
The Web66 mailing list is for discussion of web use in K-12 school classrooms, primarily focused on schools that are producers of web information. Messages should be related to the web and its use in education.

5 English and the Language Arts: Opening New Doors to Literature and Literacy

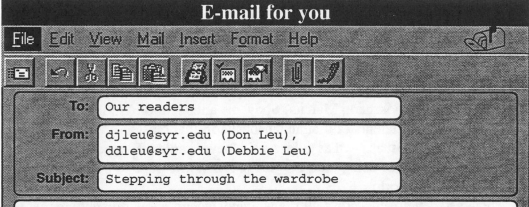

E-mail for you

File Edit View Mail Insert Format Help

To: Our readers

From: djleu@syr.edu (Don Leu),
ddleu@syr.edu (Debbie Leu)

Subject: Stepping through the wardrobe

In <u>The Chronicles of Narnia</u>, C. S. Lewis leads us through the secret door of a wardrobe, opening a magical world full of exciting, new opportunities. We believe the Internet is another door, opening new worlds for you and your students with many wonderful opportunities for literature and literacy.

The Internet enhances your English/Language Arts curriculum in many ways, providing richer, more meaningful, and more authentic literacy experiences. Your students can participate in global book clubs, communicate by e-mail with a favorite author, read reviews of books posted by students from around the world, participate in an electronic discussion about Shakespeare and other authors, quickly search on-line versions of Barlett's Quotations or Roget's Thesaurus, or engage in other wonderful experiences as you open new doors to literature and literacy.

In the first edition we noted our preference for literary experiences with real books over on-line books. While changes on the Internet have been dramatic in the past year, imagining worlds through a good book still contains richer potentials for evocative, critical, and emotional response than any current story on the Internet. Our preferences may change sooner than we expected, however. Who can tell what new literary experiences will be developed in the years ahead? Clearly, the English/Language Arts curriculum is being profoundly enhanced by the new worlds of literature, response, and literacy the Internet opens for all of us.

Don and Debbie

Document: Done

Teaching with the Internet: Alicia Meyer's Class

"I did a search for pourquoi stories like we're reading and I found a cool site!"

It was Monday morning and Marcus was participating in Internet Workshop with the rest of his sixth grade class. "Our group has Asia and Australia and I found this school. I made a bookmark. It's called the Fahan School and they made a page with all kinds of creation stories from different cultures and they had other kids e-mail them from where they were in the world . . . like from Japan, and Indonesia, and Amsterdam. Ms. Meyer, could we do that, too? You know, ask people to send us their pourquoi tales? Then we could do the same thing . . . write them on our class home page so other kids could read them."

"Yeah. Cool!" A chorus of thoughts emerged from the class.

"Did you set a bookmark, Marcus? Show me after school. We'll see."

"Yes!" several students said simultaneously. In this class, a "We'll see" from Ms. Meyer was almost as good as gold. Alicia Meyer smiled. Everyone was excited about the possibility of using their new classroom home page to post stories from other places in the world.

Alicia had developed a cross-curricular thematic unit about diversity for her 6th grade class. Her goal was to increase students' appreciation for diversity as they studied math, science, social studies, reading, writing, speaking, and listening. In math, she planned experiences for students to explore number systems from several ancient civilizations, including a study of systems using bases other than 10. In science, she was going to use the unit on biodiversity she had developed in a summer workshop at the university last year. In social studies, she developed experiences for students to better understand the cultures of both Native Americans and immigrants. Finally, in language arts, she was planning experiences around "pourquoi tales," creation myths that exist in every traditional culture. Pourquoi tales explain sources of natural phenomena such as how people obtained fire, why mosquitoes buzz in people's ears, where the moon came from, or why rivers run into the ocean.

She introduced the concept of a pourquoi tale at the beginning of the unit by engaging the class in read aloud response journal activities (Leu & Kinzer, 1998) with several examples, including *The Fire Bringer* by Margaret Hodges and *Star Boy* by Paul Goble. Then she had students work in one of three literature discussion groups. Each group had a large set of pourquoi tales to read. One group read and discussed tales from the Americas, another read tales from Asia and Australia, and a third read tales from Africa, Europe, and the Middle East. She used book club activities suggested by McMahon, Raphael, Goatley, & Pardo (1997), text set activities suggested by Short (1993), and response journal activities suggested by Hynds (1997).

Alicia Meyer gave each group this assignment: "Make a class presentation on at least one culture using only the information in the pourquoi tales for your region. Infer aspects of that culture from the stories you read, indicating what you inferred and the evidence supporting your inferences."

Pourquoi tales explain sources of natural phenomena such as how people obtained fire, why mosquitoes buzz in people's ears, where the moon came from, or why rivers run into the ocean.

Individuals chose different books to read and then members of each group got together twice a week to share their literary experiences in a student-led discussion organized around a "grand conversation" (McGee & Richgels, 1990). During each grand conversation, members of each group discussed the pourquoi tales they were reading and what each suggested about the cultures they were studying. They also made plans for their class presentation.

After school, Marcus showed Ms. Meyer the location at the **Fahan School's homepage** in Tasmania (http://anfi.pacit.tas.gov.au/fahan/stories.html). He also showed her another site, **Tales of Traditional Wisdom** (http://www.reedbooks.com.au/heinemann/global/mythstor.html), with a similar collection of stories from around the world contributed by students. These were nice models. It seemed like a great opportunity to develop a better understanding of different cultures by communicating and sharing stories with students around the world.

Then, with a telling gleam in his eyes, Marcus showed Ms. Meyer the home page for **Ms. Hos-McGrane's 5th-6th grade class at The International School of Amsterdam** (http://www.xs4all.nl/~swanson/origins/intro.html). Marcus knew Ms. Meyer's ancestors came from the Netherlands and he had saved this Internet location for last. He took her to the wonderful project this class had completed: **Creation Stories and Myths** (http://www.xs4all.nl/~swanson/origins/cstorymenu.html). As Marcus showed Ms. Meyer the extensive set of resources from around the world this class had located, he knew she would give them the green light for Internet Project.

"Marcus," she said. "You certainly know how to convince me. This is wonderful! Head on home now and let me do some work."

Alicia took the mouse from Marcus's hand and started thinking. She had to do some quick planning. She visited **NickNacks: How to Telecollaborate** (http://www1.minn.net:80/~schubert/NNglobal.html), a site with information about Internet Projects she recalled seeing posted on the RTEACHER listserv. Here, she reviewed how to develop collaborative projects on the Internet. She quickly linked to a number of useful resources that told her exactly how to set up a project, announce it to others, and post her announcement. In just a few minutes, she had posted an announcement at a number of different locations asking teachers and students from around the world to contribute pourquoi tales from their cultures. By exchanging stories, they would each develop a deeper appreciation for differences and for important aspects of other cultures. She posted her project description at four different locations, explaining the project and asking for other classes to join her class:

- **Classroom Connect's Teacher Contact Database—** (http://www.classroom.net/contact/)

- **The Global Schoolhouse Projects Registry—** (http://www.gsh.org/gsh/class/projsrch.htm)

- **Intercultural E-mail Classroom Connections—** (http://www.stolaf.edu/network/iecc/)

Figure 5-1.
The page with creation stories (pourquoi tales) created by Ms. Hos-McGrane's class at the International School in Amsterdam.

Ms. Hos-McGrane's class (http://www.xs4all.nl/~swanson/origins/cstorymenu.html)

- **Kidproject—**
  (http://www.kidlink.org:80/KIDPROJ/)

She also joined the **NCTE-talk** mailing list for English educators (majordomo@serv1.ncte.org) and the **KIDLIT-L** mailing list for educators interested in children's literature (listserv@bingvmb.bitnet). She posted a description of her project on both mailing lists, inviting other classrooms to join in her collaborative project.

By the end of the week, Alicia had received messages from eight different schools from around the world: Darwin, Australia; Bristol, England; Haifa, Israel; Kyoto, Japan; Newburgh, New York; Dublin, California; Rapid City, South Dakota; Beaumont, Texas; and Clearwater, Florida. Each had promised to collect traditional myths from cultures in or near their location and share these in two weeks via e-mail with all of the collaborating classrooms.

As Alicia announced the results of her work to the class during Internet Workshop, everyone was full of new ideas. Each group, they decided, would work with schools from their part of the world: the Asia and Australia group would coordinate work with the schools in Darwin and Kyoto; the Americas group would work with schools in the United States; and the Europe, Middle East, and Africa group would work with schools in Bristol and Haifa. Also, each group now had a new assignment, to uncover explanatory myths from cultures in their own community so that they could share these with their partner schools on this project. This would take some work interviewing parents and relatives to see what they could find. Then they would draft versions of these stories and work to revise them. Finally, they would polish off the final version using an editing conference with peers in class before sending it to their partner schools. The class was humming with excitement as each group set to work.

Lessons from the Classroom

There are at least four important lessons we can learn from this experience in Alicia Meyer's class. First, this story illustrates how important it is to learn from one another about the Internet. Marcus showed Alicia new ideas for Internet use and, as Alicia visited several classroom home pages, she discovered wonderful models for Internet use from other teachers. Alicia also relied on colleagues from the RTEACHER, NCTE-talk, and KIDLIT-L mailing lists to help develop her project. And, the collaborative relationships her class formed with other classrooms also led to many new ideas. Clearly, we depend upon others as we discover the many possibilities the Internet provides.

Second, the story of Alicia's classroom illustrates how Internet Project may be used to integrate the language arts and other subject areas into your classroom curriculum. By creating this project and connecting with other classrooms, Alicia supported her students in all of the language arts: reading, writing, speaking, listening, and viewing. Students learned much about language use as they gathered pourquoi tales, developed and refined their drafts, debated the correct punctuation, checked on the correct spelling, or reconsidered the correct way to begin or end their stories. These were important learning opportunities in the language arts. Her students also discovered new cultural experiences through Internet Project. These cross-cultural insights connected immediately with her activities in social studies and science. Internet Project provides exceptional possibilities for cross curricular integration and multicultural understanding.

This story also illustrates a third lesson: The Internet provides wonderfully authentic opportunities for supporting literacy learning by connecting reading and writing. The Internet provides natural opportunities for your students to communicate in writing about their work and to read the responses of others. This has many important benefits for your students.

Reading and writing are similar processes. They have been compared by various authors as the two wings of the same bird or two sides of the same coin. In busy classrooms, we need to seek ways in which to combine subject areas that have tradi-

The story of Alicia's classroom illustrates how Internet Project may be used to integrate the language arts and other subject areas into your classroom curriculum.

The Internet provides wonderfully authentic opportunities for supporting literacy learning by connecting reading and writing.

tionally been viewed as separate and that benefit from being combined. This is possible when we connect reading and writing with the Internet.

After she announced the project, Alicia's class read and wrote as they had never done before. Students worked hard in the ensuing weeks to gather explanatory myths from the Vietnamese, Cambodian, African American, Italian, Iroquois, and Chinese cultures in their own community. They wanted very much to have good stories to share with these classes in distant places. Not only did students read more because of this experience, but they read better because their interest was so high and they were supported by members of their literature discussion group. In addition, important new writing opportunities opened up as students collected stories from their community and carefully drafted, revised, and edited these before sending them to other schools. And, as students shared the stories they found, one often saw students helping other students read them together. The Internet can be an important tool for supporting literacy learning by connecting reading and writing.

Finally, this story also illustrates a fourth lesson: While the Internet contains many original works of literature for students to read, it is especially useful to enrich the literary experiences of students as they read books away from the computer. Immediately after Alicia announced the project, each group independently decided to search for pourquoi tales from their group's part of the world. While some of these were gathered from the Internet, many more were discovered in the school library. Virginia Hamilton's *In the Beginning: Creation Stories from Around the World* was a favorite. As one student said, "We want to be ready when we start to get our stories from Japan and Australia." As students brought their stories back to each group, many discussions took place as they shared ideas about each culture. These experiences enriched the literary potential of the initial assignment by taking students beyond their set of books and into their local community, their library, and even the rest of the world through the Internet. Many opportunities to enrich children's literary experiences may be developed by integrating the Internet into classroom instruction.

Many opportunities to enrich children's literary experiences may be developed by integrating the Internet into classroom instruction.

Internet FAQ

Sometimes I try to reach a location on the WWW and I get an error message. It says that the server is not accepting connections or that the server may be busy. What should I do?

This usually is caused by one of two conditions. First, the computer where this site is located may be down for servicing. Second, too many people may be trying to get into the server at the same time, something that occasionally happens with popular educational sites during the school day. A strategy we use is to try to contact the same location three times before we give up on a busy server. Sometimes we can sneak in, even if many people are trying to reach this location at the same time. Move your cursor to the end of the address in the location bar, click, and then press your return key. Your browser will try again to connect to this location. If, after three tries, we still cannot get in, we usually give up and try again later.

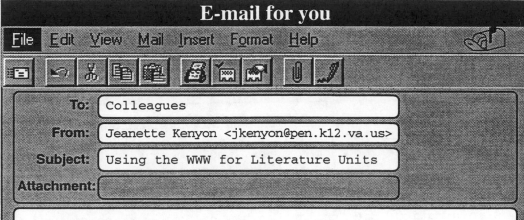

E-mail for you

File   Edit   View   Mail   Insert   Format   Help

To: Colleagues

From: Jeanette Kenyon <jkenyon@pen.k12.va.us>

Subject: Using the WWW for Literature Units

Attachment:

Dear Colleagues,

My class uses the Internet frequently to enhance various literature units. During our studies of Stuart Little by E.B.White, and From the Mixed Up Files of Mrs. Basil E. Frankweiler by Elaine Konigsburg, we located several valuable resources. We also used excellent links about Central Park to locate and research places mentioned in both books. For example, the class was able to view the lake where Stuart entered a boat race as well as tour the Metropolitan Museum of Art, where Claudia and Jamie's adventures took place. Using an enlarged map from the Central Park site, we created a bulletin board highlighting pertinent landmarks from each story. At the suggestion of several students, we even posted a quiz question on our Home Page where visitors can try to locate Claudia and Jamie using map skills with the Central Park map. Useful links:

    http://www.panix.com/clay/nyc/maps.shtml
    http://www.metmuseum.org/
    http://www.centralpark.org/~park/
    http://www.ctnba.org/CTN/mixed/basil.htm

The Narnia Series by C. S. Lewis led us to many interesting sites. Several students concluded the unit by creating a newspaper from Narnia (The Narnia Times) which is also posted on our Home Page. We received encouraging e-mail from a fellow C. S. Lewis fan, who hosts one of our favorite Narnia sites (see below for link). Useful links:

    http://www.iserv.net/~dorcasb/narnia.htm
    http://ernie.bgsu.edu/~croy/askaslan.html
    http://cslewis.drzeus.net

Don't overlook the wealth of original literature available on the Internet. I have downloaded all of

Document: Continued

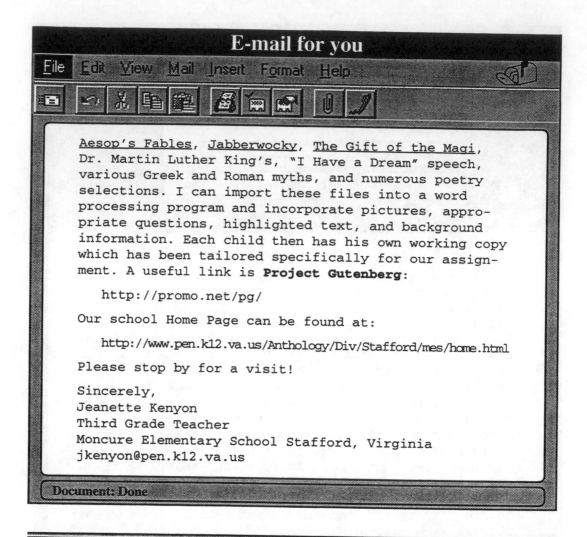

Aesop's Fables, Jabberwocky, The Gift of the Magi, Dr. Martin Luther King's, "I Have a Dream" speech, various Greek and Roman myths, and numerous poetry selections. I can import these files into a word processing program and incorporate pictures, appropriate questions, highlighted text, and background information. Each child then has his own working copy which has been tailored specifically for our assignment. A useful link is **Project Gutenberg**:

http://promo.net/pg/

Our school Home Page can be found at:

http://www.pen.k12.va.us/Anthology/Div/Stafford/mes/home.html

Please stop by for a visit!

Sincerely,
Jeanette Kenyon
Third Grade Teacher
Moncure Elementary School Stafford, Virginia
jkenyon@pen.k12.va.us

Document: Done

Central Sites for Literature

The best single location we know for young adult and children's literature is The Children's Literature Web Guide.

The best single location we know for young adult and children's literature is a site maintained by David Brown, a librarian at the University of Calgary. **The Children's Literature Web Guide** (http://www.ucalgary.ca/~dkbrown/index.html) contains a comprehensive and organized array of links to literature resources. The types of resources on this page are too exhaustive to list but they include everything from on-line works of literature, resources for teachers, locations about movies developed from literature, resources for parents, resources for storytellers, resources for writers and illustrators, discussion groups about literature, lists of award winners, and information about authors.

Resources at this location are designed to enrich your students' literary experiences without taking them away from books. As the developer of this site indicates, "If my cunning plan works, you will find yourself tempted away from the Internet, and back to the books themselves!" If you are serious about literature in your classroom, you should explore this site, set a bookmark, and incorporate its many resources into classroom learning projects.

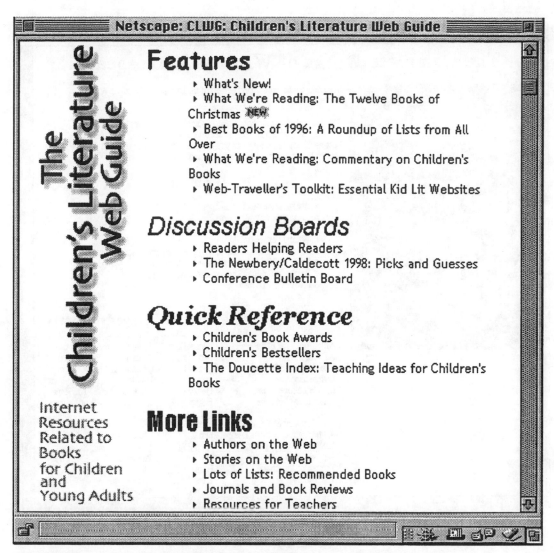

The **Children's Literature Web Guide** (http://www.ucalgary.ca/~dkbrown/index.html)

If you have an interest in Shakespeare, a marvelous central site has been developed for your classroom needs at MIT, **The Complete Works of Shakespeare** (http://the-tech.mit.edu/Shakespeare/works.html). This amazing resource contains all of the works of Shakespeare, an electronic glossary for locating the meanings of archaic terms, discussion groups where your students can ask questions and share ideas, and much, much more. Be certain to pay a visit and explore this location. There are many opportunities for classroom activities to bring Shakespeare alive for your students.

Is your class reading specific works of literature and you need some quick ideas for Internet integration, perhaps even some ready-to-go Internet activities? Be certain to visit another central site for literature: **Cyberguides: Teacher Guides and Student Activities** (http://www.sdcoe.k12.ca.us/score/cyberguide.html). This wonderful location, being developed by Don Mayfield and Linda Taggart-Fregoso in

Cyberguides: Teacher Guides and Student Activities is the best location we have found for the immediate integration of exceptional works of literature into your classroom program.

Figure 5-2.
The homepage for **The Children's Literature Web Guide,** a central site for literature.

Figure 5-3.
The homepage
for **The
Complete
Works of
Shakespeare**,
a central
site for
Shakespeare.

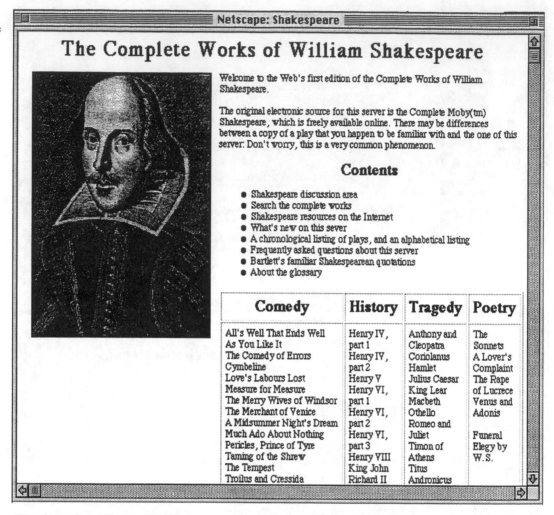

The Complete Works of Shakespeare (http://the-tech.mit.edu/Shakespeare/works.html)

San Diego, is the best location we have found for the immediate integration of exceptional works of literature into your classroom program. The site contains an extensive list of literary works, each containing classroom-tested lessons, activities, and evaluation strategies developed by teachers. Literature selections at Cyberguides are nicely organized by grade level appropriateness (K-12). This is one resource every K-12 teacher should thoroughly explore and use in the classroom. Set a bookmark today! And don't forget to drop an e-mail message to Don Mayfield and Linda Taggart-Fregoso, telling them what wonderful work they are accomplishing for all of us.

While we tend to prefer real books for most literary experiences in a classroom, it is often useful to read other works on the Internet related to ones you use in class.

In addition to these locations, there are many central sites containing on-line works of literature for your classroom. While we tend to prefer real books for most literary experiences, it is often useful to read other works on the Internet, especially if they are related to others you use in class. It is especially nice to know that any work you find on-line may be printed out so that students may read it in the class or take it home to share with their family and friends. There are several types of on-line literature collections: older classics with expired copyrights, traditional tales, and works of literature written by children.

TEACHING TIP

Amazon.com (http://amazon.com/) is a commercial bookstore on the WWW containing over a million titles. One feature of this site is the opportunity it provides to submit a review of any book you have read and quickly see it posted. As students complete independent reading projects, invite them to write a review. Have them read the initial draft of their review during Internet Workshop and seek suggestions for revision. After the review has been revised, help students to use the search engine at Amazon.com to locate their book. Then, have them post their review at this location.

You will find many older classics with expired copyrights on the Internet. Because their copyright has expired, these works may now be published by anyone. This allows them to be posted on the web without violating copyright law. Older classics often are used by teachers to provide additional literary experiences for students who have read one work by an author and are interested in reading more, especially when your library's holdings are a bit thin. The problem with these classics is that they usually appear in a text-only form without illustrations. This sometimes takes away from the literary experience. Some of the best locations for classic works of literature include:

- **Project Gutenberg**—(http://promo.net/pg/)
  This voluntary project has a goal of providing one trillion works of literature to users by December 31, 2001. Here you will find the complete texts of many classic works by authors such as Louisa May Alcott, Jane Austen, Aesop, O. Henry, Victor Hugo, Charles Dickens, and many others. Set a bookmark!

- **Lewis Carroll Home Page Illustrated**—
  (http://www.cstone.net/library/alice/carroll.html)
  The major works of Lewis Carroll are located here, including: *Alice's Adventures in Wonderland, Through the Looking Glass,* and *The Hunting of the Snark.* Each contains color illustrations.

- **Classics for Young Children**—
  (http://www.ucalgary.ca/~dkbrown/storclas.html)
  A comprehensive set of links to classic works, some of which are illustrated. These include *Little Women, The Call of the Wild, The Wonderful Wizard of Oz, The Wind in the Willows, Rip Van Winkle, The Gift of the Magi, Anne of Green Gables,* and many, many others.

Traditional tales are another form of on-line literature. These include folktales, fairytales, myths, and legends. Because so many were published some time ago and their original copyrights are out of date, many are now in the public domain and available on-line. Usually these exist in text-only versions. Occasionally, you will find illustrated versions.

Because traditional tales come from an oral tradition, there are many different versions for most stories. The richness of the web allows us to share multiple versions of the same story with students. This leads to wonderful opportunities for critical analysis as students evaluate how the versions differ, consider the types of response each provokes in readers, or determine what characterizes a "typical" traditional tale. Some of the best central sites for traditional tales include:

- **The Encyclopedia Mythica**—(http://www.pantheon.org/mythica/)
  This is an encyclopedia devoted to myths, folklore, and legends. An outstanding place to begin research in this area.

- **Tales of Wonder**—(http://darsie.ucdavis.edu/tales/)
  This is an extensive archive of folk and fairy tales from around the world— a must for any cross-cultural unit or for a unit on this genre. Set a bookmark!

- **The Little Red Riding Hood Project**—
  (http://www-dept.usm.edu/~engdept/lrrh/lrrhhome.htm)
  This site contains 16 different versions of this tale from 17th–19th century Europe. It is a nice site for comparative projects. It includes original illustrations.

- **Folklore, Myth and Legend**—
  (http://www.ucalgary.ca/~dkbrown/storfolk.html)
  A comprehensive site with many useful links to sources of information and copies of traditional tales.

Other central sites for literature contain children's voices, literature written by children. These sites are great to motivate the writers in your class.

Other central sites for literature contain children's voices, literature written by children. These sites are great to motivate the writers in your class and show them what is possible. Some of these locations include:

- **Cyberkids**—(http://www.cyberkids.com/)
  This is a quarterly on-line magazine written by kids for kids ages 7–11. It includes articles and stories by young writers.

- **KidPub**—(http://en-garde.com/kidpub/intro.html)
  A wonderful collection of more than 17,000 stories written by children and maintained by a father in Massachusetts who wanted a place for his daughter to publish her work. Many great stories here.

- **Parents and Children On-line**—
  (http://www.indiana.edu/~eric_rec/fl/pcto/menu.html)
  Sponsored by ERIC, this regular magazine contains materials written by children and is intended to support family reading at home.

Internet FAQ

I have heard that some locations have authors reading their works aloud over the Internet? How does this work? How can I get my computer to do this?

New technologies for multimedia continue to appear on the Internet. Sound and video technologies are ones that are changing especially rapidly. Some locations on the WWW are beginning to take advantage of these technologies. **Children's Voice** (http://schoolnet2.carleton.ca/english/arts/lit/c-voice/zine4.html), for example, invites your students to submit work for publication. Your students can read some wonderful writing at this location. Best of all, you may even listen as some of the authors read their stories with RealAudio technology, a special treat. RealPlayer plug-ins (containing RealAudio and RealVideo) can be added to your Internet browser (Windows or Mac / Netscape or Internet Explorer) for free at the **RealAudio** web site (http://www.real.com/products/player/index.html).

Reading a great story is one of the better experiences we can provide students. Often, though, our students' experience with a story is limited by knowing little about the author. We can provide richer literary experiences by sharing information about the person who wrote their book. This helps to contextualize the literary work and provides important information to children about why an author wrote a story, what experience in their life prompted the story, how they write, other books the author has written, and issues the author often writes about. Knowing this information enriches children's literary experiences. There are many sites on the web that will provide your students with this information. You may, of course, use one of the search engines to locate information about authors. Some of the sites we value include:

- **Ask the Author**—(http://www.ipl.org/youth/AskAuthor/)
  This location of the Internet Public Library contains information about a number of popular authors including Lois Lowry, Avi, Matt Christopher, Natalie Babbitt, Daniel Pinkwater, Jane Yolen, Gary Paulson, Charlotte Zolotow, and others. Photos of the authors, a biography, and answers to questions submitted by kids are available.

- **Into the Wardrobe: The C.S. Lewis WWW Site**—(http://cslewis.cache.net/)
  This is the best author site around. Many rich resources including a biography, an album of photographs, recordings of the author's voice, many links to other Lewis sites, a listserv address, a usenet address, and even a live chat location.

- **The L.M. Montgomery Institute**—
  (http://www.upei.ca/~lmmi/core.html)
  The official institute's site for Lucy Maud Montgomery, the author of *Anne of Green Gables* and other works. The location includes information about her life, additional links to related sites, information for subscribing to a listserv about her books, and sites on Prince Edward Island, her home.

- **My Little House on the Prairie Home Page—**
  (http://www.pinc.com/njenslegg/)

  This site contains much useful information about the author of the "Little House" series. Historical information about the characters and the locations where they lived is provided. The site also has a useful link for teachers that will take you to plans for instructional units about this author and her work.

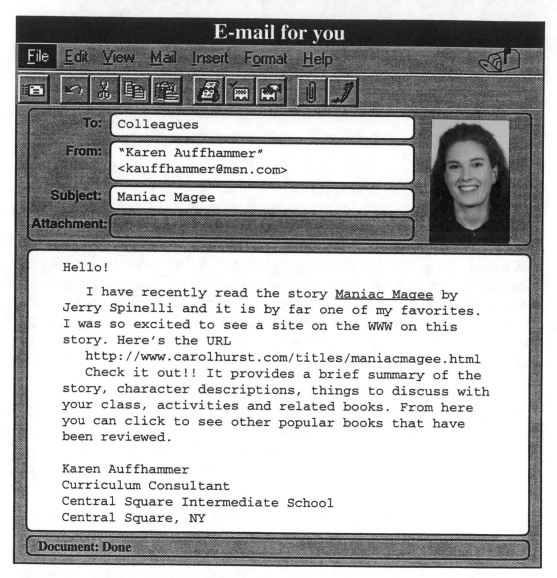

E-mail for you

File   Edit   View   Mail   Insert   Format   Help

To:	Colleagues
From:	"Karen Auffhammer" <kauffhammer@msn.com>
Subject:	Maniac Magee
Attachment:	

Hello!

    I have recently read the story <u>Maniac Magee</u> by Jerry Spinelli and it is by far one of my favorites. I was so excited to see a site on the WWW on this story. Here's the URL
    http://www.carolhurst.com/titles/maniacmagee.html
    Check it out!! It provides a brief summary of the story, character descriptions, things to discuss with your class, activities and related books. From here you can click to see other popular books that have been reviewed.

Karen Auffhammer
Curriculum Consultant
Central Square Intermediate School
Central Square, NY

Document: Done

The Internet also opens new doors to authentic writing experiences as students communicate with other writers from around the world.

Central Sites for Writing

The Internet also opens new doors to authentic writing experiences as students communicate with other writers from around the world. Students may correspond with experts about their writing, publish their work and invite comments from others, read responses to their writing, and write messages back to others. These opportunities make the Internet a wonderful resource to support student writing at all levels. There are two types of central sites in writing: those that provide a wide range of support for student writers and those that provide opportunities for students to publish their work.

Locations on the Internet That Support Young Writers

There are a number of central sites on the Internet for young writers. These locations are often important sources of support for students who are serious about their writing. Explore these locations, set a bookmark, and invite your students to take advantage of the many resources at each location.

- **Inkspot**—(http://www.inkspot.com/)
  Arguably the best location to support aspiring writers with many types of help, including words of advice from authors and editors, interviews with young writers, and a Young Writers' Forum. At the Young Writers' Forum, students can network other writers and exchange ideas.

- **For Young Writers**—(http://www.inkspot.com/young/)
  Another Inkspot location containing a rich array of sites on the WWW to support young writers.

- **The Quill Society**—(http://www.quill.net/)
  Looking for a central site for your secondary English class? Here it is. The Quill Society consists of young writers from around the world who enjoy creative expression and wish to learn from one another. This site includes a message board for discussions between young writers, a place to publish your work, a board of critics who will respond to your work with helpful suggestions, and a fun activities area. A great location for your writers!

Publishing Student Work on the Internet

The Internet provides new and exciting opportunities to publish your students' work. You may publish student work on a classroom homepage (see Chapter 12). You may also publish student work at many locations on the Internet devoted specially to this purpose. You can take advantage of these locations to engage students in comprehensive writing process activities that include prewriting, drafting, revision, editing, and publishing. When a student's work is prepared, think about submitting it to one of these locations:

- **The Book Nook**—(http://i-site.on.ca/booknook.html)
  This outstanding location provides a location for students to publish reviews of books they have read. All reviews are published. Students will find examples of reviews organized by grade level and genre. They also are given guidelines for developing their review as well as a list of books in need of reviews in a "Lonely Book Club." An excellent site that deserves a permanent bookmark on your computer.

Looking for a central site for your secondary English class? Here it is. The Quill Society consists of young writers from around the world who enjoy creative expression and wish to learn from one another.

The Internet provides new and exciting opportunities to publish your students' work.

- **Cyberkids**—(http://www.cyberkids.com/)
  This is a magazine for kids. Each year, the magazine invites submissions for writing, art, and musical compositions from students, ages 7–11, for a contest. After a preliminary screening, readers then vote for the winners, which are published. A great location for free reading time. Set a bookmark!

- **KidPub**—(http://en-garde.com/kidpub/intro.html)
  All work is published at KidPub, a publishing location for kids maintained by a parent in Massachusetts. Directions for submissions are provided. Students can even see how many people have read their work. Set a bookmark!

Keeping It Simple: Using Internet Activity with Internet Workshop

There are as many good ideas for enriching literary experiences with the Internet as there are creative teachers with a few moments to plan a new Internet Activity and weave it into a session of Internet Workshop.

There are as many good ideas for enriching literary experiences with the Internet as there are creative teachers with a few moments to plan a new Internet Activity and weave it into a session of Internet Workshop. We cannot be exhaustive here. We can, however, provide some examples that might serve to inspire you to think of your own creative ideas for developing Internet activities.

- **Julius Caesar Unit**—Take advantage of the activities developed at **Cyberguides** (http://www.sdcoe.k12.ca.us/score/cyberguide.html) to add to your unit on Shakespeare's *Julius Caesar*. This site contains resources and directions to help students complete four compositions about this classic work: an opinion/comparison-contrast essay, an expository essay, a statement of opinion, and an argumentative essay. Use Internet Workshop to share works in progress as well as completed works. This will prompt conversations about the play and about students' different interpretations of character, plot, and theme.

- **Cinderella Studies**—Engage your class in a study of Cinderella tales from around the world. Nearly every culture has its own version of this classic tale. Compare and contrast different versions to infer what these differences might suggest about the culture associated with each story. Begin with beautifully illustrated versions from your library such as *Mufaro's Beautiful Daughters* by John Steptoe. Then have students explore the web for other versions. They may wish to start at the **Cinderella Project** (http://www-dept.usm.edu/~engdept/cinderella/cinderella.html) and **Cinderella Stories** (http://www.ucalgary.ca/~dkbrown/cinderella.html). Then have students begin exploring the web using various search engines for even more versions. A great activity for combining web use and literature in very effective ways.

- **Studying Indigenous Peoples' Literature**—If you engage students in a project studying Native Americans or other indigenous peoples, be certain to set a bookmark for **Indigenous Peoples' Literature** (http://www.indians.org/welker/framenat.htm), an outstanding site developed by George Walker, or **Native American Indian Resources** (http://indy4.fdl.cc.mn.us/~isk/mainmenu.html), another site rich in informational resources. Have students explore these sites to find out information about the culture behind each of the books they read. Have them share the information they find during Internet Workshop.

- **This Door Leads to the Internet**—Cover the outside of your classroom door with butcher paper, or another type of large paper. Have a group of students design a book cover on this paper entitled "This Door Leads to the Internet." At the same time, set bookmarks to locations with collections of stories on the Internet such as **Contemporary Writing for Children and Young Adults** (http://www.ucalgary.ca/~dkbrown/storcont.html). Have students read a story that is interesting to them during their time on the computer and then print it out. Then have students sit in a "reader's chair" at the front of the room and share their favorite selection with the class. As they finish, post the printed version of their story on the bookcover door students have designed.

- **Jan Brett's Stories**—If you and your class are reading one of many excellent stories by Jan Brett, invite students to visit the **Jan Brett Home Page** (http://www.janbrett.com/) and then share what they have discovered during Internet workshop. A similar activity could be done with any author page. This is especially useful to build background knowledge about the author and his/her works.

Using Internet Project and Internet Workshop to Integrate the Language Arts

Traditionally, classrooms organize learning around separate subject areas. Recently, many teachers have explored an alternative, taking a thematic approach to organize learning. Some teachers are now beginning to take a third approach as they seek to capitalize on the learning opportunities available on the Internet. These teachers organize learning experiences around collaborative, Internet projects with other classrooms around the world. This can be a very powerful way to develop learning experiences for your students. Project-based learning experiences are especially useful to integrate the language arts; students naturally engage in reading, writing, speaking, listening, and viewing experiences during the course of a project. One sees in these classrooms a rich interplay between content learning and English/language arts activities, often combining Internet experiences with more familiar method frame-

Some teachers organize learning experiences around collaborative, Internet projects with other classrooms around the world.

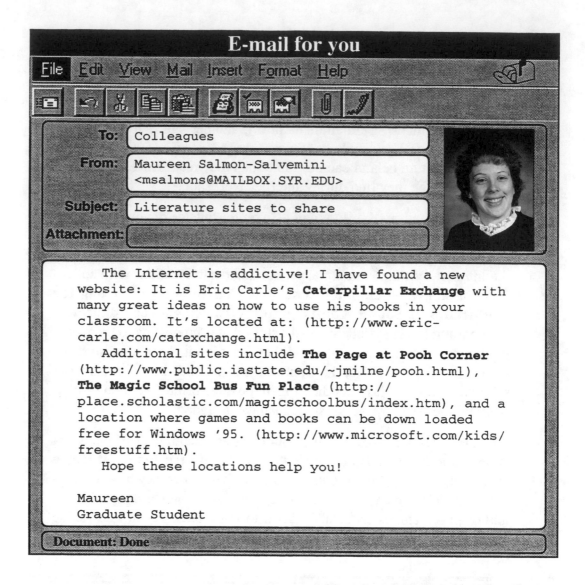

works including: cooperative group learning, response journals, readers' theater, process writing, inquiry projects, and other highly effective techniques.

Examples of Internet projects that emphasize the language arts include:

- **The Toni Morrison Book Club.**   Students from several schools read works by this exceptional author and share their responses and web resources to discover more information about her work and her life. Works are read in a certain order and weekly responses are exchanged by e-mail and posted at one English classroom's home page. Internet Workshop is used to share responses and plan new responses with collaborating classrooms.

- **Presidential Election.**   In this election research and balloting project, students research the presidential candidates in the United States, write and publish editorials at a central location to convince voters, and then conduct a mock election at school sites around the country. The results are displayed by school and state so that students can analyze voting patterns. Internet Workshop is used to coordinate much of the planning for this work as well as to discuss the results and their meanings. Math, social studies, and language arts are integrated within this learning unit.

- **Paddington Bear Travels the World.** This project sends a stuffed Paddington Bear to primary grade classrooms around the world. When Paddington arrives, he has to keep a journal describing his adventures, the cultures he visits, the sights he sees, and the students he meets. His travel journal is published at the home page of the school that first sent him on his journey and continuously updated by the classroom he is currently visiting. Other students write to him and ask him questions, which are answered by the class where he is at any point in time. Other activities such as calculating mileage and locating Paddington on the map are also used. Classrooms use Internet Workshop to coordinate the work and to share correspondence. This project integrates social studies, science, math, and language arts.

- **K-1 Students Request Postcards.** This project requests that postcards from classes around the world be sent to a K-1 class in Georgia to help them develop a better understanding of locations around the world. The postcards are read in class during Internet Workshop to initiate discussion about geographical locations and then they are fastened to a map of the world next to the country they came from. Students answer each postcard with another postcard from their area as well as with an e-mail message. This project is used to initiate contact with other classrooms for future projects.

The special advantage of Internet Project is its potential to create very powerful learning opportunities, especially in English and language arts. Communicating with students in other locations motivates your students in ways you probably have not seen in your classroom and opens the door to important cross-cultural understandings. Done correctly, Internet Project can be the cornerstone of your English/language arts program.

Done correctly, collaborative Internet projects can be the cornerstone of your English/ language arts program.

How do you get started? You may wish to visit several locations where teachers register collaborative projects for other teachers to find. Reading about other projects will give you ideas for your own Internet project. These sites were listed in Chapter 4.

Initially, you may wish to join someone else's project. After several experiences, though, you could develop your own project, post it, and see if you can get other classrooms to join you. For example, you may wish to adapt literature discussion groups to the Internet. Post the works of literature your students will be reading to see if other classes would be interested in reading the same work(s) and exchanging responses. Comparing responses to literature on the Internet will provide many opportunities to integrate the language arts.

TEACHING TIP

If you are interested in using Internet Project in your classroom but anxious about how to get started, simply join one of the mailing lists listed at the end of this chapter devoted to English and the language arts. Then, post a message asking others to share their experiences with this approach. Ask for suggestions that would be helpful to a person who is first attempting Internet Project. You will receive many great ideas from your colleagues. Others, too, will benefit from the suggestions colleagues share on the mailing list in response to your question.

A wonderful example of an Internet project using literature appeared this past year on several mailing lists, inviting classrooms to participate: "Looney Lobsters Love Regional Literature." This outstanding Internet project was developed by Marjorie Duby, a 5th grade teacher at the Joseph Lee Elementary School in Boston, Massachusetts. Her project description is one of the best we have seen so we wanted to be certain to share it with you. It was posted on the **KIDLIT-L** mailing list (listserv@bingvmb.cc.binghamton.edu), among other locations, inviting other teachers to collaborate with her classroom. Visit the home page for the 1998 project (http://bps.boston.k12.ma.us/rc328sb/titles98.shtml) to see how other classrooms have shared their regional works of literature through the travels of Larry and Lester, the "Looney Lobsters."

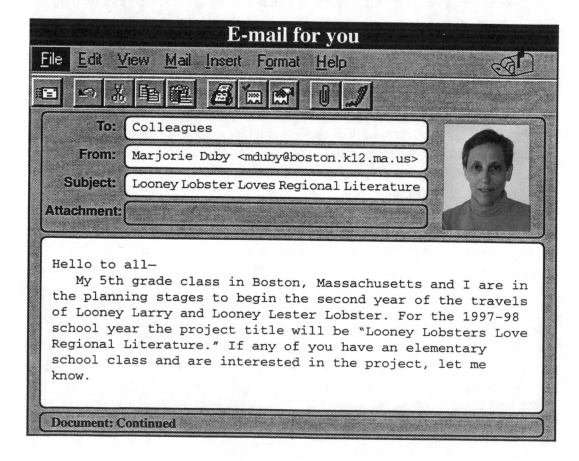

E-mail for you

File   Edit   View   Mail   Insert   Format   Help

Project Background

Last year our traveling stuffed crustaceans, Looney Larry and Looney Lester of Boston, Massachusetts accepted the gracious hospitality of elementary school classrooms across the United States for one school week and then were mailed to another classroom eventually returning to Boston.

They received cuddles, pets, and tours of local sites. They learned of local customs and culture. As we kept in touch with them and others through the Internet via electronic mail and our "Looney Lobster on the Loose" website at http://bps.boston.k12.ma.us/rc328sb/looney.html, we learned much virtually.

Our Looneys enjoyed traveling and learning so much that they would like to again travel the USA learning about local regional literature.

Our Project Announcement

Would you be willing to show hospitality in your elementary school classroom for one school week to our traveling Looney? During Looney's visit, would you be willing to read aloud picture books based on local lore—a folktale, a custom, a happening, a regionally identifiable daily life story?

What we will send:
A small box which will include:
1. a small pouch with Looney Lobster, a small, cuddly, stuffed crustacean
2. a photo-album showing our class members—on our travels around Boston and in our classroom
3. Looney Lobster's itinerary
4. a single-use camera
5. a pouch of SASE envelopes

What we will ask that you do:
1. In your message of interest, identify the title and author of a picture book/s based on your local lore—a folk tale, a custom, a happening, a regionally identifiable daily life story—which your class will read aloud to Looney during his visit to your school.
2. Immediately after being notified of your acceptance into the project, arrange to send a photo of your class (digitized, photocopy of a photo, or original photo) possibly holding a copy of the regional book they will read aloud during your school week.

Document: Continued

3. Once accepted into the project and the "Looney Lob-sters Love Regional Literature" booklist is created, begin to locate the booklist entries at your local library for read-aloud use during the scheduled school weeks.

4. Subscribe to our Looney Lobster Listserv (mailing list) which will network participants allowing students to converse about the literature and the daily experiences of Looney.

5. Send electronic mail messages related to Looney's visit to the Looney mailing list.

6. If possible, create a school-based webpage of Looney's travels and experiences linked to our "Looney Lobsters Love Regional Literature" webpage.

7. With the single-use camera, take a close-up picture of your state's license plate and two other pictures of your choice.

8. Remove one of the SASE from the box. Inside the envelope, place the front page of your local newspaper.

9. Following Looney Lobster's scheduled visit to your school, immediately send him to his next scheduled site allowing a minimum of 4 days for Priority Mail travel.

What we will be doing:

1. Calculating the accumulated mileage for our Looney Lobsters.

2. Locating the latitude and longitude of each city that our Looneys visit.

3. Becoming aware of the daily time zones for each school that Looney Lobster visits.

4. Observing the daily weather of Looney's host school and comparing it to our weather.

5. Obtaining from our local library the regional litera-ture suggested by participants for each scheduled Looney visit.

6. Reading aloud the weekly booklist suggestion to our lower grade Reading Buddies.

7. Reacting to the read aloud selections with other participant students through the mailing list.

8. Receiving the SASE information that is sent to us as our Looneys move to the next school site.

Document: Continued

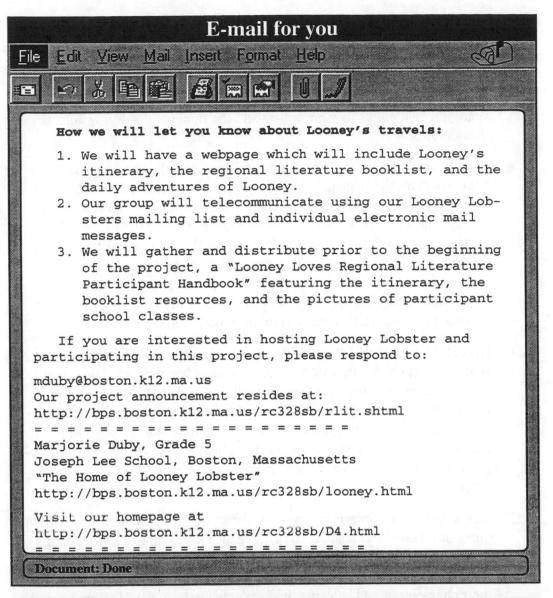

E-mail for you

File Edit View Mail Insert Format Help

How we will let you know about Looney's travels:

1. We will have a webpage which will include Looney's itinerary, the regional literature booklist, and the daily adventures of Looney.
2. Our group will telecommunicate using our Looney Lobsters mailing list and individual electronic mail messages.
3. We will gather and distribute prior to the beginning of the project, a "Looney Loves Regional Literature Participant Handbook" featuring the itinerary, the booklist resources, and the pictures of participant school classes.

If you are interested in hosting Looney Lobster and participating in this project, please respond to:

mduby@boston.k12.ma.us
Our project announcement resides at:
http://bps.boston.k12.ma.us/rc328sb/rlit.shtml
= =
Marjorie Duby, Grade 5
Joseph Lee School, Boston, Massachusetts
"The Home of Looney Lobster"
http://bps.boston.k12.ma.us/rc328sb/looney.html

Visit our homepage at
http://bps.boston.k12.ma.us/rc328sb/D4.html
= =

Document: Done

Using Internet Inquiry with Internet Workshop

Inquiry approaches to the Internet are also valuable to support learning in language arts and literature. Inquiry approaches require students to engage in self-directed reading and writing projects as they explore issues of personal interest. The personal nature of these inquiry projects motivates students in exciting ways, helping them to accomplish tasks they might have thought impossible to accomplish. The intensive reading and writing experiences required in inquiry projects provides students with authentic literacy experiences where they learn much about comprehension and composition. Using Internet Inquiry and Internet Workshop with the language arts and literature will help you to capitalize on these special opportunities. Here are several ideas and examples for using Internet Inquiry with Internet Workshop as you engage students in this important area:

The intensive reading and writing experiences required in inquiry projects provides students with authentic literacy experiences where they learn much about comprehension and composition.

- **Literature Inquiry Projects.**   As students encounter an interesting historical period, develop a favorite author, or encounter an fascinating location during their literary experiences, encourage them to complete an Internet Inquiry. Have them use the library and Internet resources to discover all they can about their topic and question. Encourage them to share the challenges they encounter and the final results during Internet Workshop.

- **Literature Fair.**   Set aside one period each month for all of your students to share their Internet Inquiry projects in literature. Use Internet Workshop to share progress and respond to questions as you build up to this special day. Have students display the results of their research on poster board or on your classroom home page. Invite students from other classes to visit during a literature fair where students can share the results of their work. After the fair, set up the poster board presentations in the school library for the entire school to see or invite other classrooms to view your students' work at your classroom home page.

- **Living Museum of Literary Authors.**   Invite students to complete Internet Inquiry on the author of a work they are reading. Have them conduct research to discover everything they can about their author. Then, invite them to dress up as the author and prepare a display, sharing information they discovered about this person. Have students pose in their costumes, without movement, as other classes visit your living classroom museum of literary authors reading the displays and viewing the authors.

- **Dress Up As A Character Day.**   Have students complete Internet Inquiry on a favorite character. Then, have everyone come to school on the same day, dressed as their character. During Internet Workshop, have students ask questions of one another, trying to discover the name of their character or author, using the format from the game "Twenty Questions."

A Final Thought

The Internet permits rapid, written communication between people around the world, quickly fulfilling the dream many have of a global village

Probably one of the most powerful uses of the Internet for the classroom is the potential that exists to support English and language arts. The Internet permits rapid, written communication between people around the world, quickly fulfilling the dream many have of a global village. As a result, you have a very special tool to support literacy learning in your classroom. As you work with the Internet in your classroom, you and your students will discover many new ways to exploit this potential. Be certain to share your successes with others by posting Internet Project ideas for others to join or by describing your successful experiences on a mailing list, inviting others to learn from your successful experiences.

Resources for the Language Arts and Literature on the Internet

Bartlett's Familiar Quotations—
(http://www.columbia.edu/acis/bartleby/bartlett/index.html)
Who first coined the phrase "Snug as a bug in a rug?" Using this classic work of famous quotations will quickly tell you it was Benjamin Franklin. This on-line resource is a tremendous source for great quotations. It contains a wonderful search engine with cross links to famous authors. Set a bookmark!

Carol Hurst's Children's Literature Site—(http://www.carolhurst.com/index.html)
A useful central site for children's literature but more commercial than others mentioned in this chapter. Still a useful resource with book reviews, instructional ideas, and links to literature sites.

Dictionaries and Encyclopedias—(http://libwww.syr.edu/isd/dictency.htm)
Visit the research shelf at Syracuse University to find links to a variety of resources including encyclopedias, dictionaries, thesauri, pronunciation guides, braille typography, and much more.

Eric Carle Web Site—(http://www.eric-carle.com/index.html)
The web site for this popular children's author. It contains a bulletin board for exchanging ideas with other teachers about how best to use Carle's books in the classroom. It also contains his snail mail address in case your children wish to write him.

Help Your Child Learn to Write Well—
(http://www.ed.gov/pubs/parents/Writing/)
A brochure for parents from the U.S. Department of Education that may be printed out and distributed at "Back-to-School Night." This provides useful information for parents about ways to assist their child with writing.

Helping Your Child Learn to Read—
(http://www.ed.gov/pubs/parents/Reading/index.html)
An on-line book for parents written by recognized experts in the field of reading for the U.S. Department of Education. This book contains useful information on how parents may help their child to read. Print out copies of one of the chapters for "Back-to-School Night" and provide this address to parents so that they may read the entire book. A great resource.

How a Book is Made—(http://www.harperchildrens.com/index.htm)
Here is a wonderful on-line book written by Aliki, a widely-recognized author/illustrator of books for young children. This is a great reading experience for younger children and provides important information about the work of a professional author. Use it in an author study on Aliki or in a unit on writing.

How the Leopard Got Its Spots—
(http://www.sff.net/people/karawynn/justso/leopard.htp)
The classic pourquoi tale by Rudyard Kipling from the *Just So Stories*. Illustrated with photographs.

Magazines—(http://www.yahooligans.com/Entertainment/Magazines/)
This is a central site with links to many outstanding on-line magazines for kids. A treasure trove of resources.

Multicultural Resources—(http://falcon.jmu.edu/~ramseyil/multipub.htm).
Here you will find articles about multicultural children's literature as well as reviews and a host of literature selections organized by cultural groups. It is a real treasure for teachers serious about multicultural literature.

Multicultural Book Review—
(http://www.isomedia.com/homes/jmele/homepage.html)
If you are looking for great multicultural literature selections, here is a wonderful resource. Many excellent reviews of great literature. Encourage your students to add their reviews of books they have read, too!

Readers Theater—(http://www.acs.ucalgary.ca/~dkbrown/readers.html)
This location contains links to locations on the WWW devoted to readers theater. Several locations contain readers theater scripts you can print out and use in your classroom. If you use this instructional method in your class, this is the location for you!

Reading Online—(http://www.readingonline.org/)
This is the free electronic journal of the International Reading Association, the best on-line journal currently found on the Internet. It contains a wealth of resources, including sections on critical issues, developments in literacy, a graduate student section, an international forum, an electronic classroom, professional materials, and research. Special features include the use of many multimedia resources and discussion forums where you may comment on articles you read. Set a bookmark!

Stone Soup—(http://www.stonesoup.com/)
Stone Soup is a hard copy magazine with stories, poetry, and art created by young children. This location takes you to a number of stories and poems written by young children and provides directions for how students may submit work.

The Doucette Index—(http://www.educ.ucalgary.ca/litindex/)
Are you looking for web sites that have teaching ideas for a particular work of literature or a particular author? Here's the site for you. This index is a search engine limited strictly to children's and young adult literature. It will find instructional resources on the web related to your literature needs.

The Internet Classics Archive—(http://classics.mit.edu/)
This wonderful resource contains a searchable collection of almost 400 classical Greek and Latin texts (in English translation) with user-provided commentary and trivia sections. The Classics Archives features, among others, such notable pieces as Homer's *Iliad and Odyssey*, Virgil's *Aeneid, The Histories of Tacitus and Thucydides*, and Plato's *Apology*. Set a bookmark!

The Reading Zone of the Internet Public Library—
(http://www.ipl.org/youth/lapage.html)
This is a good central site for literature with many opportunities for your students. Developed at the University of Michigan, your students can: ask questions of authors such as Virginia Hamilton, Timothy Gaffney, Shonto Gegay and others; read biographies and view photos of many more authors; discover links to many authors' home pages; read original stories or listen to them being read aloud; enter a writing contest; see the book recommendations of other students; and much more. Set a bookmark!

Listservs/Mailing Lists for the Language Arts and Literature

KIDLIT-L—(listserv@bingvmb.cc.binghamton.edu)
A listserv on children's literature.

NCTE-talk—(majordomo@serv1.ncte.org)
This is the main listserv for the National Council of English Teachers, an important professional association for English education. It is a high traffic list. At the NCTE web site you can subscribe to a number of different listservs/mailing lists devoted to English education, K-12 (http://www.ncte.org/chat/). Descriptions of each list may also be found here. Find the mailing list that is just right for you!

RTEACHER—(listserv@listserv.syr.edu)
A forum for conversations about literacy in both traditional and electronic contexts. The archive for these conversations may be found at http://listserv.syr.edu/archives/rteacher.html. This is a very supportive and diverse group of educators interested in using the Internet for literacy education. We also discuss non-Internet aspects of literacy education.

TAWL—(listserv@listserv.arizona.edu)
A listserv discussion group on teaching from a whole language perspective.

WAC-L—(listserv@vmd.cso.uiuc.edu)
A listserv on writing across the curriculum.

Usenet Newsgroups for the Language Arts and Literature

K-12 Teacher Chat Area—(k12.chat.teacher)
Discusses issues of K-12 instruction, including language arts.

Language Arts Curriculum in K-12 Education—(k12.lang.art)
A newsgroup on the language arts curriculum in schools.

Writing Instruction in Computer-based Classrooms—(comp.edu.composition)
Discusses issues of writing in electronic environments.

References

Hynds, S. (1997). *On the brink : Negotiating literature and life with adolescents.* New York: Teachers College Press.

Leu, D.J., Jr., & Kinzer, C. K. (1998). *Effective literacy instruction*, 4th edition. Englewood Cliffs, NJ: Prentice Hall.

McGee, L. M., & Richgels, D. J. (1990). *Literacy's beginnings: Supporting young readers and writers.* Boston: Allyn & Bacon.

McMahon, S. I., Raphael, T. E., Goatley, V. J., & Pardo, L. S. (Eds.). (1997). *The book club connection.* New York: Teachers College Press.

Short, K. (1993). Intertextuality: Searching for patterns that connect. In D. J. Leu & C. K. Kinzer (Eds.), *Literacy research, theory, and practice: Views from many perspectives.* Forty-first Yearbook of the National Reading Conference. Chicago: National Reading Conference.

6

Social Studies:
A World of Possibilities

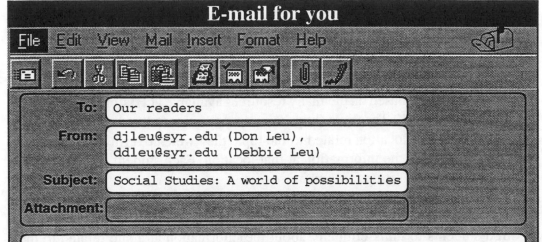

E-mail for you

File Edit View Mail Insert Format Help

To: Our readers

From: djleu@syr.edu (Don Leu),
ddleu@syr.edu (Debbie Leu)

Subject: Social Studies: A world of possibilities

Attachment:

There are more resources for social studies education than any other subject area on the Internet. The possibilities for learning experiences in this area are so rich it becomes easy to integrate social studies into every other curricular area, increasing the learning potential of the Internet for your students.

While the extensive resources for social studies make it possible to design rich learning experiences for students, this richness presents an important challenge to teachers and students: How do you quickly find the information you require on the Internet when there is so much available? Using central sites, developing search engine strategies, seeking assistance on mailing lists, and using individual bookmark folders are especially useful strategies as you explore the Internet for learning opportunities in social studies. We will share each of these strategies in this chapter.

Most important, we will also share effective strategies for teaching social studies with the Internet. These rich sources of information and communication create many new opportunities for your students to explore history, culture, politics, and important social issues. Using the Internet to visit people and locations around the world opens up a world of possibilities for you and your students.

Don and Debbie

Document: Done

Teaching with the Internet: Robert Guzman's Class

Spring was in the air as Robert Guzman entered his room in the morning. He sat for a few moments enjoying his coffee and thinking about his first full year with an Internet connection in his high school classroom. It had been a busy year, filled with new learning as he and his students explored this new resource together to enrich their study of history.

At the beginning of the year, Robert felt a bit intimidated by all of the information on the Internet related to social studies. He wondered how he was going to keep track of everything without getting lost.

He decided to start simply; he set up a single Internet Activity for students to complete each week based on the many resources available at **History/Social Studies Web Site for K-12 Teachers** (http://www.execpc.com/~dboals/boals.html). He set a bookmark to a location related to the topic they were covering that week and developed a task for the information at that location. Each student was required to complete the task he set up for them.

Initially, he developed scavenger hunts to develop navigational skills during Internet Activity. Gradually, he moved into other short learning experiences. These required students to think critically about the information at a site related to their current unit. During one week of the colonial period, for example, he set a bookmark to a wonderful site, **Benjamin Franklin** (http://sln.fi.edu/franklin/rotten.html). He then directed students to explore this site and write a short essay about what they thought was the most important accomplishment in Franklin's life, explaining why this accomplishment was so important. At the end of the week, during a short Internet Workshop session, students had a chance to compare their ideas and discuss their conclusions. The discussion really made the totality of Franklin's life come alive as students described his many accomplishments.

During the middle of the year, as he felt more confident and knowledgeable about Internet resources, Robert decided to use Internet Project, connecting with other classrooms around the world. He wanted his students to see how people in different cultural contexts interpret the same historical event. He posted a project to compare perceptions of World War II (WWII) by students from several different countries at **The Global SchoolNet Projects Registry** (http://www.gsn.org/gsn/proj/index.html) and **The Global School House** (http://www.gsh.org/class/default.htm).

After studying this event in their individual classrooms, students in each of the classes wrote an essay describing the meaning of WWII to their country. These essays were exchanged by e-mail between each of the participating classes so that students could read them and understand that history is often interpreted differently by different societies. Each student then wrote a second essay describing what they had learned from reading the essays of students in the different countries. Classrooms from Japan, Russia, Germany, England, Italy, and Canada agreed to participate in the project.

He decided to start simply; he set up a single Internet Activity for students to complete each week based on the many resources available at History/Social Studies Web Site for K-12 Teachers.

During the middle of the year, as he felt more confident and knowledgeable about Internet resources, Robert decided to use an Internet Project, connecting with other classrooms around the world.

Benjamin Franklin (http://sln.fi.edu/franklin/rotten.html)

Figure 6-1. The Home Page for **Benjamin Franklin** at the Franklin Institute Science Museum in Philadelphia.

For Robert and his students, studying about history was fundamentally changed. History was not just something they read about; it was the people they were talking with over the Internet and the experiences they shared. History had become human.

As part of the project, participating classrooms subscribed to **MEMORIES** (listserv@maelstrom.stjohns.edu), a mailing list where participating classrooms could exchange e-mail messages with survivors of WWII. This was an especially important experience for everyone involved as students asked questions about different events and received information from people who had actually lived through the experience. For Robert and his students, studying about history was fundamentally changed. History was not just something they read about; it was the people they were talking with over the Internet and the experiences they shared. History had become human.

Robert's Internet Project was a tremendous success. It was a powerful experience for each of the classrooms, making history come alive for everyone involved. Some classes in the project continued exchanging information throughout the year with his class. Each teacher promised to get together again next year so they could repeat the project.

As the end of the year approached, Robert decided to try Internet Inquiry. Students identified a question in American History they wanted to explore on their own using resources on the Internet and resources in the school library. Before they started their project, Robert set up individual bookmark folders for each student in his class so that students could keep track of good locations and not get these mixed up with those of other students. He also conducted several Internet Workshops using the different search engines to locate information. He had learned there were so many sites related to social studies education that finding useful locations required extra assistance for his students.

Robert had students complete the planning form in Figure 6-2. This helped to focus their efforts and provide a road map for their initial work during Internet Inquiry. After one week, he had individual conferences with students to check their progress and to make revisions in their project if these were necessary.

At the end of their Internet Inquiry, Robert had each student develop a Kids-Teaching-Kids Activity. This had each student develop a learning activity related to the Internet Inquiry they had just completed and then create a poster advertising this experience. Students had to provide the address of the location on the Internet, explain the learning activity for this site, and advertise the virtues of completing their activity. Robert required each student in his class to participate in at least four of these activities during the last two weeks of school. It was a nice way to wrap up their study of history during the year.

Lessons from the Classroom

Robert Guzman's first year illustrates a number of important lessons about integrating the Internet into your social studies program. First, it illustrates how beginning with Internet Activity is often the easiest way to begin using the Internet in your classroom. As you develop more confidence, it is easy to develop additional experiences for your students.

Second, we again see the power of Internet Project for bringing classroom learning alive through collaborative experiences with students at other locations around the world. Internet Project can be an especially powerful way of organizing classroom learning experiences in social studies; it enables your students to understand how students in different parts of the world view historical, political, and social events. It enables them to better appreciate the power of different cultural experiences. Participating in the MEMORIES mailing list and sharing thoughts about WWII

Figure 6-2.
The Internet
Inquiry Plan-
ning Form
Used in Mr.
Guzman's
Class.

PLANNING FOR INTERNET INQUIRY

Directions: This form will help you to plan for Internet Inquiry, help to keep you on track as you complete your work, and help you to evaluate your work when you finish. Please complete each item as completely as possible and then schedule a conference with me to discuss your planning.

Name(s): _____ Date: _____

Title of my (our) Internet Inquiry: _____

The project will be completed on _____

The purpose of my (our) project is: _____

_____

_____

As I (we) planned my (our) project, I (we) used the following resources: _____

_____

_____

_____

I (we) will do the following during this project: _____

_____

_____

_____

I (we) will evaluate the project in the following manner: _____

_____

_____

I (we) will begin by using the following Internet sites or by using the following words/ phrases with a search engine: _____

_____

_____

I (we) had a conference with Mr. Guzman about this project on the following dates:

_____   _____   _____

with other students around the world fundamentally changed the nature of historical study in Robert's classroom.

Third, Robert's experiences show how Internet Inquiry may be used to support independent learning. This helps students to develop greater responsibility for their own learning as they explore questions important to them.

Robert's experiences also show how an activity like Kids-Teaching-Kids may be used to support the social learning experiences especially important with the Internet. This activity is also a nice way to wrap up a unit in your classroom, allowing students to teach one another about what they have learned.

Finally, Robert's experiences demonstrate how extensive the resources on the Internet are for social studies. This is great for developing learning experiences but it often requires you to help students sort through the many resources to find ones that are most useful. Often it is helpful to provide special assistance with using the various search engines to locate information. It is also helpful to develop individual bookmark folders so that students may keep track of their own bookmarks.

Central Sites for Social Studies Education

Because there are so many Internet resources for social studies education, a central site strategy is often necessary for quickly locating Internet resources directly related to your learning goals.

Because there are so many Internet resources for social studies education, a central site strategy is often necessary for quickly locating Internet resources directly related to your learning goals. Fortunately, there is an exceptional central site on the Internet available for social studies education. The **History/Social Studies Web Site for K-12 Teachers** (http://www.execpc.com/~dboals/boals.html) is the best single location we know of for social studies. The home page for this location only hints at the many resources it contains. Pay a visit to this site and explore some of the many topics. You will find an amazingly exhaustive set of resources organized in an easy-to-understand hierarchical structure. Set a permanent bookmark for your classroom. You will be coming back to this location frequently.

There are several other central sites that may prove useful to you. An important one is **The Library of Congress Home Page** (http://www.loc.gov/). In Chapter 1 you discovered the extensive multimedia, historical resources available at one portion of this site, **American Memory** (http://lcweb2.loc.gov/ammem/). There are many other important resources at The Library of Congress Home Page, including: **Thomas** (http://thomas.loc.gov/), the official source of legislative information for the U.S. Congress; **Exhibitions** (http://lcweb.loc.gov/exhibits/), a collection of recent exhibitions at the Library of Congress; **Library Services** (http://lcweb.loc.gov/loc/libserv/), which provides you with access to all of the services of the Library of Congress; and **Catalogs** (http://lcweb.loc.gov/catalog/), which allows you to access the extensive catalogs of this library and many others. There is probably no better location for multimedia, historical documents of the United States. Your students can view items ranging from the original draft of the Declaration of Independence in Thomas Jefferson's handwriting to the Vietnam War POW/MIA database. It is a most impressive resource for your social studies program, especially with the recent emphasis being placed on the use of primary source documents.

Other central sites you may find useful in your work include:

- **The Cornell Theory Center Arts and Social Science Gateway** (http://www.tc.cornell.edu/Edu/ArtSocGateway/)

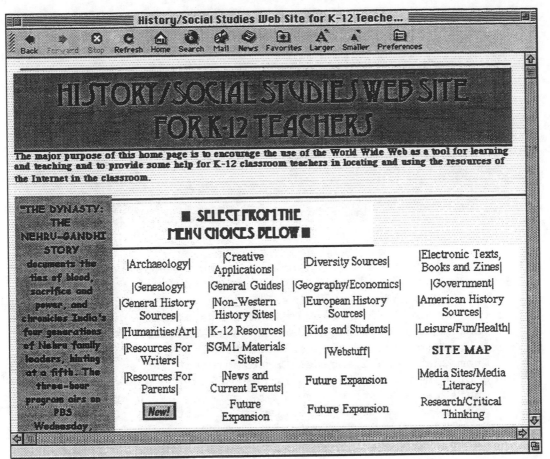

Figure 6-3. A wonderful central site for social studies education: the **History/ Social Studies Web Site for K-12 Teachers.**

History/Social Studies Web Site for K-12 Teachers
(http://www.execpc.com/~dboals/boals.html)

- **Lesson Plans and Resources for Social Studies Teachers**
  (http://www.csun.edu/~hcedu013/index.html)

- **Nebraska Department of Education Social Science Resources HomePage** (http://www.nde.state.ne.us/SS/ss.html)

Keeping it Simple: Internet Activity Assignments

Sometimes, it is easiest to begin using the Internet in your classroom with Internet Activity. This may be especially useful as you begin to explore the extensive resources available on the Internet in social studies. Simply locate a site on the Internet with content related to the learning objectives in your classroom. The easiest way to find a good location is to visit the central sites for social studies education identified earlier. Then develop an activity related to that site and assign this activity to your students. They can complete it during their weekly time at the computer. Be certain, too, to discuss their experiences during a short Internet Workshop session.

Nearly any good resource from the central sites above might be used in this fashion. If you are studying the Civil War, for example, you may wish to set a book-

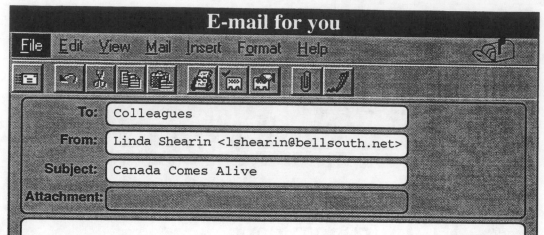

E-mail for you

File   Edit   View   Mail   Insert   Format   Help

To: Colleagues

From: Linda Shearin <lshearin@bellsouth.net>

Subject: Canada Comes Alive

Attachment:

Dear Teachers,

The Internet is a great tool for making Social Studies come alive for students. In North Carolina, 5th grade students engage in a comparative study of peoples and regions of the Western Hemisphere. I located **Canadiana** (http://www.cs.cmu.edu/Unofficial/Canadiana/README.html), a treasure trove of information on Canada.

From Canadiana I located Canadian school homepages for each province in Canada. I then e-mailed the schools to see if there was a class who would be interested in engaging in a short term research project with our students. Fifth grade classes brainstormed questions they would like answered about homes (types of building materials, size, cost) and schools (schedules, subjects, homework) in the Canadian communities. It is difficult to find current and detailed information on these particular topics in print materials.

The first year we did this it was evident our students were still stuck in the "Age of Exploration," assuming Canadians still lived in log cabins and cooked over open fires. What a wonderful opportunity this presented to correct some misconceptions about lifestyle. This worked both ways since our students were amazed at the Canadian students asking if all our students were "wanded" for weapons before entering our school. A great discussion ensued about how the Canadians might have developed this impression.

When the responses arrived from the Canadian students our 5th graders were surprised to find out that there were many similarities between themselves and their Canadian counterparts. They also enjoyed comparing the various school descriptions to our school.

The 5th graders used the correspondence and information gathered from other Canadian sources on the Web and in print to write a research paper in the form of a narrative based on a trip to their chosen province. In addition to

Document: Continued

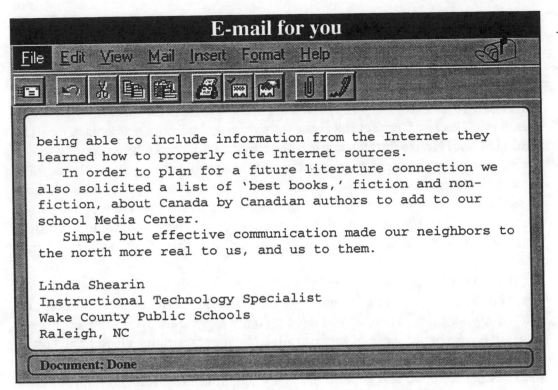

E-mail for you

File Edit View Mail Insert Format Help

being able to include information from the Internet they
learned how to properly cite Internet sources.
     In order to plan for a future literature connection we
also solicited a list of 'best books,' fiction and non-
fiction, about Canada by Canadian authors to add to our
school Media Center.
     Simple but effective communication made our neighbors to
the north more real to us, and us to them.

Linda Shearin
Instructional Technology Specialist
Wake County Public Schools
Raleigh, NC

Document: Done

For younger students studying the political geography of the U.S., set a bookmark for the interactive game, Do You Know Your State Capitals?

mark for **The Civil War Letters of Galutia York** (http://www.snymor.edu/pages/ library/local_history/civil_war/) and invite students to read the letters of this Union soldier, taking notes in a journal about this soldier's view of himself and his country. You might also set a bookmark for the **Civil War Timeline** (http://rs6.loc.gov/ ammem/timeline.html) in the **Civil War Photograph Collection** (http://rs6.loc.gov/ cwphome.html). Have your students read and view the pictures, printing out one picture and doing research about the battle to determine its significance. Post these photos and descriptions on a bulletin board in your classroom for everyone to see.

During Internet Workshop, students could share their observations after reading this diary and viewing these photos. Use your students' observations to draw conclusions about the Union soldiers of that era and the manner in which they thought about their country. These activities would serve as a powerful introduction to the human side of the Civil War.

For younger students studying the political geography of the U.S., set a bookmark for the interactive game, **Do You Know Your State Capitals?** (http:// www.cris.com/~Kraft/capitals/). During Internet Activity have them visit each state, trying to guess the capital, until they know each of the state capitals. Invite your students to play this game with partners. Use Internet Workshop to continue this game, but in a group format.

Setting up Internet Activity Assignments such as these in your classroom is a good way to ease yourself and your students into simple activities before attempting the richer, but more complex, experiences that are also possible with Internet Project and Internet Inquiry.

Setting up Internet Activity Assignments such as these in your classroom is a good way to ease yourself and your students into simple activities before attempting the richer, but more complex, experiences that are also possible with Internet Project and Internet Inquiry.

Internet Project

Previous chapters have described the important role Internet Project may play in your classroom. The chapters also identified locations such as **Global SchoolNet's Internet Project Registry** (http://www.gsn.org/project/index.html), **Classroom Connect's Teacher Contact Database** (http://www.classroom.net/contact/), or **The Global School House** (http://www.gsh.org/class/default.htm) where you may search for Internet projects others have developed. Internet projects are especially useful in social studies since they allow you to compare your students' experiences with those of students in other cultures. Often, communicating with a class in another part of the world will make your study of that culture come alive as you exchange information about experiences. This is what happened in Robert Guzman's and Linda Shearin's classes.

Internet projects are especially useful in social studies since they allow you to compare your students' experiences with those of students in other cultures.

If you are just beginning to use Internet Project, it is often easiest to find a project posted by another teacher and seek to join a learning experience that seems appropriate for your class. Then, as you develop more experience with Internet Project, you will have a better sense of where to advertise for cooperating classes and how to develop a project that others will be interested in joining. We encourage you to visit the sites listed above and explore the many opportunities available for your class through an Internet project. Examples of projects posted in the past at these sites include:

- **Menus of the World.** Posted by a middle school teacher in Washington, this project sought collaborating classrooms around the world to learn more about each other's culture through their food. Each week, classes exchanged e-mail messages containing a typical daily menu from their part of the world for four people, plus the estimated cost for each item in the meal using the local currency. The menu was used as a springboard for classrooms to ask questions about the cultural meanings for different food items: what unusual items were, how food was obtained, who prepared the food, how the meal was served, and how the meal was eaten. Each meal's cost was also converted into the currency used in each classroom to compare costs of common foods as well as the average cost for each meal.

- **Geo Game** (http://www.gsn.org/project/gg/index.html). This Internet Project is actually a contest. Each participating class completes a questionnaire about their own location, including information about latitude, typical weather, land formations, nearest river, time zone, points of interest, direction from the capital, population, and other items. These are then mailed to the project coordinator, who removes the name of the location and then returns the questionnaire items to participants. Participants try to locate the city for each set of items using maps, atlases, and reference materials on the Internet.

- **A Cultural Macbeth**. To foster the cultural exchange of ideas and interpretations of Shakespeare, three schools in Germany invited other classes to exchange their views about the characters in this play. Each week a different character was discussed via e-mail with students. Classrooms from six different countries shared different interpretations of each character. The students quickly discovered how character interpretation is powerfully influenced by one's cultural context. At the same time, students learned much about one another's culture as they discussed the reasons behind their interpretations of each character.

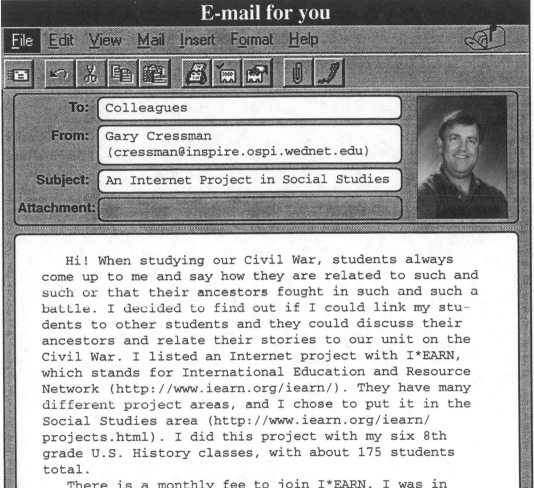

E-mail for you

File   Edit   View   Mail   Insert   Format   Help

To: Colleagues

From: Gary Cressman
(cressman@inspire.ospi.wednet.edu)

Subject: An Internet Project in Social Studies

Attachment:

Hi! When studying our Civil War, students always come up to me and say how they are related to such and such or that their ancestors fought in such and such a battle. I decided to find out if I could link my students to other students and they could discuss their ancestors and relate their stories to our unit on the Civil War. I listed an Internet project with I*EARN, which stands for International Education and Resource Network (http://www.iearn.org/iearn/). They have many different project areas, and I chose to put it in the Social Studies area (http://www.iearn.org/iearn/projects.html). I did this project with my six 8th grade U.S. History classes, with about 175 students total.

There is a monthly fee to join I*EARN. I was in contact with them from home and school using text-only e-mail. Usually I had my students compose their work during class and I would send them off at night when the I*EARN connection charges were lower. I also would collect messages during the evening at home and post them the next day on the wall. But often my students wanted to know if there was any mail that day, so I

Document: Continued

said OK and we checked our mail. It was wonderfulllllllll when a message would come in and the student it was addressed to was there to receive it. All mail came to me; my students did not have their own accounts or addresses.

One of the I*EARN moderators in Spain picked up my message and passed it on to a Belgium UN relief worker. The next day I received a message from a 16 year old Bosnian boy with a cry for help from his refugee camp in northern Bosnia. The message was actually sent in Serbo-Croatian, and an English translation came a day later; I do not know who did the translating. I had no thoughts of including our study of the US Civil War with civil wars in our society today. But things changed quickly. So I shared this message with my students and they started writing letters of support to this boy. This got my students following current events in a way that would not have been possible otherwise.

A few days later, a message came from some high school students in New York who were writing a newspaper about human rights abuses, which a civil war is. They asked if my students could join in their discussion. Of course we did. And 27 of my students were included in the paper, Liberty Bound, published by the Cold Spring Harbor High School. The age difference between the students did not make a difference as it turned out. In fact, it made my students become more concerned that they did not sound too young.

We were also contacted by a High School in northern Israel and asked if my students could help teach their students about our civil war. This connection was again made for us by one of the I*EARN moderators. In return, their students sent us stories about their experiences during the Gulf War.

Internet projects have had a powerful impact on my students' learning. I have found that the best projects are those where you have a tight bond/connection/commitment from the people on the other end to stick to the project. Often these happen in unexpected ways.

Gary Cressman
Chair, History Department and Computer Resource Teacher
Enumclaw Junior High   Enumclaw, Washington
cressman@inspire.ospi.wednet.edu

Document: Done

Internet Inquiry

Internet Inquiry helps students develop independent research skills and explore questions that are personally important. Internet Inquiry projects may be developed by small groups or by individuals. You will recall from Chapter 4 that Internet Inquiry often includes these phases: question, search, analyze, compose, and share. Sometimes Internet Inquiry will also include an evaluation phase, when the project is evaluated, often by the students themselves. Involving students in self-evaluation experiences is helpful in getting them to become more aware of how to develop successful research and learning experiences.

Some teachers introduce Internet Inquiry by reading aloud a book such as *What Did George Washington Have for Breakfast?* by Jean Fritz. In this wonderful story, the main character pursues a question that is personally very important. An introduction like this nicely illustrates the learning opportunities that happen when someone pursues the answer to a seemingly simple question.

Internet Inquiry is often effectively combined with Internet Workshop sessions. During this time, students and groups may share what they have learned in their research as well as the roadblocks they have encountered. These conversations enrich the study of your unit at the same time they provide students with useful new ideas to explore as they seek answers to their questions.

Internet Inquiry is often effectively combined with Internet Workshop sessions. During this time, students and groups may share what they have learned in their research as well as the roadblocks they have encountered.

Kids-Teaching-Kids

One of the best ways to learn something is to teach it to someone else. This is the idea behind Kids-Teaching-Kids. As your students use the Internet during a unit, consider using this type of experience at the end of the unit as you summarize and review the learning that has taken place.

During a Kids-Teaching-Kids activity, students first identify a useful web location related to their studies. Then they develop a learning experience using the web site for other students to complete. Here are several examples:

- A student completes a unit on twentieth-century U.S. history, sets a bookmark to **Langston Hughes Sites** (http://www.liben.com/Hugheslinks.html), and asks other students to read each of the poems there, selecting one and writing a response in their poetry journal about it.

- Another student, completing a unit on diversity, invites others to visit the **Indigenous Peoples' Literature** page (http://www.indians.org/welker/framenat.htm) and asks them to list the two stories they liked the best from the many wonderful stories at this site. These choices are added to a continuously updated graph using a spreadsheet program on the computer.

One of the best ways to learn something is to teach it to someone else. This is the idea behind Kids-Teaching-Kids.

- Another student, completing a unit on ancient civilizations, invites class-mates to explore **The Ancient Olympic Games Virtual Museum** (http://devlab.dartmouth.edu/olympic/), a wonderful site, and then write an imaginary letter home to their parents in Athens describing what they saw.

After students develop their learning activity, they design a poster, advertising the web site and describe what students will be required to do. These poster adver-tisements are then displayed around the room so that everyone can read them to select the site they wish to visit and the activity they will complete. Often, teachers will distribute a list of the sites and ask students to obtain the signature of the person who developed the activity they complete. This indicates that they have successfully completed their activity.

Kids-Teaching-Kids can be useful for organizing Internet activities during the final weeks of a unit in your classroom. It may be used, of course, in all subject areas but, because there are so many resources on the Internet for social studies, it is especially useful in this area.

TEACHING TIP

Kids-Teaching-Kids is a great way to culminate Internet Inquiry. If your stu-dents have been exploring individual inquiry projects, set aside at least one day for them to share their work by having each develop a short activity on the Internet. Create a page with a list of all the Internet activities and invite your students to complete as many as possible. When they complete an activity de-signed by another student, have them obtain the signature of the student who developed the activity along with a brief evaluation. This is an especially nice experience if you have access to an entire lab of Internet computers. Each stu-dent can set up their own station. Have half of the class visit the student stations and the other half share their Internet activity at a computer. Then rotate groups.

Search Strategies in Social Studies

There are so many wonderful resources on the Internet for teachers and students it is sometimes hard to find what you want. It is easy to get lost as you explore first one site and then another and then still another. There are several strategies you and your students might find useful as you explore the many resources in social studies.

The easiest strategy is to visit one of the comprehensive social studies sites listed earlier in the chapter and begin to explore the many resources located there. Usually these are organized by topics. The best of these is the **History/Social Studies Web Site for K-12 Teachers** (http://www.execpc.com/~dboals/boals.html), an extensive listing of hundreds of locations on the WWW useful for supporting social studies education. It is likely that you will find many useful resources simply by visiting this single location.

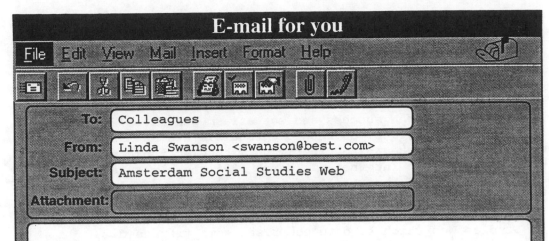

Dear Teachers,

Since 1994 students and teachers at the International School of Amsterdam have been engaged in a number of Internet-based projects. In April 1994 ESL students in the secondary school sent a request via Kidlink/Kidsphere for information on endangered species from other schools/countries. The response was overwhelming and led to a six-week intensive correspondence with schools in Canada, Russia, USA, and Finland. We exchanged letters, reports, questionnaires and even circulated a petition amongst the participants supporting the movement to save the endangered mountain gorillas of Rwanda. Students were exposed to a much wider range of issues than was available in their course book. The students also noticed the experience significantly improved their writing skills.

In January 1995 middle school students who were studying the writings of Jack London began an e-mail correspondence with students in Fairbanks, Alaska who were reading "The Diary of Anne Frank." Our students had visited the Anne Frank house in Amsterdam on numerous occasions and were able to provide the Alaskan students with additional information about The Netherlands, Amsterdam and even Anne Frank herself. The Alaskan students responded with information on the Klondike, the gold rush, native peoples of Alaska and frequent updates of the Iditarod Sled Dog Race of 1995. The correspondence lasted for several months and culminated in the visit of the Alaskan students to Amsterdam in May of that year. Our students took them on a guided visit of the Anne Frank house and in return the Alaskan students put on a series of plays illustrating the life and times of Jack London. In addition to new friendships, both groups benefited from the shared exchange of information about the places they live.

Document: Continued

E-mail for you

File　Edit　View　Mail　Insert　Format　Help

Following the success and enthusiasm generated by these two projects, a group of grade six students and their teacher began to experiment with electronic publishing on the Internet. In March 1996 the class selected some of their best social studies projects, designed a small web page and provided links to related Internet resources. Thus began the Grades 5/6 Social Studies Web which to date comprises some fifteen different projects and can be found at the following address: http://www.xs4all.nl/~swanson/origins/

Their web site has evolved in the two years since its inception to becoming an integral part of the teaching / learning program. Internet publishing has sparked the students' interest in presentation skills and good writing and design issues. Most importantly, they have discovered the benefits of publishing to a real world. To date they have corresponded with professional storytellers (in response to their project on "Creation Stories"), historians ("Ancient Civilizations"), university students ("Human Origins") and students and teachers from numerous countries.

In addition to their normal library research they have learned how to deal with the variety of registers and (often contradictory) information available on the Internet. They have corresponded with copyright holders asking permission to adapt or reproduce materials for their projects while learning how to properly acknowledge a variety of published information sources. In return, their work has been acknowledged by others in the online community—most notably, the extensive list of annotated resources which they produced for their study of ancient civilizations.

Publishing and exchanging information via the Internet has enhanced the educational experience of our students and invigorated our social studies curriculum. Most notably, we discovered first-hand what others have stressed—that many of the Net's best resources are human beings.

Linda Swanson
Internet Resource Manager
International School of Amsterdam
Amsterdam, The Netherlands
(now living in the San Francisco Bay Area, California)

Document: Done

If you are seeking something very specific on the WWW, you may wish to use one of the search engines by clicking on the "Search" button with Netscape Navigator or Internet Explorer. This will connect you to a page with several search engines such as Excite, Yahoo, Infoseek, Lycos, or Hot Bot. Here you can type in the words that best describe what you are looking for and click on the button that says "Search" or "Find." This will search the Internet for related web sites.

These search engines usually try to match the words you provide to words that appear on various pages in the WWW. Thus, it is best if you only use key descriptive words likely to be on the pages you are seeking. For example, the best way to search for something about the pyramids of Giza in Egypt is to simply type in "pyramids Giza Egypt." Avoid the use of words like "the" "of" or "a" since the search engine will look for these in addition to the other words you enter, listing every page it finds containing the word "the" "of" or "a". Some search engines will allow you to do a more advanced search by clicking on a button. At this location you can usually ask the search engine to search by the exact phrase or sentence. This will permit an even more precise search for the type of information you are looking for.

Another very useful strategy is to join a mailing list and ask other members for their recommendations of useful web sites. This often leads to great locations since these teachers will have already used them in their classrooms. You may, for example, wish to subscribe to **NCSS-L**, a listserv for teachers of social studies (listproc2@bgu.edu). Other listservs or mailing lists are described at the end of this chapter. If necessary, see Chapter 3 to review the procedures for subscribing to mailing lists.

Using Individual Bookmark (Favorites) Folders

You may face a challenge when you have an entire class doing Internet Inquiry with many individuals setting "bookmarks" (the term used with Netscape Navigator) or "favorites" (the term used with Internet Explorer). In a single-computer classroom, your list of bookmarks/favorites will become lengthy and confusing. Versions 3.0 and later of both Netscape Navigator and Internet Explorer allow you to solve this problem by making a separate bookmark/favorite folder for each student in your class.

To make individual bookmark folders with Internet Explorer, go to the menu item Favorites and select Open Favorites. Once your Favorites window is open, go to the menu item Favorites again and select New Folder for each new folder you wish to create. Type in the name of a student next to one of the folders. Repeat this for each student in your class and you will have a bookmark window that looks similar to Figure 6-4.

Now that you have a location for each student to place their favorites with Internet Explorer, you will need to show students how to keep their favorite locations organized. Each time a new favorite location is added, it will be added to the end of the folder list. Remind students to open the "favorites" window and drag and drop their

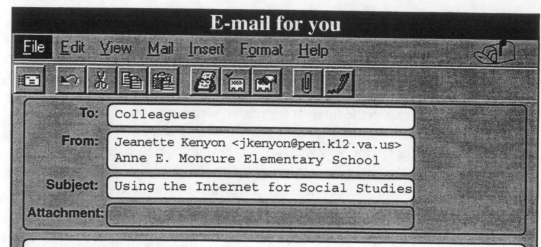

To: Colleagues

From: Jeanette Kenyon <jkenyon@pen.k12.va.us>
Anne E. Moncure Elementary School

Subject: Using the Internet for Social Studies

Attachment:

Dear Colleagues,

Every March my 3rd grade class follows the Iditarod Sled Dog Race using the Internet as our main source of information. Cooperative learning teams decide on a particular musher to follow throughout the race. A large Alaskan map is posted along with pictures, daily race information, weather reports, and interesting race news. The students move their "musher" pin along the trail daily as the race progresses. There are wonderful sites on the World Wide Web which post daily race updates as well as a wealth of background information about the race, the mushers, history of the Iditarod, and life in Alaska. This year, the sites that I found most useful included:

    http://www.newsminer.com/iditarod/
    http://www.starfishsoftware.com/idog/index.html
    http://www.iditarod.com/iditarod/

The links change nearly every year and you might wish to conduct your own search using one of the many search engines. Coverage improves greatly every year but many sites do not become functional until shortly before the race begins. This year coverage included live video and audio clips of race highlights.

It is very easy to incorporate map skills, math practice, including reading charts and graphs, weather studies, cultural lessons, geographical land forms, and even animal rights issues into the unit. There is always a high level of excitement as the students scan the latest race standings and move their musher along the trail. I use a variety of additional materials but my favorites include works by Gary Paulsen and Shelly Gill, who has compiled a very comprehensive curriculum guide for the Iditarod. These books are all available online from Amazon Books at: http://www.amazon.com

Sincerely,   Third grade teacher
Jeanette Kenyon   Anne E. Moncure Elementary School
jkenyon@pen.k12.va.us   Stafford, Virginia

Document: Done

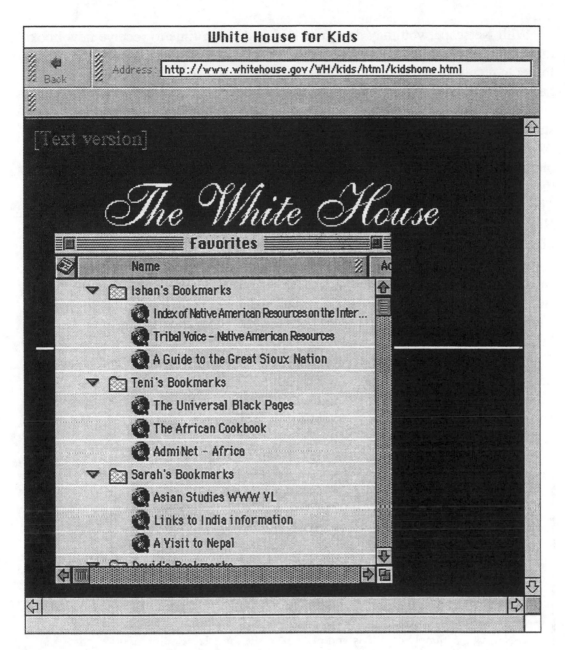

Figure 6-4. Setting individual "favorites" folders in Internet Explorer.

favorites into their bookmark folder. This will help to keep the list of favorites organized for your students.

With Netscape, the process is somewhat similar. To make individual bookmark folders you must first open the bookmark window by clicking on the Window menu item at the top of your Netscape Navigator screen. Select the item called Bookmarks. This will open a separate window for editing and adding new bookmark folders, one for each student. To add a folder for each student, click on the menu item called Item at the top of your screen and select Insert Folder. A window will then open asking you to name this new folder. Simply type in the name of a student here and then select OK to close the window.

With Netscape, you may designate one folder at a time to receive new book-marks. You will need to show students how to make certain they designate their folder to receive new bookmarks. That way, when they add a new bookmark, it will be placed within their folder and not within a folder belonging to someone else.

Designating a student's folder to receive new bookmarks is not difficult. Show students how to open the bookmark window in Netscape Navigator by clicking on the Window menu item at the top of your screen and selecting Bookmarks. As you did before, this will open the window for editing bookmark folders. Now, highlight the folder of the student who is working at the computer by clicking on it once. Then, click on the menu item at the top of your screen called Item and select Set to New Bookmarks Folder. Whenever this student adds a new bookmark, it will be placed in his or her folder, since this is now the active bookmarks folder.

Next, go back up to the menu item at the top of your screen called Item and select Set to Bookmark Menu Folder. This will make only the bookmarks in this student's folder appear when the Bookmark menu item is selected at the top of the Netscape Navigator screen. Close the bookmark window and this student is ready to begin.

Before students begins their session, have them open the bookmark window, designate their folder by clicking on it, and then select the Set to New Bookmarks Folder and Set to Bookmark Menu Folder. This will make their folder the active bookmark folder. You may wish to cover this strategy during an Internet Workshop session.

Internet FAQ

I'd like to use the same bookmark file at home and at school. Can I do this?

Sure! You can copy your bookmark file from one computer onto a floppy disk and then place it on another computer. This will then become the new bookmark file. Be careful, though, because it will replace the previous bookmark file, unless you move this to a safe location when you save it. In Netscape, your bookmark file can be found in your Preferences folder in your System file. It will be in a folder called Netscape *f*. Simply copy this and place it in the same location on another computer. With Internet Explorer, your favorites (bookmarks) can be found in the preferences folder of your system file, too. It will be in a folder called Explorer. Follow the same directions to move it from one computer to another.

Social Studies Resources on the Internet

Contacting the Congress—(http://www.visi.com/juan/congress/)
Use this location to quickly send any of the members of the U.S. Congress an e-mail message about your concerns. It may also be used to request information for your class about units you are planning.

Cybrary of the Holocaust—(http://remember.org/)
This is an incredibly extensive cyber library of resources for individuals wishing to study the Holocaust. Audio interviews from survivors, written recollections by survivors, works of literature, images, and a wide array of resources depict this dark period in our history to ensure that we do not forget.

Excite: Regions—(http://city.net/regions/)
Have your students start here to take tours of various countries and cities around the world. They travel by clicking on the location of the map they wish to visit and, once they arrive, find pictures, information about that location, and links to other sites with more information about their travel destination. A great initial activity to orient your students to the WWW. Formerly called Virtual Tourist II.

MapQuest—(http://www.mapquest.com/)
This is one of the better interactive map services on the WWW. Your students can explore maps of nearly any region, right down to locating their own home on a map of your city. This is a wonderful location to develop map reading skills with your students as you study different regions. Set a bookmark!

National Council for the Social Studies—(http://www.ncss.org/)
This home page for the major professional organization devoted to social studies education contains a nice set of links organized around the ten themes for the Curriculum Standards for Social Studies.

National Geographic Society Home Page—
(http://www.nationalgeographic.com/main.html)
The home page of the National Geographic Society provides for students a wealth of information related to the programming and books of this organization. Within the site is a great location (http://www.nationalgeographic.com/resources/ngo/education/index.html/geoed7.htm) for lesson ideas on geography, an area of the curriculum that is often neglected. Also located at this site are maps which may be printed out by students for reports.

Nova Online/Pyramids: The Inside Story—
(http://www.pbs.org/wgbh/nova/pyramid/)
Take a guided tour inside the great pyramids of Giza, read about the history of these magnificent wonders, share the recent discoveries of archeologists, and come away with a new appreciation for the accomplishments of this ancient civilization. A great site for any class studying ancient Egypt.

Our Story—(http://www.seas.upenn.edu/~cardell/africa.html)
A rich site devoted to the peoples and cultures of Africa, including people in the Americas from Africa. This site contains links to many sites with information about the history, culture, and arts of many rich heritages, all of which trace back to the African continent.

The Early American Review—(http://earlyamerica.com/review/)
An on-line journal on the people, issues, and events of 18th-century America. A wonderful scholarly resource for high school students in an American history course.

The Smithsonian Home Page—(http://www.si.edu/newstart.htm)
The Smithsonian Institution calls itself "The nation's treasure house for learning." This site certainly does it justice. Many outstanding links to the wonderful resources of this fine institution.

The White House for Kids—
(http://www.whitehouse.gov/WH/kids/html/kidshome.html)
Have your students take a tour of the White House and visit the president and his family. Students may also leave a message for the President, read a newsletter for students, and experience several important historical moments that have recently taken place. A great location for Internet Activity in the elementary grades.

Listservs/Mailing Lists for Social Studies

CIVNET—(listserv@listserv.syr.edu)
Conversations about the teaching of civics.

H-HIGH-S—(LISTSERV@msu.edu)
A mailing list for high school teachers of history.

MEMORIES—(listserv@maelstrom.stjohns.edu)
This listserv allows students to talk with survivors of World War II.

NCSS-L—(listproc2@bgu.edu)
The Instructional Technology Committee of National Council for the Social Studies has established this listserv for interested Internet users to share information and ideas about social studies education in grades K-12 and in teacher education.

SOCSTUD-L—(mailserv@hcca.ohio.gov)
Conversations about teaching social studies.

SS435-L—(listserv@ualtavm.bitnet)
Conversations about teaching social studies in the elementary grades.

TAMHA—(listserv@cms.cc.wayne.edu)
Conversations about teaching American history.

Usenet Newsgroup for Social Studies

The Social Studies and History Curriculum in K-12 Education—
(k12.ed.soc-studies)
Discusses instruction in social studies at all grade levels.

7

Science: Using the Internet to Support Scientific Thinking

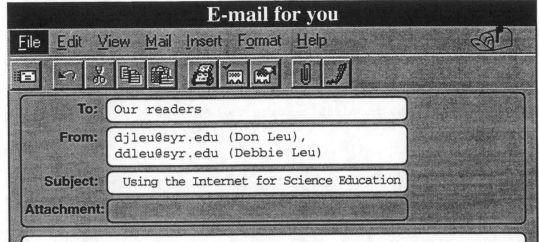

E-mail for you

File Edit View Mail Insert Format Help

To: Our readers

From: djleu@syr.edu (Don Leu),
ddleu@syr.edu (Debbie Leu)

Subject: Using the Internet for Science Education

Attachment:

It is essential that we prepare each of our students to think scientifically if we hope to prepare them for the futures they deserve. Each of us needs to help our students in this area, even if our primary teaching responsibility is not in science education.

Science education is not just about learning facts. At its core, science education helps students to think scientifically. This simply means helping them to ask questions and seek logical answers through observation, reading, writing, and critical analysis. As noted in the National Science Education Standards, science education needs to provide both a "hands on" and a "minds on" experience. Some teachers lack confidence in this area. Approached with the proper perspective, however, science education can become the center of every classroom as you use it to integrate language arts, math, social studies, and other subject areas.

The Internet can be a valuable tool in this process. Learning to use the Internet, itself, is a scientific process as you and your students make hypotheses about how the Internet works and then test them with your browser. Internet Workshop may be especially useful in these efforts.

In addition, the Internet provides extensive resources to help your students as you cultivate their

Document: Continued

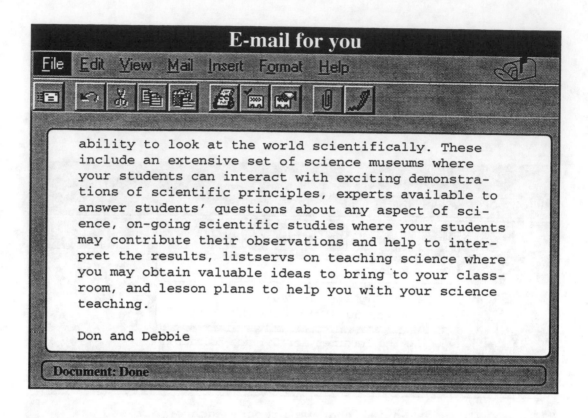

ability to look at the world scientifically. These include an extensive set of science museums where your students can interact with exciting demonstrations of scientific principles, experts available to answer students' questions about any aspect of science, on-going scientific studies where your students may contribute their observations and help to interpret the results, listservs on teaching science where you may obtain valuable ideas to bring to your classroom, and lesson plans to help you with your science teaching.

Don and Debbie

Document: Done

Teaching with the Internet: Anne Thomas's Class

As Anne Thomas walked into Room 301, a full week before school started in the fall, she saw the quotation behind her desk and smiled. It was a simple sentence, a sentence she had found during her first attempts at navigating the Internet several years ago. She had copied the quotation onto an index card and posted it behind her desk so she would see it every time she entered the room. The worn card, quoting an early rocket scientist, said:

> It is difficult to say what is impossible, for the dream of yesterday is the hope of today and the reality of tomorrow.—Robert Goddard

This card held many meanings as it greeted her each morning. It reminded her of the passionate belief she had in the potential of every child in her room. It also reminded her of all that she had accomplished in learning to use the Internet, especially in the area of science.

When Anne first started teaching, three years ago, she did not feel comfortable teaching science. She quickly formed a team teaching relationship with her friend next door. They team taught social studies and science that first year and the following year, each focusing on the subject area they knew best. Anne learned a lot about science teaching from this relationship as she increased her understanding of the Internet.

Her mind drifted to last year, the third year her school had been connected to the Internet and the first year she had actually taught science by herself. She smiled again as she recalled some of her experiences. She had started the year cautiously, doing a unit on the solar system and integrating language arts experiences by reading *This Planet Has No Atmosphere* by Paula Danzinger and *A Wrinkle in Time* by Madeleine L'Engle. She set bookmarks on Internet Explorer for **The Nine Planets Tour** (http://seds.lpl.arizona.edu/billa/tnp/), **The Hubble Space Telescope** (http://www.stsci.edu/), and the home page for the current **Space Shuttle** mission at NASA (http://www.ksc.nasa.gov/shuttle/countdown/). She developed several short Internet Activity Assignments for students to complete at these locations. She also subscribed to several listservs for science educators, following the conversations to see if she could get some good ideas for her class. One of the best conversations mentioned the **National Standards for Science Education** and gave the URL for this document (http://www.nap.edu/readingroom/books/nses/html/). She explored this site and its links, learning about the new science standards and getting several useful ideas, especially the concept of science as inquiry.

Over a holiday break, Anne discovered the location for **NASA K-12 Internet Initiative: Online Interactive Projects** (http://quest.arc.nasa.gov/interactive/index.html), a wonderful site with opportunities for her students to work directly with the men and women scientists at NASA. From here, she located the **Shuttle/Mir Online Research Experience** (http://quest.arc.nasa.gov/smore/), an Internet Project site. This contained an outstanding set of science experiences related to the Space Shuttle and MIR collaboration, including: information about science projects taking place, biographies of the scientists on the project, experiments students could complete, a discussion group for teachers and students, and many outstanding lesson plans. This allowed her students to collect data and contribute to an on-going science study through Internet Project. They enjoyed comparing their observations with observations made by other students around the world. Most important, the NASA scientists opened the world of science to her students by sharing their excitement about the important work they do.

Toward the end of the year, Anne decided to try Internet Inquiry with cooperative group science projects. Students worked in groups of twos and threes to identify an important scientific question. Then they used the Internet and their school library to try to discover the answer. Internet Workshop sessions twice a week seemed to help students a lot with their inquiry projects. At the end of the unit, the class held a science fair with each group setting up a "poster session," describing their question, their work, and what they had discovered on a large poster board. Some students even developed Kid-Teaching-Kids activities on the Internet.

Anne remembered the project Tyronne and Alex had shared at their science fair. Tyronne and Alex had both been interested in the ant farm she brought into the classroom after the winter holidays. They were fascinated by the continuous activity of these insects. The question they wanted to answer in their Internet Inquiry was "Do ants ever sleep?" When they shared this question during Internet Workshop, other students had all kinds of suggestions. They could check in the library for books about animals. They could check on the Internet by doing a search with one of the search engines for "ants" and "sleep." Someone also gave them the URL for **The**

Figure 7-1.
The home
page for
NASA K-12
Internet
Initiative:
Online
Interactive
Projects.

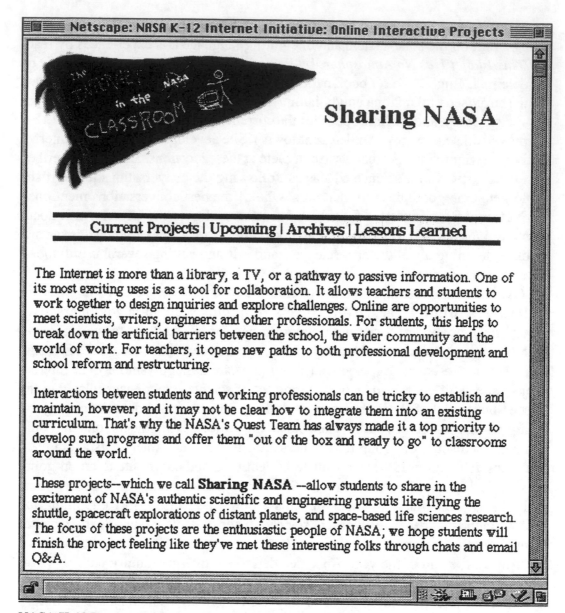

NASA K-12 Internet Initiative: Online Interactive Projects
(http://quest.arc.nasa.gov/interactive/index.html)

Mad Scientist Network, a place on the Internet where they could ask a scientist this question (http://www.madsci.org/). And, someone else suggested that they mark one ant and watch it for 24 hours to see if it ever stopped to sleep. The idea of staying up all night caught their attention and they pleaded with Anne to take the class ant farm home over the weekend. She finally relented and, after they selected one ant ("Hooty") and marked him with a non-toxic marker, Anne dropped the ant farm off at Alex's house Friday after school.

Tyronne and Alex made observations every fifteen minutes in their science journal for an entire day and learned that Hooty never stopped to take a rest and never stopped working. They even took some pictures for their poster session at the science fair. They created a wonderful poster that presented all of their work. It included photos, a written report describing their research, and the conclusions they reached. They also included the e-mail message in Figure 7-2 from a scientist in Australia. They were pleased they had figured out a way to answer their question using a method that even the adult scientist had not considered.

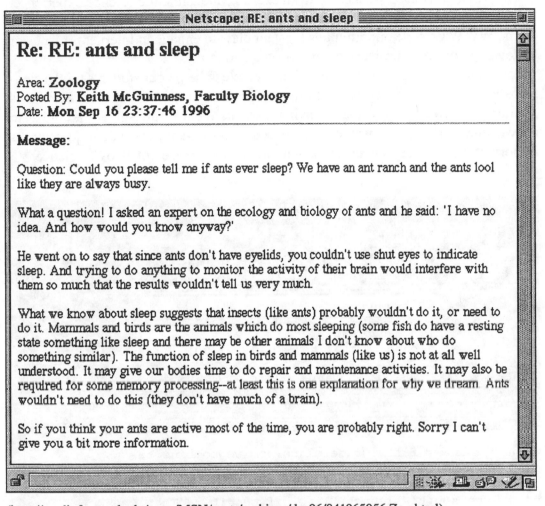

Figure 7-2. Tyronne's and Alex's response from an Australian scientist on the Mad Scientist Network.

Re: RE: ants and sleep

Area: **Zoology**
Posted By: **Keith McGuinness, Faculty Biology**
Date: **Mon Sep 16 23:37:46 1996**

Message:

Question: Could you please tell me if ants ever sleep? We have an ant ranch and the ants lool like they are always busy.

What a question! I asked an expert on the ecology and biology of ants and he said: 'I have no idea. And how would you know anyway?'

He went on to say that since ants don't have eyelids, you couldn't use shut eyes to indicate sleep. And trying to do anything to monitor the activity of their brain would interfere with them so much that the results wouldn't tell us very much.

What we know about sleep suggests that insects (like ants) probably wouldn't do it, or need to do it. Mammals and birds are the animals which do most sleeping (some fish do have a resting state something like sleep and there may be other animals I don't know about who do something similar). The function of sleep in birds and mammals (like us) is not at all well understood. It may give our bodies time to do repair and maintenance activities. It may also be required for some memory processing--at least this is one explanation for why we dream. Ants wouldn't need to do this (they don't have much of a brain).

So if you think your ants are active most of the time, you are probably right. Sorry I can't give you a bit more information.

(http://medinfo.wustl.edu/~ysp/MSN/posts/archives/dec96/841965056.Zo.r.html)

Lessons from the Classroom

The Internet provides many helpful resources that can assist you in developing an exciting and dynamic science program in your classroom.

This story from Anne Thomas's classroom has several important lessons for each of us to consider. First, the Internet provides many helpful resources to assist you in developing an exciting and dynamic science program in your classroom, a program consistent with the National Science Education Standard's emphasis on thinking scientifically through inquiry.

Second, Internet Activity may be used in your classroom to enrich your science program, especially when you are just beginning to use the Internet. These take little

Working with the scientists at NASA and other classrooms around the world provided Anne's students with an exciting and authentic science experience.

time but provide important experiences for your students as you begin to explore the Internet in the classroom.

Third, Internet projects are a powerful way of helping your students to think scientifically as they work collaboratively with others to gather data and interpret the results. Working with the scientists at NASA and other classrooms around the world provided Anne's students with an exciting and authentic science experience. They learned much about this special way of looking at the world. Several locations on the WWW provide opportunities for your class to engage in Internet projects, or to develop your own projects and invite others to join.

Fourth, Internet Inquiry is an excellent vehicle to help your students think scientifically as you develop a science-as-inquiry program in your classroom. Science is as much a verb as it is a noun. Having students identify questions they wish to answer and then helping them to develop techniques for answering their questions is important in preparing students who not only *know* science but also *do* science.

Science is as much a verb as it is a noun. Having students identify questions they wish to answer and then helping them to develop techniques for answering their questions is important in preparing students who not only know *science but also* do *science.*

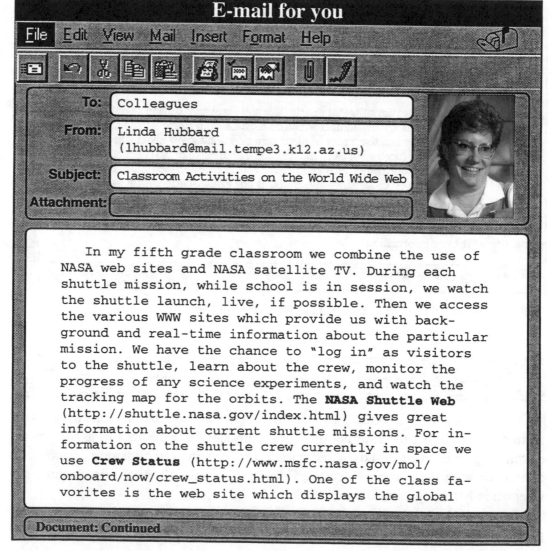

E-mail for you

File   Edit   View   Mail   Insert   Format   Help

To: Colleagues

From: Linda Hubbard
(lhubbard@mail.tempe3.k12.az.us)

Subject: Classroom Activities on the World Wide Web

Attachment:

In my fifth grade classroom we combine the use of NASA web sites and NASA satellite TV. During each shuttle mission, while school is in session, we watch the shuttle launch, live, if possible. Then we access the various WWW sites which provide us with background and real-time information about the particular mission. We have the chance to "log in" as visitors to the shuttle, learn about the crew, monitor the progress of any science experiments, and watch the tracking map for the orbits. The **NASA Shuttle Web** (http://shuttle.nasa.gov/index.html) gives great information about current shuttle missions. For information on the shuttle crew currently in space we use **Crew Status** (http://www.msfc.nasa.gov/mol/onboard/now/crew_status.html). One of the class favorites is the web site which displays the global

Document: Continued

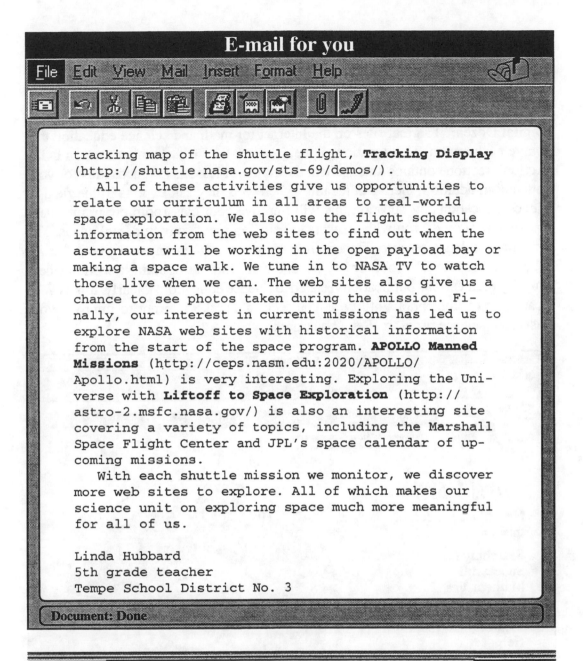

E-mail for you

File   Edit   View   Mail   Insert   Format   Help

tracking map of the shuttle flight, **Tracking Display**
(http://shuttle.nasa.gov/sts-69/demos/).
   All of these activities give us opportunities to
relate our curriculum in all areas to real-world
space exploration. We also use the flight schedule
information from the web sites to find out when the
astronauts will be working in the open payload bay or
making a space walk. We tune in to NASA TV to watch
those live when we can. The web sites also give us a
chance to see photos taken during the mission. Finally, our interest in current missions has led us to
explore NASA web sites with historical information
from the start of the space program. **APOLLO Manned
Missions** (http://ceps.nasm.edu:2020/APOLLO/
Apollo.html) is very interesting. Exploring the Uni-
verse with **Liftoff to Space Exploration** (http://
astro-2.msfc.nasa.gov/) is also an interesting site
covering a variety of topics, including the Marshall
Space Flight Center and JPL's space calendar of upcoming missions.
   With each shuttle mission we monitor, we discover
more web sites to explore. All of which makes our
science unit on exploring space much more meaningful
for all of us.

Linda Hubbard
5th grade teacher
Tempe School District No. 3

Document: Done

Central Sites for Science Education

There are a number of central sites on the Internet for science education. One type provides you with a wide array of links to useful curricular and other resources for science education. Another will provide you with information about the national science standards. Others will provide you with science units, ideas for science demonstrations, and/or lesson plans. Finally, some locations will be useful if you wish to subscribe to listservs related to science education. Each will be useful to you as you consider the broader issues of your science education program.

If you only have time to visit one central site, pay a visit to the **Eisenhower National Clearinghouse for Mathematics and Science Education** (http://

If you only have time to visit one central site, pay a visit to the Eisenhower National Center for Mathematics and Science Education.

www.enc.org:80/index.htm). This federally funded project provides K-12 teachers with a central source of information on mathematics and science education. The home page image hardly gives a hint of the tremendously useful resources available here. We have found the best resources linked to the image labeled "Action" or "Reform in Action." Click on this image. One section contains links to a monthly "Digital Dozen," 13 great sites on the Internet for math and science education that change each month. This location, alone, is worth the visit. Another section in the "Action" section contains an excellent collection of lessons and activities for your students. In addition, there is a location where you may ask experts in the field of science education any question that will improve your classroom program. These experts will provide you with answers to help you meet your students' needs. The web site also has a resource finder, allowing you to search an extensive set of instructional resources by topic or key word. Finally, this site contains a section where you may read various publications related to science education. Clearly, this WWW location is of tremendous utility as you seek to use the Internet to improve your classroom science program. Set a bookmark!

Figure 7-3. The home page for the **Eisenhower National Clearinghouse for Mathematics and Science Education,** an outstanding central site for science education.

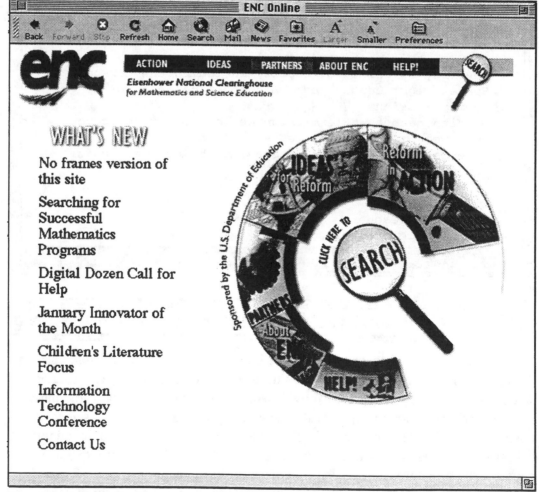

Eisenhower National Clearinghouse for Mathematics and Science Education
(http://www.enc.org:80/index.htm)

Another excellent site to use as a jumping off point is **Frank Potter's Science Gems** (http://www-sci.lib.uci.edu/SEP/SEP.html). Developed at the University of California at Irvine, this site contains over 2,000 links to outstanding science resources on the WWW. What is especially nice about this location is that resources are organized by science area (e.g., physical science, Earth science, life science, etc.) and by topic within each area (e.g., within Earth science there are locations for measurement, earth, solar system, astronomy, atmosphere, land/oceans, and natural resources). Each topic is also organized by grade level. The organizational scheme used at this site allows you to quickly find resources for units you are planning to teach in your class.

You may also be interested in taking a look at the **National Science Education Standards** (http://www.nap.edu/readingroom/books/nses/html/overview.html), a document describing science standards at different grade levels. Many teachers find that this provides important support as they review the nature of their science education program.

Another type of central site provides teaching plans for busy teachers. Many of these are good beginning points as you consider ways in which to help your students become scientifically literate and think scientifically. One of the most comprehensive sites is **Lessons and Activities for Science** (http://www.enc.org:80/classroom/index.htm), a location at the Eisenhower National Clearinghouse for Mathematics and Science Education site mentioned earlier. This site contains links to outstanding locations containing more lesson plans and activities than you would be able to complete in a lifetime of teaching. Exploring these locations will give you many good ideas for your science program.

Teachers often use demonstrations to catch students' interest and get them to think scientifically. There are a number of useful locations on the WWW with demonstrations you can provide to your class to illustrate scientific principles or to initiate conversations about causes and effects. One of the best collections of demonstrations is **The Exploratorium Science Snackbook** (http://www.exploratorium.edu/publications/Snackbook/Snackbook.html). This allows you to quickly replicate many of the exciting exhibits at one of the world's premier science museums. Another location with outstanding classroom demonstrations may be found at the site for **N.E.R.D.S.** (http://nerds.unl.edu/nerds.html), or Nebraska Educators Really Doing Science). A third location with exciting demonstrations is **Whelmers** (http://www.mcrel.org/whelmers/). Developed by Steven Jacobs, these demonstrations catch students by surprise and get them to really think about physical principles. Each is aligned with the National Science Education Standards.

One of the best collections of demonstrations is The Exploratorium Science Snackbook.

Finally, you may find it useful to follow the discussions in several listservs/mailing lists. If you are an elementary teacher, consider subscribing to **T321-L**, a discussion group for teaching science in elementary schools (listserv@mizzou1.missouri.edu). Another is **CYBERMARCH-NET**, a discussion group for teachers interested in environmental education (majordomo@igc.apc.org). Additional listservs/mailing lists as well as several science education newsgroups are listed at the end of this chapter.

TEACHING TIP

If you wish to keep up with the most recent developments in earth science, take a look at **Web Earth Science for Teachers** (http://www.usatoday.com/weather/wteach.htm), a location within *USA Today*. This has an extensive list of science links closely related to current event items in the news. There are also links to lesson plans and activities you can use in your classroom. This is an especially good resource for integrating weather resources into instruction.

Keeping It Simple: Using Internet Activity with Internet Workshop

Excellent Internet Activity assignments may be developed from the many resources located at science museums around the world. These often provide exciting simulations, demonstrations, or science puzzles for students.

Internet Activity is a good way to begin using the Internet in your classroom for science education. Internet Activity assignments are easy to set up and require minimum navigation knowledge by either you or your students. Locate a site on the Internet with content related to your science unit, perhaps by using one of the central sites described above, and set a bookmark for this location. Next, develop a thoughtful activity that requires students to use the information at the site. Then, assign the activity to your students to complete during the week. Finally, share your experiences during Internet Workshop.

Excellent Internet Activity assignments may be developed from the many resources located at science museums around the world. These often provide exciting simulations, demonstrations, or science puzzles for students. By developing appropriate Internet Activity assignments, you can engage your students in scientific thinking.

A good place to begin is the **Science Learning Network** (http://www.sln.org/), a central site for museums and science educators around the world. Their **Inquiry Resources Page** (http://www.sln.org/) contains links to outstanding, interactive science activities designed by the finest science museums we have. Activities range from a virtual cow's eye dissection for a unit on optics to a visit to Leonardo da Vinci's workshop. It also contains links to many great science activities at different museums and a searchable data base that allows you to quickly find science activities by topic and grade level. In addition, this location contains wonderful resources for collaborating with other science teachers around the world, including: an on-line chat area, a projects area, and a bulletin board. Stop by and explore this important location supported by the National Science Foundation.

The best science museum we know for students is San Francisco's Exploratorium. It used to be that only Bay Area students were fortunate enough to access the many exciting and informative science exhibits there. Now, anyone with an Internet connection can participate. Be certain to pay a visit to the **Exploratorium Home Page** (http://www.exploratorium.edu/). You won't regret it. Another museum with great interactive exhibits is **London's National Museum of Science and Industry** (http:/

/www.nmsi.ac.uk/). You may also wish to visit an excellent collection of links to interactive science museums around the world at **Hands-on Science Centers Worldwide** (http://www.cs.cmu.edu/~mwm/sci.html).

Here are several examples of Internet Activity assignments that might be developed for science units.

- **The Science of Cycling.** Invite your students to visit this Exploratorium location (http://www.exploratorium.edu/cycling/brakes2.html) to gain a scientific view of a common activity—cycling. Use a jigsaw grouping technique and assign small groups to different aspects of the science of cycling: the wheel, braking and steering, frames and materials, aerodynamics, and human power. Have each group explore their section, completing the interactive simulations of items such as braking distance under different conditions, and then prepare a short presentation during Internet Workshop to explain the science of their area.

- **A Virtual Dissection of a Cow's Eye.** If you are doing a unit on optics or physiology, you may wish to set a bookmark for The Cow's Eye Dissection (http://www.exploratorium.edu/learning_studio/cow_eye/). Here students are taken step-by-step through the dissection with supporting glossary terms for the parts of the eye; RealAudio sound clips from the Exploratorium staff explain what is taking place. This location also contains a program students can download to your computer that will help them to learn the physiology of a cow's eye. Have students explore the entire WWW location in order to draw an accurate illustration of a cow's eye with each of the important parts labeled. On a separate page, have them explain how this important body part works. Post these next to your computer as they are completed. Afterwards, have them ask an expert from the Exploratorium via e-mail a really great question about how a cow's eye works. Post questions and answers.

- **Storm Science.** During a unit on weather for third or fourth graders, set a bookmark to **Hurricane: Storm Science** (http://www.miamisci.org/hurricane/), a location at the Miami Science Museum. Have students track several hurricanes on an interactive map, make a storm hunter plane, read narratives from the members of a family that survived a hurricane, make several weather instruments, and contribute a story of a personal disaster or a work of art to the healing quilt. After the experience, have students send a really good question about the weather to a scientist at **The Mad Scientist Network** (http://www.madsci.org/). Post questions and answers as they arrive.

Internet Activity assignments such as these will enable you to support science units with Internet experiences that require little preparation time yet provide important experiences for your students.

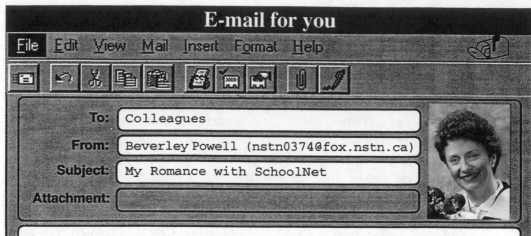

E-mail for you

File   Edit   View   Mail   Insert   Format   Help

To: Colleagues

From: Beverley Powell (nstn0374@fox.nstn.ca)

Subject: My Romance with SchoolNet

Attachment:

Based on my experience in elementary teaching and information consulting, I think that all the teachers reading the new edition of this book should be aware of the educational potential of **Canada's SchoolNet** (http://www.schoolnet.ca).

SchoolNet is a collaboration between federal, provincial, and territorial governments, the education profession and industry. It ties in Canada's elementary and secondary schools, libraries and museums. It is a world-class educational resource offering a vast range of informational opportunities. For example:

The GrassRoots Program—(http://www.schoolnet.ca/grassroots/) Motivates teachers and students to design, create and implement pedagogically sound interactive classroom projects for the Internet.

SchoolNet Digital Collections (SDC)—(http://www.schoolnet.ca/collections/) Exhibits more than 100 collections from Canadian archives, libraries, museums, etc. A federal Industry Canada program contracts with young students to produce this multimedia portrait of Canada.

Special Needs Education Network—(http://www.schoolnet.ca/sne/) Provides access to Internet resources for parents, teachers, schools and others in the education of students with special needs.

International Program—(http://www.schoolnet.ca) Increases understanding among peoples of the world. Students and teachers around the world, with the help of sponsors, collaborate on projects using cultural themes. Expertise and exemplary practices are exchanged. Global entrepreneurship is encouraged. The World Bank has been involved.

Document: Continued

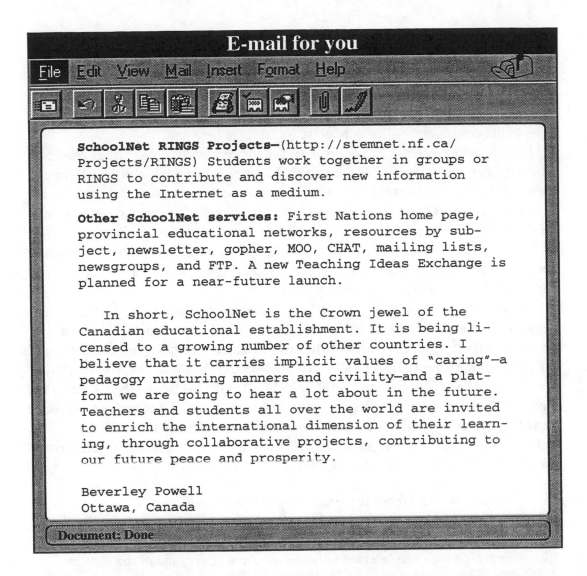

Internet Project is useful in science for several reasons. First, it creates situations where students help one another to discover important concepts. Internet Project takes natural advantage of opportunities for socially mediated learning, opportunities that are so powerful within the Internet for science education.

Second, Internet Project provides natural opportunities for curricular integration with science and other subject areas. Internet Project requires students to engage in language arts experiences as they communicate with others via e-mail. These experiences also lend themselves to social studies as students learn about different parts of the world and the social and cultural characteristics that define those locations. In addition, Internet Project often requires students to engage in math experiences. A project comparing weather patterns in different parts of the world, for example, will require students to record rain amounts, wind speed, and temperature, and calculate the means for these over an extended period of time. Students may also have to compare and perhaps graph meteorological data reported from other locations. Thus, Internet projects in science contain inherent possibilities for curricular integration, an important concern for busy teachers who have to continually squeeze new additions to the curriculum within school days that do not expand.

Finally, when Internet Project is designed appropriately it can foster scientific thinking. Thinking scientifically involves developing and evaluating best guesses about why things are the way there are. This can be an important part of any Internet project in science. Classes in different parts of the world often see the same issue in different ways because of different cultural traditions. Internet projects in science allow students to question one another, decide upon appropriate ways of evaluating competing hypotheses, gather information, and evaluate that information to reach conclusions that are agreed to by all parties.

As you begin to consider Internet projects around science topics, be certain to visit the central locations for this approach described earlier to find examples of Internet Project: **NASA's Online Interactive Projects** (http://quest.arc.nasa.gov/interactive/index.html), **Telecollaborative Learning Around the World** (http://www1.minn.net:80/~schubert/NickNacks.html), **Global SchoolNet's Internet Project Registry** (http://www.gsn.org/project/index.html), **Classroom Connect's Teacher Contact Database** (http://www.classroom.net/contact/), and **The Global School House** (http://www.gsh.org/class/default.htm). Examples of projects posted previously at some of these sites include:

- **Where in the World is Cynthia San Francisco—** (http://k12science.stevens-tech.edu/curriculum/weather/c3whome.html). This project takes your students on a real world scientific investigation in which they use Internet resources to solve "the crime of the century." For a two-week period, your students receive clues that take them to the location of the United States' leading nuclear physicist, Cynthia San Francisco, who was recently kidnapped by a hostile organization. Clues come from real-time weather data, such as satellite images, weather stations, and current weather maps. Students use interactive weather web sites in conjunction with the clues to determine the location of Dr. San Francisco. Along with each clue, your class receives a hands-on experiment/activity which your students can explore to better understand the weather concept to which the clue relates. With each new clue you also receive the answer to the last one, thus allowing teachers and students to confirm that they are on the right track. During the project, students can collaborate with other participating schools as well as with an expert meteorologist who will answer all of their weather-related questions.

- **Night Of The Comet**—(http://ccf.arc.nasa.gov/comet/index.html). Sponsored by NASA at their page for **Online Interactive Projects** (http://quest.arc.nasa.gov/interactive/index.html#archives), this project provided a forum for observing and discussing the passing of Comet Hyakutake. Students at over 100 locations around the world contributed their observations, questions, and answers to this "First Virtual Star Party." Students could ask experts at NASA questions, send in their photos of the comet for viewing by others, read about comet facts, and participate in a series of experiments. Be certain to visit the location describing current projects (http://quest.arc.nasa.gov/interactive/index.html) to discover new opportunities in space science. Set a bookmark!

- **Worldwide Weather Watch.**   A first grade teacher from Macedon, New York and second grade teachers from Mound, Minnesota posted this science project and attracted classrooms from the United States; Canberra, Australia; and Tasmania. Primary school students around the world compared global weather conditions by sharing monthly e-mail reports about their weather, what they wore, and what they were did outside. Students learned about different temperature scales, seasonal change in different hemispheres, measurement, math, cultural variation, and language arts.

- **Earth Day Groceries Project**—
  (http://www.halcyon.com/arborhts/earthday.html).
  Each year participating classes obtain grocery bags from local supermarkets, decorate them with environmental messages, and then return them to be used at the grocery store by customers. Students share photos and reports of their accomplishments at a central site. A teacher at the Arbor Heights Elementary School in Seattle, Washington has developed this wonderful environmental awareness project. Over 300 schools around the world participated last year, distributing over 120,000 grocery bags decorated with messages about the environment.

- **The Boiling Point of Water.**   A teacher in Denver posted a recent project asking classrooms at different elevations around the world to conduct a simple experiment, share data, and then analyze the data and compare results. On the same day, each class obtained the elevation for their location and then measured carefully the temperature at which water boiled. Each class shared their observation with each of the other classes. Then students in each class plotted the relationship between elevation and the boiling point of water. As classes shared their results, they discovered that water does not always boil at 100 degrees Celsius or 212 degrees Fahrenheit.

Figure 7-4.
The **Earth Day Groceries Project,** a great environmental awareness project site, developed by a teacher at Arbor Heights Elementary School in Seattle, Washington.

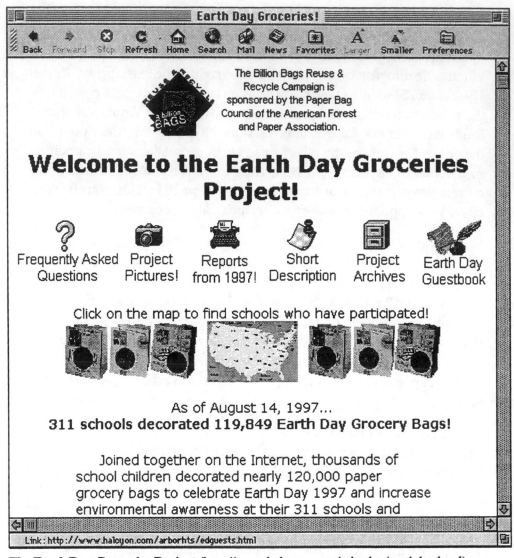

The **Earth Day Groceries Project** (http://www.halcyon.com/arborhts/earthday.html)

Internet FAQ

I am using Netscape 3.0 in my fourth grade class. Why do I always get an "Out of Memory" message after several students use the Internet in the morning?

There are a number of reasons for an "Out of Memory" message. This message is telling you that your RAM (Random Access Memory) or the memory allocated to Netscape has reached its limit. There are three possible solutions. First, see if you can obtain additional RAM. This requires inserting one or several new chips. You will need to talk to the technical support person at your school about this. Second, try having each student quit Netscape when they finish their session. Netscape keeps track of each site you visit and this list often gets lengthy, taking up much of Netscape's memory allocation. Quitting Netscape deletes this list and frees up memory. Third, you may choose to use an earlier version of Netscape. These require less RAM and will give you more memory to use as you navigate the WWW.

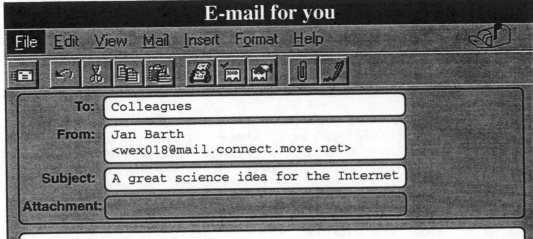

E-mail for you

File   Edit   View   Mail   Insert   Format   Help

To: Colleagues

From: Jan Barth
<wex018@mail.connect.more.net>

Subject: A great science idea for the Internet

Attachment:

Hello!
    I would like to share an idea for classroom
Internet use with you. You can use this idea if you
have one or many terminals available. If only one
terminal is available, a team of students can take
turns searching and presenting information. If several terminals are available, then students can work
either individually or in teams to get information.
Sites should be bookmarked ahead of time to make the
best use of the student's time in the classroom. A
good site to start with is for the **Oil Spill Public
Information Center's site**: (www.alaska.net/~ospi).
    In my 8th grade unit on conservation of resources,
classes used the net to research an environmental
disaster, the Exxon Valdez oil spill in Alaska on
March 24, 1989. Each student prepared a report about
how the spill occurred, the impact it had on plant
and animal life and the food chain, and the methods
of clean up after the spill. They used all their
accumulated information about the spill and clean up
efforts to devise a way to clean up a simulated oil
spill in the classroom. Teams of 3 students worked
cooperatively to determine the best way to clean up
the spill. They were to consider cost of the materials and time for the clean up. If you desire, a competition can be held between teams to determine winners. Be sure to have a scoring guide in place before
the teams begin their planning and the actual competition takes place. That way, students know what they
are working toward.
    The students loved researching about the oil spill
on the net. They found pictures, great information
about how the spill occurred and information about
the clean up and the effect of the spill on the living organisms. The great thing about researching this
particular spill is that there are follow-up research

Document: Continued

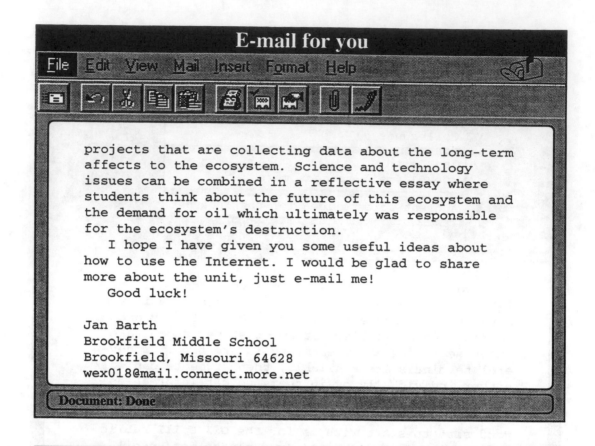

projects that are collecting data about the long-term
affects to the ecosystem. Science and technology
issues can be combined in a reflective essay where
students think about the future of this ecosystem and
the demand for oil which ultimately was responsible
for the ecosystem's destruction.

I hope I have given you some useful ideas about
how to use the Internet. I would be glad to share
more about the unit, just e-mail me!

Good luck!

Jan Barth
Brookfield Middle School
Brookfield, Missouri 64628
wex018@mail.connect.more.net

Using Internet Inquiry with Internet Workshop

Children have so many questions about the world around them and there are so many resources on the Internet to engage them in careful study of natural phenomena that Internet Inquiry should be an important part of your science program.

Internet Inquiry is a perfect vehicle for helping your students to think scientifically, critically, and carefully about the natural world. Children have so many questions about the world around them and there are so many resources on the Internet to engage them in careful study of natural phenomena that Internet Inquiry should be an important part of your science program.

You will recall that Internet Inquiry usually contains five phases: question, search, analyze, compose, and share. In the first phase, students identify an important question they wish to answer; usually this is related to the unit you are studying. You can support this phase by participating in group brainstorming sessions or by conducting an Internet Workshop around the topic of important questions that might be explored. In addition, you may wish to brainstorm individually with students who are having difficulty identifying an intriguing question. Another very nice strategy during this phase is to set a bookmark for science museums or other science sites and encourage students to explore these locations for an interesting question to address.

During the second phase, search, students look for information and/or perform experiments to address the question they have posed. They may search on the Internet for useful resources, experiments, and demonstrations. Students should also be encouraged to use more traditional resources that may be found in their classroom or school library.

During the third phase, analyze, students analyze all of the information they have in order to respond to the question they initially posed. Sometimes this phase leads to a straightforward answer derived from several supporting lines of evidence: the results of an experiment, a graph of data, an e-mail response from a scientist, documentation from several books or Internet locations, or an e-mail message from another student studying the same question. Often, the analysis phase may be supported by peer conferences where students share their results and think about their meanings. Or, you may wish to use Internet Workshop to support students' analytic skills.

TEACHING TIP

Internet Inquiry often leads students to other interesting questions and ideas about the issues they study. When students develop an especially intriguing question during their work, invite them to discuss it with an expert via e-mail. Communicating with experts via e-mail can be very helpful to students and brings them into the real world of scientists who are also exploring interesting questions. Be certain, however, that students only use these resources when they are unable to discover an answer on their own. People at ask-an-expert sites do not like to do homework for students who should really do it on their own. You can help by conducting an Internet Workshop session on how to ask the best question possible. A list of e-mail addresses and WWW locations where students may contact experts in science is provided in Figure 7-5.

The fourth phase, compose, requires students to compose a presentation of their work. This may be a written report, a poster board display, or an oral report with displays of evidence. You may wish to follow process writing procedures to support this phase by engaging students in drafting, revision, and editing conferences.

The final phase, share, is an opportunity for students to share their work with others and respond to questions about their investigation. Some teachers set aside a regular time one day a week for sharing Inquiry Projects as they are completed. You may wish to use a variation of an Author's Chair in your classroom by designating a Scientist's Chair for use during presentations of Inquiry projects. Alternatively, you may wish to have a science fair in your classroom at the end of each unit where students may display their work and answer questions as students circulate around, visiting each of the presentations. Or you may wish to conduct a Kids-Teaching-Kids activity as described in Chapter 6.

Internet Inquiry can be an exciting aspect of your classroom and your science program. It provides independent explorations of the scientific world, opportunities to contact real scientists about important issues, and opportunities to support the development of scientific thinking.

Figure 7-5.
WWW locations and e-mail addresses for contacting experts in various fields.

General Locations for Contacting Experts in Science

Ask an Expert—(http://www.askanexpert.com/askanexpert/)
This is a general site with links to a wide range of experts.

Ask a Mad Scientist—(http://www.madsci.org)
This wonderful resource will put you in touch with a wide range of scientists around the world.

Locations for Contacting Specific Types of Experts in Science

Ask an Architect—(http://www.askanarchitect.com/form.html)
Obtain answers to questions about designing spaces.

Ask an Astronaut—(http://www.nss.org/askastro/home.html)
email: rpearllman@nss.org
Obtain answers to questions about space science and being an astronaut.

Ask an Astronomer—(http://bolero.gsfc.nasa.gov/~odenwald/ask/askmag.html)
email: starman@unc.edu
Obtain answers to questions about stars, planets, comets, and other aspects of astronomy.

Ask Dr. Science—(http://www.ducksbreath.com/index.html)
Obtain answers to all kinds of questions about science.

Ask an Earth Scientist—(http://www.soest.hawaii.edu/GG/ASK/askanerd.html)
Obtain answers to questions about the natural workings and natural history of the Hawaiian Islands and the world.

Ask a Geologist—(http://walrus.wr.usgs.gov/docs/ask-a-ge.html)
email: Ask a Geologist@usgs.gov
Obtain answers to questions about rocks, geology, and earth forms.

Ask a Gravity Expert—(http://www.physics.umd.edu/rgroups/gen_rel_the/question.html)
Obtain answers to questions about gravity.

Ask an Ocean Animal Expert—(http://www.whaletimes.org/whaques.htm)
email: whaletimes@whaletimes.org
Obtain answers to questions about all types of marine animals.

Ask a Science Expert—(http://sln.fi.edu:80/tfi/publications/askexprt.html)
Obtain answers to questions about science from the Franklin Museum in Philadelphia.

Ask a Vulcanologist—(http://volcano.und.nodak.edu/vwdocs/ask_a.html)
Obtain answers to questions about volanoes from experts in this field.

Science Resources on the Internet

Bill Nye The Science Guy—(http://nyelabs.kcts.org/)
A great resource related to the popular series on your local Public Broadcasting System television station. There is, of course, information on programming including home science demonstrations and lessons for upcoming topics. There is also a location to send the science guy e-mail. More importantly, there is a search engine that will connect you to outstanding science sites on the WWW. Science rules, indeed!

Jumbo—(http://www.jumbo.com/)
Looking for shareware and freeware to download and use in your classroom for science units? Here is the location with the largest set of programs to download on the WWW. Check out the science and the education sections for many useful resources.

Live from Antarctica—(http://quest.arc.nasa.gov/antarctica/index.html)
Here are enough resources for an entire year's project on science taking place in Antarctica. Dates and times for a series of related television programs are listed as well as a teacher's guide and classroom lessons, questions and answers between students and scientists, a bibliography of related resources, links to other sites with information on the Antarctic, weekly newspapers published in the Antarctic, and contact with scientists studying the plant life and the ozone hole.

Mars Missions—(http://marsweb.jpl.nasa.gov/)
During a five-day period this past year, more than 260,000,000 visited the WWW location of the Mars Pathfinder Project to learn about the most recent developments and view the latest photos from the Martian surface. Here is the main site for all of NASA's scientific explorations of Mars, including upcoming work by the Mars Global Surveyor. Stop by to see some remarkable images and learn about some remarkable scientists!

Monarch Watch—(http://www.MonarchWatch.org/)
Here is a wonderful opportunity to participate in science studies of the Monarch butterfly, sponsored by the Department of Entomology at the University of Kansas. The site contains an extremely comprehensive set of resources for studying Monarchs and sharing your observations, especially of their migration through your area. Find out about migration patterns, join one of several science projects, learn how to raise and release Monarchs in your classroom, learn how to start a butterfly garden near your classroom, and communicate with scientists who study these beautiful creatures. Set a bookmark!

Rainforest Action Network—(http://www.ran.org/ran/)

If you are engaged in an ecology or rainforest unit, here is a great location to find out about the latest efforts to preserve these important parts of our ecosystem. Many links for those who are serious about preserving our planet and its systems.

The Franklin Museum Science Institute—(http://www.fi.edu/)

This is one of the finest science museums around, devoted to helping children think scientifically and explore the fantastic world around them. There are so many great experiences for students it is hard to know where to start. Perhaps with the science of thrill rides? Maybe an interactive exhibit on the workings of the heart? Or maybe explore the adaptations of animals to urban environments? You may even follow the life of a high school biology classroom. Wonderful. Set a bookmark!

The Hubble Space Telescope's Public Page—
(http://oposite.stsci.edu/pubinfo/)

Here is the location for the Hubble Space Telescope and all of the wonderful science taking place with this instrument. Many incredible photos of deep space illustrating a number of new insights discovered with this technology. Many links for teachers and students interested in space study are also found here.

The Nine Planets: A Multimedia Tour of the Solar System—
(http://seds.lpl.arizona.edu/billa/tnp/)

Want to get your upper elementary grade and middle school students interested in space science? Have them take this tour of the solar system, visiting each of the planets and their major moons. Many stunning photographs and the latest science resulting from recent probes to these unusual worlds. Set a bookmark!

The Why Files—(http://whyfiles.news.wisc.edu/index.html)

Funded by the National Science Foundation and located at the University of Wisconsin, this location provides you and your students with science information behind recent news stories. What evidence is there of life on Mars? Does a climatologist study changes in the Earth's climate? What causes Mad Cow disease and how do humans catch it? How does amber preserve DNA? These and many more questions are answered here along with related links to other sites on the WWW.

Virtual Frog Dissection Kit—(http://www-itg.lbl.gov/vfrog/)

An outstanding demonstration of the potential of the Internet for science education. Think of all the poor frogs that will be saved! This site, developed by the Lawrence Berkeley National Laboratory contains a great dissection experience where students learn about a frog's internal organs and systems. Videos are also available. At the end, students may also play the Virtual Frog Builder Game, where they try to put a frog back together. Set a bookmark!

VirtualEarthquake—(http://vflylab.calstatela.edu/edesktop/VirtApps/VirtualEarthQuake/VQuakeIntro.html)
VirtualEarthquake is an interactive computer program designed to introduce you to the concepts of how an earthquake epicenter is located and how the Richter Magnitude of an earthquake is determined. Concepts such as seismometer, seismograph, and epicenter are explained, and students see how scientists study earthquakes.

VolcanoWorld—(http://volcano.und.nodak.edu/)
Here is a wonderfully interactive location to explore volcano science. View maps of active volcanos, talk to vulcanologists, view videos of the most recent eruptions, explore a host of educational links. This is a tremendous resource for a somewhat unusual, but very exciting, topic.

You Can with Beakman and Jax—(http://www.beakman.com/)
Based on the television program, Beakman's World, this location is great for curious young scientists who want to figure out how the world works. It has a location where students can ask questions about the natural world and also an interactive set of demonstrations illustrating answers to questions such as: What does smoking do to your lungs? How does a thermometer work? Why does the moon look bigger on the horizon? How does a sundial work? How does the moon power the tides? A good question is a powerful thing!

Listservs/Mailing Lists for Science

CYBERMARCH-NET—(majordomo@igc.apc.org)
A discussion group for teachers interested in environmental education.

IMSE-L—(listserv@uwf.cc.uwf.edu)
A discussion group sponsored by the Institute for Math and Science Education.

T321-L—(listserv@mizzou1.missouri.edu)
A discussion group on the teaching of science in elementary schools.

TIMS-L—(listserv@uicvm.uic.edu)
A discussion group sponsored by the Teaching Integrated Mathematics and Science (TIMS) Project.

Usenet Newsgroups for Science

k12.ed.science—Discussion about the science curriculum in K–12 education.

misc.education.science—Discussion of issues related to science education.

k12.chat.elementary—Informal discussion among elementary students, grades K–5.

k12.chat.junior—Informal discussion among students in grades 6–8.

k12.chat.teacher—Informal discussion among teachers in grades K–12.

Math:
Thinking Mathematically on the Internet

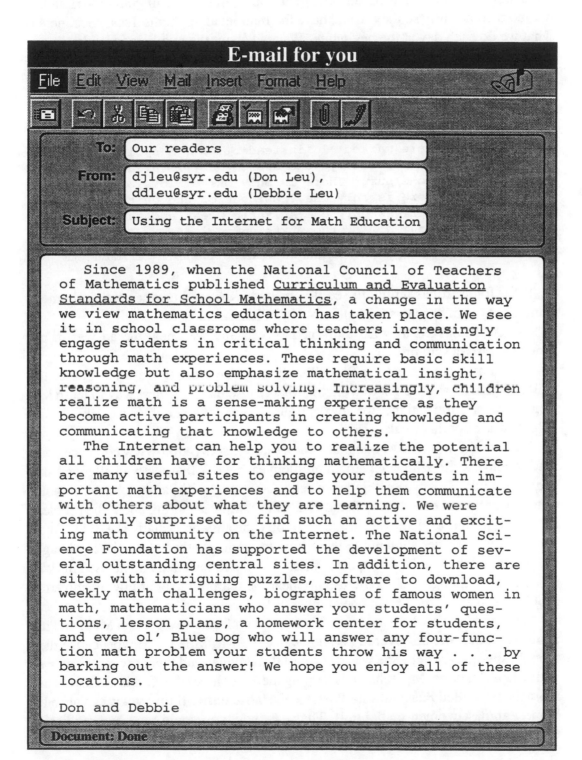

E-mail for you

File Edit View Mail Insert Format Help

To: Our readers

From: djleu@syr.edu (Don Leu),
ddleu@syr.edu (Debbie Leu)

Subject: Using the Internet for Math Education

Since 1989, when the National Council of Teachers of Mathematics published <u>Curriculum and Evaluation Standards for School Mathematics</u>, a change in the way we view mathematics education has taken place. We see it in school classrooms where teachers increasingly engage students in critical thinking and communication through math experiences. These require basic skill knowledge but also emphasize mathematical insight, reasoning, and problem solving. Increasingly, children realize math is a sense-making experience as they become active participants in creating knowledge and communicating that knowledge to others.

The Internet can help you to realize the potential all children have for thinking mathematically. There are many useful sites to engage your students in important math experiences and to help them communicate with others about what they are learning. We were certainly surprised to find such an active and exciting math community on the Internet. The National Science Foundation has supported the development of several outstanding central sites. In addition, there are sites with intriguing puzzles, software to download, weekly math challenges, biographies of famous women in math, mathematicians who answer your students' questions, lesson plans, a homework center for students, and even ol' Blue Dog who will answer any four-function math problem your students throw his way . . . by barking out the answer! We hope you enjoy all of these locations.

Don and Debbie

Document: Done

Teaching with the Internet: Sarah Johnson's Class

"I want to show you our Web Math." Clarissa pulled her mom over to the Internet computer in the Math classroom. They sat down to see what Clarissa had been talking about every night during dinner. It was Open House evening and Clarissa had her mom come early so they would have the Internet all to themselves. "See, here is what we do each day at the beginning. We read about the numbers for today."

Since today was the first of the month, they read a portion of the page for the number one at **About Today's Date** (http://acorn.educ.nottingham.ac.uk/cgi-bin/daynum), a site located at Nottingham University in England:

```
"An ace is number one in playing cards. French play-
ing cards are marked '1' instead of 'A'. A cyclops is
a creature with one eye and a dromedary is a camel
with only one hump. There is only one of lots of
things. There is only one President of the United
States, there is only one Atlantic Ocean and there is
only one you. All of these are unique."
```

(http://acorn.educ.nottingham.ac.uk/ShellCent/Number/Num1.html)

"Ms. Johnson has a quiz to see if somebody knows this when we go home. I print it out for my group so we all know it," Clarissa said.

"Today she asked us what a dromedary was and we knew the answer in my group," Clarissa said proudly.

"See, now here we got the Brain Teasers . . . These are to tease our brains and make us smarter and we got to work together 'cause that's the best way to learn Ms. Johnson says. Julie and me, we always figure it out, but sometimes we ask Alisa to help. It was easy this week. See?"

Clarissa had selected the bookmark for **Brain Teasers** (http://www.eduplace.com/math/brain/), a site with a new math problem each week that really challenged students to think. This was a regular, weekly assignment in Sarah Johnson's room. Often there would be a group of students at the computer talking about the problem and trying to figure out the best strategy to solve the answer. Usually she didn't mind since she wanted her students to learn how to learn together. Sometimes, though, she had to tell them to be a bit quieter when they got too excited and noisy. This was a good noise, though. She could usually hear them arguing about how to solve the problem as they learned from one another.

"See, and here's what I'm doin'. It's a report on famous women in Math and it's about Hypatia. She discovered parabolas but she was killed in Egypt 'cause they thought she was a witch. She was just smart. I'm gonna send them my report with e-mail when I'm done. Ms. Johnson's helping me." As she spoke, Clarissa showed her mom the site called **Past Notable Women of Mathematics** (http://www.cs.yale.edu/homes/tap/past-women-math.html). They saw how you could read biographies of famous women and how students could submit reports to be posted at this site.

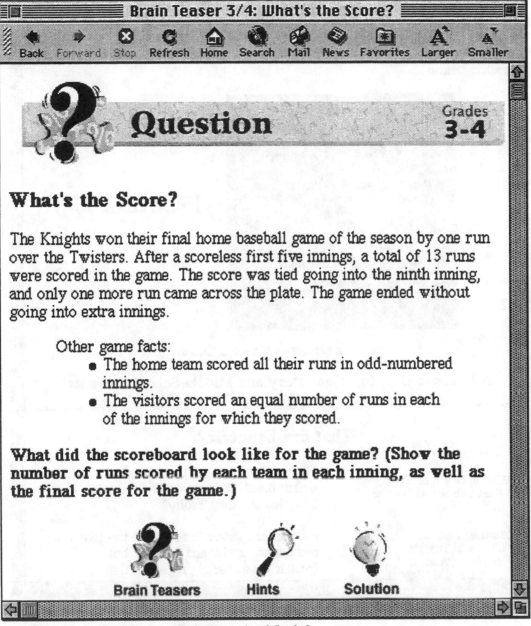

Figure 8-1. An example problem for students from the Brain Teaser site.

Brain Teaser site (http://www.eduplace.com/math/brain/)

"And here is where we did our fractals project," Clarissa said as she showed her mom the site called **A Fractals Lesson** (http://math.rice.edu/~lanius/frac/). "Fractals are cool! Here is the Sierpinski Triangle we made when we did this. We had to measure and find all the midpoints in our triangles." Clarissa pointed to the bulletin board and the large fractal made from students' separate fractals.

Then, Clarissa took her mother over to another location in the room where there was a display called food prices around the world. It showed the results of an Internet project. Their class had posted an Internet project designed to compare the price of a Big Mac, regular fries, and soda, along with other food items, around the world.

Figure 8-2.
The home
page for A
Fractals Les-
son.

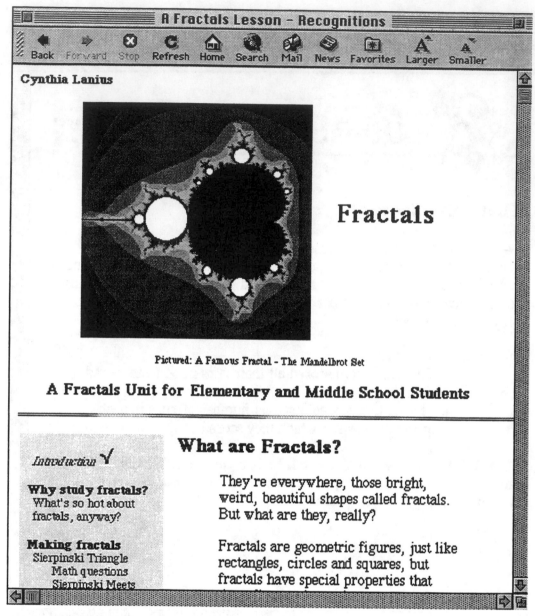

A Fractals Lesson (http://math.rice.edu/~lanius/frac/)

Each class reported on the price for each item and then used the average hourly salary for their country to calculate how long it took to earn each food item. The participating classes shared the results with one another so they could compare the price of common food items in each of their countries. Each participating class was completing a unit on statistics. They studied common statistical concepts by working through the lessons at a site called **Statistics Every Writer Should Know** (http://nilesonline.com/stats/) and then linked to an excellent resource containing economic statistics for each participating country, **Finding Data on the Internet: A Journalist's Guide** (http://nilesonline.com/data/links.shtml). "See, we need to work 11 minutes for a Big Mac," said Clarissa. "And in Russia they have to work 2 hours."

Clarissa's mom was thinking that math had certainly changed since she went to school. She had a conversation with Ms. Johnson about this because she wasn't certain how she could help Clarissa at home. Ms. Johnson gave her a copy of an article she had obtained and printed from the Internet, **Helping Your Child Learn Math** (http://www.ed.gov/pubs/parents/Math/index.html). It contained all kinds of useful ideas for parents to do at home to assist their children. "Yes," Clarissa's mom thought to herself on the way home, "Math certainly has changed."

Lessons from the Classroom

Clarissa's story from Sarah Johnson's classroom illustrates several useful lessons for us to consider as we look at the Internet for Math education. First, the Internet profoundly changes the possibilities for Math education in fundamental ways. The availability of extensive resources on the Internet enriches the nature of mathematics education and changes it as much as when school textbooks first appeared for elementary students during 18th and 19th centuries. The Internet allows teachers and students to study mathematics in important new ways consistent with the recent standards adopted by the National Council of Teachers of Mathematics and the emphasis on mathematical insight, reasoning, and problem solving. As with other areas of study, we will see that Internet Activity, Internet Project, and Internet Inquiry are all possible in Mathematics education. Each may be used to integrate learning with other subject areas.

The Internet profoundly changes the possibilities for Math education in fundamental ways.

In addition, the Internet provides a wealth of mathematical data which may be used to help students learn more about themselves and the rest of the world. Just as Clarissa's class developed new insights about living standards around the world, your class may use the Internet to reach new conclusions based on data available through the Internet.

Finally, the Internet provides opportunities for students to communicate their developing insights and to compare them with those of other students, in their class and around the world. Increasingly, math lessons ask students to communicate their insights about patterns they see in the world around them. The Internet provides important opportunities to accomplish this.

Central Sites for Math Education

You can use a number of sites for a jumping off point as you begin to explore the Internet for math education. Most of these have links that will take you to a wide range of locations designed to support your math program. These will include sites that may be used for Internet Activity, Internet Project, or Internet Inquiry. Central sites may also contain links to lesson plans and locations where you can share ideas with other teachers about math education. A few will contain links to publications that allow you to keep up with developments in math education. Usually these central sites are more permanent and stable locations; they will be less likely to move to

The Internet provides a wealth of mathematical data which may be used to help students learn more about themselves and the rest of the world.

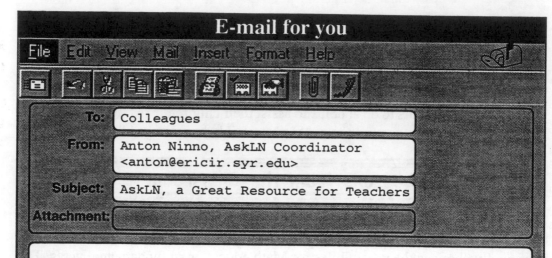

E-mail for you

File   Edit   View   Mail   Insert   Format   Help

To: Colleagues

From: Anton Ninno, AskLN Coordinator
<anton@ericir.syr.edu>

Subject: AskLN, a Great Resource for Teachers

Attachment:

Hi everyone!

    My name is Anton Ninno, and I'm the new coordinator of **AskLN** (http://www.att.com/learningnetwork/askln.html), which stands for: Ask the AT&T Learning Network. AskLN is a question-answering service, related to AskERIC and KidsConnect. At AskLN we answer questions from teachers about using educational technology in the classroom, and from parents and administrator, too. Got an educational technology question? Just let us know!

    You can read all about AskLN by clicking here: http://www.att.com/learningnetwork/. At the mentor page you'll meet our team of edtech teachers. Some of us are new to AskLN, like me. Last April I was the technology facilitator at Porter Magnet School in Syracuse, New York, and before that I taught 5th and 6th grades. The magnet curriculum theme at Porter is Technology & Career Exploration. So, I did a little career exploration myself, and moved to Syracuse University!

    It's been quite a transition, moving from an elementary school to a university. Now my work is almost entirely done with e-mail and a web-browser—amazing! There were many changes in the work culture too. For example, in a school, if you want to get anything done you have to hand someone a piece of paper (and cross your fingers!). Here, I use almost no paper at all. Educational journals and magazines are the only hardcopy materials I see. Yes, that's right; I no longer carry a 50-pound canvas bag home every day.

    Of course the most exciting element of AskLN is my communication with teachers all across the country. We recently hit a milestone—our first question from down under—Australia! Our sister service, **KidsConnect** (http://www.ala.org/ICONN/kidsconn.html), receives questions from K-12 students on six continents, so our goal is to support teachers around the globe—those students' teachers.

Document: Continued

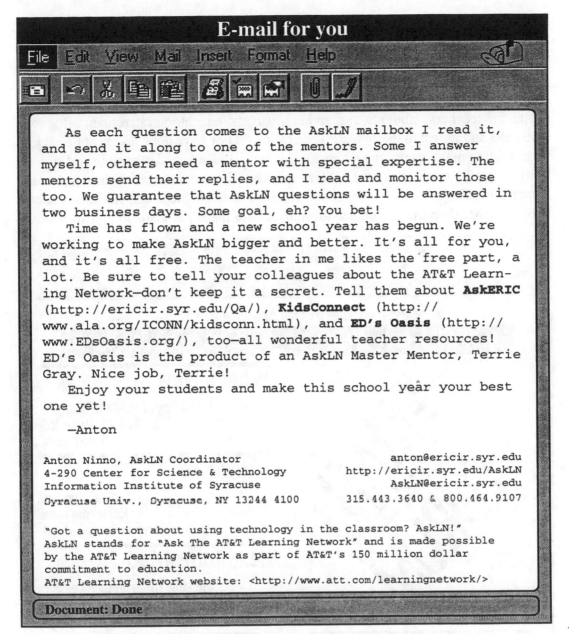

As each question comes to the AskLN mailbox I read it, and send it along to one of the mentors. Some I answer myself, others need a mentor with special expertise. The mentors send their replies, and I read and monitor those too. We guarantee that AskLN questions will be answered in two business days. Some goal, eh? You bet!

Time has flown and a new school year has begun. We're working to make AskLN bigger and better. It's all for you, and it's all free. The teacher in me likes the free part, a lot. Be sure to tell your colleagues about the AT&T Learning Network—don't keep it a secret. Tell them about **AskERIC** (http://ericir.syr.edu/Qa/), **KidsConnect** (http://www.ala.org/ICONN/kidsconn.html), and **ED's Oasis** (http://www.EDsOasis.org/), too—all wonderful teacher resources! ED's Oasis is the product of an AskLN Master Mentor, Terrie Gray. Nice job, Terrie!

Enjoy your students and make this school year your best one yet!

—Anton

Anton Ninno, AskLN Coordinator   anton@ericir.syr.edu
4-290 Center for Science & Technology   http://ericir.syr.edu/AskLN
Information Institute of Syracuse   AskLN@ericir.syr.edu
Syracuse Univ., Syracuse, NY 13244 4100   315.443.3640 & 800.464.9107

"Got a question about using technology in the classroom? AskLN!"
AskLN stands for "Ask The AT&T Learning Network" and is made possible
by the AT&T Learning Network as part of AT&T's 150 million dollar
commitment to education.
AT&T Learning Network website: <http://www.att.com/learningnetwork/>

another location, disappear, or turn into a subscription service that will require a fee. They are often supported by a state or federal unit or by a non-profit organization or university. We encourage you to begin your explorations at one of these central sites.

As with science, the best single site may be the **Eisenhower National Clearinghouse for Mathematics and Science Education** (http://www.enc.org:80/index.htm). We especially like the location here called the "Digital Dozen," 13 great sites on the Internet for math and science education that change each month. There is also an archive for sites that have received this award in the past. Another helpful feature is the "ENC Services" location where you may ask experts any question you might have about math education. In addition, there is a great selection of lesson and activity locations and a "Resource Finder" that will help you locate curriculum re-

The Internet provides opportunities for students to communicate their developing insights and to compare them with those of other students, in their class and around the world.

sources for classroom projects. Be certain to begin your exploration in math at the Eisenhower National Clearinghouse for Mathematics and Science Education.

Another outstanding central site is the **Math Forum** (http://forum.swarthmore.edu/) at Swarthmore College, funded by the National Science Foundation. The goal of this location is to ". . . to build a community that can be a center for teachers, students, researchers, parents, educators, citizens at all levels who have an interest in mathematics education." They have done an exceptional job by providing many useful resources for teachers, students, and others. In addition to links to useful math sites on the web, the Math Forum maintains chat areas and listservs/mailing lists for students and teachers to share ideas and questions about math. **Dr. Math** (http://forum.swarthmore.edu/dr.math/) is also on call to answer

Figure 8-3. The home page for **The Math Forum,** an important central site for math education.

Usually these central sites are more permanent and stable locations; they will be less likely to move to another location, disappear, or turn into a subscription service that will require a fee.

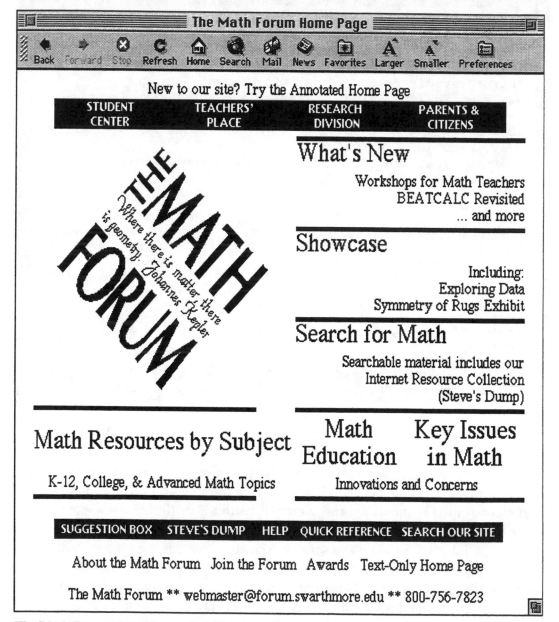

The Math Forum (http://forum.swarthmore.edu/)

questions from you or your students. Dr. Math is a great resource for homework! The Math Forum is an exceptional site on the web. Be certain to explore the many resources there.

A third central location you may wish to visit is **Math Archives** (http://archives.math.utk.edu/newindex.html). Located at the University of Tennessee, this site has an especially good collection of software you may wish to download and use in your classroom. The Math Archives provide resources for mathematicians at all levels, not just K-12 educators, but if you look in the "Teaching Materials" section you will find a category for "K-12 Materials." There is also a nice collection of links to WWW resources for math in a section called "Topics in Mathematics." You will find a visit to this location well worth your time.

The **Math Department at Canada's SchoolNet** (http://www.schoolnet.ca/math_sci/math/) may also be useful as you begin to explore links to math resources. This location contains a number of links to math sites you will find useful. At the present time, this list is not organized by topic or grade level, but SchoolNet is quickly evolving and it looks like this will be an important resource.

The **Math** (http://www.csun.edu/~vceed009/math.html#Math) section of **Web Sites and Resources for Teachers** (http://www.csun.edu/~vceed009/) is also very useful as a jumping off point into the web for math education. These locations are located at California State University–Northridge and maintained by two professors in the School of Education. At the Math location, there are many links to locations with lesson plans for busy teachers. There are also links to a number of good board games. Another section contains links to ideas and activities to support your math program. All of the sites at this location contain resources that are useful to classroom teachers. It appears to have been developed by people who really understand teachers' classroom needs.

Finally, you may wish to subscribe to one of several listservs/mailing lists and participate in the conversations that are taking place each day about math education. One of the more important conversations taking place is on **NCTM-L** (listproc@sci-ed.fit.edu), the listserv sponsored by the National Council of Teachers of Mathematics. Join in and share your questions, concerns, and insights. Other useful listservs/mailing lists and math education newsgroups are listed at the end of this chapter.

> *As with science, the best single site may be the Eisenhower National Clearinghouse for Mathematics and Science Education.*

> *Another outstanding central site is the Math Forum at Swarthmore College, funded by the National Science Foundation.*

Internet FAQ

I have heard that each time I visit a site, there is something called a cookie that captures information about me. What is a cookie? What can I do to prevent a web site from obtaining personal information about me?

Cookies are requests for information from web site administrators who record and request information about you whenever you visit their site. Internet Explorer and Netscape Navigator may be set to warn you when a cookie is being requested. In Internet Explorer, go to the View menu item, click on "options," and then select the Advanced tab. Check the box that says, "Warn before accepting cookies." In Netscape Navigator, go to the Options menu and click on "Network Preferences." Click on the "protocols" tab and check the box that says "Show an alert before accepting a cookie."

Keeping It Simple: Using Internet Activity with Internet Workshop

If you explore some of the central sites described above you will quickly find many exciting locations related to the units in your math program. These are great places to use as your assignments for Internet Activity, the fastest way to bring the resources of the WWW into your classroom for math and other areas of your curriculum. Developing an assignment for Internet Activity is easy. Locate a site on the Internet with content related to your math unit and set a bookmark for this location. Then develop an activity that requires students to use that site. Assign this activity to your students to complete during the week. Some teachers will develop a number of different activities related to the site and then ask students to complete as many as possible during their computer time. Work completed during Internet Activity may be shared at the end of the week during Internet Workshop.

Many teachers will develop Internet Activity assignments from one of several locations on the web that provide a weekly math challenge for students, a math problem that requires careful thinking to solve. Alternatively, some teachers will just print out this math problem each week and duplicate copies for their students. One location with weekly problems for students is **Brain Teasers** (http://www.eduplace.com/math/brain/) a location sponsored by Houghton Mifflin. Each week, a new problem is presented by grade level. If students require it, they may click on a "Hint" or a "Solution" button. There is also an archive of problems used in the past.

The Little Math Puzzle Contest (http://www.odyssee.net/~academy/mathpuzzle/) is another site with a weekly math problem for students. This site presents a single, ungraded problem for students. There is also an archive and a winner's list. You must have a password to access the answer at this site. Teachers may obtain the password via e-mail.

Word Problems for Kids (http://juliet.stfx.ca/people/fac/pwang/mathpage/math1.html) is another location with graded math problems. For each, there is a linked "hint" button. Answers are provided to teachers with a registered e-mail address.

Other sites, too, may be used for Internet Activity. These may be located by exploring some of the central sites for math education described earlier and creating activities related to your units of study. Here are just a few ideas to get you started with your own Internet Activity assignments:

- **Dr. FreeMath**—(http://ois.unomaha.edu/drfreemath/)
  Dr. FreeMath is an electronic mail project where one mathematics question per month will be researched and answered from each elementary class. Past examples of questions include: How much water evaporates in the ocean each year? Why is any number to the zero power equal to one? Why is pi not really equal to 22/7? Have individuals bring their

best questions to Internet Workshop and then work together to pick one that is sent to Dr. FreeMath.

- **Biographies of Women Mathematicians—** (http://www.scottlan.edu/lriddle/women/women.html) This site contains a developing set of biographies. The group creating this site is looking for others to research famous women mathematicians and submit additional biographies. Invite students to read about one of these favorite women and bring their story to Internet Workshop.

- **MacTutor History of Mathematics archive—** (http://www-groups.dcs.st-and.ac.uk/~history/) Extensive links to sites with information about the history of math. A nice location to set up a weekly question related to math history that will help students develop a richer understanding of math concepts.

- **The Fruit Game—**(http://www.2020tech.com/fruit/f752.html) A simple interactive game with a hidden trick. See if your students can explain the trick in writing. Share your best guesses during Internet Workshop.

- **Interactive Mathematics Miscellany and Puzzles—** (http://www.cut-the-knot.com/) Forget the title. Check this site out! It has an incredible list of links to games, activities, and puzzles that will keep your class busy all year with Internet Activity! Set a bookmark!

TEACHING TIP:

"Visiting Math Mentors"

If you are looking for a special type of weekly math challenge, pay a visit to the **Elementary Problem of the Week** (http://forum.swarthmore.edu/sum95/ruth/elem.pow.html). Each week a new problem is listed. There is also an archive of past problems. If you register for the yearly set of problems, your answers will be responded to by a "Visiting Math Mentor" each week. A "Visiting Math Mentor" is someone who provides advice and encouragement as you attempt to solve that week's problem. Students, groups, and classes may also apply to be a "Visiting Math Mentor." So, after participating for a while, have your class volunteer to respond to answers submitted by other students during the year. This can be very exciting for your students as they take on the role of the teacher and help others solve challenging math problems.

Internet FAQ

Sometimes when I go to a site on the WWW it tells me that I need a "Java-capable browser." How do I know if I have this? What does this mean?

You have a Java-capable browser if you are using Netscape 3.0 or later, or if you use Internet Explorer 3.0 or later. A Java-capable browser is one that will run special programs put on the web to assist with animation, sound, or video. These enhance the multimedia capabilities of web locations. You are using a Java-capable browser if you see animated objects at some web sites. These might be a message that moves along the bottom of your window or objects that spin around in place. Java-capable browsers also permit multiple windows to be open at any single web site.

E-mail for you

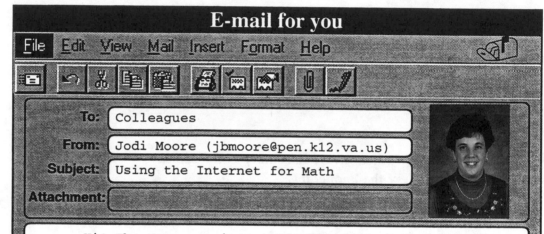

File Edit View Mail Insert Format Help

To: Colleagues

From: Jodi Moore (jbmoore@pen.k12.va.us)

Subject: Using the Internet for Math

Attachment:

Hi! The Internet is a tool that will motivate and excite all your students, especially in math. There are countless web sites available to entice even the most reluctant learners. I print a problem for my class each week from **Brain Teasers** (http://www.eduplace.com/math/brain/) or **The Elementary Problem of the Week** (http://forum.swarthmore.edu/sum95/ruth/elem.pow.problems.html). The problems provide an avenue for healthy competition as well as practice and discussion within the classroom.

My students also frequent various web sites that provide useful information for research and reference on mathematicians and related mathematical topics such as the **MacTutor History of Mathematics Archive** (http://www-groups.dcs.st-and.ac.uk/~history/). This information enhances classroom instruction and helps math take on a new and exciting face. Enlivening the classroom environment with the real world is motivating. Students display confidence locating information readily and they are able to apply the knowledge they have collected.

Document: Continued

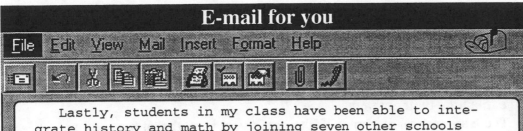

E-mail for you

File　Edit　View　Mail　Insert　Format　Help

Lastly, students in my class have been able to integrate history and math by joining seven other schools from the United States, Newfoundland (Canada), Germany, Saudi Arabia, and Australia in an Internet project. During a three-month period we all agreed to write four different articles with information about our school and the history and geography of our area. After composing each short research project, students at each school wrote five math problems based on the research. This was then sent using e-mail to the other six schools. Students in the participating schools solved the problems and sent back their answers. We were able to check the solutions as well as analyze any errors. It was especially interesting to listen as students decided if it was a computational error, an error in writing the problem, or a misinterpretation of the data. My students also benefited from the submissions of the other six schools. Each of the teachers in the project often collaborated to "lead" the problems in a particular area to provide appropriate practice and subsequent mastery.

I thoroughly enjoy the opportunities the Internet allows me to provide my students. Just like any other new toy, limits must be set and specific rules must be devised. Still, this powerful tool will literally make all the difference in the world with students. I can honestly say I am glad technology has arrived!

Jodi Moore, 6th grade teacher　　Battlefield Middle School
jbmoore@pen.k12.va.us　　　　　11120 Leavells Rd.
　　　　　　　　　　　　　　　Fredericksburg, VA 22407

Document: Done

Using Internet Project with Internet Workshop

While it may take more time and planning, Internet Project is an important instructional tool for several reasons. First, Internet Project supports cross-curricular learning experiences. Language arts is almost always a part of any Internet project in math since projects require students to communicate with others about their thinking. In addition, social studies and science are also frequently a part of these projects. An insightful teacher will plan to take advantage of these natural opportunities for cross-curricular integration.

Internet projects in math are also important because they encourage students to work together to develop the ability to think mathematically.

In math, Internet Project is important because it encourages students to work together to develop the ability to think mathematically. Part of thinking mathematically is being able to communicate problem-solving strategies to others and to listen as others describe different approaches to proofs. This is supported when classrooms are communicating with one another, modeling their approaches to solutions and explaining their answers.

There are several examples of Internet Project in math that run continuously and have a separate site on the WWW. **Good News Bears** (http://www.ncsa.uiuc.edu:80/edu/RSE/RSEyellow/gnb.html), a year-long stock market game for middle school students is one such location. Here, students participate in a contest using on-line stock market data as they do research and then buy and sell stocks in an attempt to maximize their portfolio. It is an excellent experience that brings mathematical thinking to real-world problems and solutions.

Other projects may be joined by reviewing projects posted at the traditional locations on the Internet such as **Global SchoolNet's Internet Project Registry** (http://www.gsn.org/project/index.html), **Classroom Connect's Teacher Contact Database** (http://www.classroom.net/contact/), or **The Global School House** (http://www.gsh.org/class/default.htm). If you see a project that matches your instructional needs for an upcoming unit, be certain to join.

Alternatively, you may wish to work with your class during Internet Workshop to develop an Internet project in math that you post and invite others to join. Be certain to plan this far enough in advance that you can attract enough participants and develop communication links. Examples of projects that you may wish to post for others to join include:

There are several Internet projects in math that run continuously and have a separate site on the WWW.

- **Problems for Problem Solvers—**
  (http://ccf.arc.nasa.gov/comet/index.html)
  Invite other classrooms to join you in exchanging interesting math problems to solve together. Appoint one class each week to be the lead class on a rotating basis. The lead class is responsible for developing five problems or puzzles that are sent to participating classes who then have a week to return the answers. The lead class is also responsible for responding to each class and the solutions they suggested. Each week, another class becomes the lead class and circulates five new problems or puzzles for everyone to solve.

- **Heads or Tails?** Here is a simple probability project for younger students. Invite other classes to flip a coin from their country ten times and record the number of times that heads turn up. Repeat this ten times. Then have them send the results to your class. Record the data, write up the results, and send back a report with the percentage of times heads turns up during a coin toss. You may wish to invite participating schools to exchange the coins they flipped so that young children become familiar with different currency systems.

- **Graph Your Favorite**—(http://www1.minn.net:80/~schubert/Graph.html)
  This activity was completed by students in grade 2, 4, and 6 classrooms in Michigan, Minnesota, Canada, Australia, and California. Students in eight participating classes voted each week on their favorite item in one category: pets, holidays, sports, school subjects, food. The data was calculated separately for boys and for girls. Participating classes sent their data to the project coordinator, who compiled the results each week and e-mailed it to everyone for further analysis. Students used the data in raw form to make their own spreadsheets, both manually and by computer. They also made computer bar graphs and pie graphs as well as manually drawn bar graphs. Then they analyzed the graphs and drew conclusions.

TEACHING TIP

Developing an Internet Project in Statistics

Here is a project for middle school or high school students who are exploring statistics. Invite a group of participating classes to join you in working through the experiences at **Statistics Every Writer Should Know** (http://nilesonline.com/stats/). After completing these experiences, have each class develop group projects to analyze and report comparative statistics from their country, state, or nation on some category where numerical data is kept. Use the site **Finding Data on the Internet: A Journalist's Guide** (http://nilesonline.com/data/links.shtml) to obtain these data. Then share the reports that were developed and provide responses to each report.

Using Internet Inquiry with Internet Workshop

Part of thinking mathematically involves identifying questions that are important to you and then seeking answers to those questions. Internet Inquiry allows you to support these more independent experiences among your students.

You will recall from the previous chapters that Internet Inquiry usually contains five phases: question, search, analyze, compose, and share. Students identify an important question they wish to explore, search for resources to help them understand the information related to this question, analyze the data they have obtained, compose a presentation of their work, and then share their work with others. These steps may also be used to structure Internet Inquiry in mathematics.

Sometimes, it is possible to organize Internet Inquiry around interesting sites that already exist on the Internet. Examples include the very rich sites that exist for the following:

- **Pi Mathematics**—
  (http://www.ncsa.uiuc.edu:80/edu/RSE/RSEorange/buttons.html)
  Have students read about the history of pi, view a video, complete several different activities, calculate the best deal on several pizzas, and

Part of thinking mathematically involves identifying questions that are important to you and then seeking answers to those questions. Internet Inquiry allows you to support these more independent experiences among your students.

share their favorite pizza topping with students around the world. Have them write up a report on their experiences and share it with others. Soon, you will have to have a sign up list for this site during Internet Inquiry.

- **A Fractals Lesson**—(http://math.rice.edu/~lanius/frac/)
Have students explore this site during Internet Inquiry, making a fractal, learning how fractals are related to chopping broccoli, and viewing fractals on the WWW. Then have them prepare a poster session on fractals for the class, including examples they printed out from sites on the WWW.

- **Mega Mathematics**—(http://www.c3.lanl.gov/mega-math/)
There are so many wonderful Internet Inquiry possibilities at this site that it is hard to know where to begin. From a seemingly simple coloring problem that has perplexed cartographers for centuries, to the mathematics of knots, to issues of infinity, to graphs and games, this site has enough intriguing issues to keep any student thinking mathematically for a year. Point students to this site and stand back. Set a bookmark!

Another approach to Internet Inquiry is to encourage students to explore sites containing links to many different topics in mathematics. As students explore these

Figure 8-4. The home page for **Mega Mathematics.**

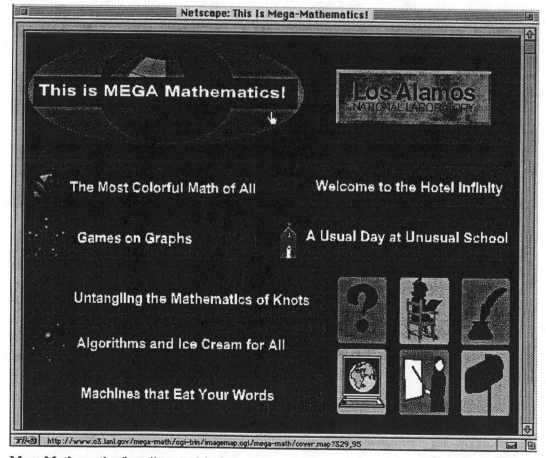

Mega Mathematics (http://www.c3.lanl.gov/mega-math/)

sites, encourage them to explore and define a project they wish to complete. You could direct them to any of the central sites described earlier in the chapter or you could direct them to some of these locations:

- **Knot a Braid**—(http://www.mta.ca/~rrosebru/kbl/knotlinks.html)
  Here is a great math location for students searching for an Inquiry project. Each week a new site is selected in math. Previous links are available so that you can go down the list until you find something really interesting. It won't be hard at this location.

- **Interactive Mathematics Miscellany and Puzzles**—
  (http://www.cut-the-knot.com/)
  Have students do Internet Inquiry on one of the puzzles or problems at this site. Be certain to encourage them to report on the history behind the problem as well as the problem itself. They may wish to visit some of the history sites mentioned earlier to gather information.

As you do more and more Internet Inquiry with your students, consider having a Math Fair where students present their projects in a "poster session." If you can, schedule this at a time when parents can attend so that they can witness all the wonderful things you are doing with your students.

Mathematics Resources on the Internet

About Today's Date—(http://acorn.educ.nottingham.ac.uk/cgi-bin/daynum)
Have students visit this page each day to find out interesting information about each of the numbers from 1 to 31. Your kids will learn a lot by just reading the information at these pages. Post the information in class, too, in your math center. Make a bookmark!

Blue Dog Can Count!!—(http://kao.ini.cmu.edu:5550/bdf.html)
Blue dog answers all your basic math problems by barking out the answers. A fun site and especially useful in the primary grades for developing basic math skills.

Classroom Links—Math—
(http://www.enc.org/classroom/claslinx/nf_resmath.htm)
Here is a set of great links to wonderful sites for mathematics education. From a fractal microscope, to a location for Googolplex, to Virtual Polyhedra, this site has outstanding sites for students and teachers. Set a bookmark!

Explorer—(http://unite.ukans.edu/)
The Explorer is a collection of educational resources including instructional software, lab activities, and lesson plans for K-12 mathematics and science education. A nice collection for busy teachers to obtain very useful resources. Set a bookmark!

Finding Data on the Internet—(http://nilesonline.com/data/)
Here is the place to get nearly every piece of statistical data on states, countries, cities, and other geographical and political units. A treasure trove for data snoopers and a great place for older students to explore during Internet Inquiry. If you work with high school students, set a bookmark!

Jumpin' Jehosaphat the Counting Sheep—
(http://www.dodds1.com/Java/Jj.html)
Here is a sheep that will solve addition, subtraction, multiplication, and division problems for your younger students. It jumps and counts out the answer, in Sheepese. Much fun! It runs better with Internet Explorer 3.0 or later than with Netscape.

KidsConnect—(http://www.ala.org/ICONN/kidsconn.html)
KidsConnect is a question-answering, help and referral service to K–12 students on the Internet. The goal of the service is to help students access and use the information available on the Internet effectively and efficiently. Useful for math, but also for other subject areas.

MacTutor History of Mathematics archive—
(http://www-groups.dcs.st-and.ac.uk:80/~history/)
Interested in the history of mathematics? Here is the URL 4 U. Find out who the mathematician of the day is or read the biographies of famous mathematicians and learn about their accomplishments. It contains many unique links to sites about the history of mathematics.

NCTM Standards—
(http://www.enc.org/reform/journals/ENC2280/nf_280dtoc1.htm)
This is the document that has had a powerful effect on the way many people think about mathematics instruction. Reading it can provide you with useful insights about this area of the curriculum.

On-line Mathematics Dictionary—
(http://www.mathpro.com/math/glossary/glossary.html)
Need to know what amicable numbers are? How about a deficient number? Or a rusty compass? Boy, could your students have fun with this page. This is a great resource when you encounter an unusual word in math.

Statistics Every Writer Should Know—(http://nilesonline.com/stats/)
This is an excellent tutorial for students learning about simple statistics, including means, medians, per cent, per capita, and more. A great interactive tutorial to help middle school students understand these concepts.

The World of Escher—(http://lonestar.texas.net/~escher/)
M.C. Escher was a wonderfully talented and self-taught artist who employed many principles of mathematics in his tessellations (repeated geometric patterns). Visit this site and marvel at the images he created. How about an Inquiry study of this person and his work?

Listservs/Mailing Lists for Math

IMSE-L—(listserv@uwf.cc.uwf.edu)
A discussion group on math and science education sponsored by the Institute for Math and Science Education.

MATHSED-L—(listserv@deakin.edu.au)
A discussion group on mathematics in education.

NCTM-L—(listproc@sci-ed.fit.edu)
A discussion group on math education sponsored by the National Council of Teachers of Mathematics.

TIMS-L—(listserv@uicvm.uic.edu)
A discussion group sponsored by the Teaching Integrated Mathematics and Science (TIMS) Project.

MATHEDCC—(listserv@vm1.mcgill.ca)
A discussion group focusing on technology in math education.

SUSIG—(listserv@miamiu.bitnet)
A discussion group on math education.

Usenet Newsgroups for Math

k12.chat.teacher—Informal discussion among teachers in grades K–12.

k12.ed.math—Mathematics curriculum in K–12 education.

pnet.school.k-12—Discussion about K–12 education.

pnet.school.k-5—Discussion about K–5 education.

Special Ideas for Younger Children: Using the Internet in the Primary Grades

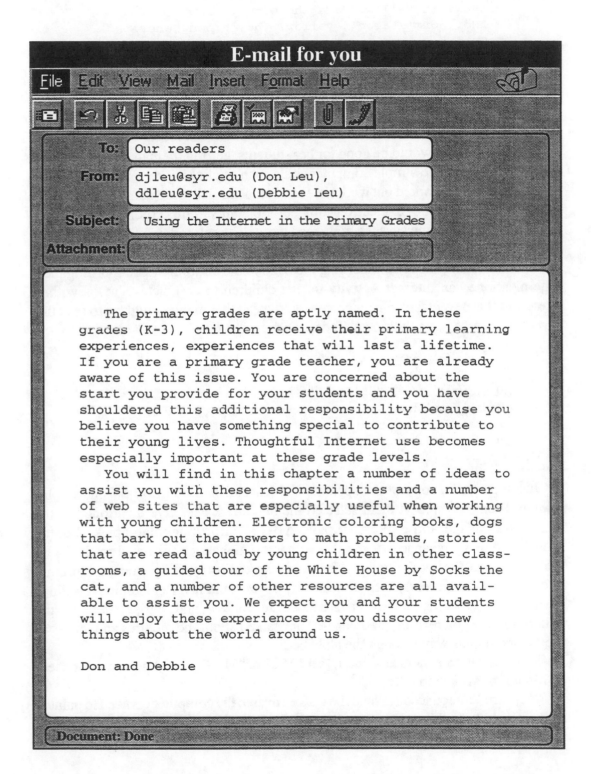

E-mail for you

File　Edit　View　Mail　Insert　Format　Help

To: Our readers

From: djleu@syr.edu (Don Leu),
ddleu@syr.edu (Debbie Leu)

Subject: Using the Internet in the Primary Grades

Attachment:

The primary grades are aptly named. In these grades (K-3), children receive their primary learning experiences, experiences that will last a lifetime. If you are a primary grade teacher, you are already aware of this issue. You are concerned about the start you provide for your students and you have shouldered this additional responsibility because you believe you have something special to contribute to their young lives. Thoughtful Internet use becomes especially important at these grade levels.

You will find in this chapter a number of ideas to assist you with these responsibilities and a number of web sites that are especially useful when working with young children. Electronic coloring books, dogs that bark out the answers to math problems, stories that are read aloud by young children in other class-rooms, a guided tour of the White House by Socks the cat, and a number of other resources are all avail-able to assist you. We expect you and your students will enjoy these experiences as you discover new things about the world around us.

Don and Debbie

Document: Done

Teaching with the Internet: Liz Dyer's Class

Justin, Leo, and Marisa were working together at the Internet computer in their kindergarten classroom.

> "Make it yellow. Make the worm yellow."
> "No. Worm's aren't yellow. They brown. Where's brown."
> "There's brown. Click brown. Now click the paint-brush. Now click the worm."
> "Cool!"

They were at **Carlos' Coloring Book** (http://coloring.com/) a site their teacher had bookmarked for her students. Liz Dye's class was exploring color names and she thought this site would be good for her students, getting them to talk about color names as they learned simple computer skills such as clicking the mouse and using bookmarks. It had worked out well; she found students using the names of the colors as they worked together to electronically color pictures in this coloring book.

"Look, the message says we gotta read the ABC book today," Marisa said. "Go to the ABC book. Click on the bookmarks and go to the ABC book."

Each morning, Liz read a morning message to the children. Each morning message mentioned an Internet Activity for her children to complete. She knew their interest in this new classroom resource would mean that many would try to read this part of the message on their own. Today the message was:

```
Wednesday, October 10
    It is a rainy day.
    Today we will have music.
    Please read the Space ABC book on the computer.
    You can listen, too!
    I made a bookmark.
Ms. Dye
```

Justin printed a copy of the apple he had just finished on the class's new color printer. Then the three of them selected the bookmark Ms. Dye mentioned in the morning message and explored **Space ABC's** (http://buckman.pps.k12.or.us/room100/ABCspace/spaceabc.html), a wonderful alphabet book developed by a K-2 classroom in Portland, Oregon. The pages were illustrated by students during a unit on space they recently completed. Many pages contained RealAudio recordings of the children reading their own pages aloud. Justin, Leo, and Marisa listened to the children in Oregon reading their pages. They talked about the pictures and letters as they worked their way through the alphabet.

"We gonna write them an e-mail," said Marisa. "Ms. Dye said we can write them an e-mail in Workshop today."

"My turn," announced Kevin as he walked over to the computer corner. He pointed to the clock. "The big hand is on 12 and Ms. Dye said it's my turn when the big hand's on 12. You gotta stop now. My turn."

Justin, Leo, and Marisa moved over for Kevin and watched as he selected the bookmark for the **What is it?** location (http://www.uq.oz.au/nanoworld/whatisit.html) of **Nanoworld** (http://www.uq.oz.au/nanoworld/nanohome.html), a site in Australia with many strange-looking photographs taken with an electron microscope. Each week, she selected a picture from the files at this location or from **Scanning Electron Microscope** (http://www.mos.org/sln/sem/index.html) and had students draw a picture of the object and then write a description of what they thought it was. It was always great fun to have students share their pictures and read their invented spelling for this activity during a brief Internet Workshop.

"Cool. It's a monster."

"No, it's a dinosaur."

"It's a monster bug."

Ignoring all of these suggestions, Kevin carefully drew his picture of the strange shape and wrote below his picture:

```
KEVIN
I THK S A KRB
```

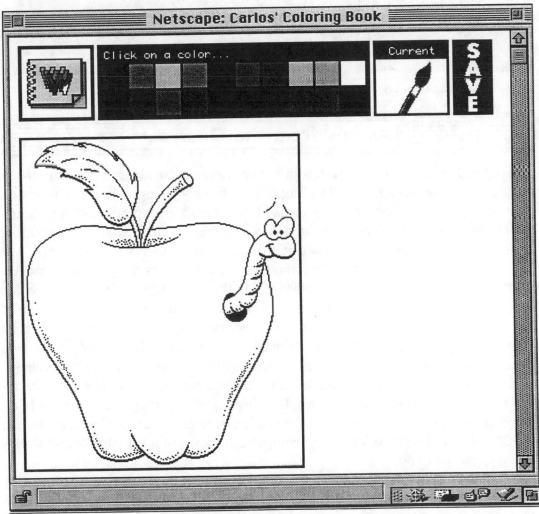

Figure 9-1. One page from **Carlos' Coloring Book,** one of several interactive coloring books available on the Internet.

Carlos' Coloring Book (http://coloring.com/)

"What you say?" asked Justin.

Proudly, Kevin read his work, "I think it's a crab."

Figure 9-2. An image from the "What is it?" quiz at the **Nanoworld Image Gallery**. These images can be used in writing activities for young children.

Nanoworld Image Gallery (http://www.uq.oz.au/nanoworld/whatisit.html)

Lessons from the Classroom

This episode from Liz Dye's classroom demonstrates how the Internet contains many locations to support classroom learning among the very youngest learners at school. In a short period of time, her students had many important experiences with letters, words, pictures, and colors. There are many locations on the Internet for supporting young children as they learn important lessons about the world around them.

The episode also illustrates how thoughtful teachers can integrate Internet Activity into their own instructional practices. In this class, Liz always began the day with a "Message of the Day." She read this with her children at the beginning of each school day as a Language Experience activity, exposing her children to print and showing them how to use print to obtain information. After taking a course on teaching with the Internet, Liz began to include Internet Activity in her "Message of the Day" for the class. She found that students paid particular attention to the activity she wrote in the message and would refer to it often throughout the school day. Children would come up to the message and point to each word as they tried to read it. Others would point to it from the computer as they reminded others of what they were supposed to do.

The episode in Liz's class also illustrates a third lesson; it is important for lower grade classrooms to receive the best technology possible. Liz had one of the few color printers in her school and a powerful multimedia computer, capable of playing

Liz began to include an Internet activity in her "Message of the Day" for the class. She found that students paid particular attention to the activity she wrote in the message and would refer to it often throughout the school day.

speech, animation, and sound very quickly. The color printer helped her children to quickly acquire color names. The multimedia computer allowed her children to listen to many things on the Internet with RealAudio technologies. A favorite right now was listening to children read their own work at the Space ABC's site.

Last year Liz wrote a memo to her principal. She pointed out that her kindergarten always had the oldest computer in the school and this limited her children's learning opportunities. She suggested that younger children really deserved the very best technologies so they could benefit from having stories read aloud to them on the Internet, so they could learn color names faster, and so they could view the memory-rich, multimedia resources available on the Internet. She pointed out that older students could read text but that her students needed the new speech technologies to assist with learning to read and write. She also noted that a color printer would ensure that her children learned color names. Apparently, her arguments were compelling; at the beginning of the year she found a multimedia computer and color printer in her classroom. Liz would take full advantage of their potential to support her young children.

It is important for lower grade classrooms to receive the best technology possible.

We have always discussed fire safety and traffic safety in primary classrooms. Now we must begin to discuss Internet safety.

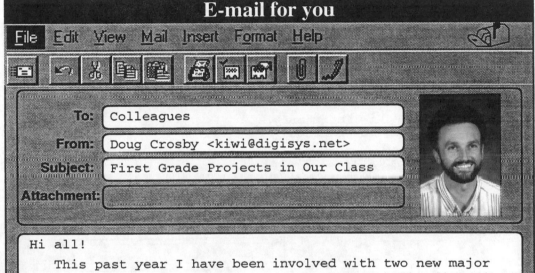

E-mail for you

File   Edit   View   Mail   Insert   Format   Help

To: Colleagues

From: Doug Crosby <kiwi@digisys.net>

Subject: First Grade Projects in Our Class

Attachment:

Hi all!
    This past year I have been involved with two new major projects that you may want to take a look at. The first is an exciting ongoing collaboration project that my first graders did with our local nursing home. We visited the residents throughout the year, reading to them and enjoying their company. Our final project was for each of my students to interview a resident, find out their family backgrounds, likes etc. and then to write a book about their partner either in fiction or non-fiction form. The culminating activity was to present these books to the residents; at the end of our school year. This was a tremendously rewarding activity both for my kids and the residents; some great friendships formed. We reported our activities on our class home page where you can see photos

Document: Continued

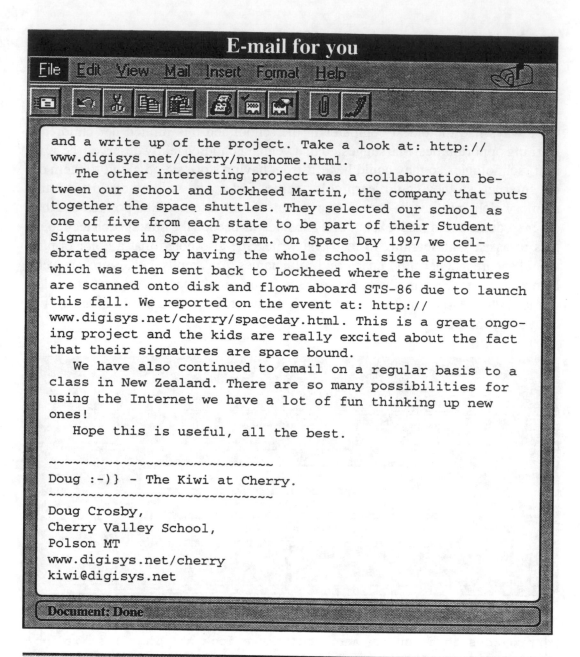

E-mail for you

File Edit View Mail Insert Format Help

and a write up of the project. Take a look at: http://
www.digisys.net/cherry/nurshome.html.
    The other interesting project was a collaboration be-
tween our school and Lockheed Martin, the company that puts
together the space shuttles. They selected our school as
one of five from each state to be part of their Student
Signatures in Space Program. On Space Day 1997 we celebrated space by having the whole school sign a poster
which was then sent back to Lockheed where the signatures
are scanned onto disk and flown aboard STS-86 due to launch
this fall. We reported on the event at: http://
www.digisys.net/cherry/spaceday.html. This is a great ongo-
ing project and the kids are really excited about the fact
that their signatures are space bound.
    We have also continued to email on a regular basis to a
class in New Zealand. There are so many possibilities for
using the Internet we have a lot of fun thinking up new
ones!
    Hope this is useful, all the best.

~~~~~~~~~~~~~~~~~~~~~~~~~~~~
Doug :-)} - The Kiwi at Cherry.
~~~~~~~~~~~~~~~~~~~~~~~~~~~~
Doug Crosby,
Cherry Valley School,
Polson MT
www.digisys.net/cherry
kiwi@digisys.net

Document: Done

General Issues for the Primary Grades

There are several issues that require special attention if you are fortunate enough to work with children in the primary grades: ensuring child safety, supporting emergent navigation skills, and seeking supportive technologies for your children. Each is essential to keep in mind as you work with young children on the Internet.

Child safety is a critical concern for young children unfamiliar with the Internet.

Child safety is a critical concern for young children unfamiliar with the Internet. As a teacher you are responsible for your students' physical safety in the classroom. You are also responsible for new safety issues that now arise because of the Internet. Chapter 2 described the nature of software filters and acceptable use policies. These help to establish rules for the appropriate use of the Internet and prevent young children from viewing objectionable locations. Chapter 4 described several locations on the Internet where all links are screened for child safety, another important strategy if you work with young children.

Primary grade teachers will need to pay particular attention to child safety on the Internet. We have always discussed fire safety and traffic safety in primary classrooms. Now we must begin to discuss Internet safety. You may wish to discuss issues of Internet safety as they arise in your class within an Internet Workshop framework as described in Chapter 2.

Teachers in the very youngest grades (K-1) will often limit children's use of the Internet to sites they have bookmarked. This limits the viewing of inappropriate locations. Others develop a rule similar to the one developed by Isabelle Hoag for her young students in Amsterdam. This too limits exposure to inappropriate locations.

Internet safety also applies to e-mail. Increasingly, school districts require that all incoming and outgoing e-mail messages for primary grade students go through the teacher's e-mail account. This way, you may monitor the e-mail communication of your students and help to ensure their safety. Should you find any inappropriate messages from strangers, you should immediately report the incident to your principal or another designated person in your district.

Another important aspect of Internet use in the primary grades is to help children learn basic navigation strategies. Learning about hyperlinks, bookmarks, mouse skills, and other emergent navigation strategies are important for the very youngest learners. You should not assume these skills in your students, but rather, plan systematically to support their development. Working with partners during computer time, using Internet Workshop, and developing very simple scavenger hunts for your young students are all ways to support this aspect of Internet use. Simple scavenger hunts that students complete in pairs or small groups are especially useful. These develop navigation strategies as students also practice functional reading and writing tasks. Here is another suggestion for the very youngest children: When you ask students to write down an answer during a scavenger hunt, look for words that are displayed on the screen so that they may copy them onto their worksheet. This will make it easier for children to successfully complete this literacy experience.

Finally, we want to speak up in support of primary grade teachers seeking and receiving supportive technologies to assist the youngest learners. Often, school districts follow a "hand-me-down" policy with computers. In these districts, primary grade classrooms receive the oldest computers that are passed down from the high school, to the middle school, and finally to the elementary school. This is unfortunate since the youngest learners benefit the most from the latest technologies and the most powerful computers. Children who struggle with decoding may play audio clips to support their reading experiences. Newer, multimedia computers also provide animations and other supportive technologies to explain challenging concepts. In order to take full advantage of these types of Internet resources you will require a computer with at least 24 MB of RAM (a type of memory). This much memory is required to run Netscape 4.0 or Internet Explorer 4.0 with multimedia plug-ins. If

Should you find any inappropriate messages from strangers, you should immediately report the incident to your principal or another designated person in your district.

Learning about hyperlinks, bookmarks, mouse skills, and other emergent navigation strategies are important for the very youngest learners.

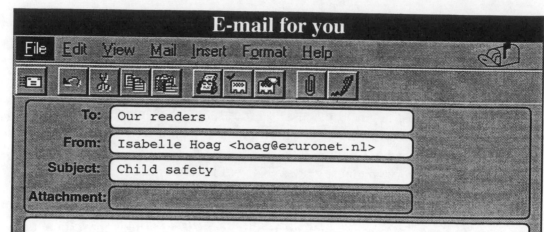

If you find yourself teaching in the primary grades without a computer capable of using the multimedia technologies at web sites, consider Liz Dye's approach— take your concerns to your principal, explaining the greater need young children have for the latest technologies.

E-mail for you

File Edit View Mail Insert Format Help

To: Our readers

From: Isabelle Hoag <hoag@eruronet.nl>

Subject: Child safety

Attachment:

Hi!

I was both nervous and excited when my class got hooked up to the Internet! I asked several people for their ideas about having the kids surf around and about making my own page. They sure helped me. I hope my ideas help you, too.

First, I was worried my third graders might find a site I would not want them to see for some reason. To guard against this, I made up the "Bookmark Plus Four Rule." My students must first ask to use Netscape. Then, they must start with a site I have saved on our list of "favorites" or "bookmarks." They can follow four links from that starting point but then they must return or start with another bookmark. They can also show me sites they would like to add to our bookmarks.

Next, I was worried that they kids would buy something or download a virus or sign up for something. There are many attractive blinking icons that scream "click here!" and children are being taught to follow instructions! So my class has strict instructions to never, ever write their name or give out any information when they are surfing. They must come and get me if they are asked for information.

Finally, when setting up my own pages, I wrote a permission slip similar to the ones I use for field trips. Only photos, work, and first names of children for whom I have permission slips are used. I only use first names and never identify children in photos.

This is a new technology and, if treated with respect and caution, it is a valuable resource in the class! Have fun!

Isabelle Hoag, Primary School Teacher
The International School of Amsterdam

Document: Done

you find yourself teaching in the primary grades without a computer capable of using the multimedia technologies at web sites, consider Liz Dye's approach—take your concerns to your principal, explaining the greater need young children have for the latest technologies.

Central Sites for the Primary Grades

As you look for central sites for young children, it is important to keep in mind child safety concerns. One place to begin your search is at **Yahooligans** (http://www.yahooligans.com/). This is one of the largest collections of useful sites for children with links that are screened for child safety before being accepted. As with all lists, though, one can never guarantee the contents of links that move away from these sites. Thus, you must still monitor student use. You may wish to set a bookmark for Yahooligans and allow students in the older primary grades access to this information. For younger students, you may wish to preview locations, set bookmarks, and only allow children to use the bookmarks you have set.

Probably the best central site screened for child safety is **Great Sites** (http://www.ala.org/parentspage/greatsites/amazing.html). This resource has been developed by the American Library Association and includes over 700 outstanding locations for children. Be certain to explore the wonderful resources here.

There is also an excellent central site for young children located at **Berit's Best Sites for Children** (http://db.cochran.com/li_toc:theoPage.db). These have been screened and rated. Each also contains a short review describing the contents. Many will indicate the approximate grade level for the activities at the location.

*Probably the best central site screened for child safety is **Great Sites**. This resource has been developed by the American Library Association and includes over 700 outstanding locations for children.*

Internet FAQ

Should I be concerned about using commercial sites in my classroom? How can I tell if a location on the WWW has commercial intentions if there aren't any advertisements?

As you consider which central sites for young children to use, you should pay attention to why a site was developed. Many central sites for young children are located at commercial locations. These can be identified by the ".com" at the end of their URL. Commercial sites sometimes seek to exploit the marketing potential available when many young children visit their location. Of the central sites identified in this chapter, only the one developed by the American Library Association is not a commercial site.

Keeping it Simple: Using Internet Activity with Internet Workshop

As you visit central sites for the primary grades, you will quickly find many locations that fit into Internet Activity. These may include coloring books, alphabet books

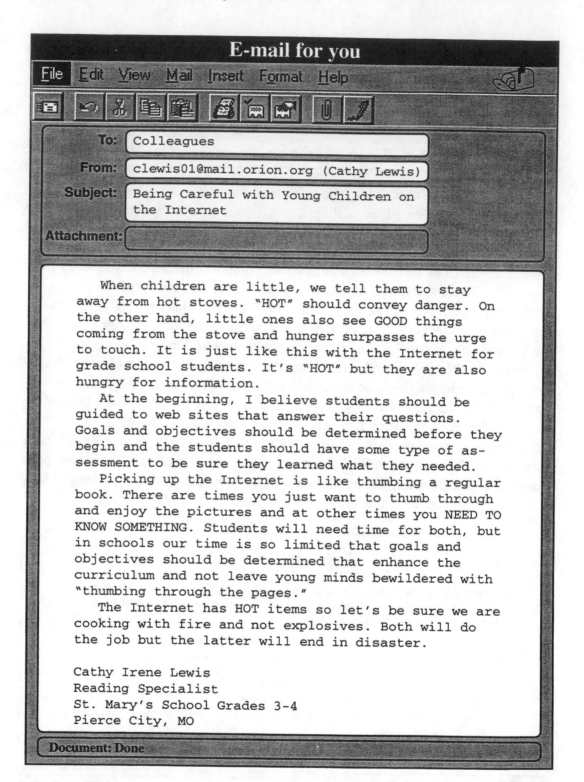

E-mail for you

File   Edit   View   Mail   Insert   Format   Help

To: Colleagues

From: clewis01@mail.orion.org (Cathy Lewis)

Subject: Being Careful with Young Children on the Internet

Attachment:

When children are little, we tell them to stay away from hot stoves. "HOT" should convey danger. On the other hand, little ones also see GOOD things coming from the stove and hunger surpasses the urge to touch. It is just like this with the Internet for grade school students. It's "HOT" but they are also hungry for information.

At the beginning, I believe students should be guided to web sites that answer their questions. Goals and objectives should be determined before they begin and the students should have some type of assessment to be sure they learned what they needed.

Picking up the Internet is like thumbing a regular book. There are times you just want to thumb through and enjoy the pictures and at other times you NEED TO KNOW SOMETHING. Students will need time for both, but in schools our time is so limited that goals and objectives should be determined that enhance the curriculum and not leave young minds bewildered with "thumbing through the pages."

The Internet has HOT items so let's be sure we are cooking with fire and not explosives. Both will do the job but the latter will end in disaster.

Cathy Irene Lewis
Reading Specialist
St. Mary's School Grades 3-4
Pierce City, MO

Document: Done

and stories, some of which are read aloud. They will also include activities in literature, math, science, and social studies. The Internet provides many opportunities to support your younger children in the classroom, especially with the use of Internet Activity.

As you have already discovered, Internet Activity is easy to develop. Simply find a location related to your classroom curriculum, set a bookmark for it, develop a brief activity, and then have your students complete this activity during the week. You may want to develop several activities for your students to explore during the week instead of just one. Often, it is useful to include a writing activity with the assignment to support young children's developing literacy ability. These writing experiences may then be shared during Internet Workshop at the end of each week.

Here are some examples of Internet Activity that might be used with students in the primary grades:

The Internet provides many opportunities to support your younger children in the classroom, especially with the use of Internet Activity.

- **Alex's Scribbles—Koala Trouble**—(http://www.gil.com.au/max/) This site from Australia features an extensive collection of wonderful stories about Max, the koala bear, by Alex Balsom (5 years old) and his dad. It is quickly becoming a classic on the Internet for young children. The stories contain hyperlinks within the illustrations; these require children to click on the correct location in the illustration in order to move

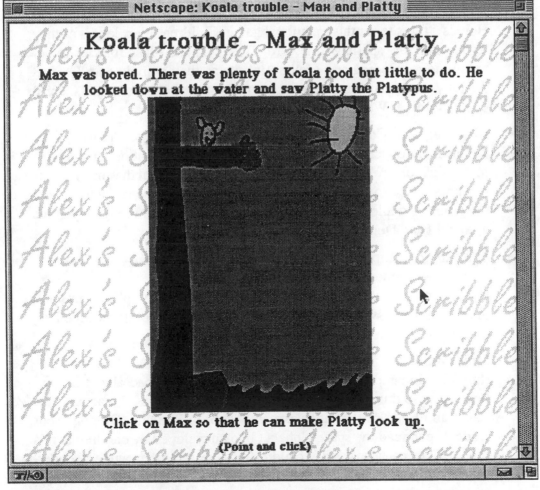

Figure 9-3. A page from a story at **Alex's Scribbles—Koala Trouble.**

Alex's Scribbles—Koala Trouble (http://www.gil.com.au/max/)

forward in the story, thus supporting reading comprehension. Have children draw a picture of Max and write their own story after reading one of these delightful adventures. Then have them read their stories during Internet Workshop.

- **Internet Coloring Books**—There are a number of coloring books on the Internet for very young children to enjoy. Have children print out their work and then write about their picture. They can read and share their work during Internet Workshop. Interactive coloring books provide opportunities to color illustrations right on the screen. Non-interactive coloring books only have black and white illustrations to be printed out and then colored. Interactive sites include: **Carlos' Coloring Book** (http://coloring.com/) and **Kendra's Coloring Book** (http://www.geocities.com/EnchantedForest/7155/). The later has started to include advertising at its new location. Non-interactive sites include: **TV Ontario Colouring Book** (http://www.tvo.org/cb_eng/) and **NASA's Space Coloring Book** (http://tommy.jsc.nasa.gov/~woodfill/SPACEED/SEHHTML/color.html).

- **Hangman at Kids Corner**—(http://kids.ot.com/cgi/kids/hangman)
  Here is a fun site for this traditional game. Children select letters as they try to guess the spelling of a word. This is a great place for kids to develop their decoding and spelling talents as they complete an Internet Activity. Invite students to print out their successful work and share it during Internet Workshop. Set a bookmark!

- **Blue Dog Can Count**—(http://kao.ini.cmu.edu:5550/bdf.html)
  At this location, children can write an addition, subtraction, division, or multiplication problem and listen as Blue Dog barks out the answer. This is a great place to check one's work. Better yet, have one student write the problem while the other predicts the answer. Then see if they agree with old Blue Dog. Great fun. Set a bookmark!

- **Jumpin' Jehosaphat the Counting Sheep**—
  (http://www.dodds1.com/Java/Jj.html)
  Here is another site like Blue Dog, only Jumpin' Jehosaphat jumps and bleets out the answer. It doesn't seem to work as smoothly as Blue Dog unless you have a very fast Internet connection.

- **Space ABC's**—
  (http://buckman.pps.k12.or.us/room100/ABCspace/spaceabc.html)
  Pay a visit to this tremendous resource developed by K-2 teachers Tim Lauer and Beth Rohloff at Buckman School in Portland, Oregon. Your students can read the space alphabet book developed by children at this school. They can also listen as children read the pages they wrote. Wonderful! Invite your children to read the book, print out their favorite page, and read it during Internet Workshop.

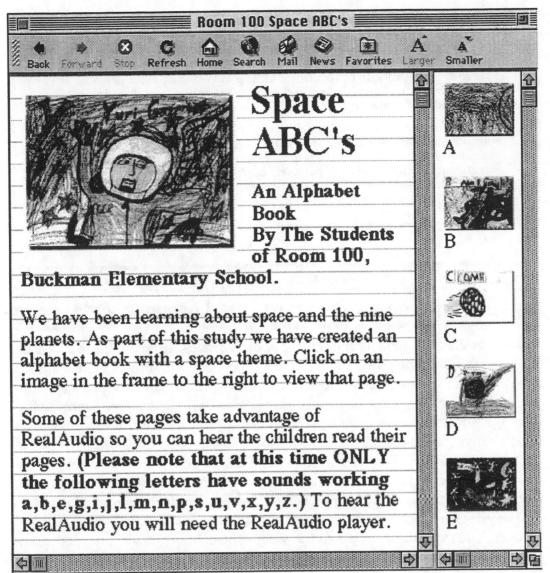

Figure 9-4. Space ABC's, a wonderful resource for young children. Your children can listen as the K-2 authors read their work aloud.

Space ABC's (http://buckman.pps.k12.or.us/room100/ABCspace/spaceabc.html)

In addition to these traditional uses of sites for Internet Activities, it is also possible to use your computer as a fixed resource to support very young children's literacy development as Liz Dye did. This is a very safe experience for your children since they only view an image you have bookmarked on the computer. For example, find an unusual image each day to display on the screen and encourage your students to draw a picture of this image and then write down what they think it is. A great source of these images is the **Nanoworld Image Gallery** (http://www.uq.oz.au:80/nanoworld/images_1.html) where you will find images taken by an electron microscope. Sometimes images will contain the label for the item. This is also useful for students who may wish to copy the word down as they write a sentence describing the picture they see. This can easily be set up as an Internet Activity for kindergarten classrooms with children's pictures and writing shared during Internet Workshop.

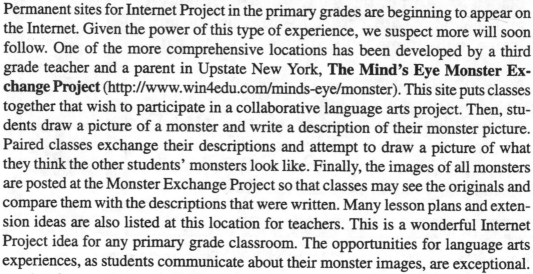

Internet FAQ

I have seen hundreds of locations on the WWW but I never know if I am looking at something "good." How can I tell if I am looking at an "outstanding" web site?

The definition of an outstanding web site is, of course, subjective. You may, however, wish to review the criteria the American Library Association uses to define outstanding web sites. They organize an extensive criteria list around these elements: authorship/sponsorship, purpose, design and stability, and content. Take a look and see if you agree. Their **Selection** page is located at http://www.ala.org/parentspage/greatsites/criteria.html.

Using Internet Project and Internet Workshop to Integrate the Language Arts

Permanent sites for Internet Project in the primary grades are beginning to appear on the Internet. Given the power of this type of experience, we suspect more will soon follow. One of the more comprehensive locations has been developed by a third grade teacher and a parent in Upstate New York, **The Mind's Eye Monster Exchange Project** (http://www.win4edu.com/minds-eye/monster). This site puts classes together that wish to participate in a collaborative language arts project. Then, students draw a picture of a monster and write a description of their monster picture. Paired classes exchange their descriptions and attempt to draw a picture of what they think the other students' monsters look like. Finally, the images of all monsters are posted at the Monster Exchange Project so that classes may see the originals and compare them with the descriptions that were written. Many lesson plans and extension ideas are also listed at this location for teachers. This is a wonderful Internet Project idea for any primary grade classroom. The opportunities for language arts experiences, as students communicate about their monster images, are exceptional.

Another permanent project location on the Internet that provides an amazing set of resources for your children is Monarch Watch. If you wish to plan a project around these beautiful creatures, this is the place for you.

Another permanent project location on the Internet that provides an amazing set of resources for your children is **Monarch Watch** (http://www.MonarchWatch.org/). If you wish to plan a project around these beautiful creatures, this is the place for you. The location contains an amazingly extensive set of resources designed for children and teachers to learn more about butterflies. Your students can raise butterflies, band them, release them into the wild, and track their progress as reports come in from observers around North America. Pay a visit to this excellent resource.

In addition to permanent sites such as these, you should also visit locations on the Internet where less permanent Internet Projects are described, inviting you and other teachers to join in classroom interchanges. Or, you may come up with your own idea for a great project and invite other teachers to join you by posting it at one of these locations. Locations where teachers post projects and invite others to join them have been described in other chapters. They include:

Figure 9-5. The home page for the **Mind's Eye Monster Exchange,** an outstanding Internet project location for primary grade children.

Mind's Eye Monster Exchange (http://www.win4edu.com/minds-eye/monster)

- **The Global SchoolNet Projects Registry—** (http://www.gsn.org/pr/index.html)

- **The Global School House: The Connected Classroom—** (http://www.gsh.org/class/default.htm)

- **KIDPROJ—**(http://www.kidlink.org:80/KIDPROJ/)

- **NickNack's Telecollaborative Learning Page—** (http://www1.minn.net:80/~schubert/NickNacks.html#anchor100100).

- **Classroom Connect's Teacher Contact Database—** (http://www.classroom.net/contact/)

Figure 9-6.
To develop an
Internet
project about
Monarch
butterflies, be
certain to visit
**Monarch
Watch.**

Monarch Watch (http://www.MonarchWatch.org/)

TEACHING TIP

Join the Read In Project

The Read In Foundation organizes an event each year to support the reading of
outstanding literature. Develop an Internet project around this event and encourage the reading of exceptional works of literature as you communicate with
popular children's authors and with other classrooms. In 1998, participating
authors include: Lloyd Alexander, Avi, Bruce Balan, Judy Blume, David Boyd,
Karleen Bradford, Eve Bunting, Bruce Coville, Paula Danziger, Ed Emberley,
Virginia Hamilton, Daniel Hayes, Joan Irvine, Jackie French Koller, James
Moloney, Ann M. Martin, Evelyn Clarke Mott, Connie Porter, Aaron Shepard,
R.L. Stine, Rob Thomas, David Wisniewski, Jane Yolen. Visit the site for **Read
In** (http://www.readin.org/TheReadIn/default.html) and participate!

Examples of projects you may wish to consider joining or developing for primary grade students include:

- **The Eric Carle Book Club.**   Invite other classes to read works by Eric Carle (or another popular author). Then, using writing process activities, share children's written responses to these works with each classroom. Also, consider polling each class about their favorite books by this author and sharing the results with other classes. When all of the results are in, have each class develop a graph to display the results. Send the results of your work to the author and see if he/she responds.

- **Amazing Insects.**   A third grade class in Minnesota studied insects during the year and shared the results of their studies with classes around the world. They exchanged information about these amazing creatures. Writing, math, literature, and science are woven into this project.

- **Playground Chants Around the World.**   Playground chants are part of every child's culture no matter where they go to school. Have your students write these down carefully and exchange them with classes at other locations around the world. Communicate with classes to find out the meanings of chants that are unfamiliar to your students. This is a wonderful way to support reading and writing in your primary grade classroom and to discover important aspects of other cultures.

- **Teddy Bears Travel the World.**   Have each participating class purchase a small teddy bear and send it to one of the other classrooms. In each class, the teddy must go home with a different child each night. Each child must then write a description of the what they did, where they went, and what it was like at their location. These should be developed with the parent/guardian and returned to school. Each day, these messages go out to each participating class to be read by the students. A map can be marked to show where each Teddy is in the world. At the end, Teddy bears can be mailed back to the home classrooms with souvenirs from its host classroom.

Using Internet Inquiry with Internet Workshop

Internet Inquiry occurs less frequently in the primary grades than it does at other grade levels. Part of the reason for this is child safety. Parents are often reluctant to have their young children independently exploring resources on the Internet. As a result, school boards often will place limits on children's independent Internet use at these younger levels. A more common reason, however, is that children at this age are still developing navigation skills. Because these skills have yet to be completely developed, it simply takes too long for many students to acquire useful information about a topic or project that interests them. Finally, the speed of obtaining informa-

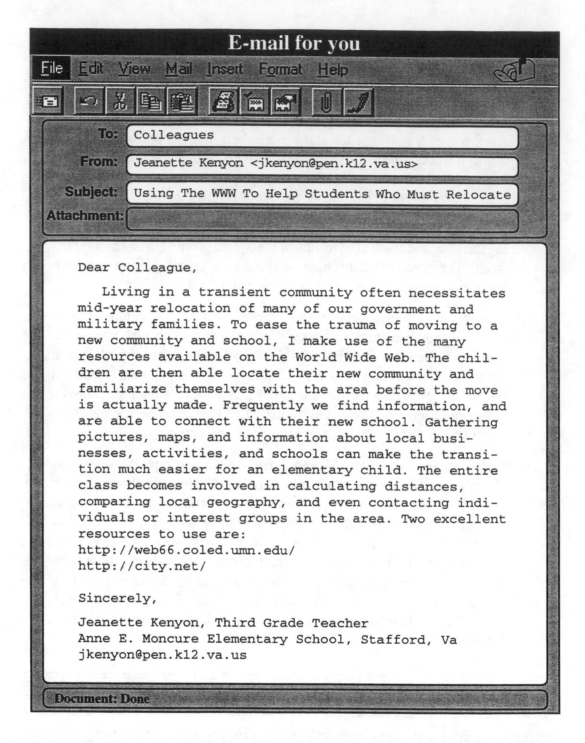

E-mail for you

File Edit View Mail Insert Format Help

To: Colleagues

From: Jeanette Kenyon <jkenyon@pen.k12.va.us>

Subject: Using The WWW To Help Students Who Must Relocate

Attachment:

Dear Colleague,

    Living in a transient community often necessitates mid-year relocation of many of our government and military families. To ease the trauma of moving to a new community and school, I make use of the many resources available on the World Wide Web. The children are then able locate their new community and familiarize themselves with the area before the move is actually made. Frequently we find information, and are able to connect with their new school. Gathering pictures, maps, and information about local businesses, activities, and schools can make the transition much easier for an elementary child. The entire class becomes involved in calculating distances, comparing local geography, and even contacting individuals or interest groups in the area. Two excellent resources to use are:
http://web66.coled.umn.edu/
http://city.net/

Sincerely,

Jeanette Kenyon, Third Grade Teacher
Anne E. Moncure Elementary School, Stafford, Va
jkenyon@pen.k12.va.us

Document: Done

tion on the Internet is also impeded by young children's emerging literacy ability. Even when children do find resources that are related to their inquiry project, they are not always able to understand the information. Thus, independent inquiry projects are less common in the primary grades than at older grade levels.

It is useful, though, to spend time supporting children as they develop navigation skills. Indeed, some teachers will focus on navigation as a subject for Internet Inquiry. Usually this is developed during Internet Workshop time when teachers encourage children to share some new strategy they have discovered and to seek advice about something they do not understand. Teachers, too, will develop navigation skills through the use of regular scavenger hunts on the Internet, usually in groups or pairs. These results will be shared during Internet Workshop as a way of discussing navigation strategies.

Primary Grade Resources on the Internet

Animal Tracks—(http://www.nwf.org/nwf/kids/)
The National Wildlife Federation has developed this site for kids interested in animals and the environment. It contains interactive games for the youngest users, riddles and jokes for older students, and even articles from past issues of *Ranger Rick*. Many articles also appear in Spanish. A nice location during units on animals and the environment. Set a bookmark!

Academic World—
(http://www.lifelong.com/lifelong_universe/AcademicWorld/default.html)
A commercial site, to be sure, but several nice examples of talking storybooks are located here. If you have downloaded the plug-in and text-to-speech software from Monster Math (see below), come to this location and visit the talking storybooks that can be used for Internet Activities. These are very nice for younger readers.

Concertina—(http://www.iatcch.com/books/intro.html)
Concertina is a new Canadian publisher of children's books. They have placed several nice selections here for young children. Some sounds are available within the books.

Kid Safety on the Internet—(http://www.uoknor.edu/oupd/kidsafe/start.htm)
This site contains questions and answers to help kids protect themselves and handle emergencies. It covers Internet safety as well as other types of situations. It may be helpful for students in the 2nd and 3rd grades. Develop an Internet activity at this site for the beginning of the school year.

Monster Math—(http://www.lifelong.com/lifelong_universe/AcademicWorld/MonsterMath/default.html)
One of the first educational sites on the Internet to use text-to-speech technology, a real boon for children in the primary grades. At this site you will find a series of easy math problems woven into a story format for young children. Directions and links are provided to obtain the plug-in that will read all of the pages aloud to children. It will even read it in Spanish. Set a bookmark!

Smokey Bear's Official Home Page—
(http://www.smokeybear.com/index.html)
Here is a great location for an Internet activity during Fire Safety Week. Kids can play several games about fire safety, take a quiz and see how they do, and even e-mail Smokey. Set a bookmark!

Stage Hands Puppets Activity Page—(http://fox.nstn.ca/~puppets/activity.html)
If you are interested in using puppets in your classroom, here is the site for you! Puppet activities are a wonderful way to support language development in the primary grades. This location is rich in resources, including an interactive experience to allow students to design their own puppet on the screen, an on-line puppet theater where you can read plays developed by other children and submit your own play, performance tips from "The Professor" (students can also ask "The Professor" questions and see the answers), paper puppets and patterns to download, ideas for using scraps to make puppets, and links to other puppet sites. Set a bookmark!

The Dr. King Timeline Page—
(http://buckman.pps.k12.or.us/room100/timeline/kingframe.html)
Here is another wonderful work of literature created by the kids at Buckman School. A great follow-up activity after reading together *My Dream of Martin Luther King* by Faith Ringgold or a unit on this important American.

The White House for Kids—
(http://www.whitehouse.gov/WH/kids/html/home.html)
Have your kids take a tour of the White House conducted by Socks, the cat. A fun activity for your students to complete as an Internet Activity. Your students can even write a letter to the president. Set a bookmark!

Listservs/Mailing Lists for the Primary Grades

ECENET-L—(listserv@postoffice.cso.uiuc.edu)
A discussion group on early childhood education (0–8 years). Message archives are located at: http://ericir.syr.edu/Virtual/Listserv_Archives/ecenet-l.html.

PROJECTS-L—(listserv@postoffice.cso.uiuc.edu)
A group interested in using a project approach in early childhood education. Message archives are located at: http://ericir.syr.edu/Virtual/Listserv_Archives/projects-l.html.

RTEACHER—(listserv@listserv.syr.edu)
A discussion group on using technology to support literacy learning sponsored by *The Reading Teacher,* a journal of the International Reading Association.

Usenet Newsgroups for the Primary Grades

k12.chat.elementary—Informal discussion among elementary students, grades K–5.

k12.chat.teacher—Informal discussion among teachers in grades K–12.

pnet.school.k-5—Discussion about K–5 education.

10 Using the Internet to Increase Multicultural Understanding

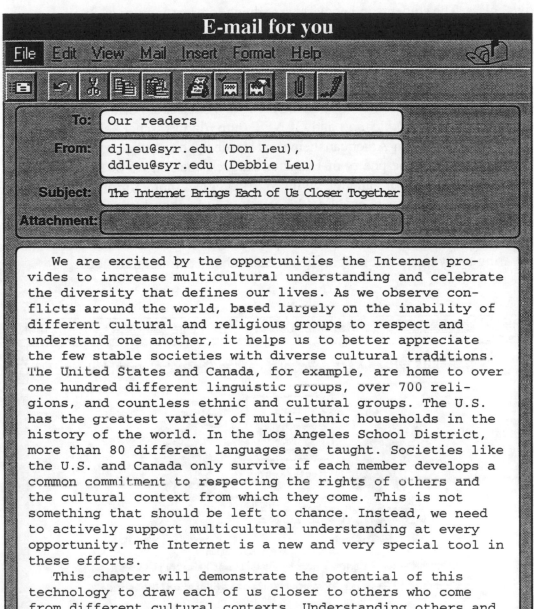

E-mail for you

File   Edit   View   Mail   Insert   Format   Help

To: Our readers

From: djleu@syr.edu (Don Leu),
ddleu@syr.edu (Debbie Leu)

Subject: The Internet Brings Each of Us Closer Together

Attachment:

We are excited by the opportunities the Internet provides to increase multicultural understanding and celebrate the diversity that defines our lives. As we observe conflicts around the world, based largely on the inability of different cultural and religious groups to respect and understand one another, it helps us to better appreciate the few stable societies with diverse cultural traditions. The United States and Canada, for example, are home to over one hundred different linguistic groups, over 700 religions, and countless ethnic and cultural groups. The U.S. has the greatest variety of multi-ethnic households in the history of the world. In the Los Angeles School District, more than 80 different languages are taught. Societies like the U.S. and Canada only survive if each member develops a common commitment to respecting the rights of others and the cultural context from which they come. This is not something that should be left to chance. Instead, we need to actively support multicultural understanding at every opportunity. The Internet is a new and very special tool in these efforts.

This chapter will demonstrate the potential of this technology to draw each of us closer to others who come from different cultural contexts. Understanding others and the cultural context from which they come is an increasingly important goal as we build a global village with this new technology.

Don and Debbie

Document: Done

267

Teaching with the Internet: Alison Meadows' Class

"But I don't understand why we can't write to Native American students," said Desmon. "I don't understand why it hurts their feelings when we say we are studying their culture."

Desmon was reporting during an Internet Workshop session in Alison Meadows' class. The students in her class were doing Internet Inquiry in a unit designed to increase multicultural understanding and build a classroom community. Celebrating different cultural traditions helped to accomplish these goals. Students had been working in groups on Internet Inquiry projects. Some had picked a Hispanic theme and were reading literature and studying about the many different Hispanic cultures. They had found many useful locations on the WWW such as the **Chicano! Homepage** (http://www.pbs.org/chicano/) and **CLNET** (http://latino.sscnet.ucla.edu/). Others had picked an African-American theme and had decided to focus on the connections they saw between the poetry of Langston Hughes, the actions of Rosa Parks and Martin Luther King, Jr., and the civil rights struggle. Another group had picked a Japanese theme and were studying the literature and cultural traditions of this culture. Through **Web66** (http://web66.coled.umn.edu/schools.html), this group had linked up with another class in Kyoto and were exchanging e-mail messages, discovering many important insights about each other's cultural traditions.

Figure 10-1. The home page for **CLNET,** a wonderful central site for Chicano/a and Latina/o cultural resources on the WWW.

CLNET (http://latino.sscnet.ucla.edu/)

Desmon's group was studying Native American literature and cultures, especially the common respect they all expressed for Mother Earth. Desmon's group had read many of the prayers, poems, and stories located at **Indigenous Peoples' Literature** (http://www.indians.org/welker/framenat.htm) as they developed a growing respect for the traditions, struggles, and views of Native Americans. **A Line in the Sand** (http://hanksville.phast.umass.edu:8000/cultprop/) had been especially useful. In addition, they read a number of books from the library, including: *Thirteen Moons on Turtles Back*, by Bruchac and London; *Giving Thanks: A Native American Good Morning Message*, by Chief Jake Swamp; *Ceremony—In the Circle of Life*, by White Deer of Autumn; *Buffalo Woman*, by Gobel; *Chief Sarah: Sarah Winnemucca's Fight for Indian Rights*, by Morrison. They had also been exploring some of the many Native American sites on the web. They were excited when they found a great location, **Native American Indian** (http://indy4.fdl.cc.mn.us/~isk/ mainmenu.html), and discovered a place to post a message (http://indy4.fdl.cc.mn.us/ ~isk/schools/schlbook.html) in hopes of linking up with Native American students who might be interested in becoming KeyPals. But then they came across a message from the author of this site saying:

```
"Non-Indians: teachers, kids, please do not say
'studying Native Americans and want to correspond
with some.' This is offensive, racist. This service
is primarily a way for Indian kids to get in contact
with each other, not a method of providing specimens
for study by your class or students."
```

Desmon was sharing his question with the rest of the class. "I didn't know that I was being racist," he said. "And I don't want to hurt anyone's feelings. I just want to understand more about their culture."

This event prompted a lively discussion in Alison's class. Some couldn't understand the reason behind the message until Michelle asked how they would feel if someone wrote: "We are studying girls, or Hispanics, or African-Americans, or boys, and we want to correspond with some."

"It makes you feel like a thing, not a person," she noted. "And, there are many different Native American cultures, not just one." This made many students think again about how the person who developed this web site must have felt when reading messages like this.

The discussion in Alison's class was useful in developing greater respect and sensitivity for others, issues at the heart of effective cross-cultural communication and understanding. It increased children's awareness of the power of words and how the words one uses in a message may unintentionally hurt people. It also helped students develop greater sensitivity to different cultural traditions and how one must be respectful of cultural differences on the WWW.

Toward the end of their conversation, Alison pointed out how important it was for Native American students to have a space on the WWW to communicate with other students from Native American cultures and that one needed to respect this right. She also noted that some Native American students were interested in com-

The discussion in Alison's class was useful in developing greater respect and sensitivity for others, issues at the heart of effective cross-cultural communication and understanding.

It is clear the Internet provides special opportunities to help everyone better understand the unique qualities in each of our cultural traditions.

municating with students from non-Native cultural traditions. She said that she had found a location on the web at the **Grassroots** section of SchoolNet (http://www.schoolnet.ca/grassroots/), where Native American and non-Native American classes who wanted to exchange e-mail could do so. She wasn't certain if this was open to their class but she said she would send a message and see if this would be possible.

Lessons from the Classroom

This episode from Alison Meadows' classroom has several important lessons for us to consider as we think about using the Internet to increase multicultural understanding. First, it is clear the Internet provides special opportunities to help everyone better understand the unique qualities in each of our cultural traditions. No other instructional resource available in your classroom is as rich in its potential for developing an understanding of the diverse nature of our global society and for helping each of your students to walk in someone else's footprints.

Children feel pride in themselves and their culture when all cultural experiences are valued for the contributions they make to a rich and vibrant society.

Alison sought to take advantage of this potential. Each group in her class defined and completed an Inquiry project celebrating a special cultural group. Alison gave each group several guidelines to follow: each project had to treat the culture with respect, it had to include literature and Internet experiences as part of the project; and, each group had to develop a learning experience for the rest of the class based on something they had learned from that culture. One group was building a display and learning center in their classroom with many cultural artifacts. Another group was planning on a poetry reading, a readers theater presentation, and an Internet Activity. Another was developing a reading corner and a bulletin board. The fourth group was planning a read aloud activity and an Internet scavenger hunt for everyone to complete.

Using the Internet to celebrate the diversity that exists in our world is important for a variety of reasons. Bringing this information into your classroom sends an important message to your students about the respect and dignity each of us needs to accord every human experience. Integrating Internet resources from different cultures into your curriculum is central to accomplishing this important goal. Children feel pride in themselves and their culture when all cultural experiences are valued for the contributions they make to a rich and vibrant society. In addition, students develop a richer appreciation of the historical forces that have shaped our societies and the contributions made by different cultural groups. Finally, the Internet allows all students to explore issues of social justice. Exploring issues of social justice is essential to preparing children for citizenship in a diverse society where these issues are fundamental to our collective well being.

E-mail allows your students to immediately communicate with others around the world from different cultural traditions in order to learn more about their unique heritage. This opportunity has never before existed in school classrooms.

The episode from Alison's class also teaches us a second lesson: e-mail experiences with others may be very useful as you consider using the Internet to increase multicultural understanding. E-mail allows your students to immediately communicate with others around the world from different cultural traditions in order to learn more about their unique heritage. This opportunity has never before existed in school classrooms; it enables your students to engage in powerful cross-cultural experiences that may be used to develop understanding and respect for others.

E-mail, however, is a two-edged sword in developing multicultural understanding. On the positive side, e-mail removes many of the visual trappings that normally impede conversations between members of different cultural groups; we tend to ignore physical differences and focus, instead, on considering the ideas and experiences of the person with whom we communicate. This is what the students who studied Japanese cultural traditions experienced in Alison's class. On the other hand, when we bring stereotypes about a cultural group to e-mail conversations, these stereotypes often appear unintentionally between the lines of our messages and may be hurtful to the recipient. This is what happened with students leaving messages at the location called Native American Indian. E-mail communication between different cultural groups requires sensitivity to the recipient and an ability to anticipate how any message might be interpreted as you compose it. Often, it forces us to confront stereotypes we may have but may not realize. These are good lessons for all of us to learn.

E-mail communication between different cultural groups requires sensitivity to the recipient and an ability to anticipate how any message might be interpreted as you compose it. Often, it forces us to confront stereotypes we may have but may not realize. These are good lessons for all of us to learn.

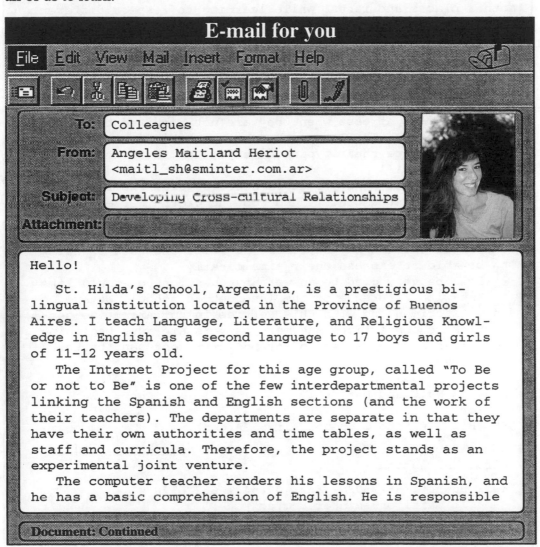

E-mail for you

File Edit View Mail Insert Format Help

To: Colleagues

From: Angeles Maitland Heriot
<maitl_sh@sminter.com.ar>

Subject: Developing Cross-cultural Relationships

Attachment:

Hello!

   St. Hilda's School, Argentina, is a prestigious bilingual institution located in the Province of Buenos Aires. I teach Language, Literature, and Religious Knowledge in English as a second language to 17 boys and girls of 11–12 years old.

   The Internet Project for this age group, called "To Be or not to Be" is one of the few interdepartmental projects linking the Spanish and English sections (and the work of their teachers). The departments are separate in that they have their own authorities and time tables, as well as staff and curricula. Therefore, the project stands as an experimental joint venture.

   The computer teacher renders his lessons in Spanish, and he has a basic comprehension of English. He is responsible

Document: Continued

for our Internet Project, and I, the teacher of English to the same group of students, provide him with translations whenever necessary. The purpose of the project is to give children a meaningful task in their computing lessons to connect our children with the outer world, since our school is located in a small suburb in the Province of Buenos Aires, and the exchange with other schools or children is scarce.

From a broader perspective, the Internet allows our young users to become aware of the geography, history, and culture of the world. It is hoped that our pupils will enlarge their knowledge, and increase their curiosity about other places and races, while learning to respect different values and ways of living and to use English to communicate effectively. The incentive to "talk" with other children all around the world is extremely powerful. The Internet is an ideal medium, since it requires an informal writing style, thus allowing the writers certain "literary licenses" (spelling, misprints, punctuation misuse). Pupils may feel more at ease when they are not required to rewrite their messages. The Internet encourages children to write and to practice their typing to enjoy the thrill of receiving a message!!!

On the other hand, teachers need to guide their pupils' work, so that the context and content of the letters are not misleading and/or inaccurate. A little time is required before children realize that no matter how instantaneous the whole process may be, there is still the need to think to be able to express their aims clearly.

I'll be very glad to answer any question you would like to ask with reference to the Internet at school. We are only experimenting with this service in our Argentine context. More connections and more servers are just beginning to appear in the market, offering lower costs and better services.

Angeles Maitland Heriot
Junior 7 Teacher
St. Hilda's School Buenos Aires, Argentina

Home address: J. de Garay 1051- (1686) Hurlingham- Buenos Aires- Argentina

tel: 00 54 1 6622392 - fax: 00 54 1 662 6378
e-mail: maitl_sh@sminter.com.ar

Document: Done

Central Sites to Increase Multicultural Understanding

There are many locations on the Internet providing a comprehensive set of resources to help your students appreciate and understand different cultural traditions. You may wish to review the resources at these sites as you develop Internet Activity and Internet Project with your students. Some locations are also useful for Internet Inquiry.

It is possible that some of the central sites we identify in this section may contain links that eventually link to locations where issues of sexual orientation are considered. While we believe these issues are important for older students to consider, we recognize that a number of communities may feel uncomfortable allowing younger students to access these sites. We mention this so that you may make informed judgments about locations you make available to your students.

The best central sites to support instruction in multicultural understanding include:

- **Cultures of the World—**
  (http://www.ala.org/parentspage/greatsites/people.html#b)
  Here is a great central site with many extensive resources selected by the American Library Association as appropriate for children from preschool to age 14. Many great resources. Set a bookmark!

- **Walk A Mile in My Shoes: Multicultural Curriculum Resources—**
  (http://www.wmht.org/trail/explor02.htm)
  If you only have time to visit one central site on multicultural issues, be certain you stop here. Developed by schools in the Albany, New York region, this location is designed specifically for teachers new to the Internet and includes many links in areas such as multicultural literature, multicultural sites for kids, locations for multicultural e-mail exchanges, sites with links on specific cultural groups, and sites with links to schools all over the world. Set a bookmark!

- **Multicultural Pavilion—**
  (http://curry.edschool.Virginia.EDU/go/multicultural/)
  Located at the School of Education at the University of Virginia, this location is very well organized and growing very rapidly. The most useful area is a "Teachers' Corner" where you will find a set of links to important locations on the WWW for multicultural education, links to on-line resources for teachers and students, several historic archives, and links to on-line literature for students.

- **Diversity—**(http://www.execpc.com/~dboals/diversit.html)
  This is an enormous collection of links to sites on the WWW related to diversity and multicultural education. It is part of the larger History/Social Studies Web Site for K–12 Teachers. Sections include: general sources, disabilities, migration and immigrant resources, Jewish resources,

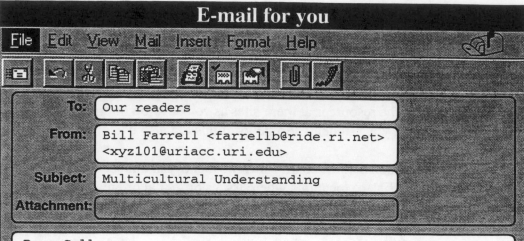

E-mail for you

File Edit View Mail Insert Format Help

To: Our readers

From: Bill Farrell <farrellb@ride.ri.net>
<xyz101@uriacc.uri.edu>

Subject: Multicultural Understanding

Attachment:

Dear Colleague,

   A topic that appeals to me is multi-cultural understanding and one of my favorite sites is **Web66** (http://
web66.coled.umn.edu/schools.html), the International Registry of schools on the web. This site has links to many,
many schools around the world. These links will tell you
about a school and many times have e-mail links to the
schools. You may be able to begin a collaboration with
another school by sending them a short e-mail message about
your school and students while requesting information about
their school and students. This is a great way for students
to begin pen pal correspondences. If they are willing, you
might be able to continue this e-mail relationship while
continuing to share information about your individual communities and customs. Students can exchange recipes from
their countries and culminate an activity with a world's
fair type of event in which the children assume the roles
of their foreign partners. I truly feel that if more and
more children are exposed to other children around the
world via e-mail and the Internet, we will ultimately have
a safer world and better place for all of us. This kind of
relationship was not possible two years ago. If you don't
succeed with one school, try another and I'm quite sure
you'll find a school that is more than willing to collaborate on a project with you. I wish you good luck on your
Internet odyssey and hope to run across your school someday
on the information superhighway.

Bill Farrell
Computer Literacy Teacher Chariho Middle School
****
William L. Farrell
Computer Specialist, Grades 5-8 Chariho Regional Middle School
455B Switch Road Wood River Jct, RI USA 02894
401 364-0651
e-mail: farrelb@ride.ri.net   http://www.chariho.k12.ri.us/cms/index.html
****

Document: Done

Asian American resources, African-American resources, Women Studies resources, Native American resources, and Hispanic resources.

- **Latin American Network Information Center—** (http://www.lanic.utexas.edu/la/region/k-12/)
A great location with many sites and resources devoted to the study of Latin America, many by students. Some of the locations are in Spanish. Set a bookmark!

Keeping it Simple: Using Internet Activity with Internet Workshop

Exploring links at these central sites will immediately give you ideas for an Internet Activity designed to increase multicultural understanding. Some teachers develop an Internet Activity related to multicultural issues as students study a unit on this theme in class. Other teachers like to have a weekly Internet Activity devoted to increasing multicultural understanding as a regular part of their curriculum, each week exploring a different cultural experience on the Internet and discussing this experience during Internet Workshop.

TEACHING TIP

Ideas for Internet Activity

When you are trying to increase multicultural understanding with Internet Activity, it is important to keep two ideas in mind. First, try to provide opportunities for students to work together on these assignments. When two students work on an Internet Activity together, opportunities develop for important exchanges to take place about these issues. This almost always leads to conversations that are important to developing greater respect and sensitivity about other cultures, especially if you establish this value in your classroom. Second, provide an opportunity to share students' thoughts and responses after they complete their activity, perhaps during Internet Workshop. This allows you to support the respect and sensitivity about other cultures that you are trying to develop.

Here are some examples of Internet Activity that might be used to support greater multicultural understanding with Internet Workshop:

- **Mancala**—(http://imagiware.com/mancala/)
This strategy game from Africa is often found in classrooms. Here it is in a virtual form. A great site for your students to play this game against the computer as you study African or African-American cultural traditions. It contains clear directions and the program will even give you hints if your game is not going very well. Set this site up as an Internet Activity during Kwanzaa. Share strategies during Internet Workshop. Make a bookmark!

- **Kid's Window**—(http://sequoia.nttam.com:80/KIDS/kids_home.html)
  Developed in a joint project between Stanford University and NTT from Japan, there are enough great resources here to design Internet Activities for an entire unit on Japan. Audio is included throughout the site. This location is probably most appropriate for the elementary grades, but everyone can enjoy the wonderfully rich insights into Japanese cultural traditions. Invite students to read one of several classic Japanese folk tales such as *Momotaro* or listen to it read aloud in Japanese and English. Have students order lunch and then write what they ordered in both English and Japanese. Have students attend language class in Hiragana, Kanji, or Katakana and then share what they learned during Internet Workshop. Have students finish up by following the directions to make an origami crane. Older students may also wish to visit a companion site, **Japan Window** (http://www.jwindow.net/). Set a bookmark for both locations!

- **Martin Luther King Jr.**—
  (http://www.seattletimes.com/mlk/index.html)
  An outstanding site designed for teachers and students to reflect on the legacy of this famous American. Developed by a newspaper in Seattle, this location includes an interactive timeline of his life and contributions, audio clips of important speeches, reflections on his life from many individuals, a photo tour of the civil rights movement, information about the national holiday in the United States, classroom ideas, and opportunities to communicate with others about the significance of Dr. King's accomplishments. A must for celebrating his life with many resources for Internet Activity. Set a bookmark!

- **Miracle: The White Buffalo**—(http://www.bossnt.com/page16.html)
  In 1994, a white buffalo calf was born in Wisconsin, a sign to many Native Americans of great significance. This location chronicles the story of this significant event and the meaning it holds for many Native American cultures. Have your students read the newspaper articles at this location to observe the way in which these are written. Then, have students use the information to write their own newspaper article of this event and its meaning. Share the results during Internet Workshop.

- **Kwanzaa Information Center**—(http://www.melanet.com/kwanzaa/)
  Kwanzaa is the African-American spiritual holiday initiated by Dr. Maulana Ron Karenga in 1966. Today it is celebrated in an increasing number of homes. This location at Melanet provides a rich set of information resources about this holiday. It explains how it is celebrated and the meaning of the important symbols. Have your students read the information at this site and come to Internet Workshop prepared to share what they have learned.

Figure 10-2. The home page for **Martin Luther King Jr.** at the *Seattle Times*.

Martin Luther King Jr. (http://www.seattletimes.com/mlk/index.html)

- **Maya/Aztec/Inca Center of the Lords of the Earth—** (http://www.realtime.net/maya/)
  A rich site with many resources designed to help students recognize the many accomplishments in history, geography, geology, astronomy, archaeology, anthropology, and art that existed in the Americas before Christopher Columbus's arrival. Have your students explore these pages and bring one important cultural achievement to share and explain during Internet Workshop. Use this time to discuss the rich heritage that existed in the Americas before their discovery by Europeans.

Using Internet Project with Internet Workshop

Internet Project is, perhaps, the best method to develop multicultural understanding among your students. When your students communicate with students from another cultural context, many important insights are shared about how we are all alike and how we are different. Children have a special way of cutting right through social trappings to share essential information with one another. Their queries, which sometimes might be perceived as offensive to an adult, are often appreciated for what they are by other children—an honest attempt to understand the world around them. Guiding children into these new types of cultural interchanges on the Internet can do much to increase your students' appreciation for cultural differences. It is a wonderful way to celebrate diversity in your classroom.

The traditional sites for Internet Project described in previous chapters may be useful as you seek out projects with classes from different cultural contexts. Sometimes, though, it takes a special effort to contact classrooms from other cultural contexts. You may have to initiate contact directly with teachers and schools. We encourage you to do so because the rewards are so great. Not every teacher or school will respond to your requests, but enough will respond to make this a valuable strategy. Locations to help you to make these contacts include:

Internet Project is, perhaps, the best method to develop multicultural understanding among your students.

- **Intercultural E-mail Classroom Connections—**
  (http://www.stolaf.edu/network/iecc/)
  This exceptional service is provided by St. Olaf College in Minnesota to bring together schools from all over the world. When you join one of the mailing lists at this location, you will have e-mail access to teachers and schools around the world. Your school can take part in a variety of e-mail exchanges and classroom collaborations as invitations appear on the list. Or, develop your own and invite others to join. Be certain to thank the organizers at St. Olaf College for their wonderful contributions, bringing many different classrooms together from all over the globe. Set a bookmark!

- **KIDLINK—**(http://www.kidlink.org/)
  The goal of KIDLINK is to create a global dialog among the 10- to 15-year-old youth of the world. It is run by KIDLINK Society, a grass roots and volunteer organization. Here you will find many wonderful forums for your students to communicate with children around the world. Language translation services are available as well as IRC chat sessions. There are locations for student-to-student as well as classroom-to-classroom contact. Both Internet projects and e-mail keypal exchanges are available at this outstanding location.
  Set a bookmark!

- **International WWW Schools Registry—**
  (http://web66.coled.umn.edu/schools.html)
  Visit this site and travel around the world to visit the home pages of schools in Australia, Japan, Canada, the United States, Europe, and many other locations. Contact some of the schools to see if they are interested in an Internet Project with your class.

Intercultural E-mail Classroom Connections (http://www.stolaf.edu/network/iecc/)

Figure 10-3. The home page for **Intercultural E-mail Classroom Connections**, a wonderful location for connecting with classrooms in other parts of the world by participating in mailing lists.

Internet FAQ

I am trying to locate a person and their e-mail address on the Internet. How do I do this?

There are several search engines devoted to locating people on the Internet. You may wish to try **Bigfoot** (http://www.bigfoot.com/) or **WhoWhere?** (http://www.whowhere.com/). Each searches large data bases of people such as phone books and e-mail directories. You may also use a regular search engine by typing in the complete name of the person you are looking for, in case they are listed on a web page somewhere on the Internet. Use the complete name and use a search engine such as **HotBot** that enables you to search for "The Person."

Examples of projects you may wish to consider joining or developing to increase multicultural understanding include:

- **Who Are Our Heroes?**   Invite classes from several different cultural contexts to participate in a heroes project. Each student in participating classes can write a description of their greatest hero, explaining what it is about this person that makes them admirable. Classes then exchange these essays in order to understand who students in different cultural contexts admire. Then, provide an opportunity for students to ask questions of one another about their essays, especially information that may relate to their culture. Use Internet Workshop to share essays and discuss the qualities each hero shares. These essays and conversations provide an ideal opportunity to discover important aspects of different cultures. This project could be extended to include heroes in different categories: parent/guardian heroes, teacher heroes, sports, heroes, politicians, etc.

- **Weekly News from Around the World.**   Invite classes from around the world to contribute two or three news articles each week from their classroom about local events. Have one class collect these articles via e-mail and distribute a weekly world newspaper to each of the participating classes. Writing about local events for students in another cultural context forces students to develop greater sensitivity to the needs of their readers from different cultural contexts. Use Internet Workshop to plan new articles and read those contributed by others. Discussing these events develops a better understanding of the cultural context in different parts of the world.

- **Explanatory Myths from Around the World.**   Every culture contains a set of explanatory myths that explains the creation of natural elements—why the sun comes up each day, where fire came from, how a mountain or lake was created, or where the face in the moon comes from. Invite schools from different cultural contexts to research, write, and share these stories with students from different cultural contexts. Read these stories during Internet Workshop and discuss what each may say about the culture from which it came.

- **KeyPals.**   During the course of the year, help your students develop keypals with several classes around the world. Share these individual messages during Internet Workshop and discuss what each suggests about its cultural context. You may also wish to visit **Intercultural E-mail Classroom Connections** (http://www.stolaf.edu/network/iecc/), **KIDLINK** (http://www.kidlink.org/), or **International WWW Schools Registry** (http://web66.coled.umn.edu/schools.html) to make contact with classes who wish to participate.

Using Internet Inquiry with Internet Workshop

Using Internet Inquiry with Internet Workshop to develop multicultural understanding can be especially powerful. Individual students often have an interest in a particular cultural context, either their own or one with which they have a special connection. Exploring these interests with Internet Inquiry can be an effective approach, since learning focuses on questions that are personally significant. Be certain to invite your students to develop inquiry projects in this area.

When students work in groups, they often share new insights, interpretations, and resources. This leads to important new directions as students pursue related questions.

There are several ideas to keep in mind as you pursue Internet Inquiry for multicultural understanding. First, where appropriate, encourage your students to work on group inquiry projects. When students work in groups, they often share new insights, interpretations, and resources. This leads to important new directions as students pursue related questions. With support, these groups may also be able to conduct their own regular Internet Workshop sessions focusing on the topic of their inquiry projects. If you can accomplish this, you and your students will have established an important vehicle for learning about multicultural understanding.

TEACHING TIP

Ideas for Internet Inquiry

Encourage your students to develop KeyPals with other students from the cultural context they are exploring. This will be an important source of information for your students. Discussing common issues that matter with someone from another cultural context is the best way to understand that context. Encourage your students to share these exchanges with their group and the rest of the class.

Second, be certain to have students share their multicultural learning within the structure of Internet Workshop on a regular basis. When many students share their new insights and their questions about a variety of cultural contexts, everyone gains new insights about the diversity that exists in this world. Moreover, discussing these matters openly helps to remove stereotypes and sends your students a powerful message about the respect we should accord each culture.

Increasing Multicultural Understanding
Resources on the Internet

Africa Online: Kids Only—
(http://www.africaonline.com/AfricaOnline/coverkids.html)
A nice location for your students to learn about Africa. They can read Rainbow Magazine—a Kenyan magazine for kids, play African games and decode messages, learn about the over 1,000 languages in Africa, meet African students on line, find a keypal, or visit the home pages of schools in Africa. Set a bookmark!

China the Beautiful—(http://www.chinapage.com/china.html)
Here is a location with all things beautiful and China. Visit the China Room and learn about calligraphy, listen to spoken Chinese, view many beautiful paintings, read a timeline of emperors, read classic poetry, participate in a discussion board about China, and travel to museums around the world with Chinese exhibits. This location also has special software for viewing the Internet in Chinese.

Cranes for Peace—(http://www.he.net/~sparker/cranes.html)
Cranes for Peace began as a project to collect paper cranes to be sent to Hiroshima for the 50th anniversary of the bombing as a wish for peace. It was based on the book *Sadako and the 1,000 Cranes*. A Japanese legend holds that folding 1,000 cranes (senbazuru) so pleases the gods that the folder is granted a wish. At the present time, this is a location to celebrate peace each year by making origami cranes and sending them to be placed at the memorial to Sadako in Seattle or to the peace shrine in Hiroshima. Visit this location to find out more about this wonderful book and the many Internet projects it has sparked for peace. Set a bookmark!

Harriet Tubman: An Unforgettable Black Leader—
(http://www.acusd.edu/~jdesmet/tubman.html)
Here is a wonderful location with great biographical information on the achievements of this remarkable woman and the Underground Railroad. All students should be familiar with her accomplishments and the important life she led. Set a bookmark!

Jewish Culture and History—(http://www.igc.apc.org/ddickerson/judaica.html)
One of the more extensive sites on the Internet on Jewish culture. It has many links to other locations, including links to Virtual Jerusalem and the Tour of Israel. More appropriate for older students.

KIDPROJ'S Multi-Cultural Calendar—
(http://www.kidlink.org/KIDPROJ/MCC/)
Here is another wonderful resource for your classroom developed by KIDLINK, a non-profit organization. This location contains a great data base of celebrations taking place each day around the world along with ideas for connecting the calendar to your curriculum. Set a bookmark and let the good folks at KIDLINK know how much you appreciate their efforts.

Multicultural Book Review Homepage—
(http://www.isomedia.com/homes/jmele/homepage.html)
Are you looking for great literature selections to use in your classroom for multicultural issues? Here it is. This location contains reviews of multicultural literature for kids. Have your students use it to find great books and have them post reviews of fine new books they have read. Set a bookmark!

Native American Indian Resources—
(http://indy4.fdl.cc.mn.us/~isk/mainmenu.html)
One of the richest locations on the Internet for the Native American community. Information about Native history, literature, biographies, herbal knowledge, environmental concerns, schools, politics, you name it. The talented webmaster for this site recently passed away, so it is not clear yet if this resource will continue its important work. We hope someone will step forward to continue her mission. Set a bookmark!

Native Web—(http://www.nativeweb.org/)
This is a great location for resources on Native cultures. It contains many useful links to a variety of Native American resources, including information about tribal units, literature, newsletters, and journals.

Listservs/Mailing Lists for Increasing Multicultural Understanding

CULTUR-L—(listserv@vm.temple.edu)
A discussion group on cultural differences in the curriculum.

MULTC-ED—(listserv@umdd.umd.edu)
A discussion group on multicultural education, K–12.

NAT-EDU—(listserv@indycms.iupui.edu)
A discussion group on K–12 education and Indigenous Peoples.

MCPavilion—(majordomo@virginia.edu)
This is the WWW location for an active discussion group at the Multicultural Pavilion web site. Directions for subscribing are located at: http://curry.edschool.Virginia.EDU/go/multicultural/issues.html

11 Including All Students on the Internet

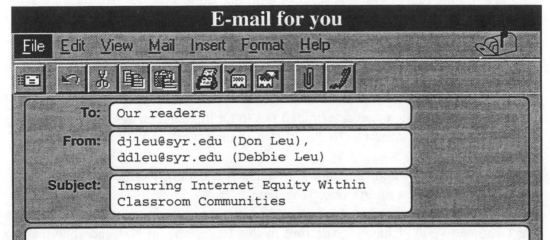

E-mail for you

File Edit View Mail Insert Format Help

To: Our readers

From: djleu@syr.edu (Don Leu),
ddleu@syr.edu (Debbie Leu)

Subject: Insuring Internet Equity Within
Classroom Communities

Internet equity has become an important issue within the educational community. It is important to provide more equitable access and ensure that we do not leave any members of our society behind. Most of this discussion, though, has focused on how to ensure equal Internet access between schools and school districts. This is one important aspect of Internet equity. Another is to do everything we can to ensure equal Internet access *within* individual classroom communities. This aspect of equity has gone largely unnoticed.

Sometimes, for example, a few students in a classroom become so excited about electronic learning they tend to dominate the use of limited electronic resources, inadvertently excluding others in the process. At other times, students who fall behind in navigational skills at the beginning sometimes fail to take full advantage of their computer time because they are uncertain about how to accomplish tasks and are too embarrassed to ask for assistance. At other times, challenged students do not always participate in Internet experiences for any of a number of reasons. This chapter recognizes each of these issues as it seeks ways to ensure equitable Internet access for each child in your class.

Don and Debbie

Document: Done

Teaching with the Internet: Jessica Hammermill's Class

Jessica Hammermill noticed the group of her students who were excited about what they had just discovered on the Internet. "Cool!" someone said again. Each time someone said "Cool!" a few more students were attracted to the computer to see what was taking place. She was pleased with the enthusiasm her students experienced about learning as they used the Internet. She was also concerned.

"Maya, isn't it your turn at the computer?" Jessica asked one of the quieter members of her class. She had noticed that Maya was reluctant to claim her computer time when others, because of their excitement, did not leave the computer according to the classroom schedule. Maya was so shy she missed her computer time several times last week. Jessica was determined not to let this happen again. She encouraged the group at the computer to quickly finish their work and allow Maya her full turn on the Internet.

"Can I help Tora when I am done?" asked Maya. Tora was a student with limited vision. Tora and Maya often worked together.

"That would be great," said Jessica. "And could you change the font size to 48 like I showed you?" Changing the font to this larger size in Netscape Navigator enabled Tora to read the information on the screen. "And then maybe ask Orlando to translate the Spanish message you two received from the class in Argentina. Have him translate your answer, and type it up, too. I would like to e-mail your message after school today."

A little later, she noticed Maya and Tora working on the Internet Activity she had developed for her class this week using the location for **Monster Math**—(http://www.lifelong.com/lifelong_universe/AcademicWorld/MonsterMath/default.html). She could tell they were using the speech-to-text plug-in because she could hear each of the story problems being read aloud for them. This helped them to understand the problem better. Tora found it especially useful as she followed along with both the text and the speech.

A little later, Jessica saw Orlando concluding the translation of Maya and Tora's e-mail message to students in Argentina. The three of them were talking back and forth as Orlando was trying to complete the translation. This activity was especially nice since it accomplished several things at once. Of course, Maya and Tora were assisted in getting their message out. In addition, however, it gave Orlando a sense of pride in his ability to speak and write in Spanish. Last year, this was seen as a handicap. After the Internet entered his classroom with opportunities to correspond in Spanish, Orlando's linguistic ability was seen in a very different light. Being fluent in Spanish was now an asset that was much in demand, especially after Jessica established connections with several Spanish-speaking classrooms around the world. Finally, working on a translation with Maya and Tora helped Orlando develop a better understanding of English at the same time it helped Maya and Tora develop a better understanding of Spanish. Listening to their conversation as they

Figure 11-1. Some locations on the Internet provide audio in both Spanish and English. This is the home page for **Monster Math.**

Monster Math (http://www.lifelong.com/lifelong_universe/AcademicWorld/MonsterMath/default.html)

worked on the translation made Jessica aware that each student was learning much about each other's language. It was a wonderful experience to observe.

A little later, Jessica noticed Orlando working on the Internet Activity with Monster Math. She noticed how he would listen to the problems in English first and then shift to the Spanish plug-in and listen to the same problem in Spanish before he sat down to solve it. Having a site with text-to-speech plug-ins in both languages was especially helpful to bilingual students like Orlando. She was hoping more sites like this would appear shortly on the Internet.

Lessons from the Classroom

The sensitive orchestration of classroom environments by an insightful classroom teacher can ensure successful Internet access for all students.

This episode from Jessica's classroom illustrates an important lesson for all of us to consider: the sensitive orchestration of classroom environments by an insightful classroom teacher can ensure successful Internet access for all students. Just having a computer connected to the Internet does not guarantee equity of access for each of your students. You must work actively to ensure equity in your classroom.

One element of this active orchestration is being sensitive to times when students' enthusiasm for their work on the Internet impedes others' access to this important resource. Having a regular schedule for Internet use, as suggested in Chapter 4, provides a certain level of equity in your classroom. In addition, however, you will have to carefully monitor student use as Jessica did, watching for those moments when students become so enthusiastic they lose track of time and prevent access by others.

Another important element in the active orchestration of equity is to be certain you are aware of ways to accommodate the unique learning needs of each child in your classroom. Adjusting the font size for Tora enabled her to access the world of text information available on the Internet. Previously, she had been limited to large-print books and the use of a special magnifier. The Internet permitted Tora to access an enormous amount of information, simply by enlarging the size of the browser font on Netscape Navigator or Internet Explorer. Text-to-speech technology also assisted her and other children who might benefit from this feature.

Instead of viewing a non-English first language as a disadvantage, linguistic diversity suddenly becomes a valuable asset when you think about ways in which to utilize this talent as you communicate with classes around the world.

Finally, orchestrating equity in your classroom will mean thinking differently about linguistic diversity. Instead of viewing a non-English first language as a disadvantage, linguistic diversity suddenly becomes a valuable asset when you think about ways in which to utilize this talent as you communicate with classes around the world. Orlando's ability in Spanish became a special talent that was valued by all members of his class when Jessica saw the potentials it provided for Internet communication. These opportunities gave Orlando a tremendous sense of self-worth as he became a central member of the classroom community. Moreover, Orlando acquired English much more rapidly as he translated messages and served as a conduit for communication with Spanish-speaking communities. While this was taking place, students in his class were also learning many new words in Spanish. Everyone gains when non-native speakers are included in classroom communities by teachers who know how to orchestrate equity.

Orchestrating Equity in your Classroom

Chapter 4 described several strategies for orchestrating equity within Internet classrooms. Posting a schedule for all students to follow, rotating assigned computer times to avoid regular schedule conflicts, and rotating partners at the computer are all useful strategies. In addition, however, there are several important issues for you

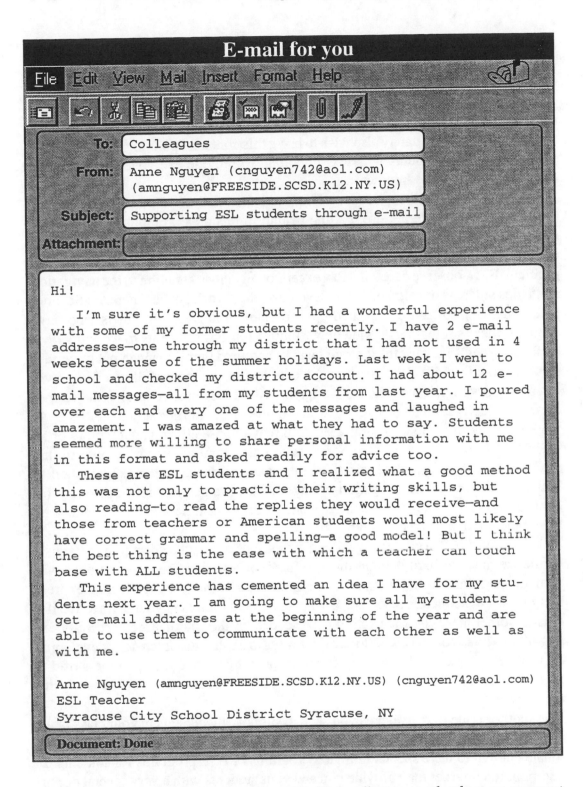

to consider. These will require you to make subtle adjustments that happen moment to moment in your classroom as you seek to individualize learning experiences for each of your students.

Jessica experienced one of these issues when she noticed a group of children at the computer excited about what they had discovered for the unit on diversity the

Be certain to use discussions during Internet Workshop to both evaluate and teach navigation strategies.

class was studying. As enthusiastic as they were, Maya was losing important time on the computer because this group had forgotten their obligation to turn the computer over to the next person on the schedule. This is a common event in most classrooms and requires you to periodically monitor the computer schedule you establish for your class, reminding students when it is time to turn the computer over to the next person. You may also wish to bring this concern up during Internet Workshop and remind students why it is important to provide everyone with an equal amount of time on the Internet.

Another issue occurs when individual students fail to develop efficient navigation strategies for Internet use. Falling behind in this area prohibits students from acquiring as much useful information as other students who have become proficient at navigating the Internet. There are several techniques to help you to minimize this problem. First, observe carefully. Pay exceptionally close attention to the navigation strategies students develop or fail to develop as they work on the computer. Second, pair students who have not picked up important strategies with others who have acquired these strategies. Provide opportunities for these students to work together on the Internet. Many useful strategies can be acquired in this manner, but be certain to also provide individual time for students to practice new skills on their own; often, when you pair a proficient navigator with a less proficient one, the former dominates navigational decisions. Third, provide short tutorial sessions for students who are weak in navigation strategies. You may choose either a small group or an individual format. In either case, focus on a central strategy you have noticed that students lack. Finally, be certain to use discussions during Internet Workshop to both evaluate and teach navigation strategies. This is a perfect time to listen to students describe how they use the Internet and, at the same time, support students who have failed to acquire these skills.

It may also be the case that gender differences exist with respect to Internet use. While we have no hard data on this phenomenon, we have noticed that boys will sometimes dominate Internet use in a classroom and that some girls may express less interest in using this resource. You should watch for this in your class to see if it exists. Sometimes, communication experiences on the Internet are especially engaging for girls. You may wish to consider ways to exploit this interest by developing an Internet Project with communication opportunities between members of different classes. This may equalize any gender differences you see in your classroom.

Just as Jessica did, you may seek out opportunities where non-native English speakers can use their skills with their native language to support classroom learning.

Another issue to consider as you seek to support all students in your class is the unique potential of the Internet for supporting ESL students. Some districts are fortunate enough to have special bilingual programs or ESL programs for students. In addition, the Internet may provide you and your students with a very special opportunity. Just as Jessica did, you may seek out opportunities where non-native English speakers can use their skills with their native language to support classroom learning. This reverses traditional attitudes about one's non-English linguistic background from a disadvantage into an asset. Many good things will result from this change in perspective.

A final issue to consider is how to support challenged students in your class who have been formally identified with special learning requirements. In some cases, technology may be able to adapt to these students' needs as was the situation with Tora in Jessica's class. In all cases, there are resources on the Internet to provide useful information about accommodations you can make in your classroom to help each student reach his/her full potential.

Opportunities for ESL Students

The Internet provides several special opportunities for ESL students in your class. You have already seen the one adapted by Ms. Hammermill. Developing an Internet Project with schools that use the same language as an ESL student in your room is a wonderful method for supporting linguistic development. Having an ESL student assist with translations places that student in a valued role within the classroom's activities. If you have your student work with others on the translations, both native and non-native speakers will develop a better understanding of one another's language. To find a school with students who speak the language of ESL students in your class, you may wish to pay a visit to **Web66** (http://web66.coled.umn.edu/) and explore their **International School Web Site Registry** (http://web66.coled.umn.edu/schools.html). Locate several possible schools and drop them an e-mail message with a list of projects you would be interested in completing together.

If you have an ESL student whose English ability is insufficient for this role, you may wish to try another approach. Pair the student with a native speaker in your class. Give them a regular Internet Activity assignment related to the country or culture from which the ESL student comes. To help you find Internet resources about this country or culture visit **Excite Travel** (http://www.city.net/), the location that has replaced Virtual Tourist II. Follow the links to the country you wish to visit. Especially useful will be the country's major newspapers. These contain many interesting news items in the first language of your student.

Or, you may wish to have your students listen to a radio station in the country or culture from which the ESL student comes. This can be done by visiting the **Live Stations** (http://www.timecast.com/stations/index.html) location at RealAudio and searching for radio stations by the student's language or geographical region. Many students will find it exciting to listen to radio stations around the world with the Internet, especially if they have a partner with whom to exchange the information.

Internet Activity about the ESL student's country will engage both students in conversation about something familiar to the ESL student. This will motivate both students and make conversation easier for the ESL student. Be certain to include a writing activity as part of the Internet Activity to foster collaborative second language learning between the two students.

You may wish to direct the two students to develop their own Internet Activity. For the first week, for example, you may ask the two students to visit the sites in the student's country of origin and create a list of Internet Activity assignments they

To find a school with students who speak the language of ESL students in your class, you may wish to pay a visit to Web66 and explore their International Registry of K12 Schools on the Web.

Many students will find it exciting to listen to radio stations around the world with the Internet, especially if they have a partner with whom to exchange the information.

Figure 11-2.
Using the
**International
WWW
School
Registry** in
Web66 to
locate schools
around the

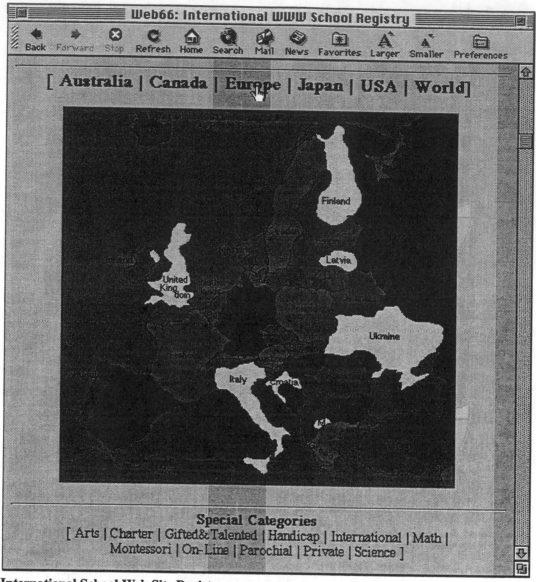

International School Web Site Registry
(http://web66.coled.umn.edu/schools/Maps/Europe.html)

want to complete. Then use this list to guide work during subsequent weeks. You might rotate partners every few weeks to allow the ESL student to meet and work with other members of your class. If you conduct Internet Workshop each week, you may wish to have the two students report the results of their assignment to the class. This provides a nice opportunity to support oral as well as written language development.

Other resources you may find useful on the WWW for supporting ESL students in your class include:

- **Dave's ESL Cafe**—(http://www.eslcafe.com)
  This is a useful site for both teachers and students containing an idiom

Dave's ESL Café (http://www.eslcafe.com)

Figure 11-3. Dave's ESL Café, a great location to support the English needs of ESL students in your classroom.

page, a quote page, a self-checking ESL Quiz Center, an ESL Help Center, a graffiti wall, student and teacher links, and an e-mail exchange. Set a bookmark!

- **Useful Resources, Lesson Plans, and Teaching Materials—**
  (http://www.ling.lancs.ac.uk/staff/visitors/kenji/teacher.htm)
  A central site with an extensive collection of ESL resources for teachers, including links to many web sites, listservs, journals, lesson plans, some bilingual education sources, and a few sites for students, too. Set a bookmark!

Netscape and Internet Explorer offer an opportunity to enlarge the print size appearing on the computer screen to nearly any size one wishes.

- **OPPtical Illusion...THEME-BASED PAGES—**
  (http://darkwing.uoregon.edu/~leslieob/themes.html)
  A series of links for instructional units and ideas for ESL students. Also
  a number of cross-cultural sources.

Opportunities for Children Who are Visually or Hearing Challenged

The Internet also provides special opportunities for children who are visually or hearing challenged. For children who are visually challenged, a common problem is often a dependency on large print texts, texts which do not always coincide with the materials used in the classroom. Alternatively, large and bulky readers are sometimes used. Both are less than ideal solutions for many students.

Netscape and Internet Explorer offer an opportunity to enlarge the print size appearing on the computer screen to nearly any size one wishes. This allows children who are visually challenged to access a wide range of information that might otherwise be inaccessible to them. To do this in Netscape 4.0, select the "Edit" item from your menu bar and then select "Preferences." Within "Preferences," select the category for "Fonts." You will see a window similar to Figure 11-4. Select the size you wish to use for both proportional and fixed fonts. You may select any size you wish. Note that one choice is "Other." This allows you to type in sizes larger than 24. In Internet Explorer, you may change font size by simply clicking on the "Larger" or "Smaller" button on the right side of the toolbar. You can see these buttons at the top of the image in Figure 11-3.

Figure 11-4. The preferences folder in Netscape 4.0, showing how to change the size of the font used to display text information on the WWW.

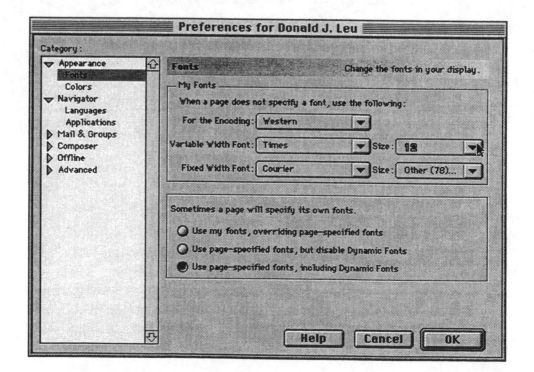

Enlarging the font size for children who are visually challenged works especially well on web pages that use a lot of text. It works less well at those sites with graphics, since graphics are not enlarged with this approach. In these situations you may wish to add software to your computer that enlarges the entire screen, not just text. You may download this software at **Visual Disability Solutions** (http://www2.apple.com/disability/visual.html) for Macintosh computers and **IBM Special Needs Home Page** (http://www.austin.ibm.com/sns/index.html) for Windows-based computers.

You may also wish to visit these central sites for visually challenged students to locate additional resources:

Blindness Resource Center (http://www.nyise.org/blind.htm)—The best central site for visually challenged and blind individuals. Set a bookmark!

TST Audio on Demand (http://www.tstradio.com/)—A location containing news, information, and entertainment all through real audio technologies. This allows visually challenged children to listen as newspaper articles, books, and information resources are read to them. A site rich in audio resources!

There are also locations on the web to support hearing-challenged students. One very useful location is **Deaf CyberKids** (http://dww.deafworldweb.org/dww/kids/), a part of the **Deaf World Web** (http://dww.deafworldweb.org/dww/). This site supports e-mail communication for children who are deaf.

Several other locations may be useful for all students in your classroom. **The Animated American Sign Language Dictionary** (http://www.feist.com/~randys/index_nf.html) provides animations for many signs. **A Basic Dictionary of ASL Terms** (http://home.earthlink.net/~masterstek/ASLDict.html) provides an extensive signing dictionary. You may wish to make these sites a regular part of Internet Activity and begin to develop the ability to sign with your hearing students. Sharing new signs during Internet Workshop helps everyone become more skilled in communicating with hearing-challenged children.

Opportunities for Other Students who are Challenged

Accommodating Internet experiences for other students in your class who have been formally identified as requiring special assistance does not differ substantially from the types of accommodations you make in other areas of your curriculum. Two ideas, though, may be useful as you seek to provide opportunities for each of your children to learn and grow.

First, our informal observations suggest the Internet may provide special motivational opportunities for those children who have been less successful in previous academic tasks. We have seen this happen enough times in school classrooms to believe something important is happening. We do not know the reason for this phenomenon. It may be that multimedia resources provide multiple sources of information

One very useful location is Deaf CyberKids, a part of the Deaf World Web. This site supports e-mail communication for children who are hearing impaired.

Our informal observations suggest the Internet may provide special motivational opportunities for those children who have been less successful in previous academic tasks.

Figure 11-5.
A great location for all students, The Animated American Sign Language Dictionary.

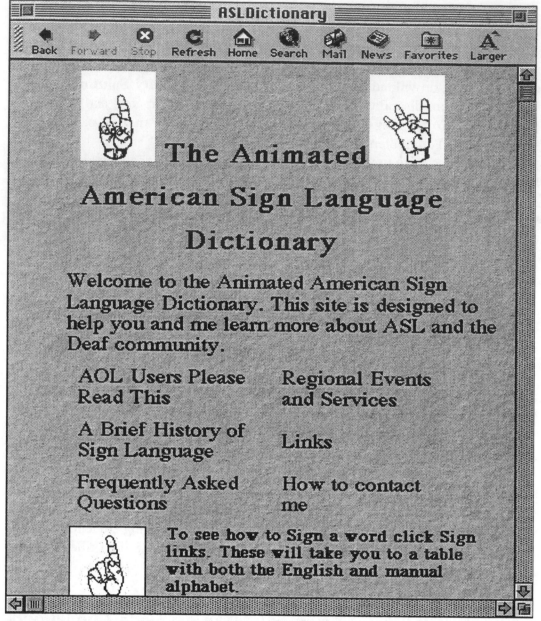

The Animated American Sign Language Dictionary (http://www.feist.com/~randys/index_nf.html)

(graphics, animations, audio, video, etc.) so that students are not just dependent on a single, textual, source for information that has always given them difficulty. It may be that the interactive nature of this environment and the new types of strategic knowledge that are necessary advantage certain types of children over others, children who have not been previously advantaged in non-electronic environments. Or, it may be that the Internet kindles a new spark of interest among students who have lost interest in learning. In any case, it happens often enough that we should think about taking advantage of the phenomenon.

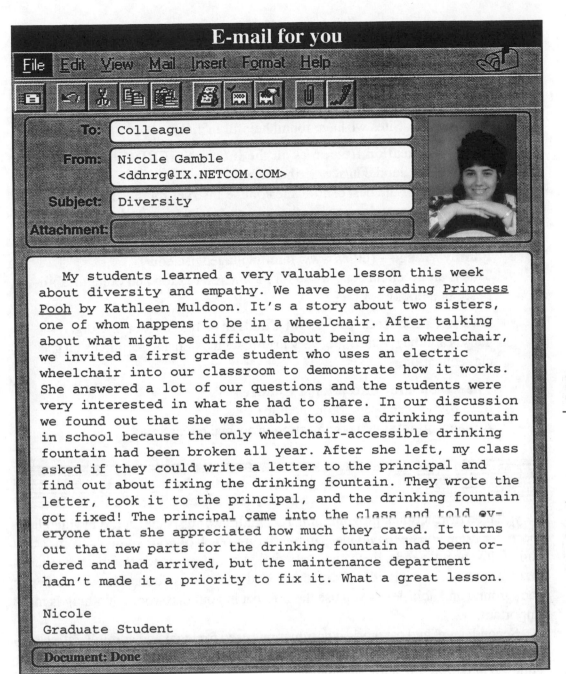

E-mail for you

File   Edit   View   Mail   Insert   Format   Help

To: Colleague

From: Nicole Gamble
<ddnrg@IX.NETCOM.COM>

Subject: Diversity

Attachment:

My students learned a very valuable lesson this week about diversity and empathy. We have been reading <u>Princess Pooh</u> by Kathleen Muldoon. It's a story about two sisters, one of whom happens to be in a wheelchair. After talking about what might be difficult about being in a wheelchair, we invited a first grade student who uses an electric wheelchair into our classroom to demonstrate how it works. She answered a lot of our questions and the students were very interested in what she had to share. In our discussion we found out that she was unable to use a drinking fountain in school because the only wheelchair-accessible drinking fountain had been broken all year. After she left, my class asked if they could write a letter to the principal and find out about fixing the drinking fountain. They wrote the letter, took it to the principal, and the drinking fountain got fixed! The principal came into the class and told everyone that she appreciated how much they cared. It turns out that new parts for the drinking fountain had been ordered and had arrived, but the maintenance department hadn't made it a priority to fix it. What a great lesson.

Nicole
Graduate Student

Document: Done

Share new information about navigation strategies with students who have been less successful in school learning tasks before you share it with others. Then, have these students teach others the new information.

One way to do this is to share new information about navigation strategies with students who have been less successful in school learning tasks before you share it with others. Then, have these students teach others the new information. This quickly puts students who have been less successful into a privileged position, a position these students seldom experience in classroom learning tasks. The effects of this strategy can sometimes be quite dramatic as less successful students suddenly feel empowered and become more interested in learning. We encourage you to try this strategy.

A second idea is also useful. Spend time exploring sites on the WWW that can provide you with more information about your students who have been formally identified as requiring special assistance. There are many useful ideas for instruction and many other informative resources on the web. Exploring these sites will provide you with important assistance as you seek to include all students in your classroom activities. Sites we have found helpful include:

- **Special Education Resources on the Internet (SERI)—** (http://www.hood.edu/seri/serihome.htm)
  This is one of the best central sites on the Internet for special education resources. It contains a comprehensive and well-organized set of links to locations important for special education issues.

- **Family Village**—(http://www.familyvillage.wisc.edu/)
  This is an excellent central site for mental retardation and other disabilities. Set a bookmark!

- **Internet Resources for Special Children**—(http://www.irsc.org/)
  This is another central site, very useful, with extensive resources on special education.

- **The Council for Exceptional Children—** (http://www.cec.sped.org/home.htm)
  A major professional organization in special education.

A Few Final Thoughts

Each and every child has unique needs that must be recognized as you make instructional decisions.

As you plan instructional programming for children with special needs in your classroom, we hope you keep two ideas in mind. First, each of your students is, in fact, a child with special needs. Each and every child has unique needs that must be recognized as you make instructional decisions. You must always consider each student's background and abilities as you use the Internet in your classroom. Nothing is more important.

Second, legal and categorical designations used for legal and administrative purposes must never limit your instructional decisions regarding individual children or your expectations for their achievement. The use of labels has brought important benefits to students whose needs have too long been ignored, but we must ensure that those labels do not prevent us from recognizing the individuality each of us expresses in our daily lives.

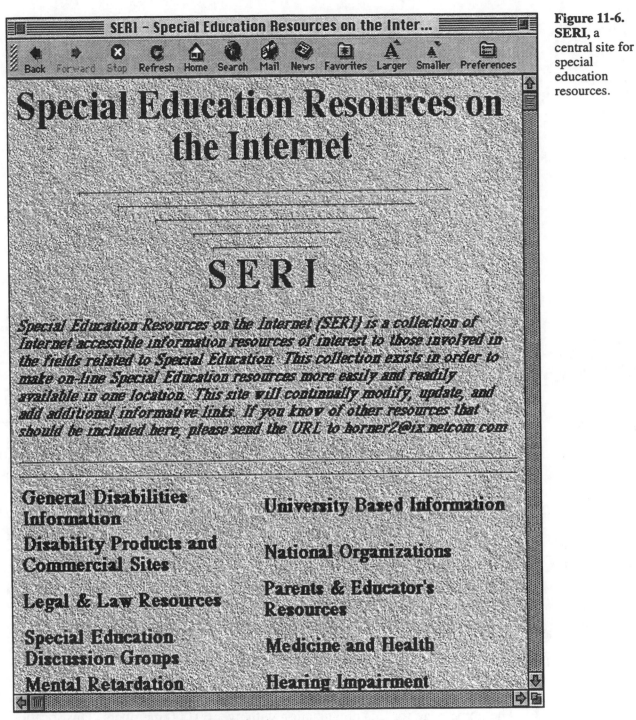

Figure 11-6. SERI, a central site for special education resources.

SERI (http://www.hood.edu/seri/serihome.htm)

Resources for Including All Students on the Internet

Apple's The Disability Connection—
(http://www2.apple.com/disability/disability_home.html)
Here is the location for getting in touch with all kinds of information about adaptive technologies provided by Apple Computer and other companies. This location also includes many free or shareware programs to use with your computer, links to disability-related resources on the WWW, and opportunities to communicate with others about disabilities and teaching/learning issues. Set a bookmark!

Autism Resources—(http://web.syr.edu/~jmwobus/autism/)
A site with many links to resources related to Autism and Asperger's Syndrome, including links to on-line discussions, mailing lists, news, treatment methods, research, and much more.

Blindness Resource Center—(http://www.nyise.org/blind.htm)
A great location with extensive information about blindness and resources to inform teachers and assist students.

Deafweb Washington's Kid Page—
(http://www.wolfenet.com/~hydronut/kids.htm)
A location for deaf and hearing-impaired children to post their stories, poetry, articles, and art.

IBM Special Needs Home Page—(http://www.austin.ibm.com/sns/index.html)
Here is the central site for all your adaptive technology needs if you use IBM or Windows-based computers in your classroom. Set a bookmark.

Inclusion Resources—
(http://www.hood.edu/seri/serihome.htm#inclusion_resources)
A nice collection of links related to inclusive education. The information at this location can provide useful background information to teachers new to inclusion.

Learning Disabilities Association of America—
(http://205.164.116.200/LDA/index.html)
The home page for this organization with over 60,000 members. This location provides links and resources for individuals interested in learning more about learning disabilities.

Learning Disabilities—
(http://www.kidsource.com/kidsource/content/learningdis.html)
This website contains a booklet from the National Institutes of Mental Health. It explains learning disabilities to parents.

International Dyslexia Association—(http://interdys.org/)
The International Dyslexia Association (IDA) is an international, non-profit, scientific and educational organization dedicated to the study and treatment of dyslexia. This location provides access to its many resources related to this important learning disability.

Scotter's Low Vision Land—
(http://www.community.net/~byndsght/welcome.html)
A site developed by a person with low vision with many links useful to the visually impaired. Wonderfully designed.

The Family Village Inclusion Resources—
(http://www.familyvillage.wisc.edu/education/inclusion.html)
Another nice location to provide resources for teachers interested in inclusive education. Contains links to locations to communicate with others, research, on-line newsletters, and web sites related to inclusion.

Listservs/Mailing Lists for Including All Students on the Internet

DEAFKIDS—(listserv@sjuvm.stjohns.edu)
A discussion group for children who are deaf.

CHATBACK—(listserv@sjuvm.stjohns.edu)
A discussion group on special education.

SPECED-L—(speced-l@uga.cc.uga.edu)
A special education discussion list.

SPEDTECH-L—(listproc@ukanaix.cc.ukans.edu)
A discussion group on technology and special education

TESLK-12—(listserv@cunyvm.cuny.edu)
A discussion group on Teaching English as a Second Language in grades K–12

12 Developing a Home Page for Your Classroom

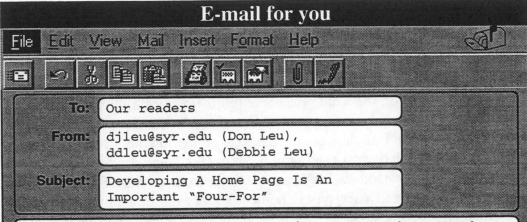

E-mail for you

File Edit View Mail Insert Format Help

To: Our readers

From: djleu@syr.edu (Don Leu),
ddleu@syr.edu (Debbie Leu)

Subject: Developing A Home Page Is An
Important "Four-For"

We are nearing the end of our journey together. You have accomplished much in a short period of time. There is one final topic we wanted to share with you: developing a classroom home page on the WWW. This isn't that hard to do. Really!

Learning to develop a home page is what we call a "four-for," something that gives you <u>four</u> important results <u>for</u> <u>one</u> activity. In a life where time is always a precious commodity, any "four-for" should be treasured. What are the important results a home page can deliver?

First, developing a home page helps your students. It provides a location for publishing student work and it allows you to organize safe links to Internet locations so students can easily access the information you want them to use. Second, developing a home page also helps others. As you develop instructional materials and links to information resources, you will find other classrooms visiting your page, benefiting from your instructional ideas. Third, developing a home page enables you to forge a tighter link between home and school. As more computers enter the home, parents can use your home page to see what is taking place in your classroom and communicate with you about their children. Finally, developing a home page helps the teaching profession. As you develop a home page for your class, it projects an important image of professionalism to the public—teachers embracing new technologies and using these in powerful ways to guide students' learning. We hope you take the time to develop a home page for your class. It will be useful for your students, other students, parents, and our profession.

Don and Debbie

Document: Done

Teaching with the Internet: Barbara Caudell's Class

It was 8:35 A.M. in Room 102.

"And I wanted to tell you that I have added a new link on our classroom home page called Virtual Tours. You may wish to visit **Virtual Tours** (http://www.dreamscape.com/frankvad/tours.html) when you are working on Internet Inquiry. There are hundreds of tours of museums, cities, and government locations related to your work." Ms. Barbara Caudell was in the middle of the morning announcements to her class before the morning got underway.

"I also wanted to remind you that since this is Friday, you should be certain to write a short message to your parents or guardians about your work this week. Do this with e-mail or on the word processor. Tell them something special you have done this week. If they have an e-mail address, send it with my e-mail account and remind them to visit our classroom home page on the Internet. You can also type your message on Clarisworks and print it out to take home. I would like to check these before you leave today." Barbara made this assignment each Friday. She found these little notes forged a new type of home-school connection, initiating important conversations at home about what was taking place at school. This helped her students.

"We have received three new messages from other schools that visited our home page yesterday. One was very impressed with our wildlife poems we did at the beginning of the year. Also, a student in Germany wanted to know if we could provide her with more information about the Battle of Lexington and Paul Revere's ride. Could you respond to this message, Katherine? You might want to send her a copy of your report. Please use my e-mail account. There was also a message from a teacher in Prince Rupert, Canada telling us how much he liked our home page. I posted a copy of each message on our 'E-mail Around the World' board next to the computer. Read these new messages about the great work you are all doing in this class."

At the beginning of the year, Barbara had taken a workshop on developing a classroom home page on the Internet. She worked her way through **Writing HTML: A Tutorial for Creating WWW Pages** (http://www.mcli.dist.maricopa.edu/tut/index.html). HTML is the programming language used on the WWW. She also learned how to use Netscape Composer, an HTML editor, to quickly make her home page. This made developing pages for the WWW as easy as typing with a word processor. She wondered why no one had told her before how easy this was to do. Somehow, she had thought that developing a WWW page required many years of experience and a lot of technical training. It only took her two hours in the workshop and then a few more hours at home trying out ideas with Netscape Composer. As she told her colleagues, "If I can do this, anyone can." She had concluded that all someone really needed was a few hours to play around with an HTML editor like Composer and an account on the school's server. The workshop and the tutorial were nice, but not necessary.

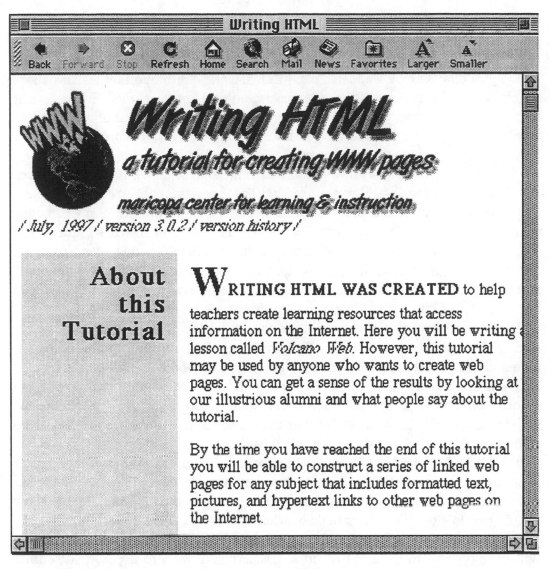

Writing HTML (http://www.mcli.dist.maricopa.edu/tut/index.html)

Figure 12-1.
The home
page of **Writ-
ing HTML,**
one of the
better tutorials
for learning
about HTML
and creating
classroom
home pages.

Barbara had scanned in the school picture of her class and set up several sections on the classroom home page. One contained the wildlife poems they did earlier, another contained a set of links she used for Internet Activity, another displayed the research they had done on the Battle of Lexington during the Revolutionary War, and another contained photos and a description of the field trip they recently took to Bunker Hill. She also put her e-mail address on the home page so parents could get in touch with her or send messages to their children when they wanted to surprise them at school. Clicking on this address immediately opened an e-mail message window.

Lessons from the Classroom

Developing a home page is not all that complex if you already are familiar with basic word processing.

This episode in Barbara Caudell's class illustrates several important lessons about developing and using a classroom home page on the Internet. First, it shows that developing a home page is not all that complex if you already are familiar with basic word processing. The new HTML editors appearing with Internet browsers make it easy to create a classroom home page.

This episode also shows how a home page helps to organize Internet resources for classroom instruction. Barbara used her home page to organize each thematic unit. She simply created a page for each thematic unit during the year and added useful links for each Internet Activity, Internet Project, and Internet Inquiry. The nice thing about this was that she could reuse the units the following year. Setting up organized sets of links in this fashion also assisted her in her Internet safety program. She always previewed the sites she included to be certain they would not lead her students off into areas of the web they should not be exploring.

Third, the episode shows how a home page may be used to publish the work that students complete in a classroom. Barbara always had a writing project for each thematic unit. These projects went through each phase of the writing process. In the final phase, students published their work on the classroom home page so that everyone in the class could read it and so that others around the world might see the wonderful writing her students did. The most avid readers of the web site, Barbara discovered, were the students themselves and their parents. Several times at the local library, she found a student showing work to parents on the Internet computer located there. She also knew that some parents viewed this work from home because several parents had left her messages. And a few told her they liked to show off their child's work to others in their office.

Notice also how a home page for your class assists other classrooms. Often, you will develop a thematic unit that other teachers may wish to use. Or, sometimes another teacher will send you an e-mail message, asking questions about your unit. One of the more powerful aspects of the Internet in school classrooms is that it allows teachers to develop curriculum that is immediately available to others throughout the world. This potential will be exploited with increasing regularity in the future.

One of the more powerful aspects of the Internet in school classrooms is that it allows teachers to develop curriculum that is immediately available to others throughout the world.

Home-school relationships are also strengthened when you develop a classroom home page. While not all families have immediate access to the Internet, this is rapidly changing as increasing numbers of families are coming on-line or using Internet connections at your school or local library. Having a home page allows your parents to view their children's work and all the fine things you are doing in the classroom. It also provides an opportunity for parents and guardians to drop you an e-mail message when they have a question. The Internet provides many new opportunities to work with the families of children in your class.

Finally, a home page for your classroom accomplishes another important goal— it projects an important image of teachers as professionals. Parents who see your classroom home page become more aware of the many wonderful things you do to

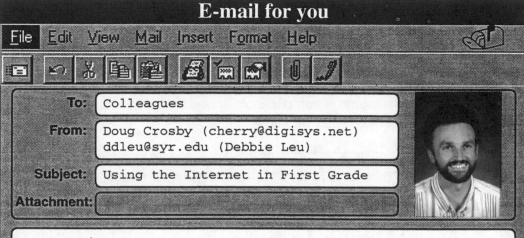

E-mail for you

File Edit View Mail Insert Format Help

To: Colleagues

From: Doug Crosby (cherry@digisys.net)
ddleu@syr.edu (Debbie Leu)

Subject: Using the Internet in First Grade

Attachment:

Greetings!

Spring had finally arrived in Montana after a particularly long and cold winter. It was time to take our first grade field trip; this year we were off to a local biological station.

All year we had been publishing class books using a variety of media, but we wanted to make our field trip report something special. Our school had recently posted a home page on the Internet so we decided to publish our field trip report for all the world to see.

It was kind of a gray day with showers threatening but we had already postponed the trip once so off we went with our digital camera in hand. It turned out to be a wonderful day with a great variety of learning activities taking place. We snapped away with our camera; there were the aquatic insects, the stream, the microscopes, and of course the big log where we all sat to eat lunch!

After returning to school we all sat around the computer to view the photos and within a short time we had come up with a whole class report which was typed directly on the screen. It looked great once we posted it on our web page. We have had a lot of fun reading e-mail from people around the world who have come across our report (http://www.digisys.net/cherry/Mr.Crosbyfield_trip.htm) and just dropped a note to say well done.

This has been a wonderful experience for my first graders in electronic publishing and a great introduction into the world of their futures.

Doug Crosby, First grade teacher   Cherry Valley School
kiwi@digisys.net   Polson, Montana
http://www.digisys.net/cherry

Document: Done

Home-school relationships are also strengthened when you develop a classroom home page.

support their children's development. We are used to many members of the tax-paying public thinking that anybody can teach children. Putting up a home page, displaying your students' work, and inviting parents into your electronic classroom displays the many talents we all have as teachers. This is of central importance when school systems rely upon taxpayers to support their efforts, especially in a period when the teaching profession is sometimes criticized by individuals who are unfamiliar with what we do and what we know.

Examples of Classroom Home Pages

Before looking at strategies for learning how to develop a classroom home page, it might be useful to view several examples to see what several outstanding teachers are doing with their own home pages. In Poulson, Montana, **Doug Crosby's classroom home page** (http://www.digisys.net/cherry/Mr.Crosby_fg.htm) shows parents

Figure 12-2. One section of the classroom home page created by Doug Crosby for his class, describing a field trip in the spring.

Doug Crosby home page (http://www.digisys.net/cherry/Mr.Crosbyfield_trip.htm)

and others what takes place in his class. At the same time, it provides students with an opportunity to publish their work, knowing that people around the world will be able to view it when it appears on their classroom home page. Projecting your classroom culture like this is important for your students. It tells them their work is valued as it prepares them for "the world of their futures." Doug also has a location on his home page for parents and others to contact him by e-mail. This enables him to stay more closely in contact with the parents of his students.

Sue Pandiani, a teacher on Cape Cod, develops a theme for each year's class. This year it is "The North Star Navigators," an idea based on a new book by Peter Reynolds. Her class has been fortunate enough to work with this author as both of them explore new worlds for students. **Sue Pandiani's classroom home page** (http://www.capecod.net/voyage/) is inspired by this book. It contains sections enabling her to publish students' work, forge links with parents, provide resources to several Internet projects her class is completing this year, and share teaching ideas with others who visit her site.

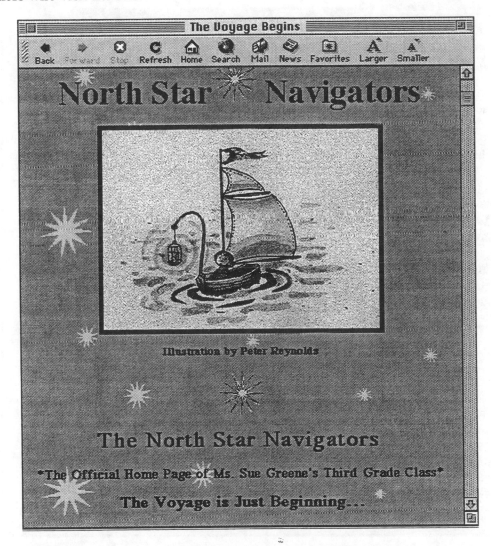

Figure 12-3. Sue Pandiani's home page: **The North Star Navigators.**

Sue Pandiani's home page (http://www.capecod.net/voyage/)

Tim Lauer and Beth Rohloff at Buckman Elementary School in Portland, Oregon also publish students' work on their classroom home page (http://buckman.pps.k12.or.us/room100/room100.html). These wonderful materials include books developed by their classes on many topics, including: Bus Safety Rules, a Space Alphabet, and a timeline of the life and accomplishments of Martin Luther King, Jr. By posting this work, Tim and Beth invite other teachers to use their curricular resources. This site is a rich one, sharing many other aspects of their classroom work, including a microscope cam and a video tour of their classroom. This amazing site provides a clear picture to parents of the many exciting things taking place in their child's classroom.

Figure 12-4. Room 100 at Buckman Elementary School in Portland, Oregon.

Room 100 at Buckman Elementary School (http://buckman.pps.k12.or.us/room100/room100.html)

Ms. Hos-McGrane and Linda Swanson, at the International School in Amsterdam, use a home page (http://www.xs4all.nl/~swanson/origins/intro_five.html) to display the wonderful work of students in social studies classes. The projects these classes are completing are really quite remarkable. Many other classrooms are beginning to use these social studies projects as resources and models to inspire their own work. A special aspect of this wonderful collaboration is that it helps students stay in touch with their class, even if they leave and travel to another location in the world. This is important because students at this school often move with their parents to new locations around the world. The home page provides a wonderful way for them to stay in touch with the work of their classmates.

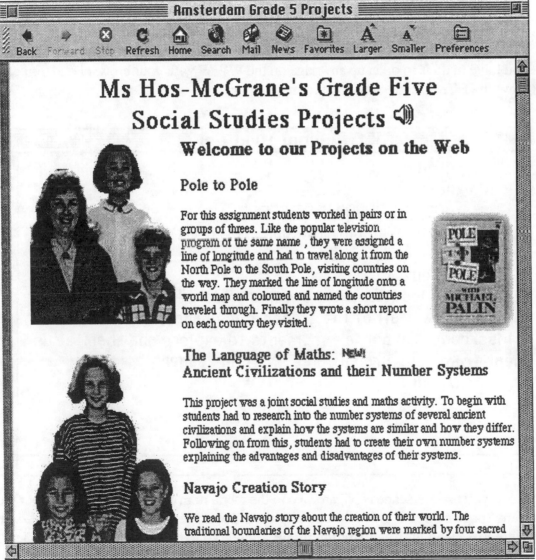

Figure 12-5. The home page of Ms. Hos-McGrane's class.

Ms. Hos-McGrane's class home page (http://www.xs4all.nl/~swanson/origins/intro_five.html)

Learning How to Develop Your Own Classroom Home Page

Developing a home page may seem intimidating. After all, a programming language is used to create pages on the web. Fortunately, though, new tools are appearing that will automatically convert what you type into the programming language used on the web. So, even knowing this programming language is not as necessary as it once was. To develop a home page, all you really need to know is how to type with a word processor. If you also know how to copy and paste graphics, that is an added bonus.

The programming language used most often to design home pages on the WWW is called HTML, HyperText Mark-up Language. It looks like Figure 12-6. When a browser such as Netscape or Internet Explorer reads a file that is written in HTML, it converts it into what you see on your computer screen. So, if a browser read the HTML file in Figure 12-6, it would appear as in Figure 12-7. This is what happens each time you view a page on the WWW; your browser reads a file written in HTML and converts it into what you see on your computer screen. To demonstrate this, all you have to do is to open up any page on the WWW with your browser and you can view the HTML code used to develop that page.

Figure 12-6.
An example of HTML (HyperText Mark-up Language).

```
Room 104.html

<html>
<head>
<BODY BGCOLOR="#FFFFFF">
 <title>Welcome to Room 104!</title>
</head>
 <body>
This is the location on the World Wide Web where you can
find out about all of the great things happening in our
classroom. Take a few moments to explore and then let us
hear from you. Drop us an e-mail message!
 </body>
 </html>
```

If you use Netscape Navigator, go to the menu item called "View" and select the item "page source." This will open up the HTML file used to create the page you were just viewing. If you use Internet Explorer, go to the menu item called "View" and select the item "source." You will see HTML code similar to what you find in Figure 12-6.

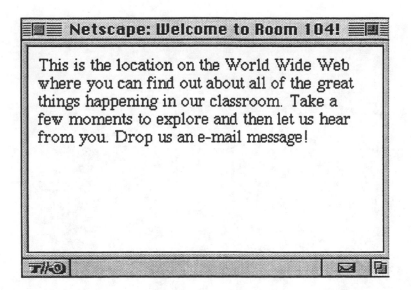

Figure 12-7.
What the information in Figure 12-6 looks like when it is read by a web browser such as Netscape.

Internet FAQ

I have heard that people often "borrow" code after viewing the HTML source code at a page they admire. They say they "borrow" images, animations, pictures, and other elements from several pages by copying and pasting and add these to their own. Is this illegal?

This, unfortunately, is all too common. Copyright issues are still being defined in this new world of the Internet. Still, it appears that web page owners possess copyright to all of the elements at their location, as long as it is original work. This means you need to request permission from a web owner before "borrowing" original text, images, or anything else from a page's source code. If you wish to read more about copyright issues on the WWW, you may wish to pay a visit to the **U.S. Copyright Office Home Page** (http://lcweb.loc.gov/copyright/copy1.html), or **Copyright Internet Resources** (http://lcweb.loc.gov/copyright/resces.html). You could also read **The No Electronic Theft Act** (ftp://ftp.loc.gov/pub/thomas/c105/h2265.ih.txt), recent legislation of the U.S. Congress. Finally, you may wish to visit the location at the New York Times devoted to copyright issues on the Internet, **Cybertimes Coverage of Copyright Issues** (http://search.nytimes.com/books/search/bin/fastweb?getdoc+cyber-lib+cyber-lib+18632+2+wAAA+copyright%7EInternet). The New York Times is currently free, but you may have to register the first time you use it.

The easiest way to develop a home page for your classroom is to use an HTML editor. This will allow you to develop your page using a program similar to a word processor.

There are two strategies for developing a classroom home page in HTML. The easiest way to develop a home page for your classroom is to use an HTML editor. This will allow you to develop your page using a program similar to a word processor. The program will automatically convert the pages you type into HTML code. Thus, all you do is type up your classroom page until it looks the way you wish it to appear, then select a converter program to convert your regular page into HTML. There are several fine programs that enable you to do this.

If you are using Netscape 4.0 or Internet Explorer 4.0 your program comes with an HTML editor already built in. The editor in Netscape is called Netscape Composer. Figure 12-8 shows an image of this program as a teacher quickly developed

Figure 12-8.
The beginnings of a home page being developed with an HTML editor, Netscape Composer.

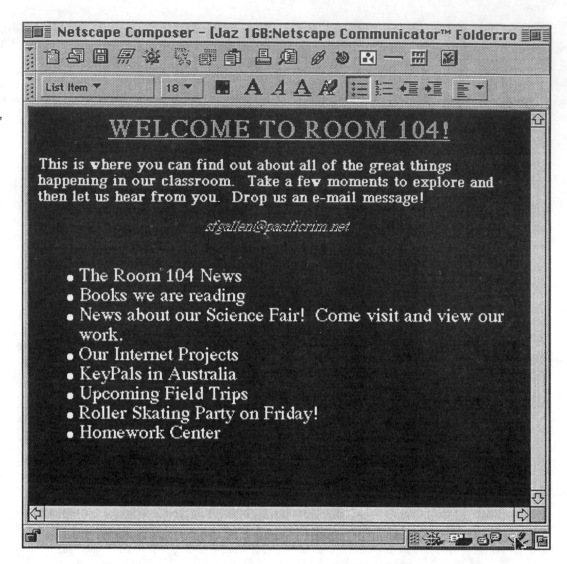

an initial version of a home page in just ten minutes. To access this HTML editor, you simply click on the pencil icon in the bottom right-hand side of the software window. This editor, like all HTML editors, requires little explanation. It works similarly to a word processor. Just begin typing away and exploring the formatting tools to design your page the way you wish it to look. You can type text, format text, insert a graphic, make a link to another page, set text to blink on and off, add color, and use many additional functions as you design your page. Simply explore each of the editing tools at the top the Composer window and in the menu items.

Another strategy is to use a word processor containing an HTML conversion program that goes with it. Microsoft Word, for example, has an attachment called Word Internet Assistant that may be obtained for free (206-882-8080). Others are also available for free or for a nominal charge. Separate HTML editors are also available, such as Adobe's PageMill (415-961-4400). You may also wish to see if one of these programs is supported by your district. Perhaps copies are already available for teachers in your district to use.

A second approach for developing a classroom home page is to spend a little time going through one of several fine tutorials that exist on the Internet. These take you step-by-step through everything you need to know to develop a classroom home page. Most of these tutorials allow you to write information in HTML and then see immediately how it will look when someone accesses your page with a browser. They are very easy to follow and get you immediately into the world of HTML without assuming any prior knowledge. The best tutorial for teachers that we have found is **Writing HTML: A Tutorial for Creating WWW Pages** (http://www.mcli.dist.maricopa.edu/tut/index.html). Others also exist, including:

- **A Beginner's Guide to HTML—**
  (http://www.ncsa.uiuc.edu/General/Internet/WWW/HTMLPrimer.html)

- **Introduction to HTML—**
  (http://www.cwru.edu/help/introHTML/toc.html)

- **Web66: Classroom Internet Server Cookbook—**
  (http://web66.coled.umn.edu/Cookbook/)

- **Setting Up A Web Site For Your School: An On-Line Presentation—**
  (http://www.fred.net/nhhs/html2/present.htm)

If you decide to use an HTML editor, we still encourage you to work your way through one of these fine tutorials. Understanding the language of HTML will enable you to easily spot problems in your HTML code should these ever arise. It also permits you to individually modify elements in your home page in a way that might not be possible with an HTML editor.

Which Elements Should I Include in My Classroom Home Page?

The design elements you include in your classroom home page will inevitably reflect your teaching style and the culture of your classroom. You may, however, wish to consider elements such as the following:

- a location where parents and others viewing your pages can send you and your class an e-mail message;

- a location where students may publish their work;

- a location where due dates for major assignments are posted;

- a location for organizing links to sites in various thematic units; and

- a location where students can publish a newspaper of classroom events and opinions.

It is important to think of your home page as a window through which the rest of the world may see your class. Thus, you will want to provide an opportunity for others to communicate with you and your students. This is easily done on a home page. You can quickly make a link that will open up an e-mail message window containing your address. This makes it easy for parents and others to get in touch with you and your students.

You should also consider using your home page as a location where students may publish their work. This allows others to see what you are doing. It also makes material and information available for others to read and enjoy. Stories, poetry, descriptions of classroom events, responses to literature . . . your home page will provide countless opportunities to allow your students to show off their best writing and art. Moreover, an HTML editor makes this very easy, as just a few clicks will enable you to copy and paste student work on your home page.

You might also wish to have a bulletin board listing due dates for major classroom assignments. Often, parents appreciate knowing when assignments are due. This is especially important in the older grades.

Another important function for your home page may be to organize links on the WWW for the various thematic units you cover during the year. You can save students much time by placing these at a single location where they are easy to access.

Finally, if you teach in the elementary grades, think about including a student newspaper on your home page. This can be a wonderful source of many writing activities. You may wish to appoint an editor for each two-week period and make this person responsible for soliciting articles and seeing that they are revised and edited to meet the standards of your home page. These provide students, parents, and others with a real understanding of all the great things that take place in your classroom.

The End of Your Journey

We are firmly convinced the world awaiting our students is one where each of them has more potential to grow and to learn.

No. This isn't the end of your journey. It is really just the beginning as you discover new resources on the web, new friends around the world, and new sources of inspiration for the important work you do with the children in your classroom. We are firmly convinced the world awaiting our students is one where each of them has more potential to grow and to learn. We also believe your role in this will be central to their success, especially with these new technologies. As we indicated in the first chapter, Internet resources will increase, not decrease, the central role you play in orchestrating learning experiences for your students. Each of us will be challenged to thoughtfully guide students' learning within information environments that are richer and more complex, presenting richer and more complex learning opportunities for both us and our students. We hope you have found the ideas we have to share useful in the important work you do to prepare children for their tomorrows. Best wishes!

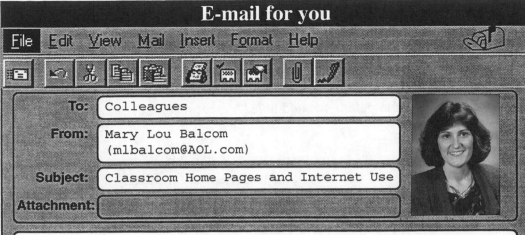

E-mail for you

File Edit View Mail Insert Format Help

To: Colleagues

From: Mary Lou Balcom
(mlbalcom@AOL.com)

Subject: Classroom Home Pages and Internet Use

Attachment:

I've been exploring the WWW for a year and still feel awestruck by the wealth of information available. My classroom is not currently wired for Internet access, so my journeys have been at home. The WWW has provided me with current information on topics I teach, actual lesson plans that I have used, great ideas to try in my classroom and lots of interesting sites that don't really relate to my curricula. As I think ahead to my eventual use of the WWW, I am excited by the avenues that will be open to my students. I feel that I will play the role of a facilitator as I guide and structure my students' use of the WWW.

I share the concerns of many colleagues regarding both the appropriate use and optimal use of the WWW. I plan to include my students in the development of appropriate use guidelines for the WWW the same way that I have typically developed classroom rules. My experience with class rules has been that students traditionally include the basics that most teachers would incorporate, and I think I could guide the process for Internet access in the same fashion.

My biggest concern is that students may waste the precious little time during which they have access to the computer on pointless meanderings around the WWW. One of the ways to avoid this is to initially give very structured assignments to ensure that students will have successful and meaningful experiences. It is also beneficial to design your own home page that organizes the topics you are studying. I recently took a class to learn how to design a home page. At first I was overwhelmed by the process, but by the end of the week had made a very simple page based on our study of ancient Egypt. I would expect the page to evolve as my students study Egypt and I would update the page. The page could change to reflect the current topic of study.

I think I'm ready to take on the challenge of using the WWW in my classroom to enhance my students' learning. Now if I could just get connected!

Mary Lou Balcom, Sixth grade teacher
Edward Smith Elementary School Syracuse, NY
mlbalcom@AOL.com

Document: Done

Resources for Developing a Classroom Home Page

ColorCenter—(http://www.hidaho.com/colorcenter/)
Are you looking for a special color or background for your classroom home page? Here is the place. You can try out different text, color, and backgrounds by moving through the palette located here. A great resource. Set a bookmark!

Guides to HTML—
(http://www.hypernews.org/HyperNews/get/www/html/guides.html)
A useful central site, but only if you have some familiarity with HTML. An extensive set of resources.

How Do They Do That With HTML?—
(http://www.nashville.net/~carl/htmlguide/)
Have you ever seen a great web page and wondered how they were able to use a special background pattern, animations, background sounds, or other tricks? Here is the page that explains everything and shows you how to include these and many other useful features in your classroom home page. Set a bookmark!

Internet in the Classroom Tutorial—
(http://www.indirect.com/www/dhixson/class.html)
See the section "Design and Post Your Classroom Home Page." This is a great place with useful ideas and useful templates for your home page.

Resources for Icons, Images, and Graphics—
(http://www.aphids.com/susan/imres)
Another nice location to obtain great visual elements for your classroom home page.

The Art of HTML—(http://www.taoh.com/)
A very rich site designed to support individuals creating home pages on the WWW. Information and resources suitable for the very beginner to the very expert are available. One of the more comprehensive locations for information on designing home pages.

The Backgrounds Archive—(http://the-tech.mit.edu/KPT/bgs.html)
A great collection of visually appealing backgrounds for use on your classroom home page.

Web / HTML / Reference—(http://www.webreference.com/html/tutorials.html)
Here is a central site with links to an extensive set of tutorials and other resources for developing your own home page. One of the better collections on the web. Set a bookmark!

webreference.com—(http://www.webreference.com/)
This is a great site to learn about creating web sites. Information ranges from basic to expert.

Web66—(http://web66.coled.umn.edu/)
This is a great general source of information for developing a classroom home page. The section on technology contains step-by-step instructions for setting up a WWW server, HTML templates you may wish to copy for your use, and much more. Set a bookmark!

Listservs/Mailing Lists for Developing a Classroom Home Page

WEB66—(WebMaster@web66.coled.umn.edu)
A discussion group for teachers preparing web pages in schools.

Glossary

acceptable use policy   A written agreement signed by parents/guardians, students, and teachers which specifies the conditions under which students may use the Internet, defines appropriate and unacceptable use, and defines penalties for violating items in the policy.

bookmark   The feature used in Netscape Navigator to mark a location on the Internet so that you might quickly be able to return to this location at a later time.

browser   A browser is a software program on your computer allowing you to connect to locations on the Internet. There are several different browsers: Netscape Navigator, Internet Explorer, Lynx, and Mosaic. Each comes in at least two flavors: Windows and Macintosh.

central site   A central site is a location on the Internet with extensive and well-organized links about a content area or important subject. Most are located at stable sites which will not quickly change. Examples include: **History/Social Studies Web Site for K-12 Teachers** (http://www.execpc.com/~dboals/boals.html), **Children's Literature Web Guide** (http://www.ucalgary.ca/~dkbrown/index.html), or **The Math Forum** (http://forum.swarthmore.edu/)

central site strategy   Often teachers find a central site strategy effective for locating useful instructional resources. Rather than using a search engine, they will locate a central site in a subject area, set a bookmark, and then use this location to find useful resources.

chat-rooms   Locations on the Internet where you may engage in simultaneous e-mail correspondence with other people.

classroom home page   A classroom home page is a location on the Internet where you can display the work your class is doing and organize links to useful resources for your students.

Content Advisor   A feature on Internet Explorer enabling you to block student access to web sites with inappropriate content. Like other software filters, this also ends up blocking access to useful sites, making it somewhat problematic.

cookies   Cookies are requests for information from web site administrators who may record and request information about you whenever you visit their site. Sometimes this is information they collect to direct you to locations you visit most often. Sometimes web sites gather information about you for statistical purposes in order to determine how many people visit their site.

favorites   The feature used in Internet Explorer to mark a location on the Internet so that you might quickly be able to return to this location at a later time.

home page location   A home page location is the page that shows up first on your screen each time students connect to the Internet. You may set the home page location to a site your prefer to see first by setting the preferences in your browser.

HTML (HyperText Mark-up Language)   HyperText Mark-up Language, or HTML, is the programming language used to design web pages on the Internet.

HTML editor   An HTML editor is a software program that allows you to design a web page they way you wish it to appear while automatically converting your design into HTML code. Netscape's Composer and Adobe's PageMill are examples.

hypertext link   Words or objects that take you to the site on the Internet linked to that item(s) when you click on it. A key navigational element for Internet use.

Internet Activity   An instructional practice often used by teachers getting started with using the Internet. It often includes these steps: locate a site, or several sites, on the Internet with content related to a classroom unit of instruction and set a bookmark for the location(s); develop an activity requiring students to use the site(s); assign this activity to be completed during the week; have students share their work, questions, and new insights at the end of the week during Internet Workshop.

Internet Inquiry   An instructional practice using the Internet in a more student-directed fashion. Usually, it consists of five phases: question; search; analyze; compose; and share.

Internet Project   A collaborative approach to instructional use of the Internet. Generally, Internet projects follow these procedures: plan a collaborative project for an upcoming unit in your classroom and write a project description; post the project description and timeline several months in advance at one or several locations, seeking collaborative classroom partners; arrange collaboration details with teachers in other classrooms who agree to participate; complete the project, using Internet Workshop as a forum in your own class for working on the project and exchanging information with your collaborating classrooms.

Internet Workshop   A regularly scheduled time used to support students' ability to acquire information from the Internet and to think critically about the information they obtain. During Internet Workshop, students share what they have learned, ask questions about issues they do not understand, and seek information to help them in upcoming work.

Internet activity page   An activity page often used by teachers to organize the activities in Internet Activity. Students complete the activities in this page and then bring it to Internet Workshop for discussion about what they learned and new questions they have.

Java   Java is a programming language often used at Internet locations to provide animations and other interactive and multimedia features. A plug-in for Java is in both Internet Explorer 4 and Netscape Navigator 4.

Kids-Teaching-Kids   During a Kids-Teaching-Kids activity, students first identify a useful web location related to their studies. Then they develop a learning experience using the web site for other students to complete. This is often done for a culminating activity for Internet Inquiry or thematic units.

plug-in   A small software program you can download from the Internet allowing you to read, view, or play multimedia elements at a web page.

pourquoi tales   Pourquoi tales are creation myths that exist in every traditional culture. Pourquoi tales explain sources of natural phenomena such as how people obtained fire, why mosquitoes buzz in people's ears, where the moon came from, or why rivers run into the ocean. Gathering and exchanging pourquoi tales over the Internet is a wonderful way for students to discover the wider world around them.

RAM (Random Access Memory)   A type of memory stored on chips in your computer. Each application you use requires a certain amount of RAM. The amount of your computer's RAM determines how many programs you can run at once. It will also determine whether or not your computer can run the latest versions of Internet browsers which require more RAM than earlier versions.

RealAudio technology   This technology permits streaming audio, a way to continuously send audio signals over the Internet to your computer. This permits you to listen to audio sources of information including radio programs broadcast from stations around the world. RealAudio has recently applied their technology to RealVideo, and developed RealPlayer a free plug-in available at their web site (http://www.real.com/products/player/index.html).

scientific thinking   Thinking scientifically involves developing and evaluating best guesses about why things are the way there are. This can be an important part of Internet Project in science as students question one another, decide upon appropriate ways of evaluating competing hypotheses, gather information, and evaluate that information to reach conclusions that are agreed to by all parties. Thinking scientifically is an important part of the new national standards for science education.

search engines   Computers on the Internet that search for sites containing words or phrases you specify. These include Yahoo, InfoSeek, HotBot, Lycos, and others.

server   A server is a computer in a network, containing information or programs that are often shared with others. A web page on the Internet is always located on a server.

software filters   These filters deny access to locations where certain words appear. Teachers and parents may edit the list of words used in the blocking software. They include: **Cyber Patrol**—(http://www.cyberpatrol.com/), **Net Nanny**—(http://www.netnanny.com/), and **SurfWatch**—(http://www.surfwatch.com/)

text-to-speech technology   This technology allows a computer to read aloud, written text. It is available for both Windows and Macintosh systems, supporting visually challenged children as well as our very youngest readers.

toolbar   A row of objects on your browser with labels underneath each object. Items in the toolbar let you do things with your browser. The toolbar often includes items such as "Back", "Forward," "Reload," "Home," "Search," "Guide," "Images," "Print," "Security," and "Stop."

Uniform Resource Locator (URL)   The address of a location on the Internet. For example, the URL of Quill Net is: http://www.quill.net/

web-site Internet Project   A web-site Internet Project is a more permanent Internet Project, coordinated by an individual at a web site.

Index

The index entries in **bold** indicate a web site address

pi, 239
Pi Mathematics, 17, 239
Pinkwater, Daniel, 163
Pitsco's Launch to Keypals, 97
Pitsco's Launch to Lists, 105
Plato, 177
Playground Chants Around the World, 261
plug-in, 55, 163, 251, 286
pnet.school.k-12, 243
pnet.school.k-5, 243, 265
Poetry HiFi, 54
POP, 87
POP ID, 73, 74
Porter, Connie, 260
posting address, 107
Frank Potter's Science Gems, 209
pourquoi tale, 152
Powell, Beverley, 212–213
Preferences, 40
preferences window, 43
prewriting, 165
primary grades, 243
Princess Pooh, 297
Print, 40
printing, 82
priority, 79
Problems for Problem Solvers, 238
process writing, 10, 168, 219
Project Gutenberg, 158, 161
PROJECTS-L, 264
Protecting Students: Guidelines and Policies, 15
Publicly Accessible Mailing Lists, 105
publishing, 165

Q

The Quill Society, 40–41, 165
Quote button, 79

R

radio stations, 291
Rainforest Action Network, 222
RAM, 216, 251
Raphael, T. E., 152
Ratings, 51–52
read aloud response journal activity(ies), 152
Read In, 260
Readers Theater, 176
readers' theater, 168
reading comprehension, 255–256
Reading Online, 176
Reading Online—The Electronic Classroom, 148
The Reading Zone of the Internet Public Library, 177

RealAudio, 163, 211, 246, 291
RealNetworks, 66
RealPlayer, 163
RealVideo, 163
Reference.com, 105, 113
Refresh, 48
Reinking, 18
Reload, 39
relocation, 262
Reply button, 79
Reply to All, 90
Reply to Author, 90
reply-to address, 107
Research, 64
Resources for Icons, Images, and Graphics, 318
response journals, 6, 168
revision, 165, 219
Reynolds, Peter, 309
Richgels, D. I., 153, 178
Rigby/Heinemann Global Keypals, 97
Rip Van Winkle, 161
Jackie Robinson and other Baseball Highlights, 1980's–1960's, 4–5
Rohloff, Elizabeth, 52–53, 310
Room 100 at Buckman School, 49
Adam Rosen's Quick Guide to Viewing the World Wide Web, 66
Ross, Cindy, 127
RSAC Ratings, 51–52
RTEACHER, 18, 102, 149, 153, 177, 264
Russia, 180

S

Salmon-Salvemini, Maureen, 168
Santa project, 103
Saudi Arabia, 237
Save button, 79
scaffolding, 20
Scanlan, Jeff, 98
Scanning Electron Microscope, 247
scavenger hunt, 30, 180, 251
scheduling computer time, 138–139
SCHOOL-L, 70, 108
SchoolNet, 146, 212, 270
SchoolNet Digital Collections, 212
SchoolNet RINGS Projects, 213
Schrand, Helen, 133
science, 16
The Science of Cycling, 211
Science Learning Network, 16, 64, 210
Science Standards, 16
scientific thinking, 213–214
Scientist's Chair, 219
SCORE Cyberguides, 146

About the Authors

Donald J. Leu, Jr. and Deborah Diadiun Leu first began teaching in the Peace Corps where they worked as elementary classroom teachers of English as a Second Language (ESL) in the Marshall Islands of Micronesia. Since then, both have worked to support language and literacy learning among many different populations using a wide variety of electronic media. Deborah has taught many types of ESL learners from engineers at the Bechtel Corporation in San Francisco to her current position where she teaches students in the English Language Institute at Syracuse University. She received her Masters degree from Syracuse University in Linguistics and English as a Second Language. Don worked as a classroom teacher and a reading specialist in California. He is currently Professor in the School of Education at Syracuse University and author of numerous books, articles, and software devoted to supporting teachers in literacy education and electronic learning environments. He received his Ed.M. from Harvard and his Ph.D. in Language and Literacy from the University of California, Berkeley. Deborah enjoys her perennial flower garden while Don enjoys fly fishing. They both enjoy spending time together with their two daughters.